AMNESTY INTERNATIONAL REPORT 1987

**This report covers the period
January to December 1986**

AMNESTY INTERNATIONAL is a worldwide movement which is independent of any government, political grouping, ideology, economic interest or religious creed. It plays a specific role within the overall spectrum of human rights work. The activities of the organization focus strictly on prisoners:

—It seeks the *release* of men and women detained anywhere for their beliefs, colour, sex, ethnic origin, language or religion, provided they have not used or advocated violence. These are termed *"prisoners of conscience"*.

—It advocates *fair and early trials for all political prisoners* and works on behalf of such persons detained without charge or without trial.

—It opposes the *death penalty* and *torture* or other cruel, inhuman or degrading treatment or punishment of *all* prisoners without reservation.

AMNESTY INTERNATIONAL acts on the basis of the United Nations Universal Declaration of Human Rights and other international instruments. Through practical work for prisoners within its mandate, Amnesty International participates in the wider promotion and protection of human rights in the civil, political, economic, social and cultural spheres.

AMNESTY INTERNATIONAL has more than 500,000 members, subscribers and supporters in over 150 countries and territories, with over 3,700 local groups in 60 countries in Africa, the Americas, Asia, Europe and the Middle East. Each group works on behalf of at least two prisoners of conscience in countries other than its own. These countries are balanced geographically and politically to ensure impartiality. Information about prisoners and human rights violations emanates from Amnesty International's Research Department in London. No section, group or member is expected to provide information on their own country, and no section, group or member has any responsibility for action taken or statements issued by the international organization concerning their own country.

AMNESTY INTERNATIONAL has formal relations with the United Nations (ECOSOC), Unesco, the Council of Europe, the Organization of American States and the Organization of African Unity.

AMNESTY INTERNATIONAL is financed by subscriptions and donations from its worldwide membership. To safeguard the independence of the organization, all contributions are strictly controlled by guidelines laid down by the International Council and income and expenditure are made public in an annual financial report.

AMNESTY INTERNATIONAL REPORT 1987

Amnesty International Publications
1 Easton Street • London WC1X 8DJ • United Kingdom

097270

First published 1987 by Amnesty International Publications
1 Easton Street, London WC1X 8DJ, United Kingdom

© Copyright Amnesty International Publications 1987

ISBN 0 86210 125 5
AI Index: POL 01/02/87
Original Language: English

Printed, designed and typeset in Great Britain by
Redesign, 9 London Lane, London E8

Cover design by Simon Knibbs

This report documents Amnesty International's work and its concerns
throughout the world during 1986. The absence of an entry in this report on
a particular country does not imply that no human rights violations of
concern to Amnesty International have taken place there during the year.
Nor is the length of a country entry any basis for a comparison of the extent
and depth of Amnesty International's concerns in a country.
Regional maps have been included in this report to indicate the location of
countries and territories cited in the text and for that purpose only. It is not
possible on the small scale used to show precise political boundaries, nor
should the maps be taken as indicating any view on the status of disputed
territory. Amnesty International takes no position on territorial questions.
Disputed boundaries and cease-fire lines are shown, where possible, by
broken lines. Areas whose disputed status is a matter of unresolved concern
before the relevant bodies of the United Nations have been indicated by
striping.

Contents

Introduction

This report is about human rights abuses by governments. It exposes the imprisonment of men and women who dissent non-violently from official views. It documents the detention of political prisoners who are held without being given the chance to defend themselves in a fair and open trial. It details brutal torture and ill-treatment in detention centres, prisons and military camps. It records the taking of life by the state in executions and political killings. The victims of such practices are in graves and prisons all over the globe.

Because it exposes the gulf between governments' commitments on human rights and the reality of their practices, Amnesty International is often attacked. It is accused of being provocative and political, of failing to appreciate the background to abuses or of giving, at least indirectly, support to the opposition. Amnesty International compares actual practice in a country with international human rights principles, and, if they have not been respected, points this out and calls for improvements. Neither the social and economic conditions in a country nor the nature of the opposition to a government can justify contravening these principles. No government is justified in claiming that it has the right to order or condone the arbitrary arrest, torture or killing of its own citizens, nor that Amnesty International has no right to intercede on behalf of the victims.

Covering the year 1986, this report places on public record the work of Amnesty International to prevent human rights violations and help victims in over 125 countries. It is an account of the movement's efforts to identify and free prisoners of conscience, to secure prompt and fair trials for political prisoners and to end torture and executions throughout the world. However, a report such as this cannot record the individual actions of the tens of thousands of active volunteers around the world who make up Amnesty International. It is their concerted efforts on behalf of the human rights of others which constitute the heart of Amnesty International's work.

Amnesty International is strictly impartial. It does not work against governments, only against human rights violations. It neither supports nor opposes any political, social or economic system. Amnesty International applies a single universal standard to all countries regardless of the ideology of their governments or the political views of the victims.

Amnesty International is often asked to compare the human rights records of different countries. It does not and cannot do this. Government secrecy and censorship obstruct the flow of information from many countries and impede efforts to verify allegations. Statistical or other generalized comparisons can never measure the impact of human rights abuses on the victims, their families and the societies of which they are part. Comparisons of governments' human rights practices can be manipulated and misused for political ends.

This report is therefore neither comparative nor fully comprehensive. The omission of a country entry should not be interpreted as indicating that no human rights violations took place in that country. Nor is the length of a country entry any basis for judging the depth and extent of Amnesty International's concerns in a country. In one entry hundreds of executions may be recorded in a single paragraph, in another the description of complex legal changes affecting the protection of human rights may occupy a page or more. To use word counts to assess the importance Amnesty International attaches to its work on a given country or the gravity of human rights violations there is a meaningless exercise.

Amnesty International works openly. It sends its information to governments before publishing reports and is always ready to correct any factual errors it may have made. The publication of this report gives governments and individuals an annual opportunity to review Amnesty International's concerns. Twenty-six years after the founding of Amnesty International, it serves once again as a reminder of how necessary the movement's work still is.

*   *   *   *   *

Another reminder of the continuing need to fight human rights abuse is the unending flow of refugees who have crossed almost every territorial boundary in the world in search of safety. While some have left their homes because of famine and others because of war, many have been forced to flee because of the human rights violations Amnesty International seeks to prevent. But the worldwide concern about the growing numbers of refugees has all too often been used to justify new restrictions on entry for asylum-seekers, rather than translated into pressure on governments to end the human rights violations that have forced so many into exile.

Confronted by the millions of men, women and children fleeing from persecution, governments have reacted by trying to turn them away, rather than by trying to stop the persecution. Unless and until human rights abuse is eradicated, desperate people, their lives disrupted and their families fractured, will go on attempting to cross borders to find freedom from incarceration, torture and death at the hands of the state.

Human rights violations are confined to no one region or political system. People have fled from political persecution in Ethiopia, Chad, Uganda, Equatorial Guinea, Angola, Zaire, Zimbabwe, Namibia and South Africa, among other countries in Africa. In the Americas refugees in large numbers have sought freedom and safety from human rights violations taking place in El Salvador, Guatemala, Chile, Colombia, Haiti and Cuba. Afghans, Vietnamese, Laotians and Kampucheans have left their countries in great numbers since the mid-1970s. This continuing movement in Asia has been augmented more recently by Sri Lankan Tamils, tribal Bangladeshis trying to escape violations in the Chittagong Hill Tracts, and by Burmese, mainly members of ethnic minority groups. In Europe, the 1980s have seen people from Poland, Romania, Spain, Turkey and the USSR seeking asylum. Human rights violations in Iran, Iraq, the Lebanon and Syria have led to large numbers of people leaving these countries to find refuge.

Amnesty International is not a refugee organization but it does seek to ensure that governments observe the principle that no person should be forcibly returned to a country where he or she can reasonably expect to be imprisoned as a prisoner of conscience, tortured or executed. Amnesty International works for prisoners. It cannot take up refugee-related problems, even if these involve departures from international standards, except in cases where possible imprisonment as a prisoner of conscience, torture or execution are at stake. When Amnesty International is asked for help by refugees outside the scope of its strictly defined mandate, it tries to refer them to other organizations able to assist. In working towards its own limited objectives, Amnesty International cooperates with national and international refugee organizations and the Office of the United Nations High Commissioner for Refugees. However, even within its limited mandate, Amnesty International has been involved in many cases where the principle that no one should be forcibly returned to a country where he or she is at risk of persecution has been threatened and violated.

A few examples must stand for countless others. One concerns Blanca de Rosal, who was two months pregnant with her second child when her husband, Jorge, a trade unionist, was abducted not far from their home in rural Guatemala. Her efforts to find him failed. In her quest to discover what had happened to her husband, she joined the Mutual Support Group, known by its Spanish acronym GAM, which is made up of relatives of people who have "disappeared". In early 1985 two GAM leaders were killed, in circumstances suggesting security force responsibility. Blanca de Rosal began to fear for her own life — a fear substantiated when she discovered that she was being shadowed. She fled to the United States of America to seek safety for herself and her children, but the US State Department recommended that she should not be granted political asylum. Amnesty International feared that if she was returned to Guatemala, the public role she played in the USA in publicizing her husband's case could place her in specific danger of "disappearance" or extrajudicial execution, despite the improvements in the human rights situation since an elected civilian government took office in January 1986.

In other cases, Amnesty International confronts situations where people have taken their own lives rather than be sent back to countries where they feared arrest, torture or execution; where refugee camps have been attacked and unarmed individuals seized, tortured and killed; where people who desperately need a safe haven are shuttled from country to country, increasing the risk that they will eventually be sent back; where those who dedicate themselves to helping the uprooted are themselves persecuted.

Several European governments have threatened to return Iranian nationals to Iran, where they risk execution, torture and imprisonment as prisoners of conscience. Amnesty International has also received reports of Iranians being turned back at the border between Iran and Turkey. In the course of 1986, the French Government expelled 26 Spanish citizens of Basque origin, handing them over to the Spanish authorities. In every case they were held incommunicado under the anti-terrorist law by the Spanish police. Several later alleged in court that they had been tortured, and produced medical evidence to support their complaints. Soviet citizens have been returned by the Finnish Government to the USSR, where they were subsequently imprisoned for trying to leave the USSR. Amnesty International knew of two people still imprisoned for this reason at the end of 1986 and worked for their release as prisoners of conscience. The Soviet Union itself expelled 10 Yemenis back to the Yemen Arab Republic in 1986 and Amnesty International believes they were imprisoned on their return and held as prisoners of conscience.

In East Africa, the governments of Kenya and Tanzania have "swapped" refugees in order to bring their political opponents back to captivity. A Kenyan who fled to Tanzania after an attempted coup failed and was granted asylum there was later returned to Kenya by the Tanzanian authorities, condemned to death by court martial, and executed in 1985. A leading member of the opposition party in Zimbabwe was handed over to the Zimbabwean authorities in 1986 by the Government of Botswana, where he had previously been given asylum. He was arrested at Dukwe refugee camp, which houses about 4,000 Zimbabwean refugees. The Zimbabwean Government has claimed that it is used as a base for "dissident" activities, a claim which is denied by both the Botswana Government and the Dukwe camp authorities. Amnesty International believed that this man, who was still in detention in Zimbabwe at the end of 1986, might have been a prisoner of conscience, and in the light of persistent reports of torture of political detainees in Zimbabwe, feared for his physical safety in custody.

A Tunisian national sentenced to death in Tunisia in his absence for assault, theft and attempted murder was arrested by the Saudi Arabian authorities, handed over to the Tunisian authorities, and executed within two weeks. Amnesty International protested to the Saudi authorities about this man's expulsion, on the grounds that no one should be returned to a country where he or she faces execution. The organization also interceded with the authorities in the United Arab Emirates when several Iranians were threatened with being expelled back to Iran, where they would be at risk of human rights violations.

In principle, most governments accept that they should not forcibly return someone to a country where they have a well-founded fear of persecution. In practice, they frequently argue that the probability is not great that the individual will suffer the human rights abuse that he or she fears. So Amnesty International's practical contribution is often to demonstrate that the person's fears are justified. It does this by providing evidence of specific human rights violations to the authorities, lawyers and organizations working on the refugee's behalf.

Unfortunately, Amnesty International has observed that the international protection of refugees has been made more difficult in recent years. Governments have become increasingly restrictive in granting asylum in the face of growing refugee numbers and deepening economic problems. Amnesty International is concerned that there appears to have been a tendency, particularly in Western Europe and North America, to treat increasing numbers of asylum applications as "manifestly unfounded". There is a real risk that this is leading to unfair and arbitrary decisions. Some governments are preventing asylum-seekers from setting foot in their countries. After 1,300 Tamils from Sri Lanka arrived to seek asylum in the United

Kingdom in May 1985, the British Government imposed a visa requirement on Sri Lankans — the first time that such a requirement had been placed on citizens of a Commonwealth country. The US authorities have intercepted boatloads of Haitian refugees and sent them back home.

All applicants are entitled to an unbiased hearing of their case, and an appeal against any negative decision, before being returned to their country of origin. Governments have an obligation to ensure that their procedures do not lead to genuine political refugees being sent back to the country they have fled. This may mean alterations in the powers and practices of border officials, it may entail providing legal representation facilities for asylum applicants. Governments are responsible for providing the facilities and acquiring the expertise to ensure that their determination of who is and is not a genuine political refugee is fully considered and fair.

Just as Amnesty International focuses on individual victims of human rights violations, so too it acts on behalf of individual refugees threatened with being sent back to face persecution. However, if abuses are committed indiscriminately against members of a particular social, religious, ethnic or political group Amnesty International may oppose the forced return of any member of the group to their country of origin. In Sri Lanka, unarmed Tamil civilians have been killed by members of the security forces, often apparently in reprisal for attacks by Tamil extremist groups on the security forces or members of the Sinhalese community. Members of the Tamil community, particularly young men, have been subjected to arbitrary arrest, torture and "disappearance". In 1986, therefore, Amnesty International maintained the position that no Sri Lankan Tamils should be sent back to Sri Lanka.

Amnesty International also opposed the forcible return of Palestinians to the Lebanon, where in recent years they have frequently been subjected to arbitrary arrest and incommunicado detention without trial, ill-treatment and torture (which in some cases has led to death) and where many have become victims of political killings. Human rights violations against Palestinians have been carried out principally by Amal, the mainly Shi'ite militia which controls territory in West Beirut and South Lebanon, and have taken place most intensively during recurrent periods of heightened tension.

As well as the forcible return of refugees to countries where they risk human rights abuse, Amnesty International has been faced by some related problems. People trying to help those seeking refuge have themselves been subjected to persecution. In the USA the church-based "sanctuary movement" has openly challenged the application of US immigration law by seeking to provide a safe haven to some of the many Salvadorians and Guatemalans who feared that they would be in danger of human rights violations if returned home. In 1986 eight people were convicted on charges of conspiring to smuggle illegal aliens from Guatemala and El Salvador into the USA and other violations of US immigration law. The defendants did not deny that they had violated the law but stated that they had been forced to take action on religious and humanitarian grounds because of the failure of the US Government to grant asylum to the vast majority of Salvadorians and Guatemalans who applied for it. They assisted refugees, they said, whose lives would be endangered if they were returned to their places of origin. Had the defendants been sentenced to terms of imprisonment, Amnesty International would have campaigned for their unconditional release as prisoners of conscience.

In El Salvador itself, church workers, including those working to assist refugees, have been arbitrarily arrested, tortured, made to "disappear" and killed.

Even when refugees have been allowed to stay in a country of asylum, they may not necessarily be safe. Military attacks on refugee camps which have led to torture and political killings are of great concern. Hundreds of Palestinians, both combatants and non-combatants, have been summarily executed or arrested and tortured, mainly by Amal, during hostilities around refugee camps in the Lebanon.

In Mozambique, Angola, Botswana, Lesotho and Swaziland, South African military forces have attacked refugee camps, killing unarmed refugees and nationals of the asylum country. Sometimes the South African Government has acknowledged its responsibility for the incursion, claiming the victims were members of armed opposition movements. On other occasions it has denied involvement, despite evidence of responsibility. Refugees have been abducted by South African security forces from the territory of the "frontline" states and taken to South Africa and Namibia and held in prison there.

Salvadorians, Guatemalans and Nicaraguans living in refugee camps in Honduras and Mexico have been subjected to torture and extrajudicial execution. Mexican doctors have shown Amnesty International delegates death certificates of refugees killed in Mexico by Guatemalan troops in 1984. The victims were men, women, old people and children, some of them mutilated after death. One woman had been 36 weeks pregnant when she was killed; the body of an 11-year-old boy was found with the genitals cut off. Salvadorian refugees in Honduras have been harassed and intimidated by Salvadorian troops. Nicaraguan refugees have been attacked in

Honduras by forces engaged in armed opposition to the Nicaraguan Government, known as the "contras". These forces, which operate from bases in Honduras with the knowledge of the Honduran authorities, have also seized Nicaraguan and foreign workers from Nicaragua and held them on Honduran soil, where there are fears for their safety.

Amnesty International is dedicated to bringing an end to human rights violations under its mandate: the responsibility for achieving this ambition lies clearly and squarely with governments. Humanitarian action for refugees is vital, but as the pages of this report clearly demonstrate, it can never be entirely successful until the human rights violations underlying so many refugee movements have been confronted and stopped. The international community has a duty not only to help those fleeing state repression, but also to work to end the human rights violations that have led so many people into unwanted exile.

Amnesty International — a worldwide campaign

"Languages are surmountable, distances can be overcome, because the heart is big and the hands warm — because we cannot live alone, because it is not just that man should imprison others. Because people like you keep alight the hope of a new day dawning." So wrote a former prisoner of conscience to the Amnesty International group that had campaigned for her release. The group had written letters to the authorities who held her appealing for her immediate and unconditional release and had also written regularly to her family and had sent them gifts and financial help.

Amnesty International is built around the idea that ordinary men and women *can* take effective action to protect the human rights of others. This idea has been demonstrated in practice for the past 25 years. Again and again, it has been pressure from ordinary people which has obliged authorities to curb torture or free prisoners of conscience, or to press other governments to do so. Without sustained pressure, it is too easy for governments to wait for international outrage to subside, to suppress information about abuses, and to employ human rights rhetoric for their own partisan purposes.

Amnesty International is an activist membership organization. Many of its members work together in groups, campaigning for the release of their "adopted" prisoner of conscience. A prisoner of conscience is someone who is imprisoned because of their beliefs, sex, ethnic origin, language or religion, who has neither used nor advocated violence. The campaigning takes many forms — besides writing appeals and supporting the prisoner's family, groups publicize their case to build pressure for their prisoner's release. An Italian group working for the release of a Uruguayan prisoner wrote some 600 letters to the Uruguayan authorities before she was released at the end of her sentence in 1983. In addition, the group contacted dozens of Italian members of parliament seeking their help, persuaded them to raise questions in the Italian and European parliaments, contacted an Italian delegation going to Uruguay and persuaded numerous Italian lawyers to intercede with the President of the Uruguayan Supreme Military Tribunal. In Canada, a group honoured their adopted prisoners — a Chilean trade union leader and his wife — by planting a Chilean tree, and using the interest generated to raise questions about what happened to the "disappeared" in Chile. A group in Mauritius received from their former prisoner of conscience in the Philippines a design which they used as the basis of a Christmas card: it is now being used by other African sections, in the Netherlands and in the United Kingdom.

If there is insufficient evidence to show whether a given prisoner is a prisoner of conscience or not, a group may be asked to investigate the case. It will write to the authorities requesting more information, and will urge that he or she should be promptly charged and given a fair trial, or else released.

No group is ever asked to work on a case of a prisoner in its own country — this is one of the important safeguards Amnesty International maintains in order to protect its impartiality.

In 44 countries Amnesty International sections coordinate the work of local groups and organize campaigns, publicity and fund-raising. For example, to commemorate Amnesty International's 25th anniversary in 1986, the Brazilian Section persuaded its national mint and post office to produce medals and stamps marking the occasion. In Denmark, too, special stamps were produced. The US Section helped organize a series of rock concerts called "Conspiracy of Hope" which culminated in a 12-hour marathon finale attended by over 55,000 people and watched by millions more on television. In Belgium, the Flemish branch built a huge prison-like structure in the centre of Brussels and invited the public to take part in a letter-writing event on behalf of prisoners of conscience. When 100 letters were signed, the first of the "cell doors" was opened. With every further batch of 100 letters another of the 60 doors was opened — when all the doors were open a painting 40 metres square was revealed depicting a prisoner being released.

Amnesty International's worldwide campaigns focus public attention on issues of particular concern. In 1986 there were campaigns against human rights violations in Pakistan, South Africa, Chile, Sri Lanka and Afghanistan. For example, Amnesty International members from all over the world wrote to more than 10,000 officials, community leaders, company executives, professionals, and members of church bodies, trade unions and other institutions within South Africa. The US Section produced facsimile passbooks which it distributed to members of Congress and other elected officials, as well as to influential community leaders. The recipients affixed photographs of themselves to the passbooks, signed them, and sent them to the South African authorities as part of the campaign for repeal of the racially discriminatory pass laws. This action was successfully followed or adapted by several other sections. Politicians, employers' federations, trade unions, law enforcement officials . . . all were approached by Amnesty International sections in various countries and agreed to write to their South African counterparts or take other forms of action. Dean Simon Farisani, pastor of the Evangelical Lutheran Church, a former prisoner of conscience and torture victim in South Africa, toured four Amnesty International sections in Asia to promote the campaign.

Many of the situations Amnesty International confronts require immediate action. In some countries, to be arrested or seized by armed agents means there is danger of torture or death. Many Amnesty International members are organized in special Urgent Action networks ready to act promptly by sending telexes and telegrams to let the authorities know the world is watching. For example, in Chile the sister of a student leader was taken from her bed by armed security forces at 4.45am on 14 October to their headquarters in Santiago, where many detainees are known to have been tortured. An Urgent Action was issued on 15 October calling for guarantees for her safety. She was released two days later. During 1986, 391 Urgent Actions were issued, of which 142 were in cases where torture was feared. An estimated 3,000-plus appeals were sent in each of these cases.

Some violations of human rights of concern to Amnesty International are better addressed by other techniques. Often, when urgency is not the most important factor, a situation will demand letters which ask more complex questions than is possible in telexes or telegrams. These letters are sent by groups which have joined one of several special networks concentrating on human rights violations in various regions of the world. In 1986, approximately one third of Amnesty International groups participated in one of 18 such regional networks.

During 1986, Amnesty International made special efforts to raise public awareness about human rights on the occasion of its 25th anniversary in May, on International Labour Day, on Human Rights Day, on International Women's Day, and during Amnesty International Week in October, when it highlighted the cases of writers and journalists in prison.

Amnesty International's members not only do the work of pressing governments to respect the rights of their citizens, they also set the organization's policy and raise its funds. The movement's governing body — the International Council — is made up of section delegates and meets every two years to decide Amnesty International's policy.

The Council elects an International Executive Committee to carry out its decisions and supervise the International Secretariat, its headquarters. All the movement's funds are raised by the membership — Amnesty International does not accept money for its program budget from governments.

The International Secretariat, based in London, collects and acts on information about Amnesty International's concerns, keeping members, groups, sections and the international news media informed about cases and campaigns. The Research Department collects and analyses information from a wide range of sources. News releases, publicity material and reports are produced and the *Amnesty International Newsletter* publishes human rights stories, including details of three prisoners of conscience, in each monthly issue. The bulk of Amnesty International's work is carried out by volunteer members, taking action on the basis of information and advice provided by the International Secretariat. This report does not attempt to catalogue the membership's activities in detail, but describes activities initiated by the International Secretariat.

Missions are organized to send Amnesty International representatives to various countries where they may have talks with government officials, collect information about human rights violations or legal procedures, or observe political trials. Reports on their findings are submitted to the International Executive Committee. (For a full list of missions during 1986 see page 380.)

One of Amnesty International's priorities is to encourage the growth of its membership in areas of the world outside Western Europe and North America where it had its early growth. For example, in Latin America and the Caribbean in the past seven years, sections have been created in Barbados, Trinidad and Tobago, Brazil, Chile and Puerto Rico, joining the already established sections in Peru, Mexico, Venezuela and Ecuador. There are Amnesty International groups in Aruba, Bermuda, Guyana, Costa Rica, Colombia, Argentina and Uruguay. In October 1986, representatives from 17 countries met in Santa Marta, Colombia, to assess their work and to plan future involvement in the movement's activities.

In Asia too, representatives of Amnesty International's Asian groups and sections met in India, for the first time in 10 years. The intervening decade saw a strengthening of existing structures in India, Sri Lanka, Bangladesh, Nepal, Hong Kong, the Republic of Korea, Australia, New Zealand and Japan, and new initiatives in Thailand, the Philippines, Malaysia and Papua New Guinea. The meeting focussed on the practical work undertaken by the membership — organizing group meetings, undertaking campaigns, fund-raising, contacting lawyers, doctors and trade unions and publicizing Amnesty International's work. Over the past five years the number of local Amnesty International groups in Asia working for adopted prisoners of conscience has increased from 87 to 260. Amnesty International material has been translated by members into many of the languages of the region including Bengali, Chinese, Hindi, Japanese, Korean, Sinhala, Tamil and Thai.

In November representatives of Amnesty International's sections and groups in eight countries in Africa gathered in the Côte d'Ivoire to discuss Amnesty International's development in the African continent. This was the eighth meeting of the African membership since the inception of Amnesty International's development program in the late 1970s. The participants were able to draw on the experience of nearly a decade of effort in building Amnesty International in Africa, and were thus better able to map out the strategy for future development. They were able to reflect on the creation of sections in Ghana, Nigeria, Senegal and Côte d'Ivoire, four sections in formation, Sierra Leone, Tunisia, Tanzania and Mauritius, and on the creation of groups in Guinea, Zambia and Sudan.

Groups are being started in the Arab-speaking world too. There are now Amnesty International members and sympathizers in Egypt, Kuwait, Jordan, Mauritania and Morocco, as well as in Tunisia and Sudan.

Campaign to abolish the death penalty

Amnesty International is unconditionally opposed to the death penalty and works for its total abolition. It regularly monitors death sentences and executions around the world and appeals for clemency whenever it learns of a case in which imminent execution is feared.

During 1986, 743 prisoners are known to have been executed in 39 countries, and 1,272 sentenced to death in 67 countries. These figures include only cases known to Amnesty International: the true figures are certainly higher. By the end of 1986, 28 countries had abolished the death penalty for all offences, and 18 for all but exceptional offences, such as war crimes.

Amnesty International noted with alarm that governments were increasingly responding to the threat of illicit drug use and trafficking by introducing the death penalty for drug-related offences. In December 1986 the organization published a survey *The Death Penalty: No Solution to Illicit Drugs* covering laws and practices in 23 countries where the death penalty was provided for drug offences. It found that despite the hundreds of executions carried out there was no clear evidence that the death penalty had had any identifiable effect in preventing drug trafficking and abuse. The death penalty appeared to have been introduced with little consideration of the risks it could entail for society. These included the danger that traffickers faced with the death penalty might kill more readily to avoid capture, thus increasing the threat to law enforcement officials; the risk that minor traffickers or drug addicts might be executed while those behind the crimes escaped detection; and the risk that increasing the severity of penalties would play into the hands of organized crime, involving hardened criminals prepared to face the attendant dangers. Moreover, in their haste to use the death penalty against drug traffickers, some countries had enacted laws which undermined internationally accepted standards for a fair trial — adding to the risks of executing the innocent which are inherent in all death penalty systems.

Refugees

While Amnesty International's statutory concerns relate to prisoners, the organization opposes the forcible return of any person to a country where he or she might reasonably expect to be imprisoned as a prisoner of conscience, tortured or executed. (See *Introduction.*) Much of Amnesty International's work in this field is done by Amnesty International sections in the countries where individuals seek asylum. This report covers the work of the International Secretariat, so references to actions taken on behalf of refugees do not reflect the work done by Amnesty International sections on behalf of individual refugees faced with being returned to countries where they would be at risk of such human rights violations.

Relief

During 1986 the International Secretariat of Amnesty International distributed £297,143 in relief payments to help prisoners of conscience and their families and to assist the rehabilitation of torture victims. Amnesty International sections and groups probably sent as much again to many thousands of prisoners and their families. This relief program is not a substitute for the primary objective of securing freedom for prisoners of conscience and an end to the use of torture, but aims to alleviate some of the suffering caused by these human rights violations. When relief payments are distributed by bodies outside Amnesty International or through individual intermediaries, the organization takes care to stipulate the precise prisoner-related purpose for which the payments are intended. Amnesty International's relief accounts, like its general accounts, are audited annually and are available from the International Secretariat.

Work with international organizations

The year 1986 was the twentieth anniversary of the adoption of the international covenants on human rights. By the end of 1986, 89 states were parties to the International Covenant on Economic, Social and Cultural Rights, 85 to the International Covenant on Civil and Political Rights and 38 to its Optional Protocol. In the course of the year Argentina, Niger, the Philippines and Sudan ratified or acceded to the International Covenant on Civil and Political Rights, Argentina and Niger acceded to its Optional Protocol, and Argentina, Niger and Suden ratified or acceded to the International Covenant on Economic, Social and Cultural Rights. In a letter to all United Nations member states Amnesty International urged governments not yet party to the covenants to commemorate the anniversary by undertaking to ratify them without further delay. Amnesty International also issued information about the work of the Human Rights Committee, the body established to monitor compliance with the International Covenant on Civil and Political Rights.

In 1986 the Human Rights Committee considered reports from the Governments of Mongolia, the Federal Republic of Germany, Czechoslovakia and Hungary. It also adopted final views on individual cases communicated to it under the Optional Protocol from Uruguay, Venezuela and Zaire (two). Amnesty International made its information available to members of the Committee.

During 1986, 14 countries ratified or acceded to the UN Convention Against Torture and Other Cruel, Inhuman or Degrading Treatment or Punishment: Argentina, Belize, Bulgaria, Cameroon, Egypt, France, Mexico, Norway, Philippines, Senegal, Sweden, Switzerland, Uganda and Uruguay. The Convention, which was adopted by the UN General Assembly on 10 December 1984, will come into force after 20 states have ratified or acceded to it. Amnesty International continued to urge ratification of the Convention in its contacts with governments.

Amnesty International was concerned during 1986 about the

continuing financial crisis facing the UN. The steps to reduce the budgetary shortfall included a 10 per cent reduction in the budget of all its programs, which seriously affected the human rights program. Of particular concern to Amnesty International were the cancellation of the 1986 session of the Sub-Commission on Prevention of Discrimination and Protection of Minorities, and its working groups on indigenous populations, slavery and communications (which means the postponement for a year of its examination under Economic and Social Council Resolution 1503 of communications concerning violations of human rights); cancellation of the October 1986 session of the Human Rights Committee; and cancellation of a meeting of the Working Group on Enforced or Involuntary Disappearances. Amnesty International had urged that the human rights program be exempted from the across-the-board cuts, given its already inadequate budget.

In September a seminar on human rights in the UN was convened in Geneva by the Special Committee of International Non-Governmental Organizations on Human Rights (Geneva). It was attended by representatives of non-governmental organizations and several members of the UN Sub-Commission (which had been scheduled to meet around that time). The seminar called for those parts of the human rights program that had been cut to be reinstated in 1987. Amnesty International sections brought these findings to the attention of their respective governments.

Throughout 1986 Amnesty International continued to submit information under the various UN mechanisms now in place to respond to violations of human rights. By 1986 special rapporteurs or representatives had been appointed by the Commission on Human Rights to study the situations of human rights in five specific countries — Chile, El Salvador, Guatemala, Afghanistan and Iran — and Amnesty International has brought its continuing concerns in all of these countries to their attention. It also brought its concerns in South Africa and Namibia to the attention of the Commission's *Ad Hoc* Working Group of Experts on southern Africa (established in 1967).

The Commission has also appointed Special Rapporteurs on torture and on summary or arbitrary executions and a Working Group on Enforced or Involuntary Disappearances. The organization alerted the Special Rapporteur on torture to reports of torture or fear of torture in the following 31 countries during 1986: Afghanistan, Bahrain, Bangladesh, Burma, Burundi, Chile, Colombia, Ecuador, El Salvador, Honduras, Indonesia, Iran, Iraq, Israel and the Occupied Territories, Mexico, Morocco, Nepal, Nigeria, Paraguay, Peru, the Republic of Korea, Saudi Arabia, South Africa, Sri Lanka, Sudan, Syria, Thailand, Togo, Turkey, Zaire and Zimbabwe.

Similarly, Amnesty International informed the Working Group on Enforced or Involuntary Disappearances of reported "disappearances" in 19 countries: the Central African Republic, Chile, Colombia, Ecuador, El Salvador, Ethiopia, Guatemala, Guinea, Haiti, Indonesia (East Timor), Iran, Kenya, Mexico, Morocco, Peru, the Philippines, Sri Lanka, Syria and Togo.

The organization also informed the Special Rapporteur on summary or arbitrary executions of reported deaths in detention or extrajudicial executions in 23 countries: Bahrain, Bangladesh, Brazil, Chile, Colombia, Ecuador, El Salvador, Ethiopia, Guatemala, India, Indonesia, Iraq, Mexico, Paraguay, Peru, the Republic of Korea, Saudi Arabia, South Africa, Sri Lanka, Suriname, Thailand, Zaire and Zimbabwe. In addition, Amnesty International sent him information on death sentences or executions imposed contrary to minimum international standards in 17 countries: Afghanistan, Angola, Bangladesh, Congo, Equatorial Guinea, Ghana, Guinea-Bissau, Indonesia, Iran, Kuwait, Libya, Nepal, Nigeria, Pakistan, Somalia, Thailand and the United States of America. In particular, the organization called for action aimed at preventing the execution of juveniles. When appropriate, the organization asked the Special Rapporteurs and the Working Group to intercede urgently on behalf of individual victims.

Under the procedure established by Economic and Social Council (ECOSOC) Resolution 728F, Amnesty International submitted information on the human rights situation in the following five countries: Benin, Bulgaria, Paraguay, Togo and Zaire. Resolution 728F authorizes the UN to receive communications about human rights violations and to bring them to the attention of the government concerned. Under Resolution 1503 the UN examines communications in confidential proceedings to determine whether there is evidence of a "consistent pattern of gross violations of human rights" in a country. In March 1986 the Chairman of the Commission on Human Rights stated that the Commission had taken action in closed session with regard to Albania, Gabon, Haiti, Paraguay, the Philippines, Turkey and Zaire; he further announced that the Commission had decided to discontinue consideration of the human rights situation in Gabon, the Philippines and Turkey.

At the 1986 UN Commission on Human Rights Amnesty International made statements on the situation of human rights in South Africa; human rights defenders; and arbitrary arrests, torture and executions in Iraq. It submitted a written statement on human rights in Iran.

In August 1986 in an oral statement Amnesty International informed the UN Special Committee on Decolonization of its concerns about the violations of the human rights of people in East Timor. In October 1986 it made a statement of its concerns in South Africa to the Special Committee against *Apartheid* on the International Day of Solidarity with South African Political Prisoners.

During a visit to UN headquarters in April 1986, Amnesty International's Secretary General met UN Secretary-General Javier Pérez de Cuéllar, other UN officials and members of the Human Rights Committee, as well as holding bilateral meetings with several UN ambassadors. In addition to raising Amnesty International's concerns in specific countries and on individual prisoners' cases, he stressed in these meetings the importance of the UN's activities in the field of human rights and how programs in this field should be protected as far as possible from budget cuts.

Amnesty International began writing a series of papers explaining various procedures available at the international level to the victims of human rights violations. It also produced further versions, in Portuguese and Arabic, of selected international standards of most direct relevance to its work — the Universal Declaration of Human Rights, the International Covenants, the Convention against Torture, the Standard Minimum Rules for the Treatment of Prisoners and the Code of Conduct for Law Enforcement Officials.

Amnesty International continued to submit information to Unesco's Committee on Conventions and Recommendations, which examines cases of violations of the human rights of writers, teachers and others within Unesco's mandate. In 1986 Amnesty International drew the Committee's attention to cases in Indonesia and Laos. In the context of preparations for an international congress on human rights teaching, the organization wrote to Unesco urging that it pursue a more active program of human rights education and dissemination of information about international human rights standards. Amnesty International continued to take part in a joint Non-Governmental Organizations/Unesco working group on human rights education.

The organization continued to make available information on violations of the right to freedom of association to the International Labour Organisation (ILO). It attended the annual International Labour Conference in Geneva as an observer.

Amnesty International attended the 16th session of the General Assembly of the Organization of American States (OAS) as a "special guest". During 1986, 13 countries signed the Inter-American Convention to Prevent and Punish Torture adopted by the OAS General Assembly in 1985. The Convention will come into force after two countries have ratified it; no ratifications had been deposited by the end of 1986. Amnesty International sent information on reported human rights violations in 11 countries to the OAS Inter-American Commission on Human Rights — Chile, Colombia, Ecuador, El Salvador, Guatemala, Haiti, Honduras, Nicaragua, Paraguay, Peru and the USA.

The African Charter on Human and Peoples' Rights, adopted unanimously by the Organization of African Unity (OAU) in 1981, came into force on 21 October 1986, three months after the OAU Secretary General received notification that a majority of the organization's 50 member states had adhered to the Charter. The Charter provides for protection of basic individual rights, including the right to life, the right to be free from arbitrary arrest or detention, the right to be free from torture and the right to freedom of conscience. It also specifies rights of peoples, duties of states and duties of individuals. The Charter provides for the setting up of an African Commission on Human and Peoples' Rights, with responsibilities including promotion of human rights in the region and examination of communications by states and others alleging that Charter provisions are not being respected. All OAU member states will participate in the election of the 11 members of the African Commission, to be nominated by states parties to the Charter. Amnesty International is encouraging OAU member states to become parties to the Charter, as well as to the international covenants on human rights and the UN Convention Against Torture. The organization sent a telex to the OAU's Secretary General, welcoming the entry into force of the Charter and looking forward to close cooperation between Amnesty International and the African Commission. Amnesty International also sent a letter to heads of all states which became parties to the Charter in 1986, congratulating them on their initiative and undertaking to encourage further ratifications of the Charter and disseminate information about it, both within and outside the region.

During 1986, 16 states deposited ratifications with the OAU. A complete list of states parties to the Charter as at the end of 1986 appears at Appendix V.

All 21 member states of the Council of Europe are parties to the European Convention on Human Rights. Amnesty International continued to seek further declarations under Article 25 of the Convention (providing for the right of individual petition) and further ratifications of Protocol No. 6 to the Convention (providing for the abolition of the death penalty as a punishment for peacetime offences). During 1986, no further declarations were made under Article 25, but France, the Netherlands and Portugal ratified Protocol No. 6, thus bringing the number of parties to the Protocol to eight.

The Council of Europe's Steering Committee for Human Rights —

at which Amnesty International has observer status — adopted two significant new draft instruments dealing with subjects within Amnesty International's mandate. On 15 May, the Steering Committee adopted a draft recommendation on conscientious objection to compulsory military service. Amnesty International welcomed it as an important step towards recognition that the right to refuse military service on grounds of conscience is implicit in the right to freedom of conscience, but considered it deficient in a number of respects. For example, it did not provide explicitly for the possibility of applying for conscientious objector status *during* military service.

On 21 November 1986 the Steering Committee adopted a draft European Convention for the Prevention of Torture and Inhuman or Degrading Treatment. The draft convention provides for an independent, international committee with powers to visit, without specific warning, places of detention in ratifying states and to interview detainees in private. Amnesty International welcomed the adoption of the draft convention and urged the Council of Europe's Committee of Ministers to adopt it without amendments.

During 1986 Amnesty International continued to send information to various committees of the European Parliament, to inter-parliamentary delegations of the European Parliament before meetings with delegations from other countries, to the European Commission and to foreign ministers. Amnesty International made a statement on its concerns on refugees before the Committee on Legal Affairs and Citizens' Rights of the European Parliament at the Committee's public hearing on the right to asylum on 25 September. It stressed that the principle of *non-refoulement* should be made explicit in the basic documents setting out the human rights policy of the European Community and its member states. It recommended that measures to harmonize and coordinate the refugee policies of member states of the European Community should be designed to conform fully with the basic principles set out in international instruments regarding the protection of refugees.

The Inter-Parliamentary Union, a non-governmental organization composed of members of parliament from 104 countries, maintains a special committee to investigate reported violations of the human rights of parliamentarians and to seek redress. During 1986 Amnesty International sent the special committee information on the situation of present or former members of parliament in 14 countries: Bangladesh, Colombia, Equatorial Guinea, Guinea-Bissau, Indonesia, the People's Democratic Republic of Yemen, the Republic of Korea, Somalia, Swaziland, Turkey, Uganda, Viet Nam, Zaire and Zimbabwe.

Africa

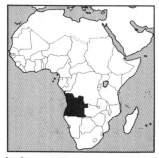

Angola

Amnesty International was concerned about the prolonged detention without trial of many suspected opponents of the government, including alleged supporters of armed opposition groups. It was also concerned about reports of torture and ill-treatment of prisoners. Most political prisoners were not brought before the courts: some 30 who were received unfair trials before military tribunals or the People's Revolutionary Tribunal and of these at least 17 were sentenced to death.

The conflict continued between the government of President José Eduardo dos Santos and guerrilla forces belonging to the *União Nacional para a Independência Total de Angola* (UNITA), National Union for the Total Independence of Angola, an armed opposition movement headed by Dr Jonas Savimbi. It was accompanied by renewed allegations of torture and killings of prisoners and civilians by both sides. It was impossible, however, for Amnesty International independently to verify specific allegations or to attribute responsibility for individual killings. The conflict appeared most intense in southern and central Angola but UNITA guerrillas were also reportedly active in some northern districts and in the Cabinda enclave. South African military forces were also active in the south, apparently in support of UNITA and in opposition to nationalist guerrillas belonging to Namibia's South West Africa People's Organisation (SWAPO), operating from Angola. SWAPO was also reported to hold prisoners, among them several former senior officials of the organization alleged to be South African spies.

During 1986 several hundred alleged UNITA supporters were reported to have been arrested. Some were accused of treason, armed rebellion or sabotage, while others were alleged to have supported UNITA in other ways, such as by providing weapons, information, shelter or food. The authorities were also reported to have detained people who were simply suspected of sympathizing with UNITA. The 200 or more UNITA guerrillas who were reported to have been arrested in 1986 by the *Forças Armadas Populares para a Libertação de Angola* (FAPLA), People's Armed Forces for the Liberation of Angola, were apparently held in security prisons or military bases in or near the provincial capitals. At least 100 people were reported to have been arrested in the Cabinda enclave on suspicion of supporting either UNITA or of one of the factions of the *Frente de Libertação do Enclave de Cabinda* (FLEC), Enclave of Cabinda Liberation Front. (One faction of FLEC was reported to have signed an accord with UNITA, while another had attempted to reach agreement with the Angolan Government.) Some detainees were reported to have been arrested because of false accusations by personal rivals and to have had little or no opportunity to test the legality of their detention. Some suspected UNITA supporters were reported to have been taken to Luanda, the capital, and held for questioning in a prison known as Estrada de Catete. Others were reportedly held in camps run by the Ministry of the Interior or in other places of detention. In some camps, detainees were apparently given political instruction with the declared object of eventually reintegrating them into society. Among them were former UNITA supporters who had taken advantage of a policy of clemency which the Angolan authorities instituted in 1978 towards members of opposition groups who surrendered.

Relatively few alleged UNITA supporters were ever brought to trial. They were apparently held for indefinite periods in administrative detention without reference to the courts and with no opportunity to appeal against their continuing detention. For example, Tito Tchikoko was detained in Huambo in 1979 on suspicion of being a UNITA supporter. Later that year he was taken to Luanda and subsequently to a detention centre in Quibala, southwest of the capital. He was not known to have been tried or released. The Angolan authorities did not respond to Amnesty International's inquiries about Tito Tchikoko and over a dozen other alleged UNITA supporters held for up to eight years.

A Zairian, Lizamoa Mongambenge, and an Angolan, Kiassonga Manuel Peterson, who had been detained without trial since 1975 and 1979 respectively, were believed to be still in detention at the end of 1986 (see *Amnesty International Report 1986*). Four other Zairians who were among a group of refugees arrested in March 1983 in Luena were also reported to have remained in detention (see *Amnesty International Report 1985*).

There were several political trials which resulted in the death penalty but it was not known if any executions were carried out. In all cases, the defendants were alleged members or supporters of UNITA who were charged with offences such as treason, armed rebellion and espionage. Amnesty International learned of six separate trials, involving a total of 30 defendants, which took place before military tribunals in Benguela, Huambo, Lubango and Ndalatando. Sixteen of the defendants were sentenced to death. In March two people accused of being members of a special UNITA commando squad were sentenced to death in Luanda by the People's Revolutionary Tribunal, a civilian court. Amnesty International was concerned that the trials failed to meet internationally recognized standards of fairness. In particular, it appeared that defendants tried by military courts were unable to appeal against their verdict and sentence, contrary to Article 48 of Law 17/78 on the reform of military justice, which stipulates that appeals against death sentences should be lodged automatically with the highest military court, the Armed Forces Military Tribunal. The two people sentenced to death by the People's Revolutionary Tribunal were not reported to have lodged appeals. The organization was also concerned that defendants did not have access to legal counsel of their own choosing and that they did not have adequate opportunities to prepare their defence. Amnesty International informed the authorities of these concerns and appealed for commutation each time it learned that a death sentence had been passed.

In August Amnesty International welcomed the commutation by the President of three death sentences. Amilcar Fernandes Freire, a 66-year-old Portuguese national, and two Angolans, all accused of spying for South Africa, had been sentenced to death by the People's Revolutionary Tribunal in September 1985. The sentences were upheld by the appeals court the following month. It was announced that the death sentence on Amilcar Freire had been commuted for humanitarian reasons on account of his age.

Amnesty International continued to receive reports that prisoners were tortured and ill-treated while held incommunicado for interrogation. The most commonly reported form of torture consisted of severe and repeated beatings. While it was unable to obtain independent confirmation of each report, Amnesty International received sufficient information to believe that control over personnel responsible for interrogation was inadequate and that prisoners were not given any opportunity to complain about their treatment.

Both government forces and UNITA claimed that their opponents committed human rights violations in areas of conflict. However, in no case was Amnesty International able to obtain sufficient verification of the reports or attribute responsibility. Journalists visiting areas controlled by UNITA reported the killing of groups of civilians and the torture and mutilation of captives by government forces.

Two armed opposition organizations were reported to be holding prisoners in Angola. UNITA continued to abduct civilians, among them foreign nationals employed in Angola. About 200 foreign nationals held by UNITA were released by the end of 1986. SWAPO, the Namibian organization which is engaged in armed opposition to continued South African rule in Namibia, was reported to be holding more than 100 of its members as alleged spies for South Africa. They were reported to include Bernadinus Petrus and Victor Nkandi, on whose behalf Amnesty International had appealed previously when they were detained incommunicado by South African security police in Namibia in the late 1970s before they went into exile. They and others were believed to be held at a SWAPO camp in Kwanza Sul province.

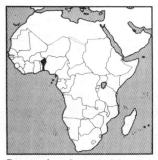

Benin

Amnesty International was concerned about the detention without trial of more than 130 suspected opponents of the government, including many prisoners of conscience, all of whom appeared to be held in breach of the provisions of the Benin Constitution. Fifty of these prisoners were released in September by presidential order but 88 others were still in detention at the end of 1986. Amnesty International was also concerned about reports of torture and ill-treatment of political detainees and the use of the death penalty. The first executions known to have taken place for several years were carried out in May when six people sentenced to death for armed robbery and murder were shot by firing-squad.

Amnesty International continued to be concerned about a large number of students and others detained in 1985 and 1986 in connection with unrest at the national university or on account of their suspected links with the banned *Parti communiste du Dahomey* (PCD), Communist Party of Dahomey (as Benin was formerly called). Some of these detainees might have been arrested because of their links with student groups and unofficial trades unions. Some were apparently held because they were suspected of supporting student demonstrations in 1985 over conditions and student union representation. Most of the detainees had been arrested between May and December 1985, but some further arrests were reported in the first months of 1986. Several of those held were prisoners of conscience who had been detained without charge or trial on previous occasions. Among them were Jerôme Houessou, a teacher previously held from March 1981 to August 1984, and Nestor Agbo, a peasant held from October 1983 to August 1984. Other prisoners of conscience whose unconditional release Amnesty International sought included Christophe Monsia Boni, a veterinary surgeon, arrested in September 1985, Alassance Tigri, a bank official arrested on 31 October 1985, and Daniel Djossouvi, a teacher who was arrested in Lomé, Togo, on 18 November 1985 and forcibly returned to Benin. In the cases of many of these detainees Amnesty International sought further information to determine whether they were prisoners of conscience, and called for their prompt and fair trial, or release. However, the organization received no reply.

The government publicly stated that the unrest in mid-1985 included demonstrations that were violent in character, and put this forward as one reason for the detentions. However, in most individual cases Amnesty International had information indicating that this was not true. The organization also noted that the government body established to investigate the events of 1985 did not examine the alleged violence of the demonstrations nor did it charge anyone with a recognizably criminal offence; rather it questioned prisoners about their political sympathies and connections. Some of those apparently detained in connection with allegedly violent student demonstrations in the capital, Cotonou, were, for example, either not in Cotonou at the time (some were in other countries) or were arrested as long as six months after the demonstrations.

A persistent pattern of detention of people associated with unofficial organizations has been observed, notably since 1979 (see previous *Amnesty International Reports*). Among the prisoners of conscience held during 1986 were Didier d'Almeida, Emmanuel Alamou and Afolabi Biaou, who had all been held as prisoners of conscience before, released in a presidential amnesty in August 1984 and rearrested later that year. Among the cases being investigated by. Amnesty International were those of Raphaël Lawani, a student arrested in June 1985, and Koffi Christophe Kinkpe, arrested by mid-1986.

All the prisoners of conscience and probable prisoners of conscience known to Amnesty International and still in detention at the end of 1986 were held either in Camp Séro Kpéra in Parakou, central Benin, or in the *Prison civile* in Segbana in the northeast of the country which appeared to have been specifically allocated for political prisoners.

All the political prisoners of concern to Amnesty International were believed to have been interrogated by the *Commission nationale permanente d'enquête de sécurité d'Etat*, National Commission of Inquiry on State Security. The purpose of this Commission, headed by a senior military officer, was apparently to establish the extent of individuals' links with opposition groupings, in particular the PCD. The Commission was apparently able to recommend to President Kerekou the continued detention or release of suspects. For example, 50 political prisoners were released on 26 September 1986 on the order of the President, apparently following a recommendation by the Commission. According to *Loi fondamentale*, Benin's Constitution, no one can be arrested and detained without a decision by a popular Tribunal or prosecuting magistrate. However, in none of the cases where people were detained for their alleged connections with the PCD or other groups were charges brought.

During interrogation by the National Commission of Inquiry, which sat first in Cotonou and later in Parakou, many prisoners were tortured or ill-treated to elicit information about opposition groups. Individuals were reported to have been beaten and whipped, sometimes until they lost consciousness. One detainee suffered a broken arm as a result of this treatment. Other detainees were subjected to the "barrel torture" — the victim is rolled around inside a barrel which contains broken glass and stones. Another method of torture was the *"rodéo"*, whereby prisoners are forced to crawl or walk barefoot over sharp stones while being beaten with sticks or rifle butts. On some occasions medical personnel were involved in determining whether a detainee was strong enough to endure torture. Medical advice was made available to some victims of torture but this was believed to have been inadequate. Torture was also reported to have been used to punish prisoners who complained about their treatment.

The death penalty was carried out in 1986 for what was believed to be the first time in several years. Six people convicted of armed robbery and murder were executed by firing-squad on 26 May. Amnesty International wrote to President Kerekou to express concern about the six executions and regret at the apparent change in policy on the use of the death penalty. The organization appealed to the President to grant clemency in any further cases of death sentences that came before him.

In August 1986 Amnesty International submitted information

about its concerns in Benin under the UN procedure for confidentially reviewing communications about human rights violations (the so-called "1503 procedure"). This submission was also sent to the government with an invitation to comment, but no reply was received.

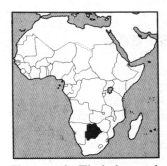

Botswana

Amnesty International was concerned about the forcible repatriation of several refugees to Zimbabwe, where they faced possible torture, and about the use of the death penalty.

In February Makhatini Guduza, a recognized refugee with political asylum in Botswana, was arrested and taken to Plumtree in Zimbabwe, where he was handed over to the authorities. He was immediately detained and was still being held without trial in Zimbabwe at the end of 1986. Amnesty International considered that he might be a prisoner of conscience and was investigating reports that he had been tortured after his forcible return to Zimbabwe. Makhatini Guduza was a leading member of the Zimbabwean minority party, the Zimbabwe African People's Union (ZAPU) who had fled to Botswana in 1983. The Botswana Government justified his expulsion on the grounds that he was directly involved in armed opposition to the Zimbabwean Government. Similar allegations had also been made by the Zimbabwean Government, which had for some time sought to obtain his return. In March Amnesty International expressed its concern to the Botswana Government about the forcible return of Makhatini Guduza to Zimbabwe.

Amnesty International also received information that a number of other refugees and political exiles had been forcibly returned from Botswana to Zimbabwe since 1983, some of whom were still in detention without charge in Zimbabwe at the end of 1986. Those returned forcibly in 1986 included Jane Mathuthu and Albert Nkomo, both of whom were reportedly served with detention orders of indefinite duration on arrival in Zimbabwe, and were later charged with assisting "dissidents". Amnesty International was investigating whether they might be prisoners of conscience.

Amnesty International remained concerned about the use of the death penalty. In June the organization appealed to President Quett Masire seeking clemency for Maxwell Mhlanga and Joseph Moyo, two Zimbabwean refugees convicted of murder. At that stage, however, their appeal against conviction and sentence had not been heard and the organization had not learned its outcome by the end of 1986. It was not known whether any executions took place.

Burkina Faso

Amnesty International was concerned about the imprisonment of prisoners of conscience and possible prisoners of conscience most of whom, however, were released before the end of 1986. New information was received about torture and ill-treatment of detainees in 1985, when one detainee was alleged to have died as a result of torture.

Some 80 prisoners were either released or had their sentences reduced at the beginning of January by the Head of State, Captain Thomas Sankara. Among them were former President Saye Zerbo and other former senior officials sentenced to prison terms in 1984 for alleged corruption or financial impropriety. At the end of the month and in early February, there were further releases. Those freed included two leading members of the *Ligue patriotique pour le développement* (LIPAD), Patriotic League for Development, both named Adama Touré and both of whom had been detained without trial since late 1984. Other supporters of LIPAD who had been among 19 people arrested in mid-January 1986 were also released uncharged. Another LIPAD leader held since late 1984, Soumane Touré, a former secretary general of one of the country's three trade union confederations, was not released at this time but remained in detention in a military camp at Pô. He had been accused of financial misdemeanours but not charged. He was reported to have demanded to be brought to trial but to have been released on the orders of the Head of State on 3 October.

Several new arrests were reported to Amnesty International in April. Those held included Drissa Touré and Joseph Diallo, two teachers accused of distributing leaflets critical of the government. In May Amnesty International expressed concern to the government about these arrests and about reports that those arrested had been held incommunicado and ill-treated. The government did not respond but subsequently Amnesty International learned that both detainees had been released uncharged at the beginning of May. Seven other people working at a gold mine at Poura, who were also reported to have been arrested as suspected critics of the government, were apparently released at the same time.

There were further releases on 4 August to mark the third anniversary of the coup which brought Captain Thomas Sankara to power. In particular, about 170 prisoners were believed to have been freed, including a number who had been detained without trial or held under house arrest for long periods. Among those released were Ali Lankoandé and Henri Guissou, two members of an opposition group, the *Front progressiste voltaïque* (FPV), Progressive Front of Upper Volta (as Burkina Faso was formerly called), who had been held under house arrest since November 1983. A number of people who had been imprisoned following bomb explosions in May 1985 at military depots in Bobo Dioulasso and Ouagadougou, the capital, were also believed to have been released.

During 1986 Amnesty International received further information about torture and ill-treatment of detainees held following the bomb explosions in May 1985. They were mostly held in Ouagadougou at the headquarters of the *Direction de surveillance du territoire* (DST), security police, where some of them were reported to have been tortured with electric shocks, burnt with cigarettes, beaten, and suspended by the wrists for long periods. Prisoners were also reported to have been made to sit in what was described as the "kangaroo position", with their knees drawn up tightly under their chins, for hours at a time. Further information was received also about the death in 1985 of Lieutenant Hamidou Zeba, one of those detained after the bomb explosions. As previously reported (see *Amnesty International Report 1986*), the government denied that his death was the result of torture and attributed it to cirrhosis of the liver. However, one report received by Amnesty International in 1986 stated that he died after being burnt with a blow torch while being interrogated. No inquest or other official inquiry into his death was believed to have been held by the end of 1986.

In March Amnesty International was invited by the authorities to send a delegate to observe the trial in Ouagadougou of Mohamed Diawara and two others, who were charged with embezzlement of funds belonging to the Economic Community of West African States. However, as it appeared to be solely a criminal matter which did not come within Amnesty International's mandate, the organization informed the authorities that it could not accept their invitation.

Burundi

Amnesty International was concerned about the imprisonment of prisoners of conscience. Some had challenged the government's restrictions on religious activities, others were imprisoned for criticizing government policies or on suspicion of organizing opposition to the government among members of the Hutu community. The majority were held without trial. The number of political prisoners was difficult to establish, but appeared often to exceed a hundred. Amnesty International was also concerned about the ill-treatment of prisoners and about the use of the death penalty.

The government maintained its policy, introduced in 1984, of restricting public religious activities to Saturday afternoons and Sundays. This resulted in arrests of members of the Roman Catholic church, the largest religious denomination; and of other Christian groups, particularly Seventh Day Adventists and Jehovah's Witnesses, both of which were banned. The government also banned several Roman Catholic organizations during the year, including the *Mouvement marial*, Movement of Mary, in March and the *Mouvement d'action catholique*, Catholic Action Movement, a youth movement, in October.

Relations between the government and the Roman Catholic church became particularly strained in September and October, when the government nationalized minor seminaries (secondary schools for boys who might become priests) and, after Bishops protested against the nationalization in a pastoral letter, prohibited pre-school classes organized by the church. At least one priest, Father André Kameya, was arrested after he read the pastoral letter in his church: he also described the background to the confrontation between church and state and called on his congregation to remain faithful to the church. Other church workers and an army officer were also reportedly arrested for criticizing these government measures and in December another priest was arrested after referring publicly to the conflict between church and state. All were, like Father Kameya, still detained at the end of the year and were adopted by Amnesty International as prisoners of conscience.

The government declared 1986 to be "Justice Year" and focused attention on the importance of respect for legal procedures. Nevertheless, in many cases reported to Amnesty International, legal procedures were not observed for political detainees, who were not referred to the procuracy or remanded in custody by a judge as laid down by law. The security forces were apparently permitted to arrest and detain suspected government opponents or critics for several months or more outside the framework of the law. Only one prisoner of conscience, Father Gabriel Secco, an Italian priest, was known to have been brought to trial. There were also many short-term detentions of people who appeared to be prisoners of conscience.

In February three Roman Catholic catechists were arrested in Nyangwa, in Gitega province, apparently because they had been organizing religious classes during the working week. They were still held at the end of 1986. In April Samuel Butoyi and more than 20 other Seventh Day Adventists were reportedly detained at the house of their pastor in Muyira, near Bujumbura, during a Saturday morning religious service. Although the women and children were released two days later, almost 20 men were held uncharged until July and then released. Some Jehovah's Witnesses were also arrested during the first half of the year and a few were reportedly still held at the end of the year.

A number of people apparently suspected of being in contact with government opponents outside the country were arrested, particularly between April and July. For example, Béatrice Mirerekano, who had Belgian nationality and was the daughter of a prominent Hutu political leader who was executed in 1965, was arrested upon arrival in Bujumbura in mid-July and detained until the end of September, while she was questioned about her contacts and activities in Belgium. Others were, like her, released uncharged after a few months. However, some were kept in custody. Ntuyengendo, a young man who had visited neighbouring Tanzania, was arrested when he returned to his village at Mugara in March: no reason was given for his detention, but he was apparently suspected of being in contact with Hutu opponents of the government who were based in Tanzania. He was not known to have been freed by the end of 1986.

In addition to these detention cases, all of which were investigated by Amnesty International, the organization remained concerned about a number of people arrested in previous years who were still held without trial. For example, Jean-Paul Banderembako, an army officer who was arrested in mid-1984 after criticizing government officials in public, was reported to have been kept in custody without being tried throughout 1986. Amnesty International also continued to investigate the case of a Protestant pastor, Siméon Nzishura, who was arrested in neighbouring Zaire, where he was a refugee, in October 1985. He was forcibly repatriated to Burundi on the grounds that he had committed non-political offences there. However, he was not tried during 1986 and Amnesty International suspected that his detention was due to his opposition to the government's restrictions on religious activities. In the cases of a number of detainees arrested before the beginning of 1986, Amnesty International was unable to find out whether they had been released or not.

Amnesty International was also concerned about the imprisonment of a former Minister of Justice, Philippe Minani, who was arrested in August 1985. He had previously been imprisoned in the 1970s after being convicted of embezzling public funds while in office, but had been released before completing his sentence. His rearrest in 1985 appeared to have been due to his support for Roman Catholic critics of the government's restrictions on religious activities; however, instead of being charged with a new offence, he was apparently imprisoned on the basis of the sentence imposed on him in 1978.

Amnesty International was aware of only one political trial during the year. This concerned an Italian Roman Catholic priest, Father Gabriel Secco, who was arrested at the beginning of June and tried in July. He had given the last sacraments to a former government official who was reputed to have taken part in the May 1972 massacres, when many thousands of people were killed in strife between the Tutsi and Hutu communities, and had later allowed his burial in a parish cemetery at Ntega. In response to criticism by members of his congregation, he explained during a religious service that the former official had asked for forgiveness. It was on account of his remarks in church that Father Secco was arrested and charged with libelling the former official, disclosing a professional secret and inciting racial hatred. He was convicted by Ngozi High Court and sentenced to six months' imprisonment. Amnesty International believed him to be a prisoner of conscience. He was released at the beginning of September after serving half his sentence.

Amnesty International remained concerned about five people convicted in December 1985 of involvement in sending an anonymous letter to the Roman Catholic Bishop of Bujumbura urging him to defy the government's ban on weekday religious services. Two of the five were convicted of insulting the head of state, on the grounds that the letter compared the government to Satan. The convictions of the five were confirmed by the Bujumbura Appeal Court in March. The Cassation Court, the final court of appeal, later turned down a complaint by one of the five, Father Gabriel Barakana, that he had not been able to present his defence adequately. All five were adopted by Amnesty International as prisoners of conscience.

As in previous years, Amnesty International was also concerned about reports of police brutality and of severe beatings inflicted on detainees. In December, for example, a Roman Catholic nun was reported to have been badly beaten while in police custody in Rumonge: she apparently fainted twice during interrogation, but was revived to be beaten again. More than 10 school teachers and other professionals belonging to the Hutu community were also reported to have been arrested in Bururi province during December and to have been severely beaten in Rumonge. The previous month, prisoners at Rumonge's Murembwe prison, who had sought refuge in neighbouring Tanzania after the 1972 massacres but had later returned home voluntarily, were allegedly subjected to a series of severe beatings. Unofficial sources claimed that some prisoners had died as a result, but Amnesty International was not able to obtain independent confirmation of this.

Death sentences were imposed during 1986 but no information was available to Amnesty International about the total number, nor about the number of executions.

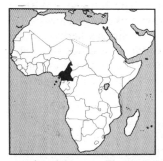

Cameroon

Amnesty International was concerned about the imprisonment of prisoners of conscience, some detained for relatively short periods but others held since 1984. Several prisoners of conscience were released during 1986. Amnesty International continued to investigate whether at least eight people who were tried and acquitted by a military court in 1984, but subsequently redetained, were prisoners of conscience. The cases of several other political detainees were also under investigation to determine whether they were prisoners of conscience. The organization continued to urge the government to disclose the identities of those executed after an armed mutiny in April 1984 and to release full details of the subsequent trials in which at least 51 people were sentenced to death.

Amnesty International adopted as prisoners of conscience 10 people arrested between late 1985 and early 1986 and held without charge or trial until August when they were released. They were among a larger group arrested after leaflets sympathetic to a banned opposition movement, the *Union des populations du Cameroun* (UPC), Union of Cameroonian Peoples, were circulated, but Amnesty International was able to confirm information only on these 10. Some of them had returned to Cameroon shortly before their arrests following assurances from President Paul Biya that former political opponents could return home. In August President Paul

Biya ordered the release of 14 people officially described as political detainees, 10 of whom were those who had been adopted by Amnesty International as prisoners of conscience. According to the Ministry of Territorial Administration, the 14 had been detained "for attempting to reconstitute banned organizations, holding clandestine meetings and distributing leaflets aimed at destabilizing institutions of the Republic".

Amnesty International also considered as prisoners of conscience several journalists who were arrested in 1986 for criticizing government policy. They included three Radio Cameroon journalists — Ebsiy Ngum, Sam Nvalla Fonkem and Johnny MacViban — who were arrested in June after a radio program critical of members of the government and following industrial action at the radio station. In mid-October the three were released from detention uncharged.

Amnesty International continued throughout 1986 to appeal for the release of André Beyegué Yakana, a Jehovah's Witness who was adopted as a prisoner of conscience in 1985. The Jehovah's Witness sect is banned in Cameroon. André Beyegué Yakana was arrested in December 1984 for attending an unofficial religious service at his home in Limbe, Southwest Province. A number of other Jehovah's Witnesses were arrested at the same time, some of whom might subsequently have been released, but Amnesty International did not obtain details of their cases. However, the organization did receive information in 1986 about two other Jehovah's Witnesses detained without trial — Olivier Nwana and Njiofack Paris — who were arrested in February 1982 and June 1984 respectively. Amnesty International took up their cases for investigation and called for their release unless they were to be charged and tried for a recognizably criminal offence. They were still held uncharged at the end of 1986.

Alhadji Hassan Tanko, whom Amnesty International had adopted as a prisoner of conscience in 1985, was reportedly released in mid-1986. He had been sentenced to two years' imprisonment in 1984 by a military tribunal sitting in camera, apparently accused of involvement in the April 1984 coup attempt. However, Amnesty International was informed that he was in fact imprisoned because he had criticized the arrests of large numbers of businessmen and women and officials in April 1984.

The cases of eight other people, among them Alain Touffic Othman and Nana Mamadou, detained shortly after the April 1984 armed mutiny, were investigated by Amnesty International to determine whether they were prisoners of conscience. They were all tried and acquitted of offences related to the mutiny but were then redetained without charge or trial. Amnesty International considered that they might be prisoners of conscience and called for their fair trial or release. The cases of at least four other people imprisoned in the wake of the April 1984 events were also investigated by Amnesty International. Some of them were believed to have been held without trial, others to have been sentenced to prison terms after trials which did not conform to international standards of fairness. The proceedings were held *in camera* and some of the accused were denied access to legal counsel of their choice. Since details of the trial were not made public, it was difficult to ascertain the legal status of those concerned and the reasons for their imprisonment. However, Amnesty International considered that the following four, at least, might be prisoners of conscience: Ahmadou Bello, the former Managing Director of Cameroon Airlines; Bobo Hamatoucour, the former Director of the *Office national de commercialisation des produits de base* (ONCPB), National Raw Materials Marketing Board; and Suzanne Lecaille and Rose Zia, both businesswomen.

Etienne Max Abessolo and Luc Minkoulou, two former soldiers detained since 1979, remained in detention throughout 1986. They were reportedly detained with others on suspicion of involvement in a plot to overthrow the former government led by President Ahidjo in 1979. However, no charges were believed to have been brought against them and they remained throughout the year in the *Prison de production*, labour camp, at Yoko. Amnesty International considered that they might be prisoners of conscience and called for their fair trial or release.

There were reports of several death sentences in 1986, but Amnesty International was not able to confirm whether any executions took place. The organization appealed for the commutation of death sentences passed on seven people about whom it obtained information. Among them were two people sentenced to death in September after being convicted of armed robbery. Amnesty International learned about four other condemned prisoners when they escaped from prison and their cases were reported in the local press. The organization continued to urge the government to release full details of all those sentenced to death in the wake of the April 1984 armed mutiny; it appeared that the families of some people allegedly involved in the mutiny still did not know the fate of their relatives.

Central African Republic

Amnesty International was concerned about the detention without trial of suspected opponents of the government and the imprisonment of one convicted prisoner of conscience.

The ban on political activities which was imposed when General André Kolingba took power in September 1981 remained in force throughout 1986. However, few arrests of opposition political party supporters were reported in comparison to previous years. In November a new constitution was approved by referendum. This confirmed President Kolingba in office for a further seven years and provided for the formation of a single ruling political party, the *Rassemblement du peuple centrafricain* (RPC), Central African People's Alliance. The constitution also provided for a Congress of two chambers, whose members were to be elected in July 1987.

Early in 1986 Amnesty International was able to confirm that many untried political detainees had been released in December 1985. Among them were a number of people who had been arrested in the Paoua area in the northwest of the country in April 1985 on suspicion of involvement with armed opposition to the government, and held without trial.

Three former government ministers and a number of other detainees who had been imprisoned for political reasons were released during 1986 under amnesties granted by President Kolingba. On 1 September, the fifth anniversary of President Kolingba's accession to power, the release was announced of Gaston Ouedane and Jérôme Allam, who had been sentenced to 10 years' imprisonment in July 1984 after being convicted of complicity in an attempt to overthrow the government in March 1982. They were then ministers in the government and were arrested when they failed to report to President Kolingba during the night of the coup attempt. Amnesty International had investigated their cases and believed that they had been unfairly convicted when tried before the Special Tribunal responsible for hearing all political cases (see *Amnesty International Report 1985*).

Also on 1 September the sentence on another former minister, François Guéret, was reduced from 10 to five years. He was adopted by Amnesty International as a prisoner of conscience after he was convicted in July 1985 of corresponding with a representative of a foreign power (by writing a letter to the son of President Mitterrand of France soon after his arrest) and insulting President Kolingba. He was released on 1 December, the anniversary of the establishment of the country's first autonomous government in 1958. Sixty-three other prisoners were also reported to have been released on the same day. Among them were 10 people who were tried in June 1983 and sentenced to 10 years' imprisonment for involvement in a bomb explosion at a Bangui cinema in July 1981. Amnesty International had been concerned that they appeared to have been convicted mainly because they had been members of the political opposition group which claimed responsibility for the bombing. However, three others who were sentenced to life imprisonment at the same trial were not released. In addition, three political prisoners convicted by the Special Tribunal in May 1982 on related charges of illegal possession of explosives remained under sentence of death during 1986. It was not known how many of the others released in December were held for political reasons.

In March 1986 students at the University of Bangui went on strike to protest against changes in the system of allocating grants and against the high level of unemployment among university graduates. Twelve students, who were either members or supporters of the *Association nationale des étudiants centrafricains* (ANECA), National Association of Central African Students, were subsequently arrested and brought to trial before the Special Tribunal in April, accused of endangering state security, causing disturbances and acting in complicity with foreign forces. They were also accused of distributing leaflets advocating the removal of French troops from the Central African Republic, following the crash of a French army plane which killed a number of civilians in Bangui. The students were reported not to have had access to defence counsel. The tribunal acquitted three of the students. The nine others were remanded in custody pending further inquiries. These nine were apparently released on 1 September, without appearing in court again. In the meantime, Amnesty International had made inquiries about their cases. Following the trial, in May 1986, the presiding judge, a military assessor and two prosecuting officials were dismissed by President Kolingba, who complained that the trial judge had allowed the defendants to attract too much publicity.

At the end of October the former head of state, Jean-Bedel Bokassa, who had been living abroad since 1979, returned to the Central African Republic and was arrested on arrival. Two French citizens accompanying him were also arrested. The death sentence imposed on Jean-Bedel Bokassa *in absentia* in 1980 was annulled and he was referred for trial by Bangui's Criminal Court on the same charges for which he had previously been tried. These included complicity in murder and embezzling state funds. The trial began on 26 November, but was postponed until 15 December at the prosecution's request. The trial was continuing at the end of 1986 and the court had heard evidence concerning only a few of the deaths in custody for which the prosecution claimed Jean-Bedel Bokassa had been responsible. The trial was attended by an Amnesty International observer.

Following Jean-Bedel Bokassa's return to the country, a journalist, Thomas Koazo, was reported to have been arrested after making remarks in a radio interview about an alleged meeting between Jean-Bedel Bokassa and President Kolingba. Amnesty International investigated the reasons for his arrest and believed that he might be a prisoner of conscience.

The organization was also concerned about the detention of Ruth Rolland, a former President of the country's Red Cross Society. She was arrested in November after distributing leaflets in Bangui accusing senior government officials of stealing diamonds found by private prospectors.

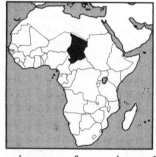

Chad

Amnesty International was concerned about the detention without trial of suspected opponents of the government, some of whom might have been prisoners of conscience. Some political detainees were released during 1986 but others remained in custody throughout the year, including at least six possible prisoners of conscience held without trial since 1983. Amnesty International was also concerned about the government's continued failure to account for a number of people who "disappeared" after being detained in previous years, who were mostly reported to have been executed extrajudicially by government security forces.

The government alleged that Libyan troops in northern Chad committed human rights abuses. The government news agency reported "frequent imprisonment, corporal punishment and physical elimination". However, when asked by Amnesty International to supply details of these allegations, the government did not do so.

There was continued conflict between the government of President

Hissein Habré and the *Gouvernement d'union nationale de transition*, (GUNT), Transitional Government of National Unity, of former President Goukouni Weddeye, which continued to occupy parts of northern Chad. In the south, there was a reduction in strife partly as a result of agreements reached between President Habré's government and groups known as *commandos* or *codos* which had previously engaged in armed opposition. This reduction in the scale and extent of internal armed conflict had a beneficial impact on human rights.

In January President Habré announced the release of 122 named political detainees. They had apparently been held in various provincial centres and in N'Djamena, the capital. It appeared that their release was linked to the conclusion of peace agreements between the government and *codo* groups. None of their cases had been known to Amnesty International.

Amnesty International pressed throughout 1986 for the trial or release of six prisoners. Abdelkarim Annadif, a former local administrator, Abbo Saleh, a trader, and four others had been detained since July 1983 when they were arrested at Abéché in eastern Chad as suspected supporters of the GUNT. Information available to Amnesty International indicated that the six might have been part of a group of Abéché citizens who signed a petition appealing to the opposition forces not to bombard the town and welcoming them. When government troops retook the town, a large number of people were arrested, including some who had signed the petition. Amnesty International was concerned that the six detained people might be prisoners of conscience and appealed to the authorities to release them without further delay if they were not to be charged and fairly tried.

Two possible prisoners of conscience detained since 1985, Clement Abaifouta and Noel Noksou, were released in May 1986, according to information received by Amnesty International. The two were apparently arrested because their names appeared on a list of people to receive grants to study abroad from an opposition group.

Information was received by Amnesty International in 1986 concerning the "disappearance" of several individuals after their reported arrests by government forces in earlier years. For example, Felix Ekeh, a Nigerian citizen, was arrested in November 1984 at his business premises in Doba, southern Chad, by government troops and taken to Doba barracks. Subsequent efforts by his family and employees to trace him were fruitless despite reported inquiries by the Nigerian Government. Amnesty International appealed in May 1986 for information about Felix Ekeh's whereabouts and legal status. Officials replied that Felix Ekeh's case was not known to them although they had undertaken an investigation, prompted by the inquiry from the Nigerian Government. They stated that he had not been arrested. Amnesty International remained concerned about the reports of Felix Ekeh's arrest by government troops and his subsequent "disappearance".

In May Amnesty International asked the government for information about Souleymane Boikete, a Chadian citizen arrested in November 1984 in Gore, southern Chad, who subsequently "disappeared". The government did not reply, despite a further request for information in October.

Comoros

Amnesty International was concerned about the imprisonment of prisoners of conscience and possible prisoners of conscience, most of whom were sentenced after trials which fell short of internationally recognized standards. A number of prisoners were released during 1986, however, either on completion of their sentences or as a result of acts of clemency by the government. An Amnesty International mission visited Comoros in August and discussed with the government the organization's concerns and the need for further measures to protect human rights.

Amnesty International was concerned about the imprisonment throughout 1986 of four civilian opponents of the government who were among 77 people tried in November 1985 on charges arising from events in March 1985, when members of the Presidential Guard mutinied against their European officers. The authorities alleged that this was part of a conspiracy involving civilian opponents who wished to overthrow the government. Moustoifa Saïd Cheikh, Secretary General of the *Front démocratique des Comores* (FDC), the Comorian Democratic Front, was sentenced to life imprisonment; FDC members Abdou Mhoumadi and Idriss Mohamed received eight-year terms; and Mohamed Abdou Soimadou received a five-year term. Sixteen members of the Presidential Guard also received sentences of life imprisonment and were held throughout 1986. All but one of those brought to trial in November 1985 were convicted but some had been released by the end of 1985. Others were freed in amnesties granted by President Ahmed Abdallah on 1 January and 13 May.

Following the November 1985 trial, as many as 70 other people were reported to have been arrested either because they had criticized the proceedings or because they were considered sympathetic to the imprisoned FDC leaders. Some were released, but in late July 42 people, most of whom had been arrested in the last two months of 1985, were brought to trial before the Correctional Court in Moroni, the capital. They were convicted of membership of an unlawful organization. The heaviest sentences were 18-month prison terms and seven of the defendants were released immediately after the trial in view of the time that they had already spent in custody. A further 17 were believed to have completed their sentences and been released by the end of 1986, at which time 18 prisoners were still believed to be held.

Amnesty International was concerned that both the November 1985 and July 1986 trials failed to satisfy internationally recognized standards of fair trial. In particular, it appeared that defendants and lawyers assigned to them were given insufficient access to the prosecution dossiers on their cases to enable them adequately to prepare their defence. It also appeared that defendants, notably those tried in November 1985, were convicted on the basis of statements made under duress while they were held incommunicado in pre-trial detention.

In February Amnesty International wrote to President Abdallah to express its concern about the conduct of the 1985 trial and the subsequent arrests. The organization welcomed the releases on 1 January and proposed that an Amnesty International delegation should visit the Comoros to discuss with the government the cases of those still held and the shortcomings of the trial. There was no response to this approach but in March it was reported that the Minister of the Interior, Information and Press, Omar Tamou, had stated in a local radio broadcast that Amnesty International had been invited to send a mission to the Comoros. No such invitation was received. However, the 30 April edition of the Paris-based magazine *Jeune Afrique* published an open letter to Amnesty International from Minister Omar Tamou. This criticized some aspects of Amnesty International's work on the Comoros but also contained a clear invitation to the organization to send a mission there. Subsequently, this invitation was confirmed by Minister Omar Tamou and an Amnesty International delegation visited the Comoros between 9 and 16 August.

In addition to Minister Tamou, Amnesty International's delegates met the Army Chief of Staff, the Minister of Justice and judicial officials. They received considerable assistance from the authorities but their requests for access to the records of the November 1985 and

July 1986 trials were denied, and they were also refused permission to visit Moustoifa Saïd Cheikh and the three other civilian prisoners. These four had earlier been adopted as prisoners of conscience by Amnesty International. Minister Omar Tamou gave the government's view that the four had been directly involved in an attempt to overthrow the state, but the authorities' refusal to permit Amnesty International access to the full documentation made it impossible to verify whether this was so. Having regard to the deficiencies of the trial, Amnesty International considered that the four prisoners should at the very least be given a new trial fully in accordance with internationally recognized standards. During the mission, Amnesty International also raised with the government the authorities' failure adequately to investigate reports of torture and ill-treatment of detainees in early 1985 and the alleged ill-treatment of some of those held following the November 1985 trial. Amnesty International's delegates stressed the need for improved safeguards against torture and ill-treatment, proposing that detainees should not be held incommunicado and that police and other security personnel should be trained to respect fundamental human rights. There was concern also about the apparent absence of statutory rules governing prison conditions. Moustoifa Saïd Cheikh, the imprisoned FDC leader, was reported to have been held in solitary confinement and to have been denied visits throughout 1986, as were the 16 members of the Presidential Guard serving life imprisonment. Noting that the Comoros had deposited its ratification to the African Charter on Human and Peoples' Rights, Amnesty International urged the government to ratify other international human rights standards, notably the International Covenant on Civil and Political Rights, the International Covenant on Economic, Social and Cultural Rights and the UN Convention Against Torture.

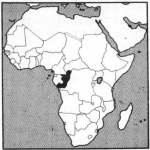

Congo

Amnesty International was concerned about the long-term detention without trial of suspected government opponents, including prisoners of conscience, and about aspects of a major political trial in August which did not conform to international standards. The organization was also concerned about new arrests of people who might be prisoners of conscience, reports of torture and the use of the death penalty.

Following an announcement by President Denis Sassou-Nguesso at the end of 1985 that those suspected of causing bomb explosions in Brazzaville in March and July 1982 were to be brought to trial, seven detainees who had been held without charge since 1983 and 1984 had their cases referred for investigation by a *commission d'instruction* (investigating commission) in April 1986. They were tried by the Revolutionary Court of Justice, a special court with jurisdiction over political cases, in August 1986. Three others were tried *in absentia*. Among the defendants were two former senior officials of the ruling *Parti congolais du travail* (PCT), Congolese Labour Party — Jean-Pierre Thystère-Tchicaya and Claude-Ernest Ndalla — on whose behalf Amnesty International had made repeated inquiries to the authorities since their arrest in 1984.

The trial sought to establish responsibility for just one of the 1982 bomb explosions, the July 1982 bombing at Brazzaville airport. Claude-Ernest Ndalla was accused of master-minding the attack, while Jean-Pierre Thystère-Tchicaya was said to have suggested the idea to him. One of the accused, Claude Kembissila, claimed in court that he had been tortured while in the custody of the state security service, the *Direction générale de la sécurité de l'Etat* (DGSE), General State Security Directorate. Other defendants retracted statements which they had made in custody on the grounds that they had been made under duress, but the presiding judge prevented several of them from giving details. The court did not investigate any of these allegations further and in general accepted the accuracy of statements made to the DGSE. The principal evidence against Claude-Ernest Ndalla and the others accused was a two-hour video-recording by the DGSE in which he confessed to the bombing and incriminated others. However, in court he denied his previous statements. He admitted that he had been in possession of explosives, but retracted all his other statements, saying that he had been "tricked" into making them. Further evidence against Claude-Ernest

Ndalla and the others came from Gaspard Kivouna, one of the accused, who was said to be an informer for the state security service. At the end of the trial all 10 accused were convicted. Claude-Ernest Ndalla was sentenced to death, Jean-Pierre Thystère-Tchicaya and one other received five-year suspended sentences and were released; the other defendants received sentences of 10 or 20 years' imprisonment. Amnesty International appealed to President Sassou-Nguesso to commute the death sentence. By the end of 1986 the sentence was not known to have been carried out.

The trial was attended by an Amnesty International observer. He concluded that the trial produced sufficient credible evidence to believe that some of the accused had been involved in some way in placing a bomb at Brazzaville airport. However, he also concluded that certain of the accused had not been involved and that two, including Jean-Pierre Thystère-Tchicaya, were prisoners of conscience. The evidence presented at the trial linking Claude-Ernest Ndalla to the possession of explosives led Amnesty International to revise its earlier belief that he was a prisoner of conscience. However, the organization remained concerned about the serious shortcomings that marked the trial and about the imposition of the death penalty on Claude-Ernest Ndalla. The procedures followed in the trial were defective in several ways. In particular, questions, rulings and statements from several of the nine judges indicated that they had made a previous assessment that the accused were lying and were guilty. Several of the judges were members of the PCT Central Committee and had been personally involved in the case at an earlier stage. The court admitted as evidence statements which the accused said had been obtained under torture or ill-treatment, when they were held in prolonged incommunicado detention. They retracted the statements in court. The court did not carry out any inquiries to establish whether the allegations of torture were true. Finally, the organization was concerned that those convicted had no right of appeal or review by a higher court.

After the trial Amnesty International asked the authorities about a number of other people arrested in 1982 in connection with the bomb explosions — notably Bernard Kolelas, Eugène Madimba, Philippe Bikinkita and Malonga — who were apparently still being held without trial. The authorities did not respond to these inquiries. At the end of 1986 it appeared that they might have been released, although this had not been confirmed.

Amnesty International learned of a number of arrests of suspected government opponents during 1986. In April Georges Mafouta-Kitoko, a civil servant, and two others were arrested, apparently because they were suspected of meeting to discuss the political situation in the country and of being in contact with government opponents abroad. Amnesty International was concerned that they might be prisoners of conscience and took up their cases for investigation. After a student demonstration in Brazzaville in November, during which three students were reportedly shot dead, there were further arrests of students and others. At the beginning of December at least seven people, including two civil servants working in the Prime Minister's office, were arrested after the authorities learned that a leaflet criticizing the government was being circulated. Most were released uncharged around the end of the year but one man, Jean-Félix Demba-Ntelo, the director of a state construction company, was still held incommunicado at the end of 1986. In all cases, those concerned were detained by the DGSE and were not remanded in custody by judicial authorities.

In early 1986 Antoine Gizenga, a former Deputy Prime Minister in Zaire, who had been detained without trial in the Congo since his arrival in April 1985, was released and allowed to remain in the country. Another Zairian who had been arrested in July 1985, Eke Akonga Nkoy, was also released during the year and allowed to leave the country. One other refugee in custody, David Kudila, was among seven Zairian refugees who were expelled from the Congo in September.

Equatorial Guinea

Amnesty International's concerns were the imprisonment of possible prisoners of conscience, an unfair political trial and the death penalty. There was one execution.

Following the reported discovery in July of a plot to overthrow the government of President Teodoro Obiang Nguema Mbasogo, 19 people were brought to trial in August before a military court (*consejo de guerra*) in the capital, Malabo. They included Deputy Prime Minister Fructuoso Mba Oñana Nchama; a member of parliament, Eugenio Abeso Mondu; other senior officials and several military officers. A member of the government, Melanio Ebendeng Nsomo, the Vice-Minister of Defence, was appointed to preside over the military court which had jurisdiction to try civilians as well as military personnel charged with crimes against state security or public order. The defendants faced a variety of charges ranging from planning a coup to insulting the head of state.

The trial concluded on 18 August. Eugenio Abeso Mondu was sentenced to death and his brother, Melchior Ndong Mondu, received a 20-year prison sentence. Five other defendants, all military officers, received 18-year sentences for failing to reveal knowledge of the alleged plot and six senior government officials, including Deputy Prime Minister Fructuoso Mba Oñana Nchama, were each sentenced to 28 months' imprisonment for insulting the head of state. Five others were acquitted and the remaining defendant was stripped of his military rank. At the end of 1986 Amnesty International was investigating reports that some of those imprisoned might be prisoners of conscience.

Amnesty International was concerned that the trial was not conducted in accordance with international standards. The trial judges could not be considered independent: one was a serving government minister and the others lacked security of tenure as, according to military law, judges could be appointed for each separate trial. In addition, it was not clear that the defendants were represented by defence counsel of their choice: their lawyers were required to be serving military officers as the trial was held before a military court. The defendants were also denied any right of appeal to a higher court, in violation of international standards.

Eugenio Abeso Mondu was executed by firing-squad on 19 August, the day after his sentence was imposed. It was not clear whether he was permitted any opportunity to petition the President for clemency. Amnesty International expressed its concern to the government about Eugenio Abeso Mondu's execution and the deficiencies of the trial. It had received no response by the end of 1986.

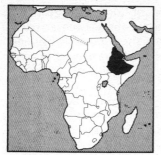

Ethiopia

Amnesty International was concerned about the imprisonment of prisoners of conscience, some of whom had been held without trial for over 12 years, and the detention without trial of many other political opponents of the government. Some political prisoners were reported to have been sentenced in secret to prison terms by a special government committee without being formally charged or tried. Amnesty International was also concerned about reports of widespread torture and ill-treatment of political prisoners. It continued to press the authorities to account for a number of "disappeared" prisoners who were feared to have been summarily executed. There were reports of summary executions of political prisoners and of people resisting resettlement into new villages.

Armed conflict between government and opposition forces continued during 1986 in many parts of the country, particularly Eritrea, Tigray, Wollega and Hararghe. Civilians in these areas suspected of having links with armed opposition groups were reportedly detained and ill-treated.

Obtaining detailed information about political arrests remained difficult as the government did not disclose any information and relatives were often afraid to report arrests for fear of official reprisal. Nevertheless about 1,000 political prisoners were believed to be being held in the Central Prison in Addis Ababa, and many more in other prisons run by the prison service, notably Sembel men's prison and Haz-Haz women's prison, both in Asmara. In addition, hundreds of prisoners were believed to be being held for interrogation in security prisons under the authority of the Ministry of State and Public Security. In the security prisons, particularly the Central Investigation Centre (*Maekalawi Mirmera Diridjit* — known informally as the "third police station" — in Addis Ababa), and the "Mariam Gimbi" Central Investigation Centre in Asmara, torture was reportedly routine. There were also reports that political prisoners were tortured in the Special Investigation (*Liyu Mirmera*) Centre of the Provisional Military Administrative Council (PMAC) in the PMAC headquarters in Addis Ababa. Many of the prisoners were believed to have been arrested on suspicion of links with opposition organizations such as the Eritrean People's Liberation Front (EPLF), Tigray People's Liberation Front (TPLF) and Oromo Liberation Front (OLF). Amnesty International also received reports of people being arrested for trying to evade military conscription or to flee the country. Relatives of those who fled were also said to have been arrested.

Political prisoners were held illegally. The Code of Criminal Procedure specifies that arrested people must be produced in court within 48 hours and either charged or released, although the court may authorize further detention without charge for up to 14 days. However, political prisoners were held for prolonged periods without charge or trial, in incommunicado detention and often without official acknowledgement. There was no effective legal remedy for such unlawful detention. Amnesty International believed that some political prisoners in 1986 were being sentenced to prison, or in some cases execution, by a secret government committee of representatives of the Ministry of State and Public Security, which is also responsible for interrogating political prisoners. Those sentenced in this way — who may have been convicted on the basis of "confessions" made under torture — were not formally charged or tried and were not permitted to appear before the committee to present a defence or to appeal against the committee's decision. They were told of the decision before being secretly executed or transferred to a civil prison. Thirteen alleged members of the Ethiopian People's Democratic Alliance (EPDA), who were arrested in December 1983 and accused of anti-revolutionary activities, were believed to be serving such secret prison sentences, ranging from five to 20 years. Amnesty International's concern that such procedures flagrantly violated fundamental principles of the rule of law received no response from justice officials in Ethiopia.

In June Amnesty International published a report, *Political Imprisonment and Torture in Ethiopia*. It contained detailed information on prisoners of conscience and other political prisoners, the legal background, torture, "disappearances" and extrajudicial execution. In submitting the report to the government Amnesty International urged the release of all prisoners of conscience and an impartial review of the cases of all other political prisoners to ensure their release or trial in accordance with international standards for a fair trial. The organization called for the immediate abolition of secret sentencing and urgent government action to stop torture and safeguard prisoners from ill-treatment. Amnesty International also urged the government to ratify the relevant international human rights instruments such as the International Covenant on Civil and Political Rights and to incorporate safeguards for the protection of human rights into a draft new constitution that had been published in June to replace the previous constitution suspended in 1974.

Amnesty International received no response to its inquiries about the arrest in mid-May of Berhanu Dinka, Ethiopia's Permanent

Representative to the UN in New York. At the end of 1986 he was still detained without charge or trial, reportedly in the Central Investigation Centre in Addis Ababa. Amnesty International was investigating whether he might be a prisoner of conscience.

Amnesty International continued to appeal for the release of prisoners of conscience arrested in previous years, including 10 members of the family of the late Emperor Haile Selassie detained since 1974. His daughter, Tenagnework Haile-Selassie, aged 74, her four daughters, a daughter-in-law and another relative, Zuriashwork Gebre-Igziabeher, were held in the women's section of the Central Prison in Addis Ababa; a grandson, Wossen-Seged Mekonnen, and his two younger brothers were held in the *Alem Bekagne* ("End of the World") maximum security section of the same prison.

The authorities gave no reason for their continued detention without charge or trial, but in 1986, for the first time since their detention began, they were permitted to receive regular medical and dental treatment in hospitals in Addis Ababa. The health of Hirut Desta continued to be of concern due to her extremely low body weight, and she was not allowed to obtain appropriate specialist treatment.

Other women prisoners of conscience still held in 1986 included Tsehai Tolessa, whose husband the Reverend Gudina Tumsa was abducted in 1979, apparently by security officers, and Martha Kumsa, a journalist. They were among many members of the Oromo ethnic group arrested in 1980 and still detained without trial, including Zegeye Asfaw, former Minister of Law and Justice, and Ababiya Abajobir, a former high court judge.

Cases of political prisoners detained without charge or trial which were being investigated by Amnesty International included that of Tesfa-Mariam Zeggay, an official of the UN Economic Commission for Africa, who was arrested in 1983 and was reported to be suffering from injuries as a result of being tortured. Amnesty International was also investigating the detention without trial of several officials of the Democratic Front for the Salvation of Somalia (DFSS), a Somali armed opposition organization based in Ethiopia.

The trial of Shimelis Teklu, an official of the Office of the United Nations High Commissioner for Refugees in Addis Ababa detained since 1984, began before the Special Court during 1986. He was charged with espionage. He was legally represented and had the right of appeal to the Special Court of Appeal if convicted.

Several prisoners of conscience were released during 1986. Negash Kebede, general secretary of the *Meseret Christos* (Mennonite) Church, and other members of the church detained since 1981, were freed in April. On 1 May the Reverend Olana Lemu and 12 other leading members of the Ethiopian Evangelical Mekane Yesus Church who had been detained without trial for several years were released. Another 50 political prisoners who had been held with them in Nekemte prison in Wollega region were also released. Tesfay Gabiso and several members of the Full Gospel (*Mullu Wongel*) Church who had been detained without trial in Yirga Alem prison in Sidamo region since 1979 were also released around the same time.

An amnesty for 775 prisoners was announced on 31 May. The identities of these prisoners were not disclosed, but they reportedly included many held since 1977 and 1978 for alleged membership of the Ethiopian People's Revolutionary Party (EPRP). A review of political prisoners' cases was said to have been undertaken after a visit to the Addis Ababa Central Prison by the Head of State Mengistu Haile-Mariam on 10 May. On 30 July, 114 detainees officially described as "former guerrillas" were released from prison in Asmara. No details were given as to whether they had been arrested on political grounds or captured in armed conflict, although several hundred people captured in combat in recent years were reported to be detained without trial in the Central Prison in Addis Ababa and in Sembel prison in Asmara.

Amnesty International continued to receive reports of torture from many parts of the country. Political prisoners were among the 1,800 inmates of Mekelle Central Prison who were freed in February by the TPLF. According to those released, many prisoners had been tortured in Mekelle Central Investigation Centre and held in harsh conditions. Amnesty International wrote to the Head of State urging a full investigation into their allegations.

Two cases were reported in which officials were prosecuted for torture. In Shoa region in July, six *kebelle* (urban dwellers association) officials were each sentenced to three years' imprisonment on charges of torturing a farmer accused of theft. In Hararghe in the same month, a court sentenced a *kebelle* chairman to death for causing the death of a prisoner by torture in 1979, and seven other officials were sentenced to life imprisonment or 25 years' imprisonment for complicity. However, despite these two prosecutions, Amnesty International was not convinced that sufficient steps were being taken to eradicate torture, investigate torture allegations and establish safeguards to protect prisoners from torture.

In January Amnesty International appealed to the government to clarify the reported "disappearance" in November 1985 of about 60 political prisoners held in Addis Ababa. Among them were Asegahegne Araya, Wube Gebre-Yohannes and Maheteme-Work Kassahun, alleged members of the EPDA who had been detained since 1983, and other prisoners held for several years for their alleged membership of the EPRP, TPLF or EPLF. Amnesty International urged the government to confirm that they were alive and well and not under threat of execution, but there was no response. Their fate was still unclear at the end of 1986 and it was feared that they might have been summarily executed. The government also failed to account for Mengesha Gebre-Hiwot, who "disappeared" from the Central Investigation Centre in Addis Ababa in mid-1985. He had been held since December 1983 for alleged membership of the EPDA and was reported to have had a foot amputated because of torture injuries. The fate of 16 other people who "disappeared" in 1979 also remained unexplained. They included prominent political detainees held since 1974 and 1977, and the leader of the Ethiopian Evangelical Mekane Yesus Church, the Reverend Gudina Tumsa, who was abducted in Addis Ababa in 1979. All were believed to have been summarily executed soon after their "disappearance".

Few details could be obtained to confirm other reports of executions of political opponents which appeared to have been carried out following secret death sentences. Four political prisoners were reported to have been secretly executed in Asmara on 3 January and two others imprisoned in Asmara were reportedly publicly executed in Segeneita, 50 kms southeast of Asmara, on 6 May. In March eight sheikhs and other Muslim leaders were reported to have been summarily executed near Hararghe, after villagers refused to participate in the official resettlement program. Many other summary or extrajudicial executions were alleged to have taken place in areas of armed conflict or of resistance to the government's mass resettlement program.

Gambia

Amnesty International was concerned about the retention of the death penalty and the introduction of new legislation extending its applicability. However, no executions were reported to have taken place.

Amnesty International learned of two cases in which critics of the government appeared to have been arrested for political reasons. In February, Boubacar Langley was arrested when he displayed a banner which appeared to criticize the government at Independence Day celebrations. He was reported to have been sentenced to 18 months' imprisonment for damaging government property, but the circumstances of his conviction were not clear. Amnesty International wrote to the Minister of the Interior in early December asking for details of his case. In October, Suntou Fatty, a leading member of the opposition Gambia People's Party, was arrested for allegedly possessing "compromising documents", but he was released after a few days.

Amnesty International wrote to the government in March after receiving reports that Pap Cheyassin Secka, a lawyer and politician convicted of participating in an unsuccessful coup attempt in 1981, was being held in solitary confinement and denied adequate medical treatment despite poor health. In response, the Minister of the Interior stated that such reports were groundless and that Pap Cheyassin Secka was in good health.

In May the President, Sir Dawda Jawara, approved an amendment to the criminal code which extended the use of the death penalty for treason, and made it mandatory in cases arising from violent attempts to overthrow the government. However, there had been no prosecutions under this provision by the end of 1986.

In early December Amnesty International wrote to the Minister of Justice about Metta Camara, a former corporal in the Gambian Field Force, who had been sentenced to death in December 1985 after being convicted of participating in an unsuccessful coup attempt in 1981. Recalling that President Jawara had previously granted clemency to others sentenced to death for participation in the coup attempt, Amnesty International appealed for Metta Camara's sentence to be commuted by the President if it were confirmed by the Court of Appeal. In response the Director of Public Prosecutions informed Amnesty International that the Court of Appeal had confirmed Metta Camara's conviction but had reduced his sentence to 20 years' imprisonment.

One other death sentence was reported to have been imposed in December at the end of a murder trial but the case was expected to go to appeal.

Ghana

Amnesty International was concerned about the imprisonment of prisoners of conscience and the detention without charge or trial of more than 50 other political prisoners. The organization was also concerned about reports of the ill-treatment of detainees subsequently tried for political offences, sentenced to death and executed. The use of the death penalty was a further concern.

Amnesty International continued throughout the year to press for the release of Jacob Yidana, a former senior police officer, who was sentenced to eight years' imprisonment with hard labour by a Public Tribunal in August 1983 on charges of assisting the escape of a criminal. Amnesty International believed that the real reason for his imprisonment was his conduct of police inquiries into the political murder of three high court judges and a former army officer in June 1982, which reportedly implicated members of the government. Amnesty International was also concerned about the procedures of the Public Tribunal which convicted him, which did not conform to internationally accepted standards of fair trial. In particular, he was not able to appeal against his sentence.

In April four people involved with left-wing groups or in trade unions were arrested. Akoto Ampaw, a former student leader, Kweku Baako, a journalist, Ralph Kugbe, an employee of a Committee for the Defence of the Revolution, and Kwesi Pratt, a public relations officer at the Ministry of Fuel and Power, were held until August 1986 when they were released uncharged. Amnesty International adopted them as prisoners of conscience because it believed the sole reason for their imprisonment was their non-violent opposition to government policy, in particular its economic policy.

At least 50 people, most of whom were believed to be former military personnel, were held without charge or trial throughout 1986 under the Preventive Custody Law, 1982 (PNDC Law 4). This empowers the ruling Provisional National Defence Council (PNDC) to authorize the indefinite detention without trial of anyone "in the interest of national security or in the interest of the safety of the person". The law of *habeas corpus* in Ghana was amended in August 1984 specifically to exclude people held under PNDC Law 4 and there was no known legal review process under this legislation.

Among those detained under PNDC Law 4 for whose fair and prompt trial Amnesty International called were six soldiers who had been members of the army's Military Intelligence branch under the government of former President Hilla Limann (1979-1981). Some reports suggested that they had been detained because they were alleged to have intimidated or assaulted members of the current government when they were in opposition (see *Amnesty International Report 1983*). Their release was announced by the Head of State on 31 December.

At least 44 other people were held under PNDC Law 4 without charge or trial throughout 1986, apparently suspected of involvement in one of the many coup attempts and plots since 1982, when the PNDC came to power.

In early November Amnesty International wrote to the Chairman of the PNDC calling for fair and prompt trials for all political prisoners. It added, however, that none should be sentenced to death or executed. In the past, some detainees prosecuted before public tribunals had been sentenced to death and executed. Among the cases raised by Amnesty International was that of George Kojo Adjei, a former detainee who had been rearrested in June 1985. At the end of 1986 he remained detained without charge or trial at Ussher Fort Prison and Amnesty International believed he might be a prisoner of conscience. Corporal Alhassan Adam, who was arrested in 1983, apparently on suspicion of involvement in a coup attempt, also continued to be held without charge or trial throughout 1986, as were Bombadier Mustapha Mohamed, Corporal Stanley Obeng Okyere, Private Rexford Ohemeng and Sergeant Emmanuel Osei. Another former soldier, Private S.K. Amponsah Dadzie, who had been tried and acquitted by a Public Tribunal in 1983 but then rearrested, was also held without charge or trial throughout 1986.

In August a former presidential candidate and leader of the Popular Front Party (PFP), Victor Owusu, was detained without charge. Press reports suggested that his detention was connected with information about an anti-government plot which the authorities obtained from Captain Edward Adjei Ampofo, who was arrested in late May, having been sentenced to death *in absentia* in 1983 on charges of treason. However, other sources suggested that Victor Owusu was detained on account of his non-violent activities in opposition to the government. His release was announced on 31 December. Following the arrest of Captain Ampofo, Amnesty International appealed to the government to commute the death sentence imposed on him in 1983 if it were confirmed on appeal.

Amnesty International was concerned about reports of ill-treatment of detainees. In particular, it noted allegations by several people tried by a Public Tribunal in May on charges of conspiring to overthrow the government that they had been hooded and beaten before their trial. An official of the Board of Public Tribunals subsequently denied that Bureau of National Investigations (BNI) personnel had ill-treated prisoners, but drew a distinction between them and the soldiers who had detained suspects. He disclosed also that the Public Tribunal had accepted that some of the accused may· have been assaulted at the time of their arrest.

Amnesty International learned of 21 death sentences passed in 1986; three of them were passed *in absentia* and two others were subsequently commuted to terms of imprisonment. Most of the death sentences were passed by Public Tribunals. The charges included conspiring to overthrow the government, armed robbery, murder and embezzlement. Amnesty International appealed for clemency in every case. However, 16 people were executed by firing-squad in late June, of whom nine had been convicted of ordinary criminal offences. The other seven had been convicted of conspiring to overthrow the government. Some of those executed for conspiring to overthrow the government alleged, as noted above, that they were ill-treated before their trial. As in all cases when Amnesty International had confirmed information about death sentences, it appealed for these to be commuted.

Guinea

Amnesty International was concerned about the government's continued failure to account for the whereabouts of some 20 prisoners who "disappeared" while in custody in July 1985 and who were alleged to have been secretly executed. Amnesty International was also concerned about the incommunicado detention without trial of at least 50 people and possibly many more, who were arrested after an unsuccessful coup attempt in July 1985, and about the continued detention without trial of some 20 people associated with former President Ahmed Sékou Touré and his government, who were arrested in April 1984. The findings of an official inquiry established to investigate the "disappearance" of many prisoners under the government of former President Sékou Touré, between 1958 and April 1984, were still awaited at the end of 1986.

Amnesty International did not learn of new political arrests during the year, but was concerned about detainees held since 1984 and

1985. Although insufficient information was available to assess whether any of them were prisoners of conscience Amnesty International was concerned that in the absence of any judicial proceedings it was likely that some detainees were being held arbitrarily and might be prisoners of conscience.

Amnesty International received further information during 1986 about prisoners arrested after the July 1985 coup attempt. This indicated that many of those arrested had played no direct part in the attempted coup on 4 July 1985, but had been detained apparently because they were regarded as supporters of Diarra Traoré, the alleged leader of the coup. Those detained were reported to include both Diarra Traoré's wife and an imam who acted as his religious advisor. It appeared that detainees suspected of involvement in the July 1985 coup attempt were held in military custody without being referred to the courts or to either the civilian or military judiciary. During 1986 they reportedly remained in detention at Alpha Yaya Diallo military camp in Conakry, where they were not allowed to receive visits from relatives, lawyers or others. Amnesty International was unable to obtain detailed information about conditions at the camp, but did receive confirmation that some of those arrested in July 1985 and during the following months had been tortured after their arrest, while in military custody. It was not clear whether the use of torture continued during 1986. Unofficial sources reported that a number of detainees held at the camp died during the year, but it was not possible to obtain independent confirmation.

No further information was made public by the government about the fate of some 20 political prisoners alleged to have been executed summarily and secretly in July 1985 (see *Amnesty International Report 1986*). Amnesty International urged the government to clarify the fate of these prisoners but received no response. In September it submitted details about them to the UN Working Group on Enforced or Involuntary Disappearances. They included 11 prisoners detained since April 1984 on account of their activities under the government of former President Sékou Touré, some of whom were alleged to have been involved in killing or torturing political detainees, and nine others believed to have been arrested in July 1985.

The government also made no further information public in relation to "disappearances" which occurred before April 1984, under the administration of President Sékou Touré. It was not clear whether the Commission of Inquiry set up after President Lansana Conté took power in April 1984 to account for missing prisoners was continuing its work, but no progress seemed to have been made towards either clarifying the fate of "disappeared" prisoners or bringing to trial those responsible for human rights abuses committed in the period before April 1984.

On a number of occasions during 1986 Amnesty International asked the authorities for information about prisoners and suggested steps to be taken to protect human rights in Guinea. In July the organization wrote to President Conté proposing eight practical measures to prevent arbitrary detention, torture and "disappearances". These were based on the 12-point program for the abolition of torture published by Amnesty International in April 1984. The proposals included introducing a procedure for bringing all detainees before a judicial authority, such as a representative of the public prosecutor's office, promptly after arrest, as required by international law, and for making judicial officers responsible for ensuring the legal procedures were respected and for checking on the detainees' well-being. Amnesty International also recommended establishing a central register in each province with the names and whereabouts of detainees, so that relatives and legal representatives could obtain this information. By the end of 1986 Amnesty International had received no response from the Guinean authorities to its July letter.

Guinea-Bissau

Amnesty International was concerned about 12 people who were sentenced to death after an unfair trial, six of whom were executed, and about reports that prisoners had been tortured and ill-treated. There was concern about the continuing detention without charge or trial of Rafael Barbosa but the organization welcomed the release of three other long-term political detainees.

Amnesty International sent a mission to Guinea Bissau from 17 to 23 June at the invitation of the government. Its delegates held discussions with President João Bernardo Vieira and a range of government, judicial and other officials. They also attended one session of the trial of the former Vice-President of the Council of State, Colonel Paulo Correia, and 55 others, both military personnel and civilians, accused of involvement in a plot to overthrow the government. The trial began before a military court on 5 June. Many of the defendants had been arrested in October and November 1985 on suspicion of planning to place a bomb in the town of Bafata where the President was due to make a speech on 14 November, the fifth anniversary of his accession to power. Following these arrests, other people were detained and charged with planning an assault on the prison to liberate the alleged coup plotters. The total number of people arrested was not known to Amnesty International. Six of the detainees died in custody and some others were known to have been released before the trial. The trial was held before the Superior Military Tribunal comprising a president, two other judges and an assessor. The hearing was observed by an invited audience which included military personnel and government officials. The defendants were assisted by legal counsel. Both those charged with plotting to overthrow the government and those accused of planning to free the alleged plotters from prison were tried together. Among the principal defendants were Viriato Rodrigues Pã, a former supreme court judge, Comandante João Biambi, who was allegedly responsible for keeping the explosive device, and Benhancaren Na Tchanda, the head of the presidential guard. Others were senior administrative, judicial and military officials, soldiers and civilians. Most of the defendants belonged to the Balanta ethnic group. On 12 July, 12 defendants were sentenced to death, 24 people were sentenced to prison terms of between one and eight years and 16 others received sentences of between 12 and 15 years' imprisonment. Four people were acquitted. There was no judicial appeal against the decision of the Superior Military Tribunal, which is the highest military court. The 12 people sentenced to death did, however, have the opportunity to appeal to the Council of State for clemency. As a result, six death sentences were commuted to 15-year prison terms. The other six people, Paulo Correia, Viriato Rodrigues Pã, Benhancaren Na Tchanda, Colonel Pedro Ramos, a high court judge, Braima Bangura, former Secretary of State for Veterans, and N'Bunhe Sanbu, a soldier, were executed by firing-squad on 18 July 1986, six days after being sentenced. On 14 July Amnesty International appealed for the commutation of the death sentences. It also informed the government of its concern that the trial had not conformed to international standards of fairness: those sentenced to death did not have the right to appeal to a higher court against the verdict and sentences; in addition, there was concern that evidence obtained by coercion had been admitted in court.

During 1986 Amnesty International received reports that some of the detainees arrested in connection with the coup plot had been beaten and otherwise ill-treated. Amnesty International's delegates were present in court when one of the defendants, a security official, claimed that he had been threatened with torture during his pre-trial interrogation. Subsequently, the organization received reports that other defendants had also told the court that they had been forced to make self-incriminating statements. No investigation of these complaints was known to have taken place. Amnesty International also received allegations that other prisoners had been beaten and ill-treated.

Six people detained in connection with the plot died in custody. João da Silva, a former Minister of Culture and Sport, was shot while attempting to escape from prison in November 1985. The other five were reported by official sources to have died of illnesses. Unofficial sources claimed that the illnesses were exacerbated by ill-treatment in custody. Amnesty International urged the government to establish an independent inquiry into the deaths and to make the findings public. It was informed by the authorities that the five who had died between February and July 1986 had been ill before their arrest and had received all possible medical treatment while in custody. While it was unable to confirm any of the allegations of ill-treatment, Amnesty International remained concerned that measures to protect prisoners from torture or ill-treatment were inadequate. The military authorities were responsible for both the custody and the interrogation of detainees implicated in the coup plot and the defendants were apparently held incommunicado for extended periods and did not have access to legal counsel until a week before the trial.

Amnesty International's concern about the death penalty was not confined to the death sentences passed on 12 July. At least one other person, Jorge Sanca, a soldier charged with homicide, was sentenced to death by a military court and executed in February. The death penalty was introduced into Guinea Bissau by the Law of Military Justice which was promulgated in 1966 by the *Partido Africano para a Independência da Guinea Bissau e Cabo Verde* (PAIGC), African Party for the Independence of Guinea Bissau and Cape Verde, in the areas which they had liberated from colonial control. However, as far as the organization knew, no other death sentences had been carried out in Guinea Bissau since the present government came to power in November 1980.

Amnesty International continued to investigate the case of Rafael Barbosa who was rearrested in June 1985 and held under an administrative restriction order on one of the islands in the Bijagos archipelago (see *Amnesty International Report 1986*).

Three long-term detainees were released in 1986. Francisco Barbosa, a relative of Rafael Barbosa, who was arrested in April 1985 and accused of distributing an anonymous leaflet criticizing the government, was released on 18 January. Fernando Delfim da Silva, arrested in Bissau in June 1985 on his return from the Soviet Union, was released in May. Amnesty International was informed by the government that the allegations leading to his arrest had proved to be false. The authorities said they had been told that he had tried to establish an opposition party among compatriot students in Leningrad. All restrictions on Victor Saude Maria, a former Prime Minister accused of plotting against the government, were removed in November. He had been detained under administrative detention or restriction orders since March 1984.

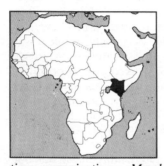

Kenya

Amnesty International was concerned about a large number of political arrests during 1986; it was investigating whether those arrested were prisoners of conscience. Over 200 people were arrested for alleged opposition to the government, many of whom were accused of having links with a clandestine opposition organization, *Mwakenya* (*Muungano wa Wazalendo wa Kukuomboa Kenya* — Union of Nationalists for the Liberation of Kenya). Amnesty International was concerned that many "disappeared" after being arrested by unidentified security officers: they were held in custody for several days or weeks without official acknowledgement or explanation. Subsequently, nine were formally detained under the Preservation of Public Security Act, 50 were convicted of political offences in trials which appeared to be unfair, and the remainder were released without charge. Amnesty International was concerned about allegations that many were tortured or ill-treated. Amnesty International was also concerned about the imprisonment since 1982 of three prisoners of conscience, one of whom was released in December. The organization was concerned about the death penalty.

In early March Ngotho Kariuki, a former university lecturer, Kariuki Gathitu and Joseph Kamonye Manje, both lecturers, Oyangi Mbaja, a businessman, and three other men were arrested — apparently for political reasons — and held without explanation of the grounds of arrest or why they were not brought to court within the normal 24-hour limit. Amnesty International inquired about their legal status, their whereabouts in custody, and the grounds for their arrests, and urged the authorities to charge or release them. The organization appealed for them to be given immediate access to legal representatives, their families and doctors. A *habeas corpus* application by Ngotho Kariuki's family on 21 March led to the disclosure by the authorities that he had been detained four days earlier under the Preservation of Public Security Act, which permits detention for an indefinite period without charge or trial. Kariuki Gathitu's detention under this act was admitted two weeks later. Under the act detainees must be given a written statement of the grounds for detention within five days. A Detention Review Tribunal reviews the case within one month and then every six months. Detainees have the right to legal representation at the tribunal hearing, which is secret. The tribunal's findings are also kept secret and are not binding.

Between 25 and 27 March Joseph Kamonye Manje, Oyangi Mbaja and the three other prisoners, one of whom had apparently been held secretly since January, were brought to court and charged with sedition. They all pleaded guilty and two were sentenced to 18 and 30 months' imprisonment for "neglecting to report a felony" (namely, the existence of an anti-government organization producing seditious publications) and three received prison terms of four and a half or five years for possession of a seditious publication. The publication, *Mpatanishi* ("The Unifier"), which was published by *Mwakenya*, was said to criticize the government and to advocate socialism in Kenya, although its contents were not disclosed in court. Amnesty International asked the authorities about their trials, in particular about whether the defendants had been allowed legal representation and whether any of the documents advocated violence or merely criticized the government. No reply was received.

At least six other people were arrested in early April and held incommunicado for a prolonged period without legal basis or official acknowledgement. Among them were Mukaru Ng'ang'a, a former prisoner of conscience detained from 1982 to 1984, and Julius Mwandawiro Mghanga, a former student leader previously imprisoned in 1985. Mukaru Ng'ang'a was detained under the Preservation of Public Security Act on 11 July after three months' unlawful detention. Julius Mwandawiro Mghanga was brought to court on 29 April and sentenced to five years' imprisonment after pleading guilty to possession of a seditious publication.

By the end of 1986 over 200 people had reportedly been arrested in similar circumstances. They were illegally held for several days or weeks without official acknowledgement in incommunicado detention before being released without charge, tried, or formally detained under the Preservation of Public Security Act. Among those formally detained under the Preservation of Public Security Act were Wanyiri Kihoro and Mirugi Kariuki, both lawyers, Katama Mkangi, a lecturer, and a businessman and two university students. A total of 50 prisoners were tried and convicted of political offences and imprisoned for periods ranging from 15 months to seven years. They included students, teachers, businessmen, civil servants and farmers. They pleaded guilty to offences such as the possession or distribution of seditious publications, neglecting to report a felony, or taking an unlawful oath (to join the *Mwakenya* organization). Several were alleged by the prosecution to be members of *Mwakenya* but this did not form part of the charges against them. Three former university students pleaded guilty in July to damaging a railway line on the instructions of *Mwakenya*, and were imprisoned for seven years.

There was particular concern at the "disappearance" of Kiboi Kariuki, former chairman of the Railways Union, after his arrest on 22 October. It was reported to Amnesty International that he was held secretly by the Special Branch in Nairobi and was being tortured. Urgent appeals were made to the government and his "disappearance" was reported to the UN Working Group on Enforced or Involuntary Disappearances. He was released at the end of December, seriously ill as a result of torture.

Amnesty International was investigating whether some of the detained or convicted prisoners might be prisoners of conscience, although it recognized that at least one of the *Mwakenya* publications named in court advocated violence. Amnesty International was also inquiring into whether those taken to court received fair trials, in view of the apparent denial of access to legal representatives. There were also allegations that "confessions" and guilty pleas had been extracted through torture.

Many of those arrested were reportedly tortured by Special Branch police officers in Nairobi to make them "confess" and plead guilty in court. Some prisoners were allegedly held naked in water-flooded cells for periods ranging from two days to a week at a time, beaten with sticks, deprived of food for several days, held in dimly-lit underground cells and denied medical treatment. Amnesty International's appeals to the authorities to ensure that prisoners were protected from torture received no response.

In December an Amnesty International delegate visited Kenya to investigate these trials. The delegate met the Attorney General and other officials and observed two trials of people charged with taking an unlawful oath to join *Mwakenya*. A report was in preparation at the end of 1986.

Amnesty International continued to appeal for the release of three prisoners of conscience held since 1982. Otieno Mak'Onyango, a newspaper editor, and Raila Odinga, a civil servant, were both detained indefinitely without trial under the Preservation of Public Security Act. Maina wa Kinyatti, a lecturer, was serving a six-year prison sentence for possession of a seditious document. Otieno Mak'Onyango was reported to be in persistent ill-health and to have been denied adequate medical treatment. Amnesty International welcomed his release by presidential order on 12 December, Independence Day, but renewed its appeals for the release of Raila Odinga and Maina wa Kinyatti, who were still imprisoned at the end of 1986. A legal action by Raila Odinga in February seeking an order for his release and complaining about ill-treatment had been unsuccessful. Maina wa Kinyatti was reportedly denied proper medical treatment for several medical complaints including one which was endangering his eye-sight. He was also denied the one-third remission of sentence for which he became eligible in October.

Six of the university students sentenced in 1982 and 1983 to prison terms of between five and 10 years for sedition (see *Amnesty International Report 1986*) were released during 1985 after being granted remission of their sentences.

Amnesty International was concerned about the poor conditions in which untried political detainees and convicted political prisoners were held. Medical treatment was inadequate, diet was poor, and prisoners slept on the cement floors of their cells with only blankets and a mat. Convicted prisoners were allowed monthly visits and regular correspondence with relatives but political detainees' contact with their families was severely restricted. Raila Odinga and Maina wa Kinyatti were held in permanent solitary confinement.

By the end of 1986 there were believed to be up to 200 prisoners held under sentence of death for murder or robbery with violence, including more than 25 convicted of these offences during the year. At least eight executions were believed to have taken place during 1986, although without official announcement.

Lesotho

Amnesty International was concerned about the detention without trial and administrative restriction of alleged government opponents. Three political detainees were reported to have died in custody in suspicious circumstances and two former government ministers and their wives were victims of politically motivated killings, alleged to have been carried out by agents of the government. Several South African political refugees or exiles were also victims of killings or abductions, which unofficial sources alleged were carried out by South African security agents acting with local support.

The government of Prime Minister Chief Leabua Jonathan, which had itself seized power in 1970, was overthrown by the armed forces on 20 January. For three weeks before the coup, Lesotho had been subject to an economic blockade by South Africa, which accused the government of permitting African National Congress (ANC) guerrilla fighters to operate from Lesotho. Five opposition political leaders who visited Pretoria briefly to discuss the blockade with the South African authorities were arrested on their return to Lesotho. They were freed several days later when the armed forces, led by Major-General Justin Lekhanya, seized power. The South African blockade was lifted when the new government agreed to deport certain South African refugees to other countries of asylum.

Following the change of government, King Moshoeshoe II was given additional powers, and a new government comprising a six-member Military Council and a subordinate Council of Ministers, both chaired by Major-General Lekhanya, took power. Subsequently, an amnesty was granted for political prisoners and exiles, which resulted in the release of Mathabiso Mosala and others awaiting trial on political charges (see *Amnesty International Report 1986*). In late March the King announced a ban on all political party activity and new legislation providing for up to two years' imprisonment for violating the ban. After the coup, the Youth Wing of Chief Jonathan's Basutoland National Party was disbanded and the Lesotho Liberation Army, a guerrilla force which had been opposed to Chief Jonathan's government, became inactive.

Following the coup, a number of people were arrested. Among them were Colonel Sehlabo Sehlabo, who had led a mutiny apparently in an attempt to prevent the coup, and Brigadier B.M. Ramotsekhoane, Major-General Lekhanya's deputy as army commander. In March the government announced that both men had died in detention: Colonel Sehlabo's death was said to have been caused by a heart attack, but no reasons were given for the deaths of Brigadier Ramotsekhoane and another soldier, Sergeant M. Tjane, whose death was also reported. Subsequently, Amnesty International received information which suggested that the deaths of Colonel Sehlabo and Brigadier Ramotsekhoane had been caused by ill-treatment. It was reported at the end of 1986 that inquests on both men were expected early in 1987.

Former Information Minister Desmond Sixishe and former Foreign Minister Vincent Makhele were also detained after the coup but they were released within a few weeks. However, in August they were among six former officials who, together with Chief Jonathan, were placed under restriction orders by the authorities. Chief Jonathan had previously been under house arrest.

On 15 November Desmond Sixishe and Vincent Makhele and their wives were abducted by a group of armed men and killed. Two friends who were abducted with them were injured but escaped. They were believed to have told the authorities that those responsible for the killings were military personnel but no arrests were known to have been made by the end of 1986.

Two months before the killings of Desmond Sixishe and Vincent Makhele, a leading church official was expelled from the country after he alleged that a death squad acting on behalf of the South African Government was operating in Lesotho. Father Michael Worsnip, General Secretary of the Christian Council of Lesotho, was deported in mid-September after he confirmed to the press the existence of widespread suspicion among South African refugees in Lesotho that this death squad was responsible for recent abductions and killings of alleged ANC activists. The victims included Joseph Mothopeng, who was reported to have been shot dead on 19 July when armed men attempted to abduct him, and Simon Makhetha, who was abducted on 22 July and widely believed to have been taken to South Africa.

Liberia

Amnesty International was concerned about the imprisonment of prisoners of conscience and the detention without trial of suspected opponents of the government. An Amnesty International observer attended two major political trials in which the authorities attempted to deny a fair trial to the defendants, although all were eventually released. There was also concern that military personnel court-martialled for their alleged involvement in an attempted coup in November 1985 might not have received fair trials. At least one death sentence was imposed although it was not known if the sentence was carried out. Amnesty International continued to urge an impartial inquiry into the extrajudicial execution of journalist Charles Gbenyon, who was killed by government troops several days after the coup attempt.

At the beginning of 1986 several hundred people arrested after an attempt to overthrow the government on 12 November 1985 were still in detention. Many appeared to have had no involvement in the coup attempt but were arrested for their opposition to the government. Some of the several hundred soldiers detained were imprisoned, Amnesty International believed, because of their ethnic group rather than their involvement in the coup attempt. Many of them were from the Gio or Mano ethnic groups, reportedly victimized by members of the Khran ethnic group which is dominant in President Samuel Doe's administration. In June President Doe ordered the release of some of the soldiers detained without trial.

On 6 January, the day of his official inauguration, President Doe ordered the release of 19 of those arrested, some of whom Amnesty International considered to be prisoners of conscience or possible prisoners of conscience. Others were released later in January and February, among them Momolu Sirleaf, a publisher, and Isaac Bantu, a journalist. Several opposition politicians, including Jackson F. Doe, Chairman of the Liberian Action Party (LAP) and a candidate in the 1985 presidential elections were also released. However, Ellen Johnson-Sirleaf, another leading member of the LAP and former prisoner of conscience, was charged with treason and indicted by a grand jury on 2 April 1986. An Amnesty International observer who attended the committal proceedings reported that some jurors alleged that they had been threatened and offered bribes by court officials to indict her. She was released on the orders of President Doe in early June. In September, she left Liberia to seek refuge abroad, reportedly after being threatened with death by a senior official of the ruling National Democratic Party of Liberia. Three other civilians were charged in 1986 with criminal offences associated with the attempted coup and brought to trial before civilian courts. A large number of others were tried *in camera* by court-martial. Most were believed to be soldiers, although details of individual trials were not available to Amnesty International.

The trial on charges of treason arising from the coup attempt of James Holder, Anthony Macquee and Robert Phillips began in February. They were alleged to have supplied weapons to the rebels. An Amnesty International observer reported that the trial judge was accused by jurors of having tried to influence them in favour of the prosecution by means of threats and bribes. Despite this, in early May the jury returned a unanimous verdict of not guilty with respect to James Holder and Robert Phillips. They were not released until June, when President Doe ordered them to be freed, together with Anthony Macquee and a number of others detained in the wake of the coup attempt. In February, Amnesty International had expressed concern to the government about reports that Robert Phillips had been tortured with electric shocks during his pre-trial detention. The government did not respond. Amnesty International subsequently learned that these reports were untrue, but did confirm that Robert Phillips had been ill-treated.

In July three opposition politicians — Jackson Doe, Gabriel Kpolleh and Edward Kessely — were detained for about two weeks, first in Monrovia, the capital, and then at the remote prison of Bella Yellah in Lofa County, for refusing to pay a fine of US$1,000. The fine had been imposed because they had formed a party coalition which was not registered with the authorities in the same way that their individual parties were. Amnesty International considered them to be prisoners of conscience. They were released when they paid the fine.

In September the death penalty was extended to cover armed robbery, and the Minister of National Defence, General Gray Allison, announced that any soldier, or civilian in uniform, accused of armed robbery would be court-martialled and immediately executed if found guilty. It was not known if anyone was court-martialled and sentenced to death under this legislation in 1986. However, at least one person was sentenced to death after being convicted of murder. Amnesty International urged the government to grant clemency in all cases in which the death penalty was imposed.

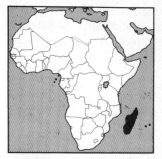

Madagascar

Amnesty International was concerned about the continued detention without trial of some 36 alleged opponents of the government, some of whom might have been prisoners of conscience. There were also new allegations of harsh prison conditions amounting to cruel, inhuman or degrading treatment.

Amnesty International continued to investigate the cases of 36 people arrested on 1 August 1985 when security forces in the capital, Antananarivo, attacked buildings occupied by members of martial arts clubs suspected of opposing the government. Between 20 and 60 deaths were reported to have occurred as a result of the attacks and more than 200 people were detained, the majority of whom were released, however, within a few weeks. Although there was a history of violent clashes between members of martial arts clubs and members of a pro-government youth organization *Tanora Tonga Saina*, Youth Who Are Aware of Their Responsibilities, it appeared that some of those detained since August 1985 might have been held on account of their peaceful opposition to the government. Throughout 1986 Amnesty International pressed for them to be brought to trial or released, but none of the 36 detainees had been tried by the end of the year.

Amnesty International received new reports of harsh prison conditions. A high incidence of deaths among prisoners was reported to have occurred as a result of severe overcrowding, malnutrition and a lack of adequate medical facilities in the prisons.

Malawi

Amnesty International was concerned about the imprisonment of prisoners of conscience, some of whom had been convicted after unfair trials in Malawi's traditional courts. Alleged political opponents and religious dissenters were detained without trial and Amnesty International investigated two reported deaths of detainees as a result of torture.

Detention without trial in Malawi is allowed under the Preservation of Public Security Regulations, 1965, if the President deems it necessary "for the preservation of public order". Detention may be for up to 28 days on the authority of an "authorized officer"; subsequently a detainee may be held indefinitely on the orders of the President. The Public Security Regulations also make it an offence to publish anything likely "to undermine the authority of, or public confidence in the government". Under the penal code individuals may be imprisoned if they further the aims of an "unlawful society", that is, any group considered to be "dangerous to the good government of the Republic".

Three prisoners of conscience adopted by Amnesty International were released in May. Jonathan Kuntambila, Sandy Kuwale and Paul Akomenji, all journalists working for Malawi's officially controlled news media, had been detained in March 1985 for reporting a speech by the country's Official Hostess, Cecilia Tamanda Kadzamira. Addressing a conference on women and development, Cecilia Kadzamira had stated: "Man cannot do without woman". She subsequently denied saying this, although it was recorded in the official UN transcript of the speech. It appeared that the remark was deemed offensive to the unmarried Life-President Dr Hastings Kamuzu Banda. The three detained journalists had included the offending remark in their reports of the speech.

In some other cases of prisoners detained without charge or trial, Amnesty International did not have sufficient information to determine whether they were prisoners of conscience. They included Ulemu Msonthi, a farmer, who was reported to have been detained in Maula prison since 1984, possibly because his father was John Msonthi, a government minister in the 1960s who was subsequently dismissed by President Banda. Amnesty International was also investigating the case of Emberson Jonas Kantefa, detained in Maula prison since November 1985, and continued to inquire into the situation of three political detainees, Aleke Banda, Ferndo Mfipa and

Francis Pollock Mhango (see *Amnesty International Report 1986*). The organization received no information to indicate that they had been released by the end of 1986.

That section of the penal code directed against "unlawful societies" had in the past been used particularly against Jehovah's Witnesses, whose religious convictions prevented them from joining political groupings and who refused to buy membership cards for the Malawi Congress Party (MCP), the country's sole party. In the late 1960s and early 1970s many Jehovah's Witnesses were imprisoned, dozens were killed and thousands fled the country to escape persecution. In recent years repression of Jehovah's Witnesses has eased, but in 1986 Amnesty International investigated reports of people being imprisoned ˙for suspected membership of the sect or possession of its literature.

In November two civil servants, Khomboka Shawa and Batwell Nkhata, were reportedly convicted by a traditional court in Lilongwe of seeking to overthrow the government. They were sentenced to two years' and nine months' imprisonment respectively, both with hard labour. They had reportedly opposed the practice of making financial contributions to President Banda, and Amnesty International adopted them as prisoners of conscience. Malawi's traditional courts do not conform to internationally accepted legal norms: for example, judges are not required to have legal training and defendants do not normally have a right to legal representation. Two other prisoners of conscience adopted by Amnesty International who remained imprisoned after having received an unfair trial in a traditional court were Ortan Chirwa, leader of the exiled opposition group, the Malawi Freedom Movement (MAFREMO), and his wife Vera Chirwa (see *Amnesty International Report 1986*). In 1983 they had been sentenced to death by the Southern Regional Traditional Court and in 1984 their appeals had been rejected by the National Traditional Court of Appeal. President Banda commuted their death sentences to life imprisonment in 1984 and at the end of 1986 they were reportedly in Mikuyu prison.

Severe beatings of political detainees and criminal suspects were reported to be common. Amnesty International investigated the cases of two prisoners reported to have died in custody as a result of ill-treatment. Medson Chilita, a civil servant from the northern region of Malawi, was reported to have died on 4 July in Maula prison in Lilongwe, after being ill-treated and denied food for several days. He had been detained without charge or trial since his arrest in early 1985, apparently for opposition to the government. Hellings Mughogho, a Jehovah's Witness, was reported to have died in custody at Rumphi, in northern Malawi, on 2 October, as a result of beatings. In both cases Amnesty International appealed to President Banda to investigate the deaths.

Mali

Amnesty International was concerned about the imprisonment of several prisoners of conscience, all of whom were released by the end of 1986. There were reports of ill-treatment of detainees and of harsh conditions at Taoudenit prison camp. Amnesty International was also concerned about the death penalty.

Eight people were detained in January after the authorities intercepted certain documents sent by an exiled opponent of the government to a student, Perignama Sylla. The documents apparently criticized the government, suggested the revival of an independent student organization and recalled the death in detention in 1980 of a student leader, Abdoul Karim "Cabral" Camara. Perignama Sylla left the country but eight of his friends and relatives, who were suspected of assisting his departure, were arrested. They were held incommunicado in police custody for 10 weeks, during which some of them were reported to have been hung up by their hands or feet and denied adequate food or medical treatment. Two were subsequently released without charge. The six others were moved in early April to Bamako prison, where their legal status remained uncertain until 20 June when a formal order authorizing their detention was issued. They were then charged with insulting the head of state, distributing false information, aiding and abetting, and harbouring criminals. Amnesty International raised the detainees' cases with the Malian authorities, on the grounds that they appeared to be prisoners of conscience. On 4 November they were brought to trial before the court of first instance in Bamako. Four of the defendants, including student Oumar Mariko, were convicted of harbouring criminals and given suspended prison sentences. Two others, one of whom was retired mechanic Bakary Diarra, were acquitted. All six were released. Perignama Sylla and another former student were tried *in absentia*, and the heaviest sentence, three years' imprisonment, was imposed on Perignama Sylla for insulting the head of state.

In November teachers went on strike in protest against delays in payment of their salaries. A number were arrested, including

Diounkounda Traore, a teacher and trade union leader who had previously been adopted by Amnesty International as a prisoner of conscience in 1981. All were apparently released uncharged after a few days in custody.

Amnesty International received new reports of harsh conditions in Taoudenit prison, a military camp situated in a remote desert area. Political prisoners were reportedly allowed no contact with the outside world, denied adequate food and medical treatment, forced to work in salt mines despite the extreme heat, and beaten if they did not work hard enough. Among those held there were prisoners convicted in 1978 of attempting to overthrow the government. The severe conditions in the camp were believed to have seriously affected the health of some prisoners, and to have led to some deaths. Of two prisoners released late in 1985, one was reported to have required surgery as a result of his treatment in the camp and another, released in a severely debilitated state, died two months later.

Five people were reported to have been sentenced to death *in absentia*: Sidi Demba Madina Soumbounou, convicted in August of treason and insulting the head of state, and four men convicted in December of theft, grievous bodily harm and possession of stolen goods. It was not known if any other death sentences were imposed during 1986, or if any executions were carried out.

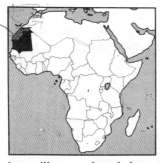

Mauritania

Amnesty International was concerned about the imprisonment of prisoners of conscience and the detention without trial of other suspected opponents of the government. Twenty-one people were imprisoned in September after a trial marked by serious inadequacies. There were reports that some detainees had been ill-treated and that prisoners generally were held in poor conditions with inadequate medical facilities.

In early September some 30 people, mostly professionals, were arrested in connection with the distribution, both within Mauritania and abroad, of a manifesto alleging discrimination by the ruling Arab-Berber population against the southern, black population. Twenty-one of them were brought to trial on 25 September charged with holding unauthorized meetings, displaying and distributing material harmful to the national interest, and making racialist propaganda. They were convicted on all charges. Four were sentenced to six-month prison terms and 17 received four- and five-year prison sentences, with fines, to be followed by five and 10 years' internal exile and loss of civil rights. The heaviest sentences were imposed on Ibrahima Sarr, a journalist, Abdoulaye Barry, an official in the Ministry of Foreign Affairs, Ibrahima Sall, a lecturer at the University of Nouakchott, and Tene Youssouf Gueye, a writer and poet who was reported to have intended to stand as a candidate in the forthcoming municipal elections. The trial lasted less than a day. The defendants were denied access to defence lawyers before the trial and the defence lawyers were given insufficient time to examine the prosecution dossiers and withdrew from the trial in protest when their request for more time was rejected. The defendants were apparently convicted largely on the basis of statements they had made while detained incommunicado in police custody. Several of the defendants were reported to have alleged in court that they had been tortured or ill-treated in detention and one woman defendant stated that she had been raped by a senior police officer at the time of her arrest, but the court apparently failed to investigate these allegations. On 13 October the Court of Appeal confirmed all the convictions and sentences despite the fact that the state had not contested appeals in four of the cases. Amnesty International expressed its concern that they might be prisoners of conscience. In a related trial, Captain Abdoulaye Kebe, an army officer, was convicted by a military court in September of revealing state secrets. He was said to have provided statistics on the racial composition of the army command for inclusion in the manifesto. He was reportedly sentenced to five years' imprisonment and 12 years' internal exile after a trial *in camera*.

Following the arrests and trials in September, there were demonstrations in various parts of the country and a second wave of arrests in September and October. The government alleged that vehicles and buildings had been attacked. At least 100 people, and perhaps many more, were detained in various parts of the country. There were reports that troops had arrested people, including some schoolchildren, in southern districts. By the end of 1986 at least 17 people had been brought to trial on charges related to the unrest and sentenced to prison terms, and at least 30 were reported to be awaiting trial.

Two other apparently politically motivated arrests were reported in September. Mahmoudi Ould Boukhreis, a businessman, and Def Ould Babana, a diplomat, were reported to have been suspected of pro-Libyan sympathies. They were believed to have been released from detention and placed under house arrest before the end of 1986.

Amnesty International was also concerned about the continued house arrest of the former head of state, Lieutenant-Colonel Mohamed Khouna Ould Haidalla and five former government officials. They were arrested following the coup in December 1984 which brought to power the government of Colonel Maaouya Ould Sid' Ahmed Taya. Their detention was authorized by presidential decrees, renewable every six months, which specifically denied them any family or other visits. Mohamed Khouna Ould Haidalla and Commandant Mohamed Lemine Ould Zein, former chief of staff of the gendarmerie, were reported to be suffering ill-health as a result of their detention. It was alleged in particular that Mohamed Lemine Ould Zein, a diabetic, had been denied a medically prescribed diet and exercise and specialist medical treatment. Amnesty International received no response to its inquiries about them.

During 1986, for the first time since the present government came to power in December 1984, Amnesty International received reports of torture. Some of those arrested in September and October were alleged to have been tortured or ill-treated in police custody, and to have required medical treatment. Kane Abdoul Aziz, an agronomist arrested on 17 October, apparently in connection with the collection of funds for the families of the 20 convicted on 25 September, was reported to have been beaten by police, as was Saïdou Kane, a student at the University of Nouakchott. No inquiry was believed to have been made by the authorities into these allegations. There were also several reports that conditions for detainees and for convicted prisoners were harsh, particularly in the Civil Prison in Nouakchott where food, exercise, hygiene and medical facilities were said to be inadequate. Both before and after their trials, political prisoners were reported to have been denied all contact with their families.

Mauritius

Amnesty International was concerned about the extension of the death penalty. Article 38 of the Dangerous Drugs Act, 1986, which came into force on 12 September, introduced a mandatory death sentence for any person convicted of importing "dangerous drugs", which included opium, heroin, cannabis and coca leaves. Unlike other serious offences under Mauritian law, which are tried before a jury of nine citizens, the offence of importation under the Dangerous Drugs Act is heard by a judge without a jury.

In the course of the parliamentary debate on the Dangerous Drugs Bill, Sir Gaëtan Duval, leader of the *Parti mauricien sociale démocrate* (PMSD), Mauritanian Social Democratic Party, who was also Minister of Justice, proposed a minimum 30-year sentence in place of the death sentence. However, this proposal was not accepted.

The death penalty was already in force in Mauritius for a number of offences, principally murder, treason and mutiny. However, on the very rare occasions that courts have handed down death sentences, they have usually been commuted to lesser sentences. In 1984 a convicted murderer became the first person to be executed in Mauritius since independence in 1968. No death sentences were reported to have been imposed under the new law. One person was reported to have been sentenced to death for murder in 1986. No executions were reported to have taken place.

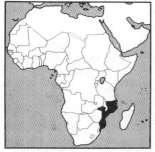

Mozambique

Amnesty International was concerned about the detention without trial of suspected government opponents including alleged supporters of an armed opposition group, the *Resistência Nacional Moçambicana* (RNM or RENAMO), Mozambique National Resistance. Some detainees arrested in the mid-1970s were considered to have "disappeared". The organization continued to investigate the cases of prisoners serving sentences after unfair trials between 1979 and 1983. There was continued concern about reports of torture and about the use of flogging as a judicial punishment. Ten people were sentenced to death by a military court from which there was no appeal.

In October President Samora Moisés Machel and 33 other people were killed in a plane crash, the causes of which were still being investigated at the end of 1986. Major-General Joaquim Chissano, the Foreign Minister, was sworn in as Head of State in November.

The RNM became increasingly active, particularly in the central provinces, and reportedly continued to receive South African assistance in contravention of an agreement between South Africa and Mozambique. There were reports of human rights abuses by both government forces and by the RNM during the conflict including torture, mutilation and killing of civilians. However, Amnesty International was unable to verify independently such reports or identify those responsible.

Amnesty International continued throughout 1986 to investigate the cases of people imprisoned since between 1974 and 1977 on account of their suspected opposition to the ruling *Frente da Libertação de Moçambique* (Frelimo), Mozambique Liberation Front. One of them, António Francisco, a former member of Frelimo, returned to Mozambique in 1974 after studying abroad. He was arrested later that year, apparently on suspicion of supporting one of the political groups which opposed the transfer of power from the Portuguese colonial government. Another, Domingos Alvares Anibal, was detained in the capital, Maputo, between March 1976 and January 1977. In 1978 he was reported to have been transferred from Ruarua prison camp in Cabo Delgado Province to another prison camp in the province of Niassa. The subsequent fate or whereabouts of both men was not known. Amnesty International also inquired about several leading members of opposition groups which opposed Frelimo before Mozambique's independence. After being arrested in late 1974 or early 1975 they were paraded at Nachingwea, Frelimo's base camp in southern Tanzania, in March and April 1975 and accused of espionage or treason against Frelimo. One of them, the Reverend Uria Simango, had been the chairman of the *Partido de Coligacão Nacional* (PCN), National Coalition Party, which was formed in August 1974 to unite the groups opposed to Frelimo. He was reported to have admitted planning to invade Mozambique in order to overthrow Frelimo. Despite repeated inquiries the authorities failed to clarify the fate of these "disappeared" detainees, giving rise to fears that they may have been secretly killed in detention.

During 1986 the arrests of over 100 alleged members or supporters of the RNM were reported in the national press. However, the actual number might have been considerably higher. Most were accused of participating in armed attacks on civilians or on industrial or commercial installations. Some four to five thousand other suspected RNM supporters were officially reported to have been arrested in previous years. Amnesty International did not know where most of them were being held. Some were known to be in the custody of the *Serviço Nacional de Segurança Popular* (SNASP), People's National Security Service. For example, several were reported to have been held since their arrest in 1980 in the SNASP headquarters in Quelimane in crowded conditions and with insufficient water and exercise. According to Decree Law No. 21/75 of October 1975, the SNASP, which is responsible for the custody of these prisoners, could detain suspects indefinitely without bringing them before a judge. In addition, security detainees did not have the right to contest the legality of their detention.

Amnesty International also investigated the cases of untried political prisoners who were not accused of participating in armed attacks but who had been detained apparently on suspicion of assisting the RNM in other ways. Although the authorities did not reply to the organization's inquiries about these detainees it was reported that one of them, Abdulla Abacar, who had been arrested in May 1985, was released in August.

Other alleged RNM supporters who had given themselves up to the authorities or who were not considered to have committed serious crimes were reportedly sent to "re-education" centres. The legal basis for their detention was not clear: they were not known to have been sentenced by a court, nor was it known whether or not they were able to appeal against their continuing detention.

Amnesty International continued to investigate the cases of 15 political prisoners who had been sentenced to periods of imprisonment after unfair trials between 1979 and 1983. One, Leonardo Mabunda, a secondary school teacher, had been accused of writing an examination essay criticizing government policies and submitting it as the work of one of his students. He was sentenced in April 1983 by the Revolutionary Military Tribunal, a court established in 1976 with jurisdiction over political cases, to eight years' imprisonment and 45 lashes. Among other things the organization was concerned that those tried by the Revolutionary Military Tribunal were not given an adequate opportunity to defend themselves in court since it was reported that they were not informed of the precise charges against them before the trial took place and were unable to call witnesses in their defence.

No alleged RNM supporters were tried in 1984 and 1985. However, in February and May 1986 two trials took place involving a total of 24 such defendants. The Revolutionary Military Tribunal sentenced to death eight defendants accused of armed activities resulting in civilian deaths. Another 15 were sentenced to between four and 30 years' imprisonment for spying, armed rebellion and other crimes against state security, and one was acquitted. One of the people sentenced to death in May, Alberto Macamo, had been arrested in December 1982 by the SNASP. In October 1984 he was reported to have admitted to the press that he had killed dozens or even hundreds of people in the course of his activities on behalf of the RNM.

Amnesty International received further reports of torture, mutilation and killing of villagers by government forces in areas of conflict. For example, it was alleged in June 1986 that a peasant woman had died in a remote northern village after soldiers seeking information about the RNM had tortured her with knives or bayonets. It was also reported that a number of prisoners in Machava prison on the outskirts of the capital, Maputo, were flogged by prison warders after some of them had allegedly committed disciplinary offences. However, the organization was unable to obtain confirmation of these and other reports of torture or ill-treatment. Although the authorities did not respond to Amnesty International's expressions of concern about the use of torture, they did respond to certain reports by local people of torture. In Nampula province a commission of inquiry was established in May to investigate allegations published in *Notícias*, the Maputo daily newspaper, that two former criminal prisoners had been beaten and tortured. One of them, Jonas Rodjas Nhabalane, was reported to have had his elbows tied behind his back for 24 hours, resulting in partial paralysis of the forearms. In another case reported in *Notícias*, local people claimed that a military commander had ordered villagers suspected of assisting the RNM in Inhambane province to be tortured. The officer was reported to have been dismissed, but it was not stated whether he or any of his subordinates were to be prosecuted. Amnesty International inquired whether or not the alleged torturers had been prosecuted but by the end of the year had received no reply. Its letter also welcomed the establishment of a commission of inquiry by the Governor of Nampula province as a potentially significant step towards the prevention of further cases of torture.

The courts, particularly those at village level, continued to impose sentences of flogging for crimes such as theft and speculation. In one case 52 Beira dock workers were each sentenced to three lashes, in addition to two-month prison sentences and a fine, for allegedly stealing over a thousand kilos of maize. Under Law No. 5/83 of 1983, which introduced this judicial punishment, flogging was made a mandatory penalty, additional to terms of imprisonment, for certain offences, including crimes against state security. However, the 15 people sentenced to prison terms for state security offences in February and May 1986 were not reported to have received additional sentences of flogging. Amnesty International continued to appeal to the authorities to abolish judicial flogging which it considers to be a cruel, inhuman or degrading form of punishment.

Ten people were sentenced to death during 1986. Two had been found guilty of murder and the others were convicted of violent crimes against the security of the state in support of the RNM. Under Article 3 of Law 3/79 which established the Revolutionary Military Tribunal there was no appeal against the decisions of this court, in contravention of the internationally recognized right of all those who face the death penalty to appeal to a higher court against their verdict and sentence. According to Article 6 of the same law executions had to be carried out within five days of sentencing. However, it was not reported whether or not these 10 people had been executed.

Human rights abuses including the torture, mutilation and killing of civilians by the RNM were reported by official sources and by people assisting refugees. There were reports that people had been hacked or clubbed to death or had had their ears or other parts of their body cut off but Amnesty International was unable to obtain independent corroboration of individual cases. The RNM was reported to have captured government soldiers but it was not known where they were being held or under what conditions. The opposition movement was also holding some 100 foreign workers captured at various times over the previous two years. At the end of 1986, 65 were released but at least two were reported to have died in captivity because of lack of medical assistance.

Namibia

Amnesty International was concerned about the detention without trial of suspected opponents of the government, some of whom might have been prisoners of conscience. There were also new reports of torture and ill-treatment of detainees, and extrajudicial killings of civilians, particularly in northern Namibia, by South African security forces. In one case, the trial of four soldiers accused of killing a civilian was prematurely terminated by order of the South African State President. Amnesty International was also concerned about the death penalty: the total number of people sentenced to death was not known but there were at least four executions.

During 1986 Amnesty International was concerned about reports that the external wing of the South West Africa People's Organisation (SWAPO) was holding prisoners in its camps in Angola. Those held were alleged by SWAPO to have spied for South Africa but other sources suggested that they had been detained as a result of political disputes within the organization.

Throughout the year, there was continued conflict between South African security forces and SWAPO guerrillas operating mostly from Angola. Both sides accused each other of responsibility for civilian killings which occurred in the war zone. South African security forces made incursions into Angola in the course of their operations against SWAPO forces. They were believed to hold a number of captured SWAPO combatants whose identities and places of detention were kept secret.

There were reports throughout the year of detentions by South African military units and security police, including particularly the former *Koevoet* (Crowbar) police unit which was renamed the Police Counter Insurgency Unit (COIN). Those held were mostly detained in the northern-most districts of Ovambo, Kavanga and Caprivi, where SWAPO guerrillas were most active. Most were believed to have been detained as suspected supporters of SWAPO, which remained a legal political party in Namibia although the organization's main leadership was based in Angola, from where a military wing continued to mount guerrilla activity inside Namibia.

The main basis for detention without trial was Proclamation AG.9 of 1977. This administrative decree empowered all members of the security forces to detain suspects incommunicado and without charge for 30 days, after which the cabinet of the so-called Transitional

Government of National Unity (TGNU) could authorize further unlimited detention. The proclamation applied in areas designated as "security districts" which extended from the capital, Windhoek, to the northern border.

In January there was a legal challenge to the use of Proclamation AG.9. In an action brought on behalf of Martin Akweenda and three other AG.9 detainees held for more than four months, it was argued that the provisions of AG.9 abrogated rights set down in a Bill of Fundamental Rights which had been attached to the proclamation establishing the TGNU in 1985. On 15 February the Windhoek Supreme Court ordered the release of the detainees on the grounds that they should have been permitted access to legal counsel after the initial period of 30 days' detention. However, Martin Akweenda was not freed: he remained in custody and was subsequently brought to trial with seven others on charges relating to SWAPO activities.

The February judgment effectively established the right of AG.9 detainees to access to legal counsel after 30 days, although in practice few detainees appeared to have benefited from this. Possibly as a result of the judgment, however, there were reports during 1986 of some detentions being carried out under Section 6 of the Terrorism Act. This was introduced by the South African Government in 1967 and made applicable in Namibia and South Africa. In 1982 the Terrorism Act was repealed in South Africa but it remained effective in Namibia. Section 6 empowered security police to detain suspects incommunicado and in solitary confinement for unlimited periods and to withhold all information about their places or conditions of detention.

The Terrorism Act and the related Suppression of Communism Act, also originally a South African law which remained applicable only in Namibia, were also challenged in the Windhoek Supreme Court as contrary to the Bill of Fundamental Rights. In February the court ruled that seven alleged SWAPO supporters should stand trial under the acts as the proclamation establishing the TGNU had not repealed the two laws. The seven were subsequently convicted and given long prison sentences for political offences involving violence.

The validity of the two laws was again challenged in August when Martin Akweenda and seven others were brought to trial. They were alleged to be SWAPO members who had participated in acts of sabotage and had been responsible for a number of deaths. The basis of the challenge was again the conflict between the terms of the Terrorism Act and the provisions of the Bill of Fundamental Rights relating to safeguards against arbitrary arrest and torture and the right to fair trial. Before the court could rule, the State President of South Africa issued a new decree, Proclamation 157 of 1986, which stated that no court would be competent "to inquire into or pronounce upon the validity of" any act passed by the South African Parliament before or after the formation of the TGNU. However, the Windhoek Supreme Court decided it should still hear the challenge to the Terrorism Act and in October decided that the act had effectively become invalid when the Bill of Fundamental Rights was introduced as part of the Proclamation establishing the TGNU. As a result, the state withdrew charges against the accused relating to incidents after the TGNU took office on 17 June 1985 but they continued to stand trial under the Terrorism Act for offences allegedly committed before that date. Their trial had not been completed by the end of 1986. In December the South African Appeal Court overturned the October judgment and ruled that the Bill of Fundamental Rights did not affect laws such as the Terrorism Act which were already in force at the time of its introduction.

In October the authorities published the findings of a judicial commission of inquiry into security legislation, which had been established in 1983 under a South African judge, H.P. van Dyk. This recommended the consolidation of existing security legislation and proposed a new draft law, which had not been made public by the end of 1986. Despite evidence of torture and abuse of detainees, the commission sought to justify the retention of detention without trial and recommended that civilians should be made liable under threat of imprisonment to provide information about SWAPO guerrillas. The commission disclosed that the military and security police did not keep records of detainees held under AG.9 although they were able to give some figures for the numbers held between 1977 and 1983. This failure to keep records, in Amnesty International's view, provided a context in which "disappearances" could occur and may have been the reason why in previous years the authorities were unable to account for people whose relatives believed they had been detained. The disclosure that records of detainees were not kept came several months after State President Botha told the South African Parliament in February that there were then nine people detained under AG.9.

There were new reports of torture and ill-treatment of detainees and new developments relating to deaths in detention in previous years. In January an inquest magistrate ruled that no one was responsible for the death of Thomas Shindobo Nikanor, who was reportedly found hanged in a cell at the secret Osire detention camp in January 1985 (see *Amnesty International Report 1986*). The inquest accepted, however, that he had been found hanged with his feet fully on the ground, which led his relatives to believe that suicide was improbable. In November the authorities announced the completion of a criminal investigation into the death in detention of Johannes Kakuva in 1980. In 1983 the Windhoek Supreme Court decided that he had been killed in detention and named security police officers allegedly responsible for his death and an ensuing cover-up, but no action was taken against them. By the end of 1986, no one had been charged in connection with the death.

Amnesty International received information that several of those brought to trial with Martin Akweenda in August had been severely ill-treated while held incommunicado. Two other notable cases were also reported, both involving children. In June it was alleged that Portas Blasius, aged 15, was badly burned by South African soldiers who held his face against the exhaust pipe of an army lorry. His mother subsequently sued the army for damages. The two soldiers responsible were convicted of the assault in October and each fined 500 rand (£150). In July a 13-year-old, Titus Paulus, alleged that he had been "roasted" over a fire by COIN personnel who interrogated him about SWAPO activities. In this case, no prosecutions had been reported by the end of 1986.

South African military personnel and security police were pro-tected throughout 1986 by an immunity from prosecution for acts committed "in good faith" in the course of their operations. Nevertheless, some soldiers and COIN personnel were prosecuted and imprisoned for assault and rape of civilians in northern Namibia, although these appeared to represent only a small minority of cases of abuse. In July State President Botha intervened to prevent the trial of four South African soldiers charged with the murder of Frans Uapota. He was among a number of people who had been seized and violently assaulted in November 1985: he died after he was beaten, kicked and trampled on by his interrogators. State President Botha used powers under Section 103*ter* of the South African Defence Act to terminate the trial on the grounds that the soldiers who had killed Frans Uapota had acted "in good faith".

Amnesty International remained concerned about the use of the death penalty but did not obtain precise figures about the number sentenced to death. At least four people were reported to have been executed.

Amnesty International was concerned also by reports that the external wing of SWAPO was holding prisoners at a camp or camps in southern Angola. Those detained were alleged by SWAPO to have infiltrated the organization and spied for South Africa, but other sources suggested that they had been detained because of internal disputes within SWAPO. In February SWAPO officials admitted that more than 100 people had been detained but they did not disclose all their identities. The detainees were reported to include at least two men who had previously been of concern to Amnesty International when they were detained by the South African authorities in Namibia in the late 1970s.

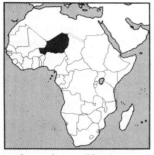

Niger

Amnesty International was concerned about the continued long-term detention of several political prisoners, some of whom had reportedly completed prison sentences imposed after an attempted coup in 1976. Some of the restrictions placed on the movement of former President Hamani Diori were reported to have been lifted. No death sentences were known to have been carried out during 1986.

Amnesty International remained concerned about reports of the continued detention without trial of more than 20 people, many of whom were arrested following coup attempts in 1976 and 1983. They included Kariman Matachi, a former army officer apparently held in Dirkou, who was reported to have been given a five-year prison sentence in 1977 in connection with the 1976 coup attempt, and who was one of seven prisoners believed held beyond the expiry of their sentence without legal sanction. Another detainee, Lieutenant-Colonel Adama Harouna, former Prefect of Niamey, was arrested in February 1983, apparently on political grounds. A group of about 20 people were also reported to be still held without trial, following a coup attempt in October 1983 which took place while President Seyni Kountche was out of the country. They included some of his closest advisors, among them Mahamane Sidikou, formerly a senior government official, who was reported at the end of 1986 to be seriously ill in prison. Other people believed by Amnesty International to be still held in detention from this time were Modieli Amadou, a former government official, and Amadou Seydou, a former army commander.

In April Amnesty International asked President Seyni Kountche about the legal status of seven long-term detainees, most of whom had reportedly been held since the coup attempt in October 1983. It called for them to be released if they were not brought to trial within a reasonable time. In the letter, the organization cited the International Covenant on Civil and Political Rights, which guarantees freedom from arbitrary arrest and the right to a fair and prompt trial, to which Niger acceded in March 1986. The government did not respond to this letter. Amnesty International later learned that one of the detainees, Dia Ardo Ibrahimou, had been released.

Amnesty International was concerned about reports that detainees continued to be held in harsh conditions. A number of detainees were reported to have been moved to a military fort in Dirkou in the east of Niger during 1986. The remoteness of this outpost made family visits almost impossible. It was alleged that prisoners in Dirkou were held in underground munitions cellars in conditions of extreme heat and cold. Conditions were also reported to be poor in the military camp at Tillabery near the capital, Niamey.

Former President Hamani Diori remained under house arrest in Niamey, although it was reported that some of the restrictions on his movements were lifted during 1986. After six years in detention without trial from 1974 to 1980, he was placed under house arrest until 1984. He was again put under house arrest in June 1985, allegedly because of the opposition activities outside the country of one of his sons.

Twelve members of the Tuareg ethnic minority who were sentenced to death following an attack on government buildings in Tchin Tabaraden in May 1985 (see *Amnesty International Report 1985*) were not known to have been executed during 1986. A stay of execution was reported to have been granted by presidential order in late 1985. *

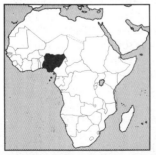

Nigeria

Amnesty International's main concerns were the imprisonment of prisoners of conscience and the frequent use of the death penalty. More than 100 people were sentenced to death, the majority of them after trials from which no judicial appeal was allowed, and more than 60 executions were recorded. However, complete statistics were not available to Amnesty International and the real number of those sentenced and executed was thought to have been considerably higher.

The only prisoner of conscience adopted by Amnesty International at the beginning of 1986, the musician Fela Anikulapo Kuti, was released in April by order of the President (see *Amnesty International Report 1986*). However, there were several short-term detentions of people believed to be prisoners of conscience. In late May Dr Junaid Mohammed, an opposition politician under the former government of President Shagari, was arrested after criticizing the government in an interview broadcast by the British Broadcasting Corporation. He was held under Decree 2, the State Security (Detention of Persons) Decree, 1984, which permits detention without trial and which was widely used by the former government led by Major-General Muhamadu Buhari. Amnesty International appealed for his release as it believed that he was detained solely because of his non-violent opposition to government policy. Dr Mohammed was released uncharged in August.

There were further politically motivated arrests in June following incidents in Máy at the Ahmadou Bello University in Zaria when security forces opened fire on a student demonstration. Leaders of the Nigerian Labour Congress led by their President, Ali Ciroma, protested against the shootings and were arrested. They were released uncharged after eight days in custody.

A large number of people who had been detained without charge or trial since early 1984, some of whom may have been prisoners of conscience, were either released under judicial review procedures in 1986 or prosecuted for criminal offences or due to be prosecuted. Most were members of former President Shagari's administration. For example, both President Shagari himself and his deputy, former Vice-President Ekueme, were released in July. However, three top officials of the military government which overthrew the Shagari administration — former Head of State Major-General Muhamadu Buhari, Major-General Tunde Idiagbon and Alhadji Rawal Rafindadi — remained in detention without charge or trial throughout 1986.

The death penalty remained a major concern. Amnesty International learned of the imposition of 111 death sentences but the real total was believed to be considerably higher. There were at least 64 executions. Of those sentenced to death, 101 had been convicted by special Robbery and Firearms Tribunals, each composed of a High Court judge, one military officer and one police officer. All the 64 people known to have been executed had been convicted by Robbery and Firearms Tribunals.

The Robbery and Firearms Tribunals, which were re-established in 1984, had jurisdiction over cases of robbery in which the accused was alleged to have been armed or to have used personal violence. There was no right of appeal to a higher court for those sentenced by the tribunals, in contrast to cases involving other serious offences such as murder which were tried before the High Court, from which appeals could be made to the Appeal Court and then the Supreme Court. Although the law governing the Robbery and Firearms Tribunals did not allow any appeal against their sentences, there was a "confirmation" process which was believed to vary from state to state. In some states the confirmation involved consideration of the sentence by a state Prerogative of Mercy Committee, and then a final decision on whether to execute from the state's military governor. This process was more akin to a clemency hearing than a judicial appeal to a higher court, and Amnesty International believed it provided insufficient legal safeguards for people sentenced to death. In addition, Amnesty International was concerned that some of the Prerogative of Mercy Committees were chaired by state Attorney Generals, who would have been ultimately responsible for the original prosecution, a situation that may not have been conducive to impartiality in consideration of clemency.

Throughout 1986 Amnesty International appealed to state and federal authorities to grant clemency. For example, on 8 September the Plateau State Robbery and Firearms Tribunal sentenced Alexander Takunde Genga, a teacher, to death by hanging after convicting him of robbing a student at gunpoint on 22 April 1985. Amnesty International appealed to the military governor for clemency, but did not learn whether he was executed. On 12 September a priest and seven other people were sentenced to death for armed robbery by the Oyo State Robbery and Firearms Tribunal, and again Amnesty International appealed for clemency but five of the seven were subsequently executed.

Thirteen death sentences were passed in February by a special military tribunal composed of senior officers on army and air force officers convicted of plotting to overthrow the government. Their alleged leader was Major-General Mamman Vatsa, who, according to official reports, had been planning the coup since soon after the takeover of power by President Babangida in August 1985. Three of the 13 death sentences were subsequently commuted to prison terms after appeals for clemency but the other 10 were carried out. Amnesty International believed that the appeals for clemency had not been considered with sufficient thoroughness and impartiality; for example, appeals for clemency were made in the first instance to the armed forces' service chiefs who were the superior officers of the convicted men, and sentences were then confirmed by the Armed Forces Ruling Council (AFRC). The executions took place just a few hours after the AFRC convened to consider the confirmation of the sentences. Amnesty International and prominent Nigerian figures appealed for commutation of all the death sentences passed.

Amnesty International was particularly concerned about a new method of execution for convicted armed robbers introduced in Niger State, central Nigeria. According to press reports in July, execution by successive volleys of bullets fired at intervals, starting with shots aimed at the ankle, were ordered by the state governor. According to the reports, two people were executed in this way. Amnesty International appealed to the state governor concerned, as well as to the federal authorities, to stop this particularly abhorrent method of torture and execution.

Amnesty International was also concerned about the case of Nasiru Bello who, according to a Supreme Court inquiry in 1986, was executed illegally in 1981 after being sentenced to death by a High Court for murder; his appeal had not yet been heard by the Appeal Court. In a unanimous decision announced on 5 December, seven Supreme Court judges held that Nasiru Bello's constitutional right to an appeal hearing had been infringed. The Attorney General of Oyo State, where the original death sentence had been passed, agreed under examination at the Supreme Court that the execution had been "unlawful".

Amnesty International welcomed an announcement in July by the Minister of Justice that the death penalty would no longer be used for people convicted of offences under SMC Decree 20, the Special Tribunal (Miscellaneous Offences) Decree of 1984, which covered offences including drug trafficking and illegal oil sales. Three people had been sentenced to death and executed under the provisions of this decree in 1985 (see *Amnesty International Report 1986*). The organization was also pleased to note that the death penalty was removed from the provisions of the Counterfeit Currency (Special Provisions) Decree No. 22 of 1984.

Amnesty International welcomed an invitation in July by the Minister of Justice for the organization to send a delegation to Nigeria to discuss the use of the death penalty and other issues, but by the end of 1986 dates and arrangements for the visit had not yet been finalized.

Rwanda

Amnesty International was concerned about the continuing imprisonment of several prisoners of conscience convicted in 1981 and about the arrest and imprisonment of several hundred people convicted in October of belonging to illegal religious groups. Amnesty International was also concerned that more than 500 prisoners were under sentence of death, although no executions were reported to have been carried out.

Two Amnesty International delegates visited Rwanda in May at the invitation of the government and met representatives of the judiciary, law enforcement agencies and the prison services. They visited a number of prisons and detention centres. The delegates were given information about a range of safeguards introduced to prevent arbitrary detention and ill-treatment of detainees, including measures to ensure that laws on detention procedures were respected. The delegates also discussed with the authorities the cases of 167 people arrested between November 1985 and May 1986 for belonging to four unofficial religious sects, the *Abantu b'Imana bihana* (Repentant People of God), the *Abarokore* (the Elect), the *Abatampera* (Temperance Movement) and the *Abayohova* (Jehovah's Witnesses).

In September Amnesty International submitted a 19-page memorandum to the government, summarizing its observations and presenting nine recommendations on human rights. These included measures aimed at preventing the imprisonment of prisoners of conscience and stopping the use of torture and ill-treatment. The organization also expressed concern that at the time of its mission in May, 560 prisoners were reported to be under sentence of death although no executions had been reported since 1982, and it recommended steps to reduce the use of the death penalty. The government replied in December with comments on a number of the points raised in the memorandum and referred to safeguards already introduced to prevent arbitrary detention and the use of torture.

At the beginning of 1986 Amnesty International was concerned about eight prisoners of conscience convicted by the State Security Court in November 1981 and August 1984 on charges of sedition. Five were still in prison at the end of the year, while three were released on or shortly before the expiry of their sentences. One, Alphonse Utagirake, who was sentenced to three years' imprisonment in August 1984, was seriously ill with tuberculosis when he was freed in September. Another, Apollinaire Bikolimana, was released in April after completing a six-year sentence imposed in 1981, but was rearrested in June on the orders of the national security service. His relatives were not informed of his arrest or where he was being detained. His case was taken up for investigation by Amnesty International and in December the Minister of Justice informed the organization that Apollinaire Bikolimana was awaiting trial on charges of subversion, but did not give details of the allegations against him.

In October 296 people were tried and convicted by the State Security Court on charges relating to membership of four religious sects which the authorities considered to be subversive. The main group involved, the *Abarokore*, some 200 of whom were among those convicted, are part of the revival movement in the East African Protestant churches, which began in Rwanda in the 1930s. This was the first time since the present government came to power that members of the *Abarokore* were known to have been detained, although Jehovah's Witnesses had been arrested since they began recruiting in the early 1980s when a formal request for legal recognition of their sect was refused. The number of arrests increased sharply from November 1985 onwards. Amnesty International's delegates were told in May 1986 that 167 people had been arrested and referred for possible prosecution in connection with their membership of sects, but arrests continued until at least August when a prominent civil servant, Augustin Murayi, Director General in the Ministry of Education, was arrested with his wife after refusing to recant his beliefs as a Jehovah's Witness. The 296 people tried in October were charged with a variety of offences, including distributing subversive information, encouraging people to disobey government orders and holding illegal meetings. The charges arose from the four sects' refusal to take part in *séances d'animation* (political meetings) organized by the ruling party, the *Mouvement révolutionnaire national pour le développement* (MRND), Revolutionary National Movement for Development. Under the terms of the constitution, all Rwandese are required to be members of the MRND and to pay dues to it. All the defendants were convicted. One, who renounced his religious views during the trial, was sentenced to two months' imprisonment. The 50 or so Jehovah's Witnesses were mostly sentenced to 10 years' imprisonment, but three were given 12-year sentences: they were Augustin Murayi, his wife, Rachel Ndayishimiye, and a reserve soldier, Justin Rwagasore, who had told the court that he would not be willing to take up arms if Rwanda was invaded. Most members of the three other sects received eight-year sentences, while 11 who were aged 18 or less at the time of their arrest were sentenced to four years' imprisonment.

Following the trial Amnesty International sought information about the charges on which each defendant was convicted in order to establish if they were prisoners of conscience. Most of those convicted were apparently sentenced simply for belonging to one of the four sects. Amnesty International was concerned that, as at previous political trials, the law on sedition was interpreted by the authorities so as to make the expression of non-violent views punishable by imprisonment. Amnesty International was also concerned that members of sects which preached non-involvement in politics were sentenced to terms of imprisonment for refusing to take part in political activities. By the end of 1986 it had adopted Augustin Murayi and Rachel Ndayishimiye as prisoners of conscience and was investigating the cases of some 290 others imprisoned.

Amnesty International was also concerned that those convicted may not have received a fair trial as none of those tried in October had legal counsel. Nor did three other people tried by the State Security Court at the beginning of October. The court deferred judgment on one on the grounds that he might be mentally unstable, but Boniface Kanyabitabo and Charles Ndoli, who had spent six years in pre-trial detention, were both convicted of helping a suspected government opponent to evade arrest and of illegal possession of firearms. During the trial, Charles Ndoli reportedly alleged that he had been tortured while in detention. He was found guilty and sentenced to 20 years' imprisonment, while Boniface Kanyabitabo was sentenced to 10 years.

In addition to the allegations of torture made in court, Amnesty International was also concerned by other reports that some prisoners were subjected to severe beatings. For example, a group of Jehovah's Witnesses arrested in Nyakabanda in August were reported to have been severely beaten and to have been bleeding from injuries when they arrived at prison.

Although the death penalty continued to be imposed no executions were reported. The 560 people reportedly under sentence of death in May had been convicted of a variety of offences, including murder and armed robbery, and had all had their appeals turned down. Others were still awaiting the outcome of appeals. Amnesty International was particularly concerned that very few of those sentenced to death had had legal counsel at their trials and recommended to the government that legal assistance be made available in all capital cases.

Amnesty International was concerned about five people, including Théoneste Lizinde, the former head of the security service, who were sentenced to death in June 1985 after being convicted of participating in extrajudicial killings of political prisoners in the mid-1970s.

Although their convictions were due to be reviewed by an appeal court, by the end of 1986 no appeal hearings were known to have occurred. Amnesty International expressed concern to the authorities that the five prisoners under sentence of death, as well as others convicted with them, were not permitted visits.

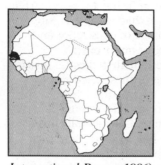

Senegal

Amnesty International was concerned about the imprisonment of possible prisoners of conscience and reports of ill-treatment of prisoners.

Thirty-three people who had been among 105 people tried in 1985 for alleged participation in violent events in the Casamance region (see *Amnesty International Report 1986*) were sentenced in January to prison terms ranging from two years to life imprisonment, although in one case the sentence was suspended. An Amnesty International observer attended part of the trial. A number of those brought to trial were alleged to have been tortured or ill-treated after arrest, but no formal inquiry into the allegations was undertaken by the authorities. An Amnesty International delegate who visited Senegal before the trial had noted scars consistent with such allegations. In October the Minister of Justice observed that such scars might have been received in clashes with police at the time of arrest. However, those interviewed by Amnesty International's delegate all claimed to have been beaten or otherwise ill-treated in police custody. Moreover, Amnesty International's delegate had noted that a fairly high proportion of the arrests appeared to have taken place some time after the demonstrations, and that many were alleged to have been arbitrary. At least seven prisoners died before the trial but no formal inquests appeared to have been conducted.

On the 26th anniversary of independence in April, President Diouf announced that eight people sentenced for their part in the Casamance events of 1982 and 1983 were to be amnestied. A similar measure led to the release of Moustapha Touré, a transport union leader, and nine other trade unionists sentenced to prison terms after strike action in September 1985. On 27 March Boubacar Diop, editor of *Promotion* magazine, was released from detention. He had been arrested on 9 August 1985, accused of insulting republican institutions and the head of state, and of spreading false information, after publishing an interview with an opposition personality.

On 1 October Amnesty International wrote to President Abdou Diouf asking the reasons for the arrest of El Hadj Mamadou Sow Sarr on 20 July and about his state of health. Amnesty International had learned that he was accused of having distributed copies of *Ferñent*, a newspaper critical of the government, and was charged on 1 August with state security offences and distributing unauthorized literature. He was tried by the State Security Court in November and received a four-month prison sentence. However, he was released on 1 December in view of the time he had already been held.

Further arrests took place in the Casamance region in November and December. At least 40 people were known to have been transferred to Dakar awaiting trial. They were charged with offences against state security and with founding an illegal association.

Seychelles

Amnesty International was concerned about the imprisonment of prisoners of conscience and possible prisoners of conscience, all but one of whom had been released by the end of 1986.

Amnesty International continued throughout the year to call for the release of Royce Dias who was adopted as a prisoner of conscience after he had received a prison sentence in 1985 on criminal charges that appeared to have been fabricated for political reasons (see *Amnesty International Report 1986*). However, three other prisoners of concern to Amnesty International were released on 24 June. Jean Dingwall, also adopted as a prisoner of conscience, had been held since September 1984; Joachim and Robin Sullivan, two brothers, had been in prison since mid-1985. All three had been detained without trial under the Preservation of Public Security (Emergency Powers) Regulations. Under the regulations the President is empowered to order the indefinite detention without trial of any person "concerned in acts which might . . . be prejudicial to the public safety and the maintenance of public order". A detainee does not have the right to challenge the grounds for detention in a court of law. A Review Tribunal exists to consider each detainee's case within a month of detention and thereafter every six months. However, this tribunal sits *in camera* and its recommendations are not binding upon the President.

There were new politically motivated arrests in early June. Several known critics of the government of President France-Albert René, including Richard Ponwaye and Philip d'Offay, both businessmen, and Philip Boule, a lawyer, were alleged to have endangered state security. They were reportedly held incommunicado at Victoria Central Police Station but no formal charges were brought against them. Amnesty International wrote to the Attorney General in July seeking clarification of their status but received no reply. However, all those arrested were released uncharged in October.

Sierra Leone

Amnesty International was concerned about the imprisonment of ordinary criminal prisoners in conditions reported to be so harsh that they amounted to cruel, inhuman or degrading treatment and caused many deaths. Amnesty International was also concerned about the use of the death penalty; at least two people were sentenced to death but it was not known if there were any executions.

Throughout 1986 Amnesty International received reports from diverse sources that criminal prisoners and suspects held on remand in Pademba Road Prison in Freetown were subject to grossly inadequate conditions. In particular, prisoners were reported to be denied adequate food and medical attention. As a result, the mortality rate among such prisoners was reported to be high and Amnesty International considered that their conditions constituted cruel, inhuman or degrading treatment. Amnesty International wrote to President Joseph Saidu Momoh in December calling for urgent government action to improve prison conditions. In doing so, Amnesty International stated that it had received no suggestion that prisoners had been starved as a matter of deliberate policy, but rather had suffered because of an apparent lack of resources at the prison. Amnesty International maintained, however, that the government had a responsibility to ensure that sufficient resources were made available to ensure that all prisoners were treated in accordance with standards laid down by the UN Standard Minimum Rules for the Treatment of Prisoners. Amnesty International cited the cases of a number of prisoners reported to have died in prison in 1985 and 1986, including four prisoners who died on one particular day, 30 June 1986. Amnesty International asked for confirmation from the government of this information and for details of what measures were being taken to correct the situation.

Amnesty International learned of two death sentences passed in 1986, one passed in June for murder and one passed on a police officer convicted of murder in November. Amnesty International appealed for clemency in both cases. The organization did not learn of any executions. There were believed to be a number of prisoners on "death row" in Pademba Road Prison and other prisons outside the capital.

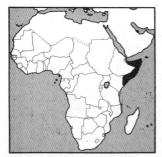

Somalia

Amnesty International was concerned about the imprisonment of prisoners of conscience, one of whom had been held without trial for over 11 years. Many other political prisoners arrested in 1986 or in previous years were detained without trial or imprisoned after unfair trials. The organization was also concerned about reports of torture and ill-treatment of political prisoners and about the use of the death penalty.

Armed conflict continued in 1986 between government forces and two opposition organizations, the Somali National Movement (SNM) and the Democratic Front for the Salvation of Somalia (DFSS). In the north, civilians suspected of contact with the SNM were arrested, ill-treated and in some cases summarily executed. There were also reports of killings of government officials or sympathizers by opposition forces.

In late January about 50 school students and up to 100 other people were arrested in Hargeisa in northern Somalia on suspicion of links with the SNM shortly after an attack in the vicinity by SNM guerrillas. Amnesty International asked the authorities about their legal status and treatment in custody and appealed for them to be released if they were not to be charged and brought to trial. Several of the prisoners were released in the following months but some were brought to trial before the National Security Court on 30 June. Abdi Dahir Ainanshe, a student, was sentenced to death for possessing weapons. Amnesty International appealed for the commutation of his death sentence and expressed concern that those convicted by the National Security Court have no right of appeal. He was still under sentence of death at the end of 1986.

In February there were unofficial reports that the presidential review of the death sentences imposed for treason on seven secondary school students by the National Security Court in Hargeisa in October 1984 (see *Amnesty International Report 1986*) had been completed. The death sentence imposed on Abdi Dama Abbi was upheld and he was secretly executed in Mandera in March, although the government would not confirm this. The other six students had their sentences commuted to life imprisonment. Amnesty International had been investigating whether the seven might be prisoners of conscience and believed that they had not received fair trials and that they had been tortured. The organization had appealed for clemency for all seven students.

Large-scale arrests of Islamic religious leaders and members of their organizations took place in Burao on 16 April. Over 300 men, women and children were reportedly detained without charge or trial for their religious activities. They were believed to have been critical of the government's policies of "scientific socialism". Many other members of Islamic organizations were arrested in Mogadishu and Merca the following month after the announcement in Mogadishu on 9 May of the formation of the Somali Islamic Movement (SIM). The SIM said that it would seek to educate society to follow "moderate Islamic beliefs and laws". It criticized the repression of religious activities by the authorities, particularly the regulations affecting mosques and religious teaching which were issued in August 1985. Among those arrested in Mogadishu were Sheikh Mohamed Moallim Hassan, a former Director General in the Ministry of Justice and Religious Affairs and a prisoner of conscience from 1976 to 1982, and Sheikh Mohamed Nur Qawi, who was alleged to have been tortured. Amnesty International appealed for their release as prisoners of conscience. Several of the prisoners were released over the following months but by the end of 1986 Sheikh Mohamed Moallim Hassan and several other religious leaders, including Sheikh Ahmed Ali Aden, the Imam of the central mosque in Burao, were still detained without charge or trial.

On 31 May, 23 people, some of them school students, who were arrested in Hargeisa in July 1985, were brought to trial before the National Security Court in Hargeisa, charged with treason. They were reportedly accused of involvement with the United Somali Students Organization, an unofficial opposition organization. Three of the students — Saeed Dahir Jama, Ahmed Abdi Omar and Hassan Osman Omar — were sentenced to death for distributing subversive literature. Other defendants were sentenced to prison terms ranging from five years to life imprisonment for lesser offences. Amnesty International appealed for the commutation of the death sentences and expressed concern that the prisoners did not receive fair trials — they were reportedly denied legal representation as well as having no right of appeal. Several were alleged to have been tortured and to be held in harsh conditions. Amnesty International was investigating whether they were prisoners of conscience. At the end of 1986 the death sentences had neither been carried out nor commuted.

Amnesty International continued to press for the release of several long-term prisoners of conscience. Abukar Hassan Yare, a law lecturer detained without trial since 1981, was released in March. Others still held at the end of 1986 included Yusuf Osman Samantar (*"Berda'ad"*), a politician and lawyer detained without trial since 1975 and Abdi Ismail Yunis, an educationalist, and Suleiman Nuh Ali, an architect, both imprisoned without trial since 1982. Amnesty International also continued to appeal for the release of 17 doctors, teachers and civil servants imprisoned in 1982 on charges of participating in a subversive organization. Three of these prisoners were released in October 1986 by presidential amnesty, but the others, including Aden Yusuf Abokor, director of Hargeisa hospital, were still in prison. Appeals continued to be made for the release of Ismail Ali Abokor, a former Vice-President of Somalia, Omar Arteh Ghalib, a former Foreign Minister, Mohamed Aden Sheikh, a doctor and former President of the Somali Academy of Sciences, and three former members of parliament detained since 1982. They were publicly accused of treason shortly after their arrest but had been continually refused access to their lawyers and families. Despite rumours in early 1986 of an imminent trial, all were still held at the end of 1986 without formal charge or trial.

Other prisoners whose cases were under investigation by Amnesty International included those of four former army officers detained without charge or trial since a coup attempt in 1978; two students detained without trial since 1984 for refusing to be conscripted into the army; and 11 prisoners sentenced to life imprisonment by the National Security Court in Burao in December 1984 for alleged links with the SNM. Amnesty International believed that these were a small proportion of the total number of political prisoners in the country, which the organization was unable to estimate. The government published no figures on political prisoners and in most cases did not reply to Amnesty International's inquiries.

On 21 October, Revolution Day, 2,506 prisoners were released and 30 sentences of death or life imprisonment were commuted by presidential order. Amnesty International welcomed the commutation of the death sentences and requested details of any political prisoners released in the amnesty. A few political prisoners were believed to have been released, among them some of the prisoners arrested in April and May 1986 for their religious activities.

Amnesty International continued to be concerned about the detention without trial of several hundred Ethiopian civilians, abducted from Ethiopia by Somali forces in 1977. They were held in a rural settlement in Hawai under the control of the National Security Service. Their detention has not been acknowledged by the government. A number of refugees who had fled from Ethiopia to avoid political persecution were also believed to be detained, some of them for alleged security offences and others apparently because they had criticized the treatment of refugees by the Somali authorities.

Political prisoners were subject to harsh prison conditions. Those detained in Lanta Bur and Labatan Jirow prisons were denied contact with their families and several were held in prolonged solitary confinement. There were reports of prisoners held in National Security Service custody, particularly in Mogadishu, being tortured and ill-treated. Conditions in government prisons, such as Mogadishu Central Prison and Hargeisa Prison, were also harsh, with prisoners being given only occasional access to their families.

Amnesty International appealed to President Mohamed Siad Barre to commute 15 death sentences imposed by the National Security Court in 1986 for treason, armed robbery and homicide. It was believed that many more death sentences were imposed during the year. In February, Amnesty International's concern at the considerable number of executions that had taken place in the previous year — probably over 100 — led the organization to appeal to the government for an inquiry into the use of the death penalty. Amnesty International noted, in particular, the wide range of offences for which the death penalty was imposed; the absence of any right of appeal for defendants before the National Security Court, which tried all capital cases; and reports that several executions had taken place in public within 24 hours of confirmation by the President. No reply was received.

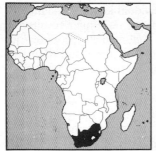

South Africa

Amnesty International was concerned about the detention without trial of several thousand critics and opponents of the government, including many prisoners of conscience, under state of emergency regulations and other security laws. Other prisoners of conscience were among hundreds of people brought to trial for alleged political offences. There were new reports of torture and ill-treatment of uncharged detainees, and there were further deaths in detention in suspicious circumstances. Administrative banning orders were effectively invalidated by an Appeal Court ruling but the government used its emergency powers to restrict critics. The death penalty remained a major concern: there were 121 executions in Pretoria Central Prison and others were carried out in nominally independent "homelands".

South African security forces abducted political opponents from neighbouring countries, killing others in the process, and appeared closely connected with attacks on opponents of the government carried out by armed vigilante groups in areas such as Cape Town and KwaNdebele. The police and military were also accused of unprovoked killings of civilians and there was suspicion that people acting on behalf of the government may have been responsible for the murder of a leading black doctor and his wife in December. No arrests were made in connection with killings of several political opponents which had occurred in 1985.

In January, Amnesty International published *South Africa: Imprisonment under the Pass Laws* to document its concern about the imprisonment of up to a quarter of a million black people each year, effectively on grounds of race. The report criticized the so-called pass laws as flagrantly discriminatory in their nature and application and said that they provided a context for systematic and extensive violations of fundamental human rights. The report also criticized the conditions under which pass law prisoners were held and a parole system which appeared to be close to a system of forced labour. Amnesty International called for the total abolition of the pass laws as a necessary step to ending the imprisonment of black people on account of their race.

A few days after publication of the report, State President P.W. Botha announced the government's intention to withdraw the pass laws, and this was accomplished on 1 July. However, the law continued to provide for registration of the population by race and required that all adults should possess individual identity documents, although failure to produce these on demand no longer resulted in immediate arrest. The Group Areas Act, which provides for residential segregation, was retained and it appeared that the authorities were using anti-squatter legislation to control the flow of black people to the cities.

In March Amnesty International launched a worldwide campaign against human rights violations in South Africa and published a briefing on its concerns. It called on the government to end imprisonment on racial and political grounds, torture and other human rights abuses. The organization published an open letter to State President P.W. Botha in which it urged the immediate release of prisoners of conscience, an end to arbitrary detention, removal of the immunity from prosecution protecting police and other security forces, and the establishment of impartial inquiries into reports of torture, killings and abductions alleged to have been committed by agents of the government. Amnesty International also called for the abolition of the death penalty. During the campaign, it wrote to more than 10,000 individuals and organizations in South Africa urging them to support the open letter's proposals and work for the protection of human rights.

The state of emergency in force in some districts since July 1985 was lifted in early March and many uncharged detainees were then released. However, following continued widespread civil unrest, the government imposed a new nationwide state of emergency from midnight on 11 June. It was not announced until several hours after it came into force, by which time security police had raided homes throughout the country and detained many critics and opponents of the government. They included prominent churchmen, trade union and black community leaders, and leaders of the United Democratic Front (UDF) and the Azanian People's Organisation (AZAPO). Young whites belonging to the End Conscription Campaign were also detained. The emergency regulations empowered all police and other security force personnel to arrest people and hold them incommunicado and without charge for 14 days, after which the Minister of Law and Order was empowered to authorize continued indefinite detention without trial. The police, other security forces and government officials were given legal immunity for acts committed "in good faith" in connection with their use of emergency powers. Curbs were placed on reporting of incidents involving the security forces.

The emergency was accompanied by an unprecedented number of politically motivated arrests. By the end of 1986, more than 20,000 people were believed to have been detained under the emergency regulations. A significant proportion were young people, including children as young as 11 or 12, some of whom were detained for several months and still held at the end of 1986. Amnesty International adopted many of those detained and investigated the cases of others as possible prisoners of conscience.

Government efforts to suppress dissent resulted in the detention of entire church congregations at Elsies River, near Cape Town, at Graaff-Reinet and at Duncan Village, near East London, on 15 and 16 June. In all, more than 1,000 people were arrested for attending services on these days to commemorate the killings of student protestors in 1976. Some were soon released but others were held for several months.

Some children and youths were released from detention only after being sent to so-called "rehabilitation camps" run by the security forces. The existence of the camps was revealed in September after initial government denials.

A number of people released from detention under the emergency were restricted by the Minister of Law and Order to curtail their movements, attendance at meetings and participation in organizations opposed to the government. Similar restrictions under the emergency regulations were also imposed on several anti-apartheid activists who had not been detained. In previous years, such people might have been restricted under banning orders under the Internal Security Act, but an Appeal Court ruling in March had invalidated all such banning orders then in force.

There were also many detentions during the year under Section 29 of the Internal Security Act, which empowers security police to detain suspects incommunicado and in solitary confinement without charge indefinitely. Those held under this provision included Pinda Molefe, a mother of three, whose husband was on trial throughout 1986 at Delmas (see below). She was detained in early June and still held incommunicado at the end of the year. Amnesty International called for her release if she was not to be brought promptly to trial on criminal charges. Others detained under Section 29 included leaders of the Kagiso Residents Association who had brought a court case against the government alleging politically motivated killings by the security forces.

Two new security provisions were introduced. Section 50A was inserted into the Internal Security Act to empower police to hold uncharged detainees for 180 days, after another detention provision of the act, Section 28, was undermined by an Appeal Court ruling. The Public Safety Act, the law permitting the declaration of a state of emergency, was also amended in order to empower the Minister of Law and Order to declare "unrest areas" in which emergency-style powers could be authorized.

Amnesty International received many new reports of torture and ill-treatment of detainees during 1986, particularly after the imposition of the state of emergency. Father Smangaliso Mkhatshwa, a prisoner of conscience and leading Catholic churchman, was assaulted and humiliated during 30 hours' continuous interrogation following his arrest in June. Afterwards, he could hardly stand. His detention and ill-treatment were challenged in the Supreme Court: this resulted in an official undertaking that he would not be further ill-treated and his removal to another place of detention, but he was not released. Military personnel were reported to have been responsible for his ill-treatment, but in other cases the security police were accused of torture. Often, the victims were children or young people, some of whom were alleged to have been tortured with electric shocks, severely beaten or threatened with death. In one case five girls aged 15 to 18 were among a group of detainees tortured with electric shocks at Heilbron Police Station in the Orange Free State. There was considerable evidence that police and security forces committed abuses in the knowledge that they were protected from prosecution under the emergency regulations.

In the first half of 1986 there were many reports of police violence towards detainees and civilians in the Lebowa "homeland". Two deaths in detention occurred within a few days in April. Makompo Kutumela, an AZAPO official, was reported to have been beaten to death in police custody at Mahwelereng on 5 April. Three others arrested with him were also severely assaulted and required hospital treatment. Six days later, Peter Nchabaleng, a UDF leader and former political prisoner, also died in Lebowa police custody. The authorities said he had collapsed but they at first withheld his body: subsequently, there were reports that he had died from an assault. Neither case had been the subject of a formal inquest by the end of 1986. However, the Lebowa "homeland" authorities introduced retroactive immunity provisions under which they and the police would be protected from prosecution for acts committed "in good faith".

There were further deaths in detention under the emergency regulations. The victims included Xoluso Jacobs, who was reported to have been found hanged in his cell in Upington Prison on 22 October. He had been held without charge since 15 June. Student leader Simon Marula died in detention in late December having been held without charge since 20 June.

Inquests began into the deaths in detention in 1985 of Sipho Mutsi and Andries Raditsela (see *Amnesty International Report 1986*) but neither had been completed by the end of 1986. At both, there was evidence that the detainees had been assaulted by police shortly before their deaths. In December the government agreed to pay compensation to Andries Raditsela's family who had sued for damages in the Supreme Court. In the Transkei "homeland" two policemen were charged with the death of student leader Batandwa Ndondo in September 1985, but their trial had not begun by the end of 1986.

There were many politically motivated arrests in the Transkei and Ciskei "homelands" under local laws similar to the Internal Security Act. In both "homelands" detainees were reported to have been tortured and ill-treated. For example, Synod Madlebe was reported to have had his head repeatedly thrust into a water-filled bag, following his arrest in Transkei in late July, and the Reverend Arthur Stofile, a former prisoner of conscience, was reported to have been severely assaulted after he was detained by Ciskei security police in October.

Another former prisoner of conscience and torture victim, Dean T.S. Farisani, was detained without charge by security police in the Venda "homeland" on 24 November. The local head of the Evangelical Lutheran Church, he was still held incommunicado at the end of 1986 and was adopted as a prisoner of conscience by Amnesty International. Earlier, he had visited several countries in support of Amnesty International's campaign against human rights violations in South Africa.

There were many political trials during 1986, some of which resulted in the imprisonment of prisoners of conscience. In June the Natal Supreme Court acquitted the last four of 16 UDF leaders who had been brought to trial on treason charges in 1985. In a separate trial, 22 other leaders of the UDF and Black Consciousness movement were brought to trial at Delmas charged with treason and other offences relating to the outbreak of civil unrest in the "Vaal Triangle" in late 1984. The trial was still in progress at the end of 1986, by which time three defendants had been acquitted.

Amnesty International remained concerned about the use of the death penalty. There were 121 executions in Pretoria Central Prison and an unknown number of hangings in Transkei and other nominally independent "homelands". Three people, all alleged members of the banned African National Congress (ANC), were executed for politically motivated offences on 9 September. They included Andrew Sibusiso Zondo who was sentenced to death in April for causing a bomb explosion which killed five people. At least 10 others were believed to have been sentenced to death for politically motivated offences but not executed by the end of 1986.

There was evidence that South African security forces were

responsible for politically motivated killings of suspected government opponents at home and in neighbouring countries. In a number of areas, there appeared to be close links between security forces and armed vigilante groups who carried out attacks on community leaders and opposition political activists, such as Chief Ampie Mayisa, who was killed at Leandra in January. In June vigilantes attacking residents at the Crossroads squatter camp near Cape Town were seen to be directed by white security force personnel. There was suspicion of such involvement also in the fatal shooting of Dr Fabian Ribeiro and his wife, both known opponents of the government, in December at Mamelodi township, Pretoria. No arrests in connection with these killings had been made by the end of 1986, nor in connection with the murders in 1985 of other prominent government opponents such as Matthew Goniwe and Victoria Mxenge (see *Amnesty International Report 1986*). Police and army shootings of township protestors remained common and resulted in many civilian deaths, some of which may have constituted extrajudicial executions. In August more than 20 people were killed by police in Soweto during protests against the forcible eviction of township residents supporting a widespread rent boycott.

Amnesty International submitted information on its concerns in South Africa to the UN Commission on Human Rights and its *Ad Hoc* Working Group of Experts on Southern Africa, and to the UN Special Committee against *Apartheid*.

Sudan

Amnesty International was concerned about the detention without trial of political prisoners, some of whom appeared to be prisoners of conscience; about allegations of torture and ill-treatment of prisoners; about sentences of amputation and the retention of laws providing for judicial amputation; and about the use of the death penalty.

Armed conflict continued in several parts of the country between government forces and the Sudan People's Liberation Army (SPLA). Human rights abuses were reported on both sides of the conflict. These included the shooting down of a civilian aircraft in Malakal by the SPLA on 18 August, killing all 60 passengers, and the killing by government soldiers in Kosti in mid-December of 22 captured SPLA guerrillas who had been wounded in battle.

The first multi-party elections in the country since 1968 took place in April, one year after the overthrow of the government of President Gaafar Mohámed Nimeiri and the assumption of power by the Transitional Military Council (TMC). On 6 May the TMC handed power to the elected government of the new Prime Minister, Sadiq el-Mahdi.

In February Amnesty International submitted a memorandum to the government prepared following its mission to Sudan in December 1985. It welcomed the progress made since April 1985 in the protection of human rights but called for the repeal of legislation which continued to permit the imprisonment of prisoners of conscience. The organization also expressed concern about recent cases of detention without trial of political prisoners, calling for them to be charged and tried or released. Amnesty International also urged the abolition of the penalties of amputation, flogging, retribution (*qisas*), crucifixion and the death penalty and for the commutation of all such sentences. Safeguards to prevent torture or ill-treatment of prisoners were proposed and ratification of international and regional human rights instruments recommended.

During 1986 several measures were taken by the authorities which coincided with the organization's recommendations, notably the accession on 18 March to the International Covenants on Civil and Political Rights and on Economic, Social and Cultural Rights and the signature on 4 June of the UN Convention Against Torture and Other Cruel, Inhuman or Degrading Treatment or Punishment.

About 90 officials or supporters of the former government of President Nimeiri detained since April 1985 were released by April 1986. A few were tried by State Security courts. They included former Vice-President Major General Omar Mohamed El-Tayeeb, who was convicted in April on charges of treason, espionage and corruption, and sentenced to life imprisonment. In December Major General Khalil Abbas Hassan and three other former army officers were convicted of rebellion for their part in the May 1969 coup which brought President Nimeiri to power. They were sentenced to life imprisonment.

Twenty-one civilians, six police officers and 220 military personnel were held without charge or trial at the beginning of 1986 in connection with an alleged conspiracy against the government in September 1985. All the civilians were released uncharged, including the Reverend Philip Gabboush, leader of the Sudan National Party. The six police officers were charged with treason, tried and acquitted in July. The detained military personnel — mostly members of the Nuba ethnic group — were charged with mutiny and other related offences and were to be court-martialled, but the trials had not started by the end of the year.

Amnesty International was concerned that 24 members of the Nationalist Socialist Alliance for the Salvation of the Country, arrested in December 1985 after launching their party, appeared to be held for their non-violent political opinions. They had criticized the government and expressed support for several aspects of President Nimeiri's rule. All were released on 23 March.

On 23 March the presidential power to form special State Security courts was abolished, thus ensuring that trials of political prisoners would in future be held before normal criminal courts, with the exception of the State Security court trials then in progress. On 1 April the State Security Act, which provided for detention without charge or trial for indefinitely renewable three-month periods, was also abolished. However, administrative detention without charge or trial for an indefinite period was still permitted under the Code of Criminal Procedure and also under the state of emergency, which remained in force throughout 1986. Several people were detained during 1986 under emergency regulations, including people holding banned demonstrations. In most instances they were released within hours or days, but Amnesty International learned of the detention of civilians by the military authorities in southern Sudan for longer periods. Mike Kilongson, a British Broadcasting Corporation (BBC) reporter, was detained in Juba on the order of the military governor of Equatoria Region from 14 March to 13 May. He subsequently alleged that he had been tortured, and that of the 34 civilians who were detained with him, one was summarily executed and two died of starvation and medical neglect. Amnesty International appealed to the authorities to investigate the allegations of torture and harsh treatment of political prisoners and to ensure that all prisoners were either formally charged and brought to court or released. The organization called for them to be given immediate access to their families, lawyers and doctors.

In Malakal in mid-August 200 or more people were reportedly arrested and accused of links with the SPLA after the SPLA shot down a Sudan Airways aircraft. Most were soon released but 27 or more senior civil servants were still detained at the end of 1986 without charge or trial. They included Daniel Dhanho, Director of Roads in the regional administration, Amos Awan Gak, Director General of Agriculture, and James Tuch, a pharmacist. Amnesty International urged that they should be either charged or released, and was investigating whether they might have been arrested for their political opinions rather than any proven links with the SPLA.

No judicial amputations took place during 1986 but Amnesty

International was concerned that about 40 prisoners remained under sentence of judicial amputation. On 4 February the Supreme Court confirmed 42 sentences of amputation and retribution but in August a resolution to the Constituent Assembly (parliament) by the Islamic National Front calling for the sentences to be carried out without further delay was defeated. By the end of 1986 the sentences were still under review by the Council of State.

The 1983 laws providing for penalties of amputation, retribution, flogging and crucifixion were technically still in force but only floggings continued to be imposed and carried out during 1986, mostly for alcohol offences. Proposals to abolish or amend these laws were under discussion during 1986. Amnesty International initiated a special relief project to provide artificial hands and feet for amputees, of whom there were 120 or more.

Amnesty International was investigating reports that prisoners sentenced to death and amputation were being held in leg irons. The organization was also concerned about reports that civilians detained in military custody on political grounds were subjected to ill-treatment and harsh conditions.

No executions were known to have taken place in 1986, although about 50 people were under sentence of death from previous years. In January Amnesty International appealed to the government to establish an inquiry into the execution in January 1985 of Mahmoud Mohamed Taha, leader of the Republican Movement, who was executed for his opinions and religious beliefs. No such official inquiry took place but on 25 April the Sources of Judicial Decision Act (1983), under which he had been charged, was amended to ensure that advocating a new interpretation of Islam could not be a criminal offence. On 18 November the Constitutional Court ruled that his execution had been unconstitutional.

Swaziland

Amnesty International was concerned about the death penalty and about the forcible abduction from Swaziland of suspected opponents of the South African Government.

At the beginning of January Amnesty International welcomed the release of former Finance Minister Sishayi Nxumalo and four other prisoners of conscience released from detention on 31 December 1985. At the same time, Amnesty International urged the government to abolish the renewable 60-day detention provision under which they had been held for a year, or to amend it in accordance with the requirements of international human rights law. The detention provision was not known to have been used in 1986, but it had not been amended by the end of the year.

In May Prince Mfanasibili Dlamini, a member of the royal family, and former Police Commissioner Majaji Simelane were tried and convicted in the High Court on charges of defeating the ends of justice. They were alleged to have fabricated accusations of treason against Sishayi Nxumalo and four others for political reasons. They were sentenced to seven and five years' imprisonment respectively.

The year was marked by continuing insecurity for South African refugees and exiles resident in Swaziland. Some alleged members of the African National Congress (ANC) of South Africa were arrested but deported to other African countries by the Swazi authorities, but other alleged opponents of the South African Government, including suspected ANC supporters, were the target of assassination or abduction by South African security forces. In some of these cases, there was a suspicion of collusion between local police officers and those responsible for the attacks. In early June three South African exiles were shot dead by what was officially described as a "hit squad" believed to have entered the country from South Africa. The same month, Sidney Msibi, an ANC member, was abducted from Manzini by South African agents. He was held incommunicado in South Africa until November, when he was released shortly before a legal challenge to his detention was to be heard in the South African Supreme Court.

In August an ANC member was taken by unidentified armed men from Mankayane police station to which he had been transferred shortly before. The ANC denied that they had freed him and it appeared that he too might have been abducted to South Africa.

Further abductions occurred in December when six people were seized by South African security forces in night raids on houses in Manzini and Mbabane. Danger Nyoni, a Swazi national whose 13-year-old son was shot dead by his kidnappers, was released within a few hours and two Swiss nationals, Corinne Bischoff and Daniel Schneider, were released and returned from South Africa two days after their abduction. Another victim, Matthews Maphumulo, a registered refugee, was reported to have been killed by his abductors. Two others, Grace Cele, also a registered refugee, and Ismail Ibrahim, an alleged member of the ANC, were still detained in South Africa at the end of 1986. Amnesty International feared that they might be tortured.

Amnesty International continued to be concerned about the use of the death penalty. However, there were no precise figures on the number of people sentenced to death and it was not known whether any executions took place. On 29 April it was reported that all death sentences then in force had been commuted at the initiative of Queen Regent Ntombi to mark the coronation of her son, Prince Makhose-tive, as King Mswati III. Amnesty International welcomed this act of clemency but received no response from the government to its request for information on the number and identities of the prisoners who benefited.

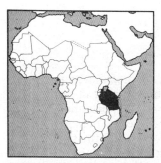

Tanzania

Amnesty International was concerned about the detention without trial of two possible prisoners of conscience and about the death penalty.

In October James Mapalala and Mwinyijuma Othuman Upindo were detained without trial, apparently because they had petitioned leading officials of the government and the country's sole legal political party, *Chama Cha Mapinduzi* (CCM), Party of the Revolution, calling for a repeal of the 1965 law that made Tanzania a one-party state. Since September 1984, when this petition was made public, James Mapalala was reported to have been detained for brief periods at least six times and Mwinyijuma Othuman Upindo at least three times. The Preventive Detention Act, under which they were held, authorized the President to order the indefinite detention without trial of anyone deemed "dangerous to peace and good order". The

Act was revised in 1985 to allow detainees to challenge the legality of the detention order before the High Court and to require the detaining authorities to release detainees if they failed to provide written grounds for detention within 15 days. Relatives of the two men filed a *habeas corpus* application before the High Court in November but the judge ruled that they had been legally detained and did not need to be produced in court. However, their detention orders were signed by the President only on 31 October, the day that the *habeas corpus* application had been filed, suggesting that they had been held since 21 October in breach of the law. The organization was further concerned to learn that relatives of the two men had been refused access to them and had not been notified of their whereabouts by the end of 1986. In November Amnesty International informed the Prime Minister of its concerns and called for James Mapalala and Mwinyijuma Othuman Upindo to be released if they were not to be charged.

Amnesty International was also concerned about the death penalty. At least 10 people were sentenced to death after being convicted of murder or other criminal offences. In December Amnesty International appealed to President Ali Hassan Mwinyi to exercise clemency on behalf of Asha Mkwizu Hauli, a woman whose sentence of death imposed for murder in 1983 had been confirmed by the Court of Appeal. There were no executions reported during 1986.

Togo

Amnesty International was concerned about the imprisonment of prisoners of conscience and the detention without trial of other suspected opponents of the government. New information was received during 1986 about the torture and ill-treatment of detainees in late 1985; a commission of inquiry established after these allegations were first made appeared either to have been inadequately conducted or to have had some of its findings suppressed prior to their publication in January. Amnesty International was also concerned about the death penalty: in December, 13 people were sentenced to death, three of them *in absentia*, for alleged involvement in a coup attempt, but they had not been executed by the end of 1986.

In June Amnesty International published a report, *Togo: Political Imprisonment and Torture*, which described the long-term detention of government opponents without trial or after unfair trials. It detailed also the use of torture and cases of deaths in detention, and called for urgent government action to end human rights abuses. In particular, Amnesty International sought the release of all prisoners of conscience, the release or trial of other uncharged political detainees, and action to prevent torture – the publication of all detainees' names and places of imprisonment, impartial and thorough investigation of torture allegations and deaths in custody, and regular, independent inspection of prisons and interrogation centres. Amnesty International also called for the repeal of legislation introduced in December 1985 which empowered the police to hold people in custody for an unlimited period, on the grounds that this would facilitate torture.

On 1 January an Amnesty International delegation which had gone to Togo to seek information about the progress of the commission of inquiry was expelled from the country. Following this, Amnesty International appealed publicly to the government to publish the commission's findings. It did so on 14 January.

The day before publication of the commission's report President Gnassingbé Eyadéma released several political detainees to mark the anniversary of his accession to power in 1967. They included seven prisoners of conscience adopted by Amnesty International, all of whom had been arrested in August or September 1985 as suspected opponents of the government. Some of them were reported to have been tortured following arrest and while detained incommunicado, and in October 1985 had been seen by Amnesty International delegates while still suffering injuries. It was in connection with their treatment that the commission of inquiry had been established. Among those freed were Aluka Kodjo Kokou, an agricultural engineer, who had been in hospital at the time of the Amnesty International mission in October 1985, and Alessi de Medeiros, a bailiff, who had a broken arm and broken ribs as a result of beatings inflicted in detention.

Among those who remained in detention following the 13 January releases were Komlakuma Doe and Kossi Assinyo, both of whom had been detained without trial since December 1984 and adopted as prisoners of conscience by Amnesty International. In addition, a number of other detainees arrested in 1985 were still held. Three of these, Adeyinka Randolph and her brother, Ati Randolph, together with Yema Gu-Konu, a university lecturer, were sent for trial on charges of possessing or distributing subversive literature. They had been arrested in September 1985. In January Amnesty International received information about further arrests in late 1985 in which as many as 30 people were reported to have been detained for possessing or distributing leaflets critical of the government. They included Tanko Diasso, a university lecturer, his brother, Ibrahim Adamou Diasso, and Fousseni Maman, a hotel worker. In late January Amnesty International issued an urgent appeal on behalf of these detainees and subsequently adopted the Diasso brothers, Fousseni Maman and five others as prisoners of conscience. One, Kodjo Ekpe, was reported to have been released in early March but the others were held until July, when all seven were apparently freed.

In April the government released four other detainees whose cases had been taken up for investigation by Amnesty International following their arrest in September 1985, including Yawo Sémanou Dobou, a telecommunications engineer. Thereafter, Komlakuma Doe and Kossi Assinyo were released in July, and in September the authorities freed Mensah Messanvi Biova and three others who had been held since August 1985 in connection with bomb explosions in Lomé. They were released after several other people were arrested in possession of explosives and charged with the previous year's bomb explosions. The four had been held incommunicado for several weeks in breach of the law, which required detainees to be brought before a magistrate or released within 48 hours. Amnesty International had taken up their cases for investigation in late 1985 and expressed its concern to the government about the illegality of their detention. The authorities then introduced new legislation to empower the police to hold people in custody for unlimited periods.

At the end of July Adeyinka Randolph and the two others charged with her were brought to trial before the Correctional Court in Lomé. All three were convicted of producing and distributing leaflets opposing the government. Ati Randolph and Yema Gu-Konu received five-year sentences. Amnesty International continued to appeal for their release as prisoners of conscience. Adeyinka Randolph received a three-year sentence but was freed on 31 July, the day after the trial, on President Eyadéma's orders. After charges were brought against the three defendants, Amnesty International told the government that it wished to send an observer to their trial. In response, however, the government stated that no such observer from Amnesty International would be permitted.

During the trial Ati Randolph made detailed allegations of torture following his arrest in late 1985. From the report of the commission of inquiry published on 14 January it was not clear whether he had been interviewed or his treatment investigated by the commission. The report, as published, did not give the number or identities of detainees interviewed and provided few details concerning the proceedings and the conduct of the inquiry.

The commission of inquiry did not report that detainees had been tortured but criticized the detention of suspects beyond the 48-hour legal limit and the standards of hygiene in places of detention. It concluded that the death in custody of Aka Adote in September 1985 was the result of natural causes. However, it apparently failed to order an autopsy and did not appear to have investigated thoroughly allegations that Aka Adote had been severely tortured shortly before his death.

The commission's findings did not accord with information received by Amnesty International in 1985. Nor did it accord with the findings of another non-governmental organization and two French lawyers who inquired into the use of torture and made public their findings in January. The two lawyers, who had been commissioned by two French organizations, alleged that detainees had been systematically tortured with electric shocks; the *Association des juristes africains*, the African Jurists Association, which had visited Togo at the government's request, reported that several detainees had been severely beaten in police custody and criticized the detention of suspects beyond the 48-hour limit. Amnesty International received information suggesting that some of the commission of inquiry's findings had been suppressed by the authorities between the completion of the commission's report in November 1985 and its publication on 14 January, but it was not possible to confirm this.

Thirteen people were sentenced to death in December after a trial before the State Security Court. This trial arose out of an unsuccessful attempt to overthrow the government on 23/24 September in which a number of people were killed. In all, 35 people were charged, including several nationals of neighbouring states, but 10 of them were tried *in absentia*. Of the defendants in court, 10 were sentenced to death, seven were sentenced to life imprisonment, five received sentences of up to one year's imprisonment, and three were acquitted. Following the trial Amnesty International appealed to President Eyadéma to extend clemency to those under sentence of death and expressed concern that defendants tried by the State Security Court were denied the right of appeal to a higher court. None of those sentenced to death had been executed by the end of 1986.

In July Amnesty International submitted information about its concerns in Togo to the UN under its procedure for confidentially reviewing communications about human rights violations (the so-called "1503 procedure").

Uganda

Amnesty International continued to investigate reports of the detention of government opponents and of the ill-treatment, "disappearance" or extra-judicial execution of civilians in areas of armed conflict between government and rebels. However, Amnesty International noted a significant improvement in respect for human rights in Uganda in 1986.

In January the capital, Kampala, fell to the National Resistance Army (NRA), which had waged a guerrilla war against successive governments since 1981. A new government was formed, headed by NRA leader Yoweri Museveni and including representatives of all the country's political parties. By March the government had established control over the entire country. With the formation of the new government and the replacement of the previous army, the Uganda National Liberation Army (UNLA), by the NRA, abuses by soldiers against the civilian population reportedly came to a halt. Although Amnesty International later received reports of ill-treatment and killing of civilians by the army, it nevertheless appeared that this general improvement was maintained as a consequence of the government's clear public statements on the need to protect human rights and the high level of discipline in the NRA.

In May the government announced the formation of a commission of inquiry, headed by a High Court judge, to investigate violations of human rights from independence in 1962 until the NRA came to power. The commission began hearing evidence in December and it was expected to sit for some years. Although it was not part of the commission's brief to initiate prosecutions, both the Minister of Justice and the commission's chairman said that they expected the Director of Public Prosecutions to initiate prosecutions as a result of the commission's findings. In 1986 charges relating to human rights violations were brought against several ministers and officials of previous governments. The new government also established the post of Inspector-General of Government, or Ombudsman, whose terms of reference included investigating complaints of human rights abuses by the government in power.

In April an Amnesty International mission visited Uganda. The delegates were able to confirm the impression of other outside observers that an atmosphere of general respect for human rights prevailed in the areas that they visited. They travelled to the "Luwero triangle", the area to the northwest of Kampala which had seen many of the worst human rights violations under the governments of President Milton Obote and Major General Tito Okello. In Luwero the delegates saw large quantities of human remains and heard accounts from local residents of widespread and systematic torture and extrajudicial killing by soldiers of the previous governments. Amnesty International's delegates met government members, including the Prime Minister, the Minister of Internal Affairs and the Minister of Justice. Amnesty International submitted a memorandum to the government in September, detailing the organization's recommendations for safeguards against future human rights violations. These included: ratification of international human rights instruments; repeal of laws permitting detention without trial; tightening of legal safeguards against incommunicado detention; regular independent inspection of places of detention; introduction of human rights training for members of the police and armed forces; and abolition of the death penalty.

Many hundreds of prisoners were reported to have been detained without trial during 1986, although the government stated that no one was held under the provisions of the Public Order and Security Act, 1967, which permits indefinite detention. However, Amnesty International had some difficulty in establishing how many of these were held for political reasons, since large numbers of criminal suspects were also detained without trial by the army. In the course of its April mission, Amnesty International asked the government about the arrest of members of former President Obote's party, the Uganda People's Congress (UPC), in the eastern Ugandan area of Busoga in February and March. The reason for their arrest was their alleged association with an organization called Force Obote Back Again (FOBA), which apparently sought the armed overthrow of the government. In all the named cases that Amnesty International drew to the government's attention, the prisoner was either subsequently released or charged with a criminal offence, or else had already been charged or released.

In the second half of 1986 Amnesty International expressed concern to the government about the detention of many people, mainly Acholis from northern Uganda, in the aftermath of armed incursions from southern Sudan by guerrillas loyal to the previous governments of President Obote and Major General Okello. Among the cases mentioned by Amnesty International was that of Pasca Lalweny Okello, the younger daughter of lieutenant General Basilio Okello, chief of the armed forces under the government of Major General Okello. She was arrested in Kampala in late August and held at Lubiri barracks in the capital until her release without charge in November. Also reported to have been arrested was Milton

Odongopiny, aged 17, an adopted son of Major General Okello. He was said to have been arrested by soldiers in Kampala in June and taken to various private houses, where he was beaten, before being transferred to police custody and released in July. In both cases Amnesty International believed that they may have been detained solely because of their family associations with members of a previous government. Amnesty International remained concerned about the large number of apparently arbitrary arrests, particularly in the north, in the course of operations against the insurgents.

In August, 25 alleged supporters of the restoration of the monarchy in the southern region of Buganda were arrested and charged with treason. They were alleged to have plotted to overthrow the government by force. In October about 20 people were arrested and charged with treason; again the allegation against them was that they had plotted the violent overthrow of the government. Those charged included three government ministers: Evaristo Nyanzi of the Democratic Party, which was strongly represented in the government; Andrew Kayiira, leader of the Uganda Freedom Movement (UFM); and David Lwanga, leader of the Federal Democratic Movement of Uganda (FEDEMU). Both the UFM and FEDEMU were small guerrilla organizations which had participated in the armed struggle against the government of former President Obote. Also arrested was the former Vice-President in President Obote's government, Paulo Muwanga. He was subsequently charged with alleged human rights violations when he was in government. Among the 20 charged in October was Anthony Ssekweyama, editor-in-chief of the Democratic Party paper *The Citizen*, who had been detained several times under President Obote's government and had been adopted by Amnesty International as a prisoner of conscience. In the cases of all those charged with treason, Amnesty International sought assurances from the government that they were being properly treated, that they had access to lawyers of their choice and that they would receive a fair and prompt trial. None of them had been brought to trial by the end of 1986.

Amnesty International was concerned about reports of the detention without charge of members of the UFM and FEDEMU by the NRA, particularly around the time of the arrest of their party leaders. At the end of 1986 Amnesty International was still trying to establish the numbers involved and to investigate whether the reason for their detention was their affiliation to a minority political group.

In previous years Amnesty International had been concerned about the widespread and systematic use of torture against political detainees. This practice did not apparently continue in 1986. The conditions of imprisonment of political detainees in military custody were reported to be very poor but did not appear, in general, to constitute deliberate ill-treatment by the detaining authorities. However, Amnesty International was concerned about the persistent use of a practice known as *kandoya* or "three piece-tying", which involved a prisoner's upper arms being tied tightly together behind his or her back. It was reported that this sometimes led to restricted breathing and death. It was unclear to Amnesty International whether *kandoya* was intended as a method of torture or a severe means of restraint, but in either case the organization considered it to be a form of ill-treatment. In October Amnesty International asked the government to investigate two reported instances of the use of *kandoya* by NRA soldiers. In one case Valent Okello was reported to have been arrested at Lacor trading centre in Gulu District, northern Uganda, in August, apparently because his poll tax card was said not to be in order. He was reported to have been tied *kandoya*-style, causing him to collapse and die on the spot. In the other instance, Geoffrey Okumu of Pece, in Gulu district, was reported to have been arrested at his home in late August, tied *kandoya*-style and taken away. He was reported not to have been seen since.

Another reported "disappearance" investigated by Amnesty International was that of Ben Ocan, of Pece Gulu. He was reported to have been arrested by NRA soldiers on 28 August during an army raid on his village. He was said to have been shot and then taken away in a military vehicle. Amnesty International asked the government to investigate these reports and said that if Ben Ocan was found to be in the custody of the NRA he should be handed over to civilian custody where he should either be charged or released. The government later stated that it was investigating this case, as well as the reported cases of *kandoya* submitted by Amnesty International, but it had not made any results available by the end of 1986.

Amnesty International received a number of reports of killings of civilians in the course of army operations against rebels in northern Uganda and sought to establish whether these were extrajudicial executions. In one incident, an elderly couple, John and Magdalene Omoya, were reported to have been killed by the NRA in October at their home in Opette village near Kitgum. John Omoya was a retired teacher who was partially paralysed and bedridden. In another incident, also in October, Valenta Otto, an elderly woman, was reported to have been shot dead on the road near Kitgum by NRA soldiers. In neither case was Amnesty International able to establish the exact circumstances, but the identities of the victims, who were unlikely to have been engaged in armed opposition to the government, gave rise to fears that they had been the victims of extrajudicial executions on account of their political affiliations or ethnic origin.

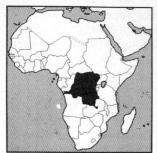

Zaire

Amnesty International was concerned about the imprisonment and banishment of prisoners of conscience for supporting an illegal opposition political party and also about reports of torture and killings in eastern Kivu region. Amnesty International was also concerned about reports of torture in other parts of the country and about the long-term detention without trial of prisoners of conscience and other political detainees.

The number of political prisoners known to Amnesty International varied considerably from month to month as people were released and new arrests made. After a wave of arrests in June of supporters of the opposition *Union pour la démocratie el le. progrès social* (UDPS), Union for Democracy and Social Progress, Amnesty International campaigned for the release of 70 people who were detained or banished because of their links with the UDPS. The total number of people imprisoned for political reasons for all or part of the year was significantly higher, but could not be estimated accurately by the organization.

Major reforms were announced at the end of October when the military security service, *Service de renseignements militaires et d'action* (SRMA), Military Intelligence and Action Service, was disbanded and a new Department (Ministry) for Citizens' Rights and Freedoms (*Département des droits et libertés du citoyen*) was established. Explaining these changes President Mobutu Sese Seko confirmed publicly that human rights violations had been committed by the armed forces. Referring to an Amnesty International report published in March 1986, *Zaire — Reports of Torture and Killings Committed by the Armed Forces in Shaba Region*, the President said that an official inquiry had been carried out after the report was published which had confirmed that some of the abuses described by Amnesty International had occurred. However, the inquiry's findings and the types of abuses it had documented were not made public. President Mobutu Sese Seko also said that the new department would deal with complaints brought by the victims of human rights violations and that the new department would be represented at all levels of the community, right down to village level.

After the dissolution of the SRMA, the Secretary of State for Defence announced that a disciplinary commission would investigate the activities of a number of SRMA officials. By the end of 1986 no details were available about the findings of this commission.

The arrest of non-violent opponents of the government continued throughout 1986. In March the Jehovah's Witness sect, which had been legalized in 1980, was banned. Amnesty International received reports of the detention without trial of Jehovah's Witnesses in Shaba region, and it appeared that arrests also occurred in other parts of the country. Efforts were also made to enforce legislation which prohibited other religious sects which had not obtained official recognition from practising. Information about the repression of these sects was difficult to obtain across the country as a whole, but in April 20 sects were prohibited in Lingwala, a district of Kinshasa.

Amnesty International was concerned about the imprisonment or banishment of UDPS supporters. About 40 people arrested in Kinshasa during the last three months of 1985 were believed to have remained in detention or under restriction throughout 1986. One group of eight people, which included Bossassi Epole Kodya, a leader of the UDPS and President of the Zairian Human Rights League was detained by the National Gendarmerie in Kinshasa until February. All eight were then banished to villages around the country.

Two UDPS leaders charged with insulting the head of state were tried in January. Kanana Tshiongo and Tshisekedi wa Mulumba, both former members of the National Assembly, were arrested in October 1985. They were both convicted by the State Security Court and sentenced to 18 months' imprisonment. However, at the end of February they were pardoned and released. They were released within a week of the release of another prisoner of conscience, Ronald van den Bogaert, a Belgian national who had been arrested in July 1985 on his arrival in Zaire and later sentenced to 10 years' imprisonment on charges of conspiring to change the country's one-party system.

Further arrests of UDPS supporters began on 11 June when seven UDPS leaders were served with administrative banishment orders. All seven had been repeatedly imprisoned or banished since 1981 or 1982. One of them, Bossassi Epole Kodya, was already restricted to Bolomba, a village in Equateur region, when the new restrictions were announced. The others were sent to villages in Kasaï Oriental, Kivu and Shaba regions. They included the two UDPS leaders released in February and two other former members of the National Assembly, Kibassa Maliba, a former government minister, and Birindwa ci Birkashirwa, a businessman. No charges were brought against them but the authorities accused them of inciting people against the government and of encouraging students to paint slogans hostile to the government on Kinshasa University's campus. Despite this accusation it appeared that the real reason for their rearrest was their persistence in seeking to have the UDPS officially recognized. One of the seven, Kibassa Maliba, was transferred a few days after his arrival in a village to Shaba's provincial capital, Lubumbashi, where he was kept under house arrest for the rest of 1986. One other, Makanda Mpinga Shambuyi, became seriously ill in July and was transferred to hospital. He requested permission to leave the country for treatment unavailable in Zaire. His request was still under consideration at the end of 1986.

At least 20 other UDPS supporters and possibly many more were arrested in June and July. They included Lusanga Ngiele and Lumbu Maloba Ndiba, also former National Assembly members and leaders of the UDPS who had been imprisoned and banished before. Also detained were Mbwankiem Niaroliem, a member of one of the first governments formed after independence in 1960, and Mpindu Buabua. At the end of 1986 Amnesty International was working for the release of some 70 UDPS supporters who were believed still to be detained or banished and whom the organization considered to be prisoners of conscience.

Amnesty International was also concerned about other political prisoners arrested in previous years. Kianzila el Busi and five others arrested in 1984 after two bomb explosions in Kinshasa remained in detention without trial. Unofficial sources suggested that the six were questioned by State Security Court investigators in early 1986, but that there was insufficient evidence against them to bring them to trial. Amnesty International continued to investigate their cases as possible prisoners of conscience.

Five prisoners of conscience, including Ngwashi Chola, who had been detained without charge in Lubumbashi since January 1984 were released in May, on condition that they reported every week until the end of the year to the local office of the *Agence nationale de documentation* (AND), the national security service. Other prisoners of conscience detained by the AND in Lubumbashi were also released during 1986. Nkamba Ilunga, who was arrested in July 1984 after disputing the result of an election in his village, was freed uncharged in April.

In southeast Kivu region the army continued to detain villagers suspected of being in contact with government opponents in neighbouring Burundi and Tanzania. They were held without being charged or referred to the local judiciary, and were only released after the payment of a ransom. The organization was also concerned by the detention for several months, on the island of Idjwi, of a young man called Moudhama, reportedly for possessing a newspaper article referring to extrajudicial executions carried out on the island in 1985 (see *Amnesty International Report 1986*).

In 1985, in Kivu's Kabare district, the appointment by the government of the younger son of the former *mwami* (king or paramount chief) in preference to the eldest son led to violent clashes between troops and civilians in which about 40 people were killed. After a senior local official was murdered about 80 people were arrested and accused of complicity, although it appeared that some had been detained solely because of their opposition to the new *mwami*. Most of them were released uncharged during 1986, but in September 15 were reported to be still detained. Amnesty International sought information from the Procurator General of Kivu region about their cases, but had received no reply by the end of 1986. Weregemere Bingwa Nyalumeke, a former government minister and prominent political figure in Kivu region, who had been opposed to the appointment of the new *mwami*, was adopted by Amnesty International as a prisoner of conscience. He had been expelled from the Central Committee of the ruling party in September 1985 and then banished to a remote farm in Katana, near Kabare. Although he was suffering from glaucoma the authorities refused permission for him to have an eye operation. Other opponents of the new *mwami* were arrested in Kabare in early 1986 and detained in unofficial prisons on the orders of local chiefs supporting the new *mwami*. Following moves by the local procurator in Bukavu to prevent such arbitrary arrests, some of the local leaders resorted to acts of terror against their opponents. There were reports of the burning of huts and houses. rape, and beatings and torture of prisoners. Amnesty International was concerned that the detentions carried out by the local leaders were outside the framework of the law and that torture and killings took place. One man, Matabaro Bagula, a villager from Kakongola, was reportedly burnt alive at the *mwami*'s court at Cirungu in May, after being held prisoner there for 10 days. In another case, also in May, a local Red Cross worker was arrested and so severely beaten and tortured that he required three months' hospital treatment. In August a retired policeman, Nyongola, was reported to have been castrated and then burnt alive in Cirungu.

Amnesty International also received reports of torture from other parts of Zaire, but not on the same scale as in 1984 and 1985 when there were widespread abuses in areas affected by counter-insurgency operations. However, in September, it was reported that a man named Radi, who was suspected of having contacts with government opponents based in Tanzania, was killed by soldiers in Moba who forced him to drink petrol until he died. A number of suspected UDPS supporters arrested in Mbuji-Mayi in March were reported to have been severely beaten. Those arrested had been among a crowd of several hundred people who welcomed Kanana Tshiongo when he arrived in Mbuji-Mayi, following his release from prison in February. Amnesty International received details of the injuries sustained by 10 individuals, which included wounds inflicted by blows, mainly to the face, arms and body.

Amnesty International remained concerned about the use of the death penalty but did not know the number of sentences imposed or how many executions took place. In July the authorities announced that four people convicted of murder and armed robbery had been executed. The previous month it was reported that a woman convicted of witchcraft and sentenced to death by the paramount chief of the Bakuba in Kasaï Occidental region had been executed. However, it was not clear whether she had been tried by a court empowered by law to impose a death sentence, nor whether her rights to appeal and to petition the head of state for clemency had been respected.

Amnesty International submitted information about its concerns in Zaire under the UN procedure for confidentially reviewing communications about human rights violations (the so-called "1503 procedure").

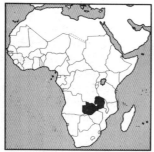

Zambia

Amnesty International was concerned about the detention without trial of alleged opponents of the government, some of whom were reportedly tortured or ill-treated, and about the death penalty. At least 18 people were sentenced to death but in November five prisoners awaiting execution for treason had their sentences commuted to life imprisonment.

Three political prisoners held without trial since their arrest in 1981 remained in detention throughout 1986. Major Ronald Chansa, an army major, Flight Sergeant Manfred Mwangana Mukumbuta, and Faustino Lombe, a teacher, were suspected of plotting the escape of several people awaiting trial on charges of treason. However, no charges had been brought against them and Amnesty International continued to investigate whether they were prisoners of conscience.

In May Peter Chiko Bwalya, a former clerk, Henry Kalenga, Joseph Chitalu and Stanslous Kachenjela were detained under the Preservation of Public Security Regulations, accused of belonging to a clandestine anti-government organization, the People's Redemption Organization (PRO), and recruiting students at the University of Zambia into it. No political parties, other than the governing United National Independence Party (UNIP), are permitted. Amnesty International expressed its concern at their detention without trial and asked the government to charge or release them. The organization was investigating whether they were prisoners of conscience.

The Preservation of Public Security Regulations, under which about a dozen political detainees known to Amnesty International were held, empower the President to authorize detention without trial for an unlimited period. The grounds for detention under these regulations may not be challenged in court. Detainees are told the formal grounds for their detention and their cases are reviewed by a special tribunal which can recommend release or continued detention, but it sits *in camera* and the President is not obliged to implement its confidential recommendations.

A civilian pilot, Captain Pasco McLeo Chansa, who had been arrested and detained in February 1985, was released uncharged in June 1986. He had been detained for `allegedly holding meetings outside the country with a person wanted by the Zambian authorities in connection with a 1980 coup plot and for failing to report these meetings to the authorities. Amnesty International had called on the authorities to charge or release him.

In May South African security personnel attacked a Lusaka suburb, ostensibly against members of the African National Congress (ANC) of South Africa which has headquarters in the Zambian capital. A number of people, most of them foreign nationals, were arrested and questioned by police after the attack. A group of seven foreign nationals on a visit to Zambia were arrested in early May. Three were released uncharged after a few weeks but the other four, all white South Africans, were still in detention under the Preservation of Public Security Regulations at the end of 1986. It was reported to Amnesty International that all seven foreigners had been tortured or ill-treated during interrogation at Lilayi police training centre near Lusaka. The reported ill-treatment included being beaten, hung upside down, forced to hold weights in outstretched hands, and made to perform physical contortions for long periods. In August the organization urged President Kenneth Kaunda to order an investigation into these allegations and to either charge the four South Africans and bring them to trial or release them. The President replied that no torture or ill-treatment had been inflicted on the South Africans and that their cases would be reviewed in accordance with the law. Amnesty International was investigating whether they were possible prisoners of conscience, imprisoned on account of their national or racial origins.

There were renewed reports of torture following the arrest of five other foreign nationals in July. No charges were brought against them and they were released in August. They alleged that they had been tortured by police in an attempt to make them confess to spying for the South African Government and had been beaten on the head, stomach and kidneys and sexually abused. President Kaunda was reported to have said that if any ill-treatment had taken place, those responsible would be punished. No investigation or prosecution had been reported by the end of 1986.

Amnesty International remained concerned about the death penalty. At least 18 people were sentenced to death in 1986, mostly for murder or armed robbery, although no executions were reported. In November, five prisoners sentenced to death for their role in the 1980 coup plot had their sentences commuted to life imprisonment by President Kaunda. The five, on whose behalf Amnesty International had appealed, were former High Court Commissioner Edward Shamwana, a Zairean politician Deogratias Symba, Thomas Mulewa Mpunga, Yoram Godwin Mumba and Albert Chimbalile. Amnesty International welcomed the commutations and urged the President to extend clemency to all others under sentence of death.

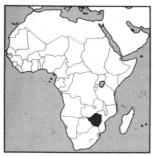

Zimbabwe

Amnesty International's main concerns were the detention without trial of large numbers of political opponents of the government, including prisoners of conscience, and the torture of prisoners in the custody of the Central Intelligence Organization (CIO). However, many political detainees were released during 1986. The organization was also concerned about continued use of the death penalty.

In January Amnesty International submitted a memorandum to the government detailing evidence of torture by the police and CIO gathered by the organization during a mission to Zimbabwe in October 1985. The memorandum recommended that the government establish an independent inquiry into reports of torture and proposed a further Amnesty International mission to the country to discuss the organization's concerns. The government did not reply to this document, which was made public in May, but on many occasions during 1986 there was public criticism of Amnesty International by members of the government and in the semi-official press. In particular, it was repeatedly claimed that Amnesty International had failed to respond to a government invitation to visit Zimbabwe. In fact the only such invitation received by the organization, in November 1985, was conditional upon Amnesty International providing the government with the names of people in Zimbabwe who had given it information, which it was not prepared to do. In its memorandum to the government, Amnesty International pointed out that international human rights instruments, such as the UN Declaration Against Torture, recognized that torture victims would often be reluctant to make a complaint to the authority which was alleged to have tortured them and that any investigation should not be conditional upon such a complaint. In August government ministers declared that Amnesty International was an "enemy of Zimbabwe" and threatened that anyone who supplied the organization with information would be detained.

At the same time, however, Amnesty International noted the release of at least 70 untried political detainees in July and August and welcomed the government's announcement that it would review the cases of all other security detainees and those serving sentences for political crimes. Also, in July the Minister of Home Affairs stated that the government would not tolerate the use of torture by the police. Earlier, in January, Stops Camp in Bulawayo — a major torture centre named publicly by Amnesty International — was emptied of political detainees, although reports later in the year indicated that the centre was still used on occasions for political detention and torture.

In May Nicholas Ndebele, acting director of the Catholic Commission for Justice and Peace in Zimbabwe (CCJPZ), was detained under emergency powers regulations. This followed a statement by the Home Affairs Minister that Amnesty International had "infiltrated" local churches. In its annual report, published in April, the CCJPZ stated that it had investigated a number of reports of torture similar to those reported by Amnesty International: "All reports were investigated and found to be correct, with remarkable similarity in the methods used in all cases." The report pointed out that the CCJPZ had not collaborated with Amnesty International in gathering evidence of torture. The same point was made clear by Amnesty International in its appeals to the government to release Nicholas Ndebele, whom the organization believed to be a prisoner of conscience. On 4 June the High Court ordered Nicholas Ndebele's release, but he was briefly redetained by police along with the

Commission's chairman, Michael Auret. Both were released apparently on the orders of Prime Minister Robert Mugabe.

Two prisoners of conscience adopted by Amnesty International were released in December: Dumiso Dabengwa and Norman Zikhali, both senior officials of the minority Zimbabwe African People's Union (ZAPU). They had been held under regulations in force under the state of emergency which has existed since the 1960s and which must be renewed every six months by parliament. Dumiso Dabengwa, a former leader of ZAPU's military wing during the country's war of independence, was acquitted of treason and arms charges in 1983. Three others acquitted with him were also still detained at the beginning of 1986 and had been adopted as prisoners of conscience: Lookout Masuku died of meningitis shortly after his release from custody in March, while Tshaka Moyo and Nicholas Nkomo were released on the orders of the High Court in June. The Constitution provides for a specially established tribunal to review all detainees' cases at six-month intervals. In October the Review Tribunal for the first time recommended Dumiso Dabengwa's release. This decision was overruled by presidential order but the government ordered his release less than two months later. Norman Zikhali, a pioneer of the Zimbabwean trade union movement and a former long-term prisoner of conscience for his opposition to the Rhodesian Government, was arrested in November 1984 when he was sent by ZAPU leader Joshua Nkomo to investigate inter-party disturbances in the southern town of Beitbridge. He was not charged, but was detained indefinitely under section 17 of the Emergency Powers (Maintenance of Law and Order) Regulations until his release in December 1986.

Other prisoners of conscience released during 1986 included Welshman Mabhena, a ZAPU member of parliament, and Nevison Mukanganga Nyashanu, an unsuccessful ZAPU parliamentary candidate in the 1985 general election. They were apparently held as state witnesses against 10 prominent politicians and army officers charged with plotting to overthrow the government. They were reported to have been ill-treated to force them to incriminate the accused but both men apparently made it clear later that they were not prepared to testify against the accused. In August charges against the 10 were withdrawn and Welshman Mabhena and Nevison Nyashanu released with them.

At the beginning of 1986 Amnesty International was investigating the cases of large numbers of uncharged political detainees to determine whether or not they were prisoners of conscience. Most of these were members or supporters of ZAPU who were alleged to have supported armed anti-government "dissidents" who were active in the south and west of Zimbabwe. The government repeatedly alleged that the "dissidents" were supported by ZAPU, an allegation that the minority party denied. Amnesty International was concerned that in many cases it was the detainee's political allegiance rather than any evidence of armed opposition that was the reason for imprisonment. The organization received the names of more than 100 detainees released in 1986. In December the Minister of Home Affairs stated that 31 remained in detention.

Among those still in detention at the end of 1986 was Makhatini Guduza, a former member of ZAPU's central committee who fled to Botswana in 1983. The government repeatedly alleged that he had recruited refugees in Botswana to join the armed opposition to the Zimbabwean Government. In February he was arrested by the Botswana authorities and handed over into Zimbabwean custody. He remained uncharged and was apparently held incommunicado at the end of 1986. In August the Zimbabwean Government acknowledged to Amnesty International that Makhatini Guduza was in custody but did not disclose his place of imprisonment or the legal basis for his detention.

Also still detained at the end of 1986 were two senior customs officials, Neil Harper and John Austin, who were first arrested in February. They were initially detained under the Emergency Powers (Maintenance of Law and Order) Regulations and subsequently charged under the Official Secrets Act with spying for South Africa. However, the Supreme Court released them in April, finding no reasonable suspicion "such as would make it lawful to deprive them of their liberty". A month later they were redetained under the emergency powers regulations. Their detention without trial was repeatedly challenged in the courts. On several occasions judges ordered their release, only for them to be redetained by the CIO.

Amnesty International continued to receive reports of torture in 1986, although considerably fewer than in 1985. In February a delegation from the CCJPZ is reported to have visited Stops Camp, a police detention centre in Bulawayo where torture had been frequently reported. They found few prisoners there and no evidence of ill-treatment. Reports reaching Amnesty International indicated that this improvement was maintained for those detained in police custody. However, the organization remained concerned about continuing reports of torture of prisoners in the custody of the CIO, some of whom were held in Stops Camp. A number of such reports referred to Esigodini, near Bulawayo, where prisoners are reported to have had their heads forced into bags filled with water, causing them to lose consciousness. Sometimes this was reported to have been accompanied by the use of electric shocks. Amnesty International also received reports of prisoners of the CIO being held naked and handcuffed for days, and deprived of sleep and food.

In July Kembo Mohadi, a ZAPU member of parliament who had been detained without trial for several months during 1985, was awarded 30,000 Zimbabwe dollars' compensation for illegal arrest and torture. He told the Harare High Court that he had had his head forced into a canvas bag full of water and that his stomach had been trampled on. In another case the same month, five ZAPU supporters were acquitted of the murder in 1984 of government senator Moven Ndlovu, when the High Court found that they had been tortured into making confessions. The accused testified that they had been whipped and had had their heads forced into buckets of water.

In January and February Amnesty International appealed to the government to set up an impartial investigation into the killing of Luke and Jean Kumalo, a Methodist headmaster and his wife, at Thekwane school near Plumtree in November 1985. Evidence gathered by Amnesty International cast serious doubt on the official version that the two had been killed during an attack on the school by "dissidents", who were responsible for many killings in western Zimbabwe throughout 1986. There were fears that their killing may have been an extrajudicial execution by the security forces. In particular Amnesty International believed that an inquiry should seek to establish: why soldiers at an army camp three kilometres away did not intervene, although the attackers were reportedly at the school for several hours, firing shots and burning buildings; why the attackers were wearing military uniform; and why the attackers left a note stating that Luke and Jean Kumalo were being killed for passing information to Amnesty International. The government rejected the call for an inquiry and said that it had captured a member of the "dissident" band responsible for the killings. At the end of 1986 Amnesty International was still seeking to establish whether he had been charged in connection with the killings.

Amnesty International remained concerned about the use of the death penalty, which had sharply increased in 1985 compared with previous years since independence, and which remained at a similar level in 1986. At least 18 people are reported to have been sentenced to death, all for murder. Most were members of "dissident" bands. Four were members of the army convicted of a politically motivated killing of a superior officer and one was a member of the ruling Zimbabwe African National Union-Patriotic Front (ZANU-PF) convicted of the murder of members of a minority party during the 1985 general election campaign. At least five executions are reported to have been carried out, all at the same time in April amid considerable publicity.

The Americas

Argentina

Amnesty International continued to follow the trials of members of the security forces accused of gross human rights violations, including the torture and "disappearance" of thousands of individuals, during the period of military rule between 1976 and 1983. The organization's concern was that the truth regarding the fate of the "disappeared" should be established and the rights of the defendants respected. During 1986 Amnesty International monitored official guidelines and new legislation introduced by the government to limit further prosecutions linked to past abuses. Amnesty International also followed the progress of investigations to trace the whereabouts of approximately 100 children who "disappeared" with their parents or were believed to have been born in secret detention centres. (See *Amnesty International Report 1986*.) A further concern was the continued imprisonment of people convicted of politically motivated crimes in unfair trials under the former government.

During 1986 Amnesty International continued to follow developments in more than 600 cases before the Supreme Council of the Armed Forces – the highest military court in Argentina – which had jurisdiction over all cases involving members of the police, military and security forces accused of offences committed between 1976 and 1982 in the course of anti-subversive operations. Proceedings before the Supreme Council were conducted *in camera* but Amnesty International received information that by the end of 1986 no progress had been made in the majority of the cases. Following reforms to the Code of Military Justice introduced in 1984, all judgments of the Supreme Council in such cases were subject to review by civilian appeals courts, which were also empowered to take over a trial if there was evidence of unwarranted delay or negligence. Several major trials were in fact taken over by civilian appeals courts during 1986. On 24 April the Minister of Defence issued a series of instructions to the Military Prosecutor of the Supreme Council. The Military Prosecutor was directed to exempt all lower-ranking officers from prosecution on the grounds that they had been obeying orders, except where there was evidence that they had committed atrocities or exceeded their orders. Furthermore, the Military Prosecutor was to call for acquittal or order the case to be dropped whenever superior officers had already been acquitted of corresponding offences. Apparently in response to public criticism, on 1 May President· Alfonsín announced to Congress that new instructions would be issued concerning prosecutions of those who could not necessarily claim to have been obeying orders.

While clarification of the government's instructions was awaited, prosecutions of former military officers were taken over by the Federal Criminal Appeals Courts from the Supreme Council. One such was the case against retired General Ramon Camps, Chief of Police in Buenos Aires Province between 1976 and 1979, and six former members of the police and army. This was the first trial involving senior, middle- and lower-ranking officers. The charges against the defendants included 32 murders, 120 cases of torture, two of torture leading to miscarriage, 214 kidnappings for ransom and the subsequent "disappearance" of 47 of the victims and 10 kidnappings of minors. The hearings before the Federal Criminal Appeals Court in Buenos Aires began in September and on 2 December General Camps was found guilty and sentenced to 25 years' imprisonment on 73 charges of torture. His deputy, Miguel Etchecolatz, received a 23-year sentence on more than 90 counts of torture and General Camps' successor as police chief, General Ovidio Riccheri, was sentenced to 14 years on 20 torture charges. Two retired senior police officers were acquitted and two junior officers — police doctor Jorge Bergés and Corporal Norberto Cozzani — received prison sentences of six years and four years respectively. The convictions were seen by Argentine jurists as a landmark decision in that responsibility for human rights abuses had been extended to lower-ranking military and police officials. The judges' ruling clarified the principle of "due obedience". The court rejected the defence plea that some military officers should be acquitted of human rights crimes because they were acting under orders from junta members and superior officers. In its ruling the court stated that "there is no authority superior to the law" and upheld the principle that subordinates must disobey an order that does not conform with the law.

Another major trial brought before the Federal Criminal Appeals Court of Buenos Aires was the prosecution of Navy Lieutenant Alfredo Astíz for the grievous wounding and abduction of 17-year-old Dagmar Hagelin, who had dual Swedish and Argentine nationality, in 1977 (see *Amnesty International Report 1980* and *1986*). Following a ruling by the Federal Criminal Appeals Court in 1985, proceedings against Lieutenant Astíz were reopened in the Supreme Council and in April the military court again brought in a verdict of not guilty for lack of evidence. On 5 December the Federal Criminal Appeals Court handed down its decision, which was to clear Lieutenant Astíz of the kidnapping and wounding of Dagmar Hageli, not for lack of evidence but because the six-year statute of limitations on the crime of kidnapping had expired.

On 9 December the government presented to Congress a draft bill — popularly known as the *Punto Final* (Full Stop) — proposing the introduction of a statute of limitations on future trials. The bill proposed that there should be no further prosecutions of members of the security and prison services for human rights violations committed before December 1983 unless the accused received a summons to testify in preliminary hearings within 60 days of the promulgation of the law. On 19 December Amnesty International wrote to the leaders of both houses of Congress about the draft legislation. The organization was concerned that given the difficulty victims and their relatives had encountered in pursuing their complaints against members of the security forces, who in the past had been able to act in secrecy and with impunity, the proposed curtailment of judicial investigations might make it impossible to establish the truth. Amnesty International pointed out the Argentine Government's obligations under international law to investigate past abuses and urged members of Congress to take these obligations fully into account when considering the draft legislation. Despite widespread opposition, Congress approved the legislation which entered into force before the end of 1986. Congress introduced two amendments: the statute of limitations applied also to civilians who had participated in subversive acts against previous governments; and cases involving "disappeared" children were excluded. The courts had until 22 February 1987 to start further criminal prosecutions.

Amnesty International continued to study the cases of a group of prisoners who were convicted of politically motivated crimes of violence in the 1970s: those of 13 men in Villa Devoto Prison and of one woman in Ezeiza Prison (see *Amnesty International Report 1986*). Hernán Invernizzi and Juan Carlos Vallejos, two of the prisoners, were released by order of the Federal Criminal Appeals Courts of Buenos Aires and Rosario in May and September respectively. In

September Amnesty International wrote to President Alfonsín about the legal position of the remaining prisoners, whose trials the organization believed had failed to conform to internationally recognized standards. The prisoners were reportedly subjected to torture while in custody, testimonies extracted under duress were presented as evidence against them in the trials and they had been denied the right to an adequate defence. Amnesty International asked the government to consider a full judicial review of their trials. Draft legislation permitting a judicial review of the trials had not been debated by the end of 1986.

Amnesty International continued to monitor efforts to locate children reported missing after the abduction or killing of their parents by the military or security forces in the 1970s. Since 1977 the main organization concerned with this problem, the *Abuelas de Plaza de Mayo*, Grandmothers of Plaza de Mayo, formed by grandparents of missing children, had succeeded in tracing 39 children. Of these, four were known to have died; 18 were returned to their real families; nine were living with adoptive families but were in contact with remaining relatives; and, at the end of 1986, the cases of eight children were awaiting decisions by the courts.

Argentina ratified the International Covenant on Civil and Political Rights and the UN Convention Against Torture in August and September respectively.

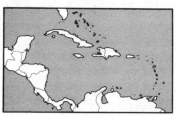

Bahamas

Amnesty International was concerned about reports of Haitian illegal immigrants being detained in inhuman prison conditions in the Bahamas pending deportation procedures. According to the reports, some 49 children under the age of three were held with their mothers in one room in Fox Hill Prison, Nassau, following arrests in Bimini and Cat Cay on 20 February 1986. Many became ill but only once in the following two weeks did a doctor visit them. Most were deported to Haiti in mid-April. Another group of about 60 men were allegedly confined for over a week in an insect-infested room without bedding, beds or proper toilets. The room was so small that they had to take turns to sleep on the concrete floor. Drinking water was inadequate and contaminated, causing stomach disorders. Many of this group had been transported to

Nassau from Grand Bahama by ship and had allegedly been confined below deck during a sea journey of 13 hours without toilet facilities, seats or other amenities.

In July Amnesty International wrote to the Minister of National Security, calling on the government to institute a thorough, impartial inquiry into these reported conditions. The Minister had not replied by the end of 1986; however the Prime Minister, to whom a copy of the letter had been sent, replied briefly saying that the claims were "outrageous" and that Amnesty International should investigate further. Amnesty International wrote to the Prime Minister again in September, reiterating its request that the government conduct a full investigation. No further reply had been received by the end of 1986.

Barbados

Amnesty International wrote to the government in December about two prisoners under sentence of death. Patrick Greaves and Michael Taylor were convicted in October 1984 of a murder committed in March of the same year. Both were 17 years old at the time of the crime. Their convictions and death sentences were upheld on 18 November 1986 by the Barbados Court of Appeal. Amnesty International called on the government to bring Barbadian law into line with international treaties and guidelines prohibiting the imposition of death sentences on people aged under 18 at the time of the crime. It also urged the government to commute. the death sentences passed on Patrick Greaves and Michael Taylor.

The last executions in Barbados took place in 1984 when three men were hanged. Amnesty International believed that about 17 prisoners were under sentence of death at the end of 1986.

Bolivia

Amnesty International's concerns continued to centre on the short-term detention of people held solely for their suspected, non-violent, opposition activities. Over 50 people, including church workers, human rights activists, labour leaders and political opposition figures were sent into internal exile following the declaration of a state of siege in August. Amnesty International continued to follow the progress of judicial investigations into extrajudicial executions which occurred during the military government of General Luís García Meza (1980-1982) and was concerned about reports of harassment of lawyers acting on behalf of complainants. Seven political prisoners who were arrested in October 1983 and whose cases had been under investigation by Amnesty International were released during 1986. Amnesty International noted with concern that the Bolivian Congress was considering the reintroduction of the death penalty for certain crimes.

On 28 August the government declared a nationwide 90-day state of siege and arrested over 160 people in several cities including La Paz, Potosí, Oruro and Cochabamba. Among those detained were labour leaders, church workers, journalists, human rights activists and political opposition figures. Amnesty International believed that most of them were prisoners of conscience. Government sources said that the state of siege had been imposed in response to "serious political and social disturbances", including a march from the mining town of Oruro to La Paz by over 5,000 miners protesting against government plans to restructure the state-owned mining company *Corporación Minera de Bolivia* (COMIBOL). While many of those detained under the provisions of the state of siege were released after several days in incommunicado detention, over 50 people were sent into internal exile to remote regions in the north of the country where they were held in detention camps. Amnesty International expressed concern about the arrests and urged the government to release all the prisoners immediately and unconditionally unless they were to be charged with criminal offences. On 14 September a church-mediated meeting between representatives of the government and the *Federación Sindical de Trabajadores Mineros* (FSTMB), the Trade Union Federation of Bolivian Mineworkers, agreed to modify plans for the reorganization of COMIBOL. By 18 September all those in internal exile had been released. Amnesty International received reports, however, that several were subject to continuing control and harassment by the authorities in their home towns, and had to report daily to their local police stations.

Amnesty International continued to monitor investigations into human rights abuses which occurred under previous governments. In February 1986 the joint Constitutional and Justice Commission of the National Congress concluded the initial proceedings stage of the "*Juicio de Responsabilidades*" (responsibilities trial) in which former president General Luís García Meza and his closest collaborators during the period of military government from July 1980 to October 1982 were charged with responsibility for human rights abuses. The proceedings were initiated in February 1984 when two left-wing political parties presented Congress with a petition against General García Meza and 54 of his collaborators on charges including assassination of political opponents, genocide, sedition, organization of irregular armed groups and misappropriation of public funds. Under Bolivian legislation the initial stage of trial proceedings against former heads of government must be conducted by Congress. In February, following the recommendation of the Commission, the case was sent to the Supreme Court of Justice. Although the final stage of the trial in the Supreme Court began on 7 April, there were many delays and the trial was still in progress at the end of 1986. Amnesty International was concerned about reports that lawyers acting on behalf of relatives of the alleged victims of the accused had been threatened and intimidated in the course of their work by paramilitary groups reportedly linked to the armed forces.

During 1986 Amnesty International learned of the release of seven political prisoners who had been arrested in the Luribay area in October 1983 (see *Amnesty International Report 1984, 1985* and *1986*). The five Bolivians and two Chileans were released on completion of sentences of two and a half to three years each handed down by the *Tribunal Permanente de Justicia Militar* (TPJM), the Permanent Tribunal of Military Justice. Amnesty International had reiterated its concern to successive governments about the refusal of the TPJM to implement an amnesty decreed by former president Hernán Siles Zuazo in October 1984, and its belief that the prisoners had been tortured during the initial period of their detention.

In October Amnesty International wrote to President Victor Paz Estenssoro expressing its concern that Congress was considering the reintroduction of the death penalty, following the killing of eight-year-old Alvaro Rolando Tavera Nava, which had caused a public outcry. The death penalty was abolished in Bolivia in the State Political Constitution of 1967 and although it was reintroduced in the penal, code and code of military justice adopted during the period of military rule in the 1970s, the constitutional prohibition of the death penalty was not modified. In September two bills were presented to Congress, proposing the modification of Article 17 of the State Political Constitution to allow the death penalty for the abduction and murder of minors. Amnesty International pointed out that Article 4(3) of the American Convention on Human Rights, to which Bolivia is party, prohibits the reintroduction of the death penalty in countries that have abolished it. The organization urged the government to oppose the reform of the State Political Constitution and to adopt measures to eliminate the death penalty from Bolivian legislation.

In December, the judge recommended the death sentence for one of those accused of Alvaro Tavera Nava's murder; two received sentences of two years' imprisonment and a further two were acquitted.

Brazil

Amnesty International was concerned about the failure of the authorities to investigate and prosecute those responsible for numerous killings of rural workers, community leaders and trade unionists and their advisers, allegedly committed by hired gunmen in the pay of local landowners, in the context of land disputes. Amnesty International believed that the apparent unwillingness of local, state and federal authorities to investigate these killings effectively and to prosecute those responsible could constitute acquiescence in these crimes. The organization also received a number of reports of uniformed police killing criminal suspects in circumstances suggesting they were victims of extrajudicial executions. Amnesty International also investigated torture and ill-treatment of detainees in police stations and prisons throughout the country.

In February Amnesty International wrote to the President of the Republic, José Sarney, about human rights abuses in rural areas in the context of disputes over land ownership. In July and August an Amnesty International mission visited areas of the states of Pará, Goiás, Maranhão and Bahia, where the highest incidence of violence related to land conflicts had been reported. Amnesty International was concerned about the growing number of peasants, rural community leaders, trade unionists, lawyers and church workers who received death threats, some of whom were killed, allegedly by hired gunmen in the pay of local landowners. Amnesty International believed that the victims of such threats and assaults were targeted because of their role in disputes over land and labour rights. There were also reports that private militias were being organized to threaten and attack rural workers.

Of particular concern to Amnesty International was the evidence of a persistent failure by local and state authorities to investigate these killings effectively or to bring criminal prosecutions, with the result that those responsible acted with impunity and further abuses were encouraged.

Amnesty International's preliminary findings from the mission were that the authorities at local, state and federal levels had consistently omitted to take the necessary measures to prevent attacks on rural workers and their advisers. The total number of killings related to land disputes officially reported in 1986 was 298. Amnesty International's delegates also received reports of an increase in the number of short-term arrests without warrant of peasants engaged in land disputes. For instance, over 700 peasants were reported to have been arrested in the state of Pará during 1986. Although Amnesty International could not verify the circumstances of all these arrests, it appeared that many were arbitrary and carried out in order to harass the victims rather than to enforce the law. In the majority of cases reported, no charges were brought following the arrests. Amnesty International's delegates were also told that peasants were beaten and ill-treated in the custody of military police during land evictions. In a number of such cases the military police appeared to have been accompanied by men known locally to be hired gunmen.

On 12 May the organization expressed its concern about the assassination of Father Josimo Moraes Tavares, a Roman Catholic priest who was shot on 10 May by a gunman in the town of Imperatriz, Maranhão state, in what is known as the Bico do Papagaio region of northern Brazil. Five bishops had previously appealed to the federal government in person about the level of violence towards rural workers seeking land rights in the Bico do Papagaio region, and had sought guarantees for the priest's life following an earlier attempt on his life on 15 April. Amnesty International believed that Father Tavares was killed because of his activities as coordinator of the Church Land Commission for the Diocese of Tocantinopolis, his work advising rural workers of their land and labour rights, and his reporting of human rights abuses against them. A gunman who confessed to having killed Father

Tavares was arrested in June, and claimed to have been employed by a local politician and landowner to carry out the assassination. Amnesty International had previously appealed on Father Tavares' behalf following his arrest in November 1984 (see *Amnesty International Report 1985*). Two weeks before Father Tavares' arrest in 1984, four peasants were arrested and reportedly tortured in an attempt to make them implicate him in an ambush in which a landowner had been killed. Amnesty International had appealed on their behalf.

In its letter to President Sarney in February, Amnesty International said that for some of Brazil's law enforcement agencies, torture had apparently become an established practice during criminal investigations. The organization noted that a number of official inquiries had been established to investigate reports of torture, and asked to be kept informed of their findings and of any prosecutions or disciplinary measures against law enforcement officers alleged to be responsible.

In October an Amnesty International delegate visited Brazil to investigate allegations of torture and ill-treatment in police stations and prisons in São Paulo, Rio de Janeiro, Porto Alegre and Brasília. One of the cases examined was that of Antonio Clovis Lima dos Santos and Cleber Leal Goulart, who were tortured in the central police station in Porto Alegre, Rio Grande do Sul State, in September 1984 (see *Amnesty International Report 1986*). The organization received no reply from either the President or the state governor to its inquiries on this case. On 1 March 1986, three weeks before he was due to testify to an official inquiry into the torture allegations, Antonio Clovis Lima dos Santos was killed in suspicious circumstances. Following the death of the main witness, the inquiry absolved four police officers who had been suspended and accused of torture, for lack of proof. The court refused to accept as evidence authenticated photographs, taken by another police officer, which appeared to show the dead youth and Cleber Leal Goulart being tortured at the central police station. Cleber Leal Goulart, who went into hiding in fear for his life after Antonio dos Santos' death, did not testify. He claimed that he was tortured again by military police when they rearrested him in November 1986 in connection with another offence.

A number of prison riots took place during 1986 and the press reported prisoners' allegations of regular torture and ill-treatment in Brazilian prisons. In December Amnesty International asked the Minister of Justice for information about an escape attempt at Papuda prison in the federal district of Brasília on 17 September. One of the prisoners was reported to have been killed in police custody when he was recaptured and members of the special federal commission investigating the incident were reported to have discovered "torture cells" in regular use in Papuda prison. Amnesty International also asked the São Paulo authorities about the findings of an official inquiry into a prison riot protesting about conditions in the prison in Presidente Venceslau, in the interior of São Paulo state, on 15 September. The inquiry report confirmed that 13 unarmed prisoners were beaten to death by the military police. Nine of them had remained in their cells and not taken any part in the rebellion. The other four prisoners were killed after surrendering.

Amnesty International examined reports that the frequent use of lethal force by police in certain urban areas suggested a pattern of deliberate killings of criminal suspects, who were often unarmed, and many of whom were juveniles. According to official statistics the military police of São Paulo shot dead 220 people in the first nine months of 1986. In one of the rare cases which led to convictions, three military police officers were sentenced to 32 years' imprisonment on 10 June for the murder of Teodoro Hoffman and Dirley Rodriguez Matos. Both boys were 17 years old and had no criminal record. They were detained near the shanty town of Heliopolis, São Paulo city, on 28 January, beaten, shot, their throats cut and their bodies dumped on a rubbish pit outside the city. Although the police authorities originally denied the boys' arrest, persistent campaigning by the boys' families led to the discovery of the bodies on 17 March. All three of the military police officers sentenced had previously been investigated for killing criminal suspects and juveniles, but had never been convicted.

On 11 July Orlando Correia, a sugar worker, and Sibele Aparecida Manoel, aged 19, were shot dead and seven sugar workers were wounded when military police fired into a crowd during a sugar workers' strike in the town of Leme, in São Paulo state. A number of trade unionists were beaten by military police in their homes and in police custody. Amnesty International was concerned at evidence that particular strikers and members of the *Partido dos Trabalhadores*, Workers' Party, were singled out for beatings. A state inquiry into the shootings had not been completed by the end of 1986.

Amnesty International urged the government to establish a commission of inquiry to investigate the "disappearance" of 125 political prisoners between 1964 and 1977 under previous military governments. There was evidence that a number of the "disappeared" had died under torture in custody and been secretly buried. Following national pressure including representations from relatives and human rights groups, the Minister of Justice announced in December that the government's human rights council would set up a commission to investigate the "disappearances".

Amnesty International was concerned about prosecutions under the National Security Law. In April Ruth Escobar, a member of the São Paulo legislature, and Vicente de Paula da Silva, a São Paulo Metal Workers Union leader, were sentenced by military courts to six months and one year's imprisonment respectively. Ruth Escobar was convicted of "offending the honour of the armed forces" because of election speeches she made in 1982, and Vicente de Paula da Silva was convicted of making statements at a metalworkers' assembly in 1983 which might "generate an adverse psychological war between the group and the President". Ruth Escobar was given a suspended sentence, and the union leader's conviction was overturned by a higher military court.

In May Amnesty International's Secretary General met the Congressional Foreign Affairs Committee, representatives from the Foreign Ministry, and the Minister of Justice. He urged Brazil to ratify the UN Convention against Torture, the American Convention on Human Rights and the International Covenant on Civil and Political Rights. The Secretary General was assured that the government intended to forward these human rights instruments to Congress for ratification, and by the end of 1986 Amnesty International had welcomed the news that this had been done.

Chile

Amnesty International's main concerns were short-term arbitrary arrests, torture and human rights violations by clandestine groups linked to the security forces. Judicial irregularities in the trials of political prisoners were reported and there was little or no progress in judicial investigations into human rights abuses. Some critics of the government were arrested and sent for trial for non-violent activities and were considered by Amnesty International to be prisoners of conscience. Students, journalists, human rights workers, political activists, church workers and inhabitants of *poblaciones* (poor neighbourhoods) were the main targets of human rights abuses.

On 3 September Amnesty International published a Briefing on Chile. It focused on the illegal activities of the official security forces and the "new strategy of terror" which had developed since 1983 using clandestine forces to intimidate and harass. Acting with impunity in broad daylight and during curfew hours, clandestine forces operated from secret detention centres and had considerable financial backing, their own communications networks, vehicles and weapons. Their victims were subjected to death threats, abducted in cars and interrogated while being driven around, or in detention centres, and sometimes tortured before being abandoned. Some were killed. The report concluded that these groups were made up of members of the security forces acting under cover with civilian collaborators. To coincide with the publication, the organization launched a worldwide campaign to end human rights abuses in Chile and issued nine recommendations considered essential to restore the rights to life and to freedom from arbitrary arrest and torture.

In a public response to the report, the government accused Amnesty International of hiding "the magnitude of Marxist attacks on the Chilean Government" and said it had not cooperated with the organization because "as shown by the report, Amnesty International's internal procedures offer no guarantees of objectivity and clarity." In September Amnesty International wrote to the Foreign Minister reiterating its concerns and pointing out that the government had supplied no information on the cases raised. By the end of 1986 it had received no response.

Emergency legislation remained in force throughout 1986. A state of emergency and a "state of danger to internal peace" (provided for by interim provision 24 of the Constitution) gave the Executive broad powers of banishment and detention (see *Amnesty International Report 1986*). Many political detentions were carried out under these provisions but for the first year since the Constitution came into force in 1981, no one was banished under interim provision 24.

On 6 September there was an assassination attempt on President Pinochet in which five of his bodyguards died. The next day a state of siege was imposed which remained in force in most regions until the end of 1986. It empowered the authorities, among other things, to authorize indefinite detention without charge, suspend publications, and restrict the right to *amparo* (similar to *habeas corpus*).

The government maintained that the state of siege and other emergency measures were needed to combat violence by armed opposition groups. Such groups were involved in armed incidents and claimed responsibility for numerous bomb attacks on public installations. Several police officers were injured or killed. In August a number of arms caches allegedly belonging to the *Frente Patriótico Manuel Rodríguez* (FPMR), Manuel Rodriguez Patriotic Front, were found and the following month the FPMR claimed responsibility for the assassination attempt on General Pinochet. Amnesty International recognizes the responsibility of governments to maintain law and order, but in doing so they must respect international human rights standards.

Politically motivated arrests increased in 1986. When combined military and police personnel, often supported by tanks and army vehicles, raided some 40 *poblaciones* mainly in Santiago, 30,000 local people were rounded up for identity checks or interrogation. Many others were detained during peaceful protests, among them hundreds of students, some as young as 11, arrested during sit-ins, strikes and demonstrations. Demonstrators, and also journalists and photographers, were sometimes badly beaten while held by uniformed police. Unidentified men in civilian clothing and heavily armed military personnel participated in arrests and beatings.

Rodrigo Rojas, a 19-year-old photographer recently returned from exile, and 18-year-old student Carmen Quintana were arrested by a military patrol at the start of a national two-day stoppage on 2 July. They were beaten, doused in inflammable liquid and set on fire. They were then wrapped in blankets and driven to the outskirts of the city where they were abandoned with severe burns. Rodrigo Rojas died on 6 July. The army at first denied involvement but later said they had carried out the arrests. They maintained, however, that the fire had been started accidentally. In spite of extensive evidence that they had been deliberately burned by the military patrol, the civilian judge appointed to look into the case only charged one of the patrol with negligence – for failing to ensure the two received proper medical treatment. The charges were increased on appeal to "unnecessary violence resulting in death" by a military court but no one else in the patrol was charged. Three witnesses left the country after receiving death threats and lawyers acting for the victims were subjected to intimidation. Amnesty International called for full investigations into the incident and into the deaths of a number of other people who were killed when uniformed police, military personnel or civilian agents fired on demonstrators and bystanders.

After the declaration of a state of siege on 7 September the scale of human rights abuses increased. Clandestine forces intensified their campaign of intimidation, especially against journalists and human rights workers. Within days of the declaration of the state of siege, four members of opposition groups had been abducted and murdered, including José Carrasco, international editor of *Analisis*, an opposition magazine. A clandestine group claimed responsibility and said that a staff member of the Vicariat of Solidarity, the church human rights organization, would be next. Hooded civilians later tried unsuccessfully to abduct Vicariat lawyer Luis Toro. Amnesty International called for full investigations.

President Pinochet warned on 9 September that "all those involved in human rights organizations should be expelled or locked up" and several were arrested or went into hiding after arrest warrants were issued against them. Amnesty International called for the release of several student, political and community leaders who had been detained without charge in police stations, some for three months. It also appealed on behalf of three French priests, among them Father Pierre Dubois, outspoken defender of human rights in the *poblaciones*, who were arrested and deported.

The organization worked for the release of a number of prisoners of conscience, among them several journalists, student leaders, and 14 leaders of the National Civic Assembly who were charged under the State Security Law after calling for a two-day national stoppage in July. The assembly, made up of representatives of professional, trade union and community groups, had called for peaceful demonstrations for a return to democracy. Six people, including a 13-year-old girl, were shot dead by military, police or civilian agents and some 800 were arrested during the two days. By the end of August the leaders had been released on bail.

Amnesty International was concerned about the increasing persecution of human rights workers. Many received death threats or suffered other acts of intimidation by clandestine groups. Some were imprisoned by the authorities. Two staff members of the Vicariat of Solidarity were arrested in May. Following these arrests Amnesty International sent a delegate to Chile to look into these and other such cases. Lawyer Gustavo Villalobos and Dr Ramiro Olivares, together with three other doctors and a medical auxiliary from a clinic, were arrested in May after assisting a man with bullet wounds who had gone to the Vicariat for help. They said later that they were unaware that, according to official reports, he had taken part in an armed attack in which a police officer had died. Amnesty International was seriously concerned that they had been arrested because of their human rights work with the Vicariat and that the authorities were using the case in order to investigate and discredit the work of the Vicariat.

Amnesty International received persistent reports of the use of torture in the interrogation of political suspects held incommunicado by police or security forces. The number of victims rose sharply during the last five months of the year and Amnesty International interceded on behalf of numerous detainees. Most testimonies cited the *Central Nacional de Informaciones* (CNI), state security police, as responsible for the routine use of torture, although some reports were also received of torture by members of *Investigaciones*, criminal investigations police, and by uniformed police. Among the methods described were mock executions, the "parrot perch" (the victim is suspended upside-down from a pole), electric shocks, the "submarine" (the victim's head is submerged in water), disorientating drugs, sexual abuse, and threats.

Attempts by some courts to protect detainees by dealing promptly with petitions for *amparo* were obstructed by CNI refusals to obey court orders. These refusals continued despite assurances given in October by President Pinochet, after complaints by three appeals courts, that the CNI would comply with judicial orders.

Hundreds of complaints submitted to the courts by victims of human rights abuses or their relatives made little or no progress, either because of the unwillingness of the courts to question the activities of the security forces or because the security forces themselves obstructed the investigations. The courts refused, for example, to investigate several complaints of killings of political prisoners in 1973 in spite of new evidence, citing a law passed in 1978 which amnestied those responsible for criminal acts between 1973 and 1978. In a number of cases witnesses and lawyers were subjected to acts of intimidation.

Efforts by a few judges led to significant progress in some investigations into human rights abuses, but in most cases evidence submitted by investigating judges was rejected by the higher courts. In January the Supreme Court revoked charges against a group of uniformed police in connection with the abduction and murder of Manuel Guerrero Ceballos, José Manuel Parada Maluenda and Santiago Nattino Allende, and the kidnapping and torture of four teachers' leaders and a union employee in March 1985 (see *Amnesty International Report 1986*).

Another ruling by the Supreme Court ended all hope of rapid progress in clarifying the fate of some 700 prisoners who "disappeared" following their arrest between 1973 and 1977. In September it amnestied 38 members of the armed forces and two civilian collaborators accused of involvement in the illegal arrest of two Communist Party members in 1976. The 40 men had been charged with "unlawful association" by civilian judge Carlos Cerda. In the course of his investigations he found conclusive evidence of the existence of secret military groups set up to eliminate members of the opposition. The higher court however ruled that the law of amnesty had to be applied at that stage, and the case closed. Judge Carlos Cerda was suspended for two months for contesting the ruling on the grounds that his investigation had not been completed.

Amnesty International investigated the cases of several prisoners whom it believed had been charged solely on the basis of confessions extracted under torture and was concerned about a number of judicial irregularities in the trials of political prisoners. It called for faster progress in the trials of political prisoners, some of which had been in the investigative stage for several years, and for better medical treatment for political prisoners. Treatment was often delayed, particularly when detainees needed facilities not available in prison. Amnesty International was concerned also that a number of detainees were held in prolonged incommunicado detention after their transfer to prison. There was strong evidence that some had been tortured while held by the security forces.

No judicial executions were carried out in 1986. Three political prisoners were sentenced to death on 28 November, but the sentences were revoked temporarily by the military appeals court because of procedural irregularities. A fourth political prisoner under sentence of death was awaiting the results of his appeal. There was no progress in the trials of 10 others who had had death sentences recommended by the prosecution.

Amnesty International submitted information on human rights violations in Chile to the Organization of American States and to the relevant UN bodies.

Colombia

Amnesty International's concerns centred on a sharp rise in extrajudicial executions and "disappearances". The victims were scores of students, teachers, trade unionists and supporters of opposition parties and civic movements, as well as alleged petty criminals, vagrants, squatters and homosexuals, believed to have numbered over a thousand. The government attributed most killings to "death squads": mysterious gunmen it described as civilians whom it could neither identify nor control. However, Amnesty International believed that actions attributed to "death squads" were in fact carried out by police and military personnel, sometimes in uniform, and by civilian gunmen working with them — acting on the apparent authority of the army high command. Long-standing concerns included persistent reports of torture, the failure of the authorities to account for hundreds of prisoners who had "disappeared" in recent years, and the paralysis of most announced investigations into "disappearances" and apparent extrajudicial executions. Amnesty International appealed on behalf of 33 people it believed to be prisoners of conscience, most of them peasant farmers seized during land disputes who were released after relatively brief periods.

Execution-style killings of captives by several guerrilla groups were reported, in particular by the *Frente Ricardo Franco*, Ricardo Franco Front. Amnesty International condemns in all cases the torture or killing of captives — whether by governments or opposition groups.

Detention procedures leading to short-term or prolonged "disappearance" continued to be the norm in political cases, although detentions were frequently acknowledged by the authorities after some days or weeks. As a rule arrests by the military were not, to the knowledge of Amnesty International, acknowledged to civilians unless release or consignment to the courts was imminent. The civilian authorities had no access to military intelligence prisoner records.

The authority to punish human rights abuse was delegated exclusively to military courts. With few exceptions this meant that security force personnel and their civilian auxiliaries responsible for torture, "disappearances" or political killings operated with impunity. Those identified by civilian prosecutors as criminally liable in political cases generally remained in their posts, or, in some cases, were promoted: whenever civilian investigators found evidence involving police or military personnel, cases were transferred to military courts, where military prosecutors generally declined to pursue them.

Amnesty International appealed on behalf of 11 prisoners whose detentions were initially denied by the authorities. Some of these prisoners later described prolonged interrogations by military and National Police intelligence personnel involving physical and psychological torture: from threats of summary execution to systematic beatings, near-drowning and electric shocks. However, others remained missing. Jaime Casas, a teacher at a rural school in Norte de Santander department, was reportedly detained by soldiers of the "García Rovira" Battalion on 22 March near Cubara, in Boyacá department. Army spokesmen denied any knowledge of his arrest. Edilberto Cardenas Cardenas was reportedly seized on 10 October in Bogotá by men in plain clothes travelling in an unmarked car, backed by two armed men on a motorcycle. Although uniformed police were also reportedly at the scene, in a stationary patrol car, they did not intervene. The authorities subsequently denied any responsibility.

Other "disappeared" prisoners were found dead, their bodies tortured or mutilated not long after their detention. Poet and singer Jesús Peña was seized by armed men believed to be members of the security services in Bucaramanga, Santander, on 4 May. He was found dead in a rural area two days later with his right hand cut off and other mutilations. Other cases raised by Amnesty International were those of victims shot in their homes or in public where the method of the killing, the description of the killers, and the response of law enforcement agencies suggested official complicity. Amnesty International issued repeated appeals for measures to halt the wave of apparent extrajudicial executions, and for inquiries into 24 specific cases.

Human rights activists were among the victims. Antonio Hernández Niño, a member of the Colombian organization of relatives of the "disappeared", ASFADES, was seized on 8 April after leaving a human rights meeting in Bogotá. On 10 August his body, bound hand and foot, was found with four gunshot wounds, on the outskirts of the capital. Another man, Guillermo Marín, was detained on the same night. He was interrogated under torture, and early on 11 April shot twice in the head. He survived, however, and gave extensive testimony to civilian public prosecutors which directly implicated the army's Bogotá Intelligence and Counter-Intelligence Battalion (BINCI). Amnesty International appealed to the authorities to investigate the detention, torture and shooting of the two men, and to guarantee the safety of Guillermo Marín. As the army was implicated, however, further investigation of the case 'fell under the exclusive jurisdiction of the military itself. In July the Chief Military Procurator said the case was to be closed as it had been proved that the allegations of army involvement were false, and that in any case Guillermo Marín was "a vulgar kidnapper and common criminal". However, the military investigation dossier, a copy of which was sent to Amnesty International by the government, did not disprove the allegations.

Eberth Marín Cotrini, who worked in a Cali human rights office, was to have left Colombia on 10 October following a series of death threats. On 9 October he was seized in a Cali street and "disappeared". Amnesty International appealed for his safety on 10 October, but the next day his body, bound and apparently tortured, was found. Amnesty International believed Eberth Marín was tortured and killed by government forces or with their acquiescence because of his role as a human rights monitor. On 13 October the organization told President Virgilio Barco, who took office on 7 August, that the case of Eberth Marín was similar to numerous others in which "disappearance", torture and extrajudicial execution had been carried out with impunity in Colombia.

Most victims of killings attributed by the authorities to "death squads" came from the urban poor: residents of slums and squatter settlements, vagrants, and, in several cities, homosexuals. The murder or "disappearance" of political activists took place in a context of daily "death squad" killings of victims described by some authorities and news media as dangerous criminals best eliminated. "Death squad" killings of victims who could not be identified, or were described by the news media as "delinquents" or "transvestites", were not systematically chronicled within Colombia. The number of victims of "death squad" killings could therefore only be estimated, although trade unions and political groups provided documentation on cases involving members of their own organizations. The legal left-wing political coalition *Unión Patriótica* (UP), Patriotic Unity, said in late 1986 that since its formation in 1984 over 350 members had been killed by "paramilitary groups" it said were directed by the armed forces, including in 1986 three of its 12 elected members of the legislature and some 30 elected municipal officers. In mid-September a Bogotá television station broadcast the findings of its own survey, and reported that there had been over 1,200 victims of unsolved "death squad" killings since January, most of them with criminal records, but also union leaders and journalists. More than 350 killings were attributed to "death squads" in the city of Cali alone in the first half of 1986. Many of the victims remained unidentified — some of them disfigured by acid or fire — and were buried in mass graves.

Colombia's Attorney General expressed dismay on 10 May 1986 at the "rising wave of official violence". He protested that police and military personnel remained untouchable for crimes committed while carrying out "the dirty work of counter-insurgency and counter-delinquency", and named Cali's National Police commanders — among others — as meriting prosecution.

Amnesty International reported its own mid-year estimate in a news release on 18 July. It believed that more than 600 Colombians had been seized and killed or shot on the spot in the first six months of the year by troops, police and gunmen working with them. The organization estimated the number of victims to number over 1,000 by the end of 1986.

Overwhelming evidence of official responsibility emerged from hundreds of Amnesty International case studies. "Death squad" gunmen openly carried military weapons in the presence of uniformed troops and police and travelled in military vehicles or unmarked cars without licence plates — some of which were seen parked in police and military compounds. The gunmen passed freely through ubiquitous army roadblocks — Colombia was under a state of siege — and were sometimes observed handing over prisoners at military bases and barracks. In many individual cases witnesses identified by name police and military personnel, and several "death squad" victims survived and described their detention, interrogation under torture, and attempted murder by regular army forces.

Although denying responsibility for the killings, army publicity campaigns against "subversion" appeared to support "death squad" actions. Wall slogans — sometimes painted by men working from army trucks — warned that the killings were "cleaning operations" to exterminate criminals, bandits and "all the Communists bleeding the Nation". Similar campaigns were launched throughout the country in the name of ostensibly civilian groups: in Pereira, *"Mano Negra"*, the "Black Hand"; in Cartagena, *"Ejército Popular Unido"*, United Popular Army; in Popayán, *"Falange"*; in Buga, *"Bandera Negra"*, Black Flag"; in Tuluá, *"El Justiciero"*, "The Justice Bringer"; and in the capital "MAS", *"Muerte a Secuestradores"*, "Death to Kidnappers". Although over 40 names of alleged "death squads" emerged in wall slogans, leaflets and news reports during 1986, Amnesty International was unaware of a single case in which alleged "death squad" members were convicted by the courts. No cases were known in which such supposedly independent armed units clashed with police or military forces patrolling the same areas.

In a letter of 22 April — made public in July — Amnesty International called on outgoing President Belisario Betancur to take steps to halt the rise in "disappearances", torture, and political killings and to establish procedures for police or military personnel who violated human rights to be investigated and prosecuted by an independent — not military — judiciary. It said that torture, "disappearance" and extrajudicial execution appeared to form part of a comprehensive counter-subversion policy of the Colombian armed forces. A public debate on the human rights situation followed, including a series of statements by civilian and military authorities. Some civilian ministers agreed with the need to take action. On 26 July the Minister of the Interior said that what was unquestionable was that there was an "authentic crisis in the administration of justice" requiring urgent reforms, including restrictions on the scope of military justice to consider only internal organization and discipline and performance of service.

Military spokesmen did not dispute the estimated death toll, but characterized the victims as "criminals" and "subversives" and their killers as mysterious civilian vigilantes. They rejected as one-sided Amnesty International's denunciation of the "death squad" killings. The Minister of Defence protested that he saw no reference in the statement to "the 630 guerrilla crimes committed this year". The head of the armed forces attributed the actions to "paramilitary" groups, but said "the armed forces have nothing to do with them".

Although grave abuses of human rights increased during 1986, Amnesty International welcomed the Colombian Government's copying to it of documentation prepared for the UN Working Group on Enforced or Involuntary Disappearances on investigations into specific cases of "disappearance" and political killing. Amnesty International received a copy of a dossier prepared by the office of the Chief Military Procurator on an investigation into 313 cases of "disappearance" reported by Colombian organizations. The dossier summarized evidence said to confirm the reappearance of 50 — some of these were disputed by Colombian rights groups — and the deaths of nine. The Procurator concluded that the investigation absolved the military of any wrong-doing.

Some information on cases of murder or torture before the military courts was also sent to Amnesty International, including a list of 242 cases of allegations of ill-treatment under investigation by the Chief Procurator of the National Police during 1985. Nine of these had led to disciplinary penalties ranging from "reprimand" to fines of five days' salary, and, in one case, suspension for 30 days. Police investigations had been opened into 18 cases of alleged forcible "disappearance", with a recommendation in one case that criminal charges be brought. Although in most cases known to Amnesty International, military court or disciplinary hearings into alleged human rights abuse led, at most, to fines or brief suspension, some prison sentences were reported. The Chief Military Procurator told a press conference in June that two soldiers had been sentenced to 18 years' imprisonment for the murder of guerrilla suspects, although the details of the case were not made public, and in November an army captain and a sergeant were sentenced to 18 and 24 years respectively by a court martial for a much publicized murder of six miners in 1985 — a case without apparent political elements.

Cuba

Amnesty International continued to be concerned about the detention of prisoners of conscience and possible prisoners of conscience, prolonged incommunicado detention, detention without trial, and prison conditions amounting to cruel, inhuman or degrading treatment.

Following the intercession of French oceanographer Jacques Cousteau, about 33 prisoners were released in May, including Raúl Pérez Ribalta who had been sentenced in 1979 to 20 years' imprisonment for espionage and whose case Amnesty International had been investigating (see *Amnesty International Report 1986*). In September, 69 former prisoners who had been released as a result of the intervention of a delegation of US Catholic Bishops arrived in the USA. Most had been released between July and September, although a few had been released during 1984 and 1985. Many had been long-term prisoners who had been arrested in the late 1950s and early 1960s, and who had been given sentences of up to 30 years' imprisonment. Other prisoners were released individually either upon expiry of their sentence or, in some cases, before; for example, Bay of Pigs (Playa Girón) veterans Ricardo Montero Duque and Ramón Conte Hernández, and former revolutionary leader Eloy Gutiérrez Menoyo, who was released following the intervention of Spanish Prime Minister Felipe González.

At the end of 1986 Amnesty International knew of approximately 450 political prisoners, of whom 10 were adopted as prisoners of conscience. It was seeking further information on a number of other cases. The organization had only fragmentary information on most of the 450, who included some 80 *"plantados históricos"* ("historical *plantados"*), convicted in the 1960s, and a group of at least 43 *"nuevos plantados"* ("new *plantados"*), mostly convicted in the 1980s. *"Plantados"* is the unofficial term for prisoners who refuse on political grounds to obey certain prison regulations such as wearing prison uniforms worn by ordinary criminal prisoners. Both the historical *plantados* and the new *plantados* were held on a variety of charges such as sabotage, espionage, conspiracy to overthrow the government, trying to leave the country illegally and "enemy propaganda".

On 22 September Elizardo Sánchez, Vice-President of the unofficial *Comité Cubano Pro Derechos Humanos* (CCPDH), Cuban Committee for Human Rights, gave an interview to two foreign journalists in Havana, in which he denounced the arrests of CCPDH members Dr Domingo Delgado Fernández and José Luis Alvarado Delgado in the week before 27 August, when Ricardo Bofill Pagés, President of the CCPDH, sought refuge in the French Embassy in Havana. On 25 September Elizardo Sánchez was himself arrested, together with CCPDH members Adolfo Rivero Caro and Enrique Hernández. The journalists were expelled from the country on the same day. The five men detained were all thought to have been taken to the headquarters of the *Departamento de Seguridad del Estado* (DSE), Department of State Security Police, in Havana, also known as Villa Marista. Amnesty International received reports suggesting that they were ill-treated during the initial period of detention. In early November Elizardo Sánchez was transferred to the military hospital after going on hunger-strike for a week. His treatment was said to have improved once he was in hospital, where he was allowed weekly visits from his mother. Adolfo Rivero Caro and Enrique Hernández received at least one or two visits from relatives at the DSE headquarters where they were still thought to be held at the end of 1986. The place of detention of Domingo Delgado and José Luis Alvarado at the end of the year was not clear, although some reports suggested that after they had both been released conditionally from prison a few months earlier, they had been returned to Combinado del Este prison on the outskirts of Havana, the main detention centre for political offenders. All five CCPDH members had been arrested on previous occasions, and in the cases of Elizardo Sánchez and Adolfo Rivero Caro, Amnesty International had taken action on their behalf. By the end of 1986 none of the five had been charged and all were still in detention, in apparent violation of the Cuban Code of Penal Procedure, which stipulates that detainees must be formally informed of the charges against them within 10 days of arrest. Amnesty International appealed for the immediate and unconditional release of the five on the grounds that they were prisoners of conscience.

Another prisoner of conscience adopted by Amnesty International during the year was Andrés José Solares Teseiro, who was arrested on 5 November 1981. He was sentenced by the *Sala de Delitos contra la Seguridad del Estado del Tribunal Provincial Popular de La Habana*, Court of Crimes against State Security of the Havana Province People's Tribunal, to eight years' imprisonment on charges of "enemy propaganda", on the grounds that he was thinking of organizing a political party in opposition to the Cuban Communist Party, and that he had drafted several letters about this to eminent personalities abroad asking for their opinions. All the documents seized by the authorities, which appeared to be the only evidence produced against him, were ordered by the court to be burned after the trial.

Rafael Lanza, another adopted prisoner of conscience, was arrested in 1982 and sentenced to eight years' imprisonment, also for "enemy propaganda". He was reportedly accused of writing a number of letters to diplomats in Havana in which he criticized the economic, social and human rights record of the Cuban Government.

Other prisoners of conscience convicted of "enemy propaganda" whom Amnesty International adopted during 1986 were Julio Vento Roberes, arrested in 1982 and sentenced to six or eight years' imprisonment, apparently on the grounds that he had drawn cartoons considered detrimental to the government and to the person of Fidel Castro in particular; Pascual Andrés Hernández Murguía, arrested in 1982 and sentenced to six years' imprisonment, reportedly for having expressed ideas considered detrimental to the state, both in writing and in conversations with friends; and Gregorio Peña Estrabao, arrested in July 1982 and sentenced to eight years' imprisonment. The charge against him was reportedly based on a letter he had received from abroad which contained a press cutting criticizing the Cuban Government. (He had previously been arrested in 1979 for trying to leave the country illegally.)

Amnesty International was investigating the case of Dr Alfredo Samuel Martínez Lara, a psychiatrist, formerly employed at the Calixto García Hospital in Havana and at the *Instituto de Investigaciones Científicas sobre el Cerebro*, Institute of Scientific Research on the Brain. Arrested in September, he was still held in the DSE headquarters on unknown charges at the end of 1986. Some reports suggested that he might have been detained after providing foreign journalists with information. Amnesty International wrote to the authorities asking for information on the precise charges against him, but received no reply.

Amnesty International was also investigating the cases of brothers Sebastián and Gustavo Arcos Bergnes, arrested in December 1981 when they were trying to leave the country illegally, after having tried for many years to obtain permission to leave. Amnesty International was concerned about reports that Gustavo Arcos was suffering from high blood pressure and had lost a lot of weight. He and his brother had been kept in cells known as *"los candados"* ("padlocked" cells), described by former prisoners as dark and wet. Gustavo Arcos was allegedly not being given appropriate treatment for his medical problem, which was aggravated by prison conditions. The organization also sought information about the health of prisoners of conscience Edmigio López Castillo, who was reportedly suffering from glaucoma and hypertension, and Ariel Hidalgo Guillén, who reportedly went on hunger-strike in protest at the arrest of the five CCPDH members. Amnesty International also continued to appeal for their immediate and unconditional release.

The conditions in which long-term political prisoners were confined continued to be of concern to Amnesty International. In January, 19 *plantados* went on hunger-strike in Combinado del Este prison. They were protesting at the suspension of six-monthly visits normally permitted to one family member, at being kept in small cells without ventilation, at the lack of medical attention, and at the existence of punishment cells where detainees were reportedly sent for periods of up to 21 days for making their demands known. Amnesty International did not know how long the hunger-strike lasted or whether conditions improved as a result.

The *plantados'* grievances were consistent with a number of testimonies which Amnesty International had received over the years on conditions in Cuban prisons. Lázaro Jordana, an art teacher, was sentenced after his arrest in March 1980 to 20 years' imprisonment on charges of trying to leave the country illegally and piracy, and was released in May. He described to Amnesty International his detention in a punishment cell in Combinado del Este prison after he had smuggled some drawings out of the prison. Between April and September or October 1984 he was kept in solitary confinement in a small cell with no clothes other than his underwear, and no bed. After two or three months and a hunger-strike his clothes were returned and he was given a sheet and mattress. The only light in the cell came from a light bulb which at one point broke and was not replaced for a week, during which time only very faint light filtered through the small hole through which his daily meals were passed. During his time in solitary confinement Lázaro Jordana was kept incommunicado and received no visitors.

Amnesty International received reports of the release and subsequent departure from the country of two political prisoners, Silvino Rodríguez Barrientos and Guillermo Casasús Toledo, who had been forcibly removed from Boniato prison in May 1983 and taken to an unknown destination (see *Amnesty International Report 1986*). In a public testimony Silvino Rodríguez said they were taken to the DSE building in Santiago de Cuba from where he was transferred after 54 days to the DSE headquarters in Havana. He said he spent a total of 18 months in solitary confinement during which he had no contact with the outside world, before being taken back to Boniato. Amnesty International had repeatedly asked the government (without receiving any reply) to disclose the whereabouts of these two prisoners since they had been removed from their cells.

Dominica

Amnesty International was concerned to learn of the first execution to take place in Dominica since 1973: that of Frederick Newton on 8 August 1986. He had been sentenced to death in June 1983 for the murder of a police officer during an attempted coup. Five soldiers who were sentenced to death with him had their sentences commuted in March 1986. Amnesty International wrote to the Attorney General in June 1986 welcoming the news of the five commutations, but expressing its concern that clemency had not been extended to Frederick Newton. The news that the warrant for his execution had been prepared was made public only two days before the scheduled date of execution. Amnesty International appealed to the President for clemency, urging him to maintain Dominica's record of not executing prisoners under sentence of death. However, the execution took place as scheduled.

Amnesty International also appealed for clemency on behalf of Eric Joseph, a 33-year-old Rastafarian under sentence of death for the murder of a prominent landowner in 1981. His case came before the Judicial Committee of the Privy Council in the United Kingdom in 1986 but was dismissed in June because he could not afford to retain a lawyer to argue his case. He subsequently obtained legal representation and in November the Privy Council granted him leave to appeal to them.

There were believed to be six prisoners on death row at the end of 1986.

Dominican Republic

Amnesty International was concerned about allegations of deliberate political killings by the police.

In June the organization appealed to the authorities to undertake an independent investigation into the killings of Daniel Valdez de la Rosa and Charles Henry Tejada Jackson, who were shot dead on 6 June by police in an alleged armed confrontation. According to eye-witness reports published in the press, the two men were not armed at the time of the shooting and pleaded for mercy before being killed. Amnesty International was concerned that the killings may have been motivated by their political activities: they both had a background of political activism. In its appeals Amnesty International expressed concern at allegations that deliberate killings by the police were a widespread practice and called for measures to ensure that this was not so. The organization urged the government to distribute the UN Code of Conduct for Law Enforcement Officials in order to ensure that all law enforcement officials were aware of their responsibilities with regard to human rights. Amnesty International also recommended that, if it were proved that the National Police had carried out these killings unlawfully, the victims' families should be afforded redress and compensation in accordance with national law. The two cases caused considerable public concern in the country, and the Public Prosecutor promised that there would be an exhaustive investigation. The newly-elected President of the Dominican Republic Dr Joaquín Balaguer was quoted as saying before he took office in August that such killings were not new and had been happening for years. He went on to say that he had evidence that people who were released in a presidential amnesty in 1978 had been gradually eliminated by the police. In October, in response to appeals from Amnesty International, the President of the Republic sent the organization documentation related to the trial and acquittal by a police court of the two police officers involved in the killings. The documentation included death certificates and documents stressing the alleged criminal activities of the victims and supporting the police account that there had been an exchange of fire and that the police had acted in legitimate self-defence. It was not clear from the documentation enclosed whether the witnesses challenging the police account had been interviewed and their testimony taken into account. In his letter the President stated that his government was "engaged in an arduous process to purge the armed institutions of the nation, with the purpose of guaranteeing, in the most effective way possible . . . [the] free exercise of human rights", and that he had taken "the firm decision to prevent abuses under "[his] rule, by carefully selecting members of forces of order and by punishing any who were directly or indirectly guilty of any violation".

Amnesty International continued to press the government to investigate the whereabouts of Samuel Roche, a Haitian refugee who "disappeared" following his arrest on 4 June 1982, and Pablo Liberato Rodríguez, who "disappeared" after his arrest under the previous government of Dr Joaquín Balaguer in 1974. However, Amnesty International was not aware of any steps taken during 1986 to clarify the "disappearances" and to bring to justice those responsible.

Ecuador

Amnesty International's concerns centred on evidence of torture; the introduction of detention procedures under which political suspects were held incommunicado and had their detention denied; and the failure to institute satisfactory inquiries into a series of killings that may have been extra-judicial executions. Political suspects frequently "disappeared" temporarily: detentions were generally acknowledged by the arresting authorities only after interrogation, or immediately before release or transfer to the custody of the prison service and the courts.

Government representatives made unprecedented public attacks on Ecuadorian church and human rights groups which actively campaigned for a halt to torture and "disappearances", accusing them of supporting subversive groups. In October police spokesmen told the news media that the Roman Catholic Bishops of Riobamba, Cuenca and Babahoyo and members of Ecuador's leading human rights organization, the *Comisión Ecuménica de Derechos Humanos* (CEDHU), Ecumenical Commission for Human Rights, were "collaborators" with the group *Alfaro Vive, Carajo* (AVC), Alfaro Lives, which had carried out a series of bank robberies and kidnappings in recent years. Human rights leaders and the Ecuadorian Conference of Bishops rejected the charge, which the authorities did not pursue. The government news media campaign coincided with anonymous threats of violence towards individual human rights workers, including members of CEDHU in Quito, the capital, and the Permanent Committee for the Defence of Human Rights based in the port city Guayaquil. In rural areas, particularly in Esmeraldas and Chimborazo provinces, Roman Catholic clergy and lay workers engaged in education and development projects were harassed and publicly denounced by the authorities as "subversives". Church workers were reported to have been detained in rural areas, although none were known to have been formally charged. On 10 September, for example, Father Aurelio Vera and church workers Susana Andrade and Bolivar Franco were reportedly detained without warrant in Guamote, Chimborazo. Although held for just one night, they were reportedly forced to sign statements accusing the Roman Catholic church in Riobamba of "subversive acts". In December Amnesty International called on the government to ensure the safety of church and human rights workers.

In May Amnesty International published a summary of its evidence of torture, including detailed testimonies and medical affidavits. The organization stated that a decrease in reports of ill-treatment and torture since 1979, when elections ended eight years of military government, appeared since 1985 to have been reversed. Detainees in the custody of police and military agencies in major cities were frequently reported to have been hooded or blindfolded, systematically beaten, sexually abused, and subjected to near-drowning and to electric shocks. Threats to relatives were also reported. Several prisoners testified that they had received medical attention for bruises, abrasions and swellings before being transferred from incommunicado detention, apparently to reduce the physical evidence of ill-treatment. However, in a number of cases medical examinations found evidence of injuries consistent with prisoners' allegations of torture.

Torture was reported in the context of detention procedures not previously used in Ecuador. Suspects were seized without warrant and their detention denied while they were being interrogated, usually for between 24 and 72 hours. A number of prisoners testified to having been seized by agents of the *Servicio de Investigación Criminal* (SIC), Criminal Investigation Service, briefly interrogated, and then transferred to secret military interrogation centres. Many of the victims were alleged by the authorities to be collaborators with AVC, or relatives of alleged members of the group.

Amnesty International appealed throughout 1986 on behalf of victims of incommunicado detention and torture. Lidia Caicedo, an 18-year-old student, was reportedly detained without warrant in Quito on 13 October by SIC agents. In later testimony she said she was tortured for two days with beatings, electric shocks, application of toxic gas into the pillow case which hooded her and threats to harm her family. A medical examination on 27 October reportedly confirmed burns on her face. She was in the Quito women's prison at the end of 1986 pending trial on charges of collaboration with the AVC group.

Amnesty International asked for information on the fate of Alberto David Troya, an army conscript, who "disappeared" for about 45 days after being detained in mid-April. It was later established that he was secretly transferred to a garrison at Yahuarcocha, and taken on 4 May to a detention centre in which he was held in a small lightless underground cell. The authorities admitted in mid-June that he was in custody, and stated that he was to be charged with theft of military equipment for the AVC group. According to his subsequent testimony, he was repeatedly tortured by intelligence officers. The arrest of Alberto David Troya followed the arrests of two of his brothers. His younger brother, a minor, was detained on 25 March in Quito, and interrogated — apparently under torture — about the activities of his brother Marco Troya, an alleged AVC member then in hiding. Following his release on 7 April, a medical examination reportedly found he had a fractured sternum, apparently from being beaten. On 27 March Marco Troya was detained, reportedly after an exchange of gunfire between members of AVC and the security services. He and Alberto David Troya were in custody pending trial at the end of 1986.

Torture was the subject of frequent public discussion in Ecuador in 1986. On 25 May in a news release headed "There is Torture in Ecuador", the President of Ecuador's *Tribunal de Garantías Constitucionales*, Tribunal of Constitutional Guarantees, reported on a meeting with the Minister of the Interior to discuss the rise in human rights violations. Despite the efforts of this tribunal, to the knowledge of Amnesty International the government initiated no investigations in 1986 into allegations of torture and unacknowledged detention in political cases. In cases on which Amnesty International appealed, the authorities responded by declaring that prisoners were members of AVC, and that abuses had not occurred.

Amnesty International was concerned about 11 prisoners who reportedly remained "disappeared" after being detained in 1985, and one who "disappeared" in 1986. Jorge Villegas Bajaña, a municipal council member for Babahoyo in Los Rios province, was reportedly seized on 8 February 1986. Amnesty International appealed for information on his legal status after conflicting reports were received: the local police denied that he had been detained but the news media reported a statement by the Minister of the Interior that "Villegas Bajaña is a prisoner, and is not disappeared".

The organization also continued to press for information on the fate of sociologist and teacher Consuelo Benavides Cevallos. She was reportedly detained on 4 December 1985 in Quinindé, Esmeraldas province, with peasant leader Serapio Ordóñez by a unit of the army's Fourth Military Zone. According to eye-witnesses both were severely beaten, and when last seen Consuelo Benavides appeared to have been seriously injured. Although army spokesmen denied the arrests, the two were reportedly taken to the headquarters of the *Fuerzas Especiales del Ejército*, Army Special Forces, in Latacunga, Cotopaxi. Although Consuelo Benavides remained unaccounted for, Serapio Ordóñez was released without charge several days later and subsequently said he had been accused of being the leader of a "subversive" group, and interrogated under torture.

Amnesty International called for an inquiry into the killing on 28 June of suspected AVC leader Ricardo Merino at his home in

Cuenca, Azuay province. Although police said he was shot when he attacked police officers, an autopsy reportedly supported claims by relatives that he had been killed while helpless — the cause of death was said to have been three bullet wounds from very close range.

Amnesty International was also concerned about the prolonged administrative detention in Quito of two Basque refugees — Alfonso Echegaray and Angel Aldana — who in July and December 1985 respectively were forcibly expelled to Ecuador by the Government of France. On the night of 8 January, according to detailed testimonies, the two were taken from house arrest by Ecuadorian police to a secret interrogation centre outside the city where they were interrogated for 16 hours by Spanish police officers. They alleged that they were subjected to torture, including electric shocks. On 21 January Amnesty International telexed the Foreign Minister to express its concern. On 30 January a reply was received denying that the two had been "tortured by Ecuadorian police". On 12 March the organization reiterated its request for an investigation, pointing out that the previous response did not address the allegation that Spanish police had ill-treated the prisoners, and stressing that the Ecuadorian authorities were responsible for the treatment of prisoners in its custody. On 11 August Alfonso Echegaray was expelled from Ecuador to São Tomé. Angel Aldana remained in custody in Ecuador.

The Government of Ecuador signed the Inter-American Convention to Prevent and Punish Torture on 30 May.

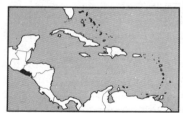

El Salvador

Amnesty International continued to be concerned about widespread torture of people from all sectors of Salvadorian society detained without trial on suspicion of subversive activities. Although still of concern, there appeared in 1986 to have been fewer "disappearances" and extrajudicial executions of opponents of the government by the Salvadorian military and police forces. However, the collection of information on human rights abuses was hindered by a wave of arrests of human rights workers and by interference in the work of journalists. The number of occasions on which human rights violations were attributed to the so-called "death squads" also fell substantially during 1986. Further evidence emerged that these groups were not extremist groups of the left and right, as successive administrations had maintained, but were customarily made up of regular police and military personnel, acting in plain clothes but under the orders of higher officials. By contrast, the number of acknowledged arrests, both short and long-term, rose in 1986. By the close of 1986 the combined political prisoner population at La Esperanza, Mariona, men's prison and the *Centro de Reorientación Femenina*, Women's Reorientation Centre, at Ilopango, where most known political detainees were held, was estimated at more than 1,000, apparently leading to problems of over-crowding.

Detainees were held under Decree 50 of February 1984, governing penal proceedings against people accused of offences against the state, while constitutional guarantees were suspended under the state of siege originally declared in March 1980. Although the government stated that it allowed visits by the International Committee of the Red Cross (ICRC) after eight days of detention under Decree 50, this was not always the practice. Under the decree, detainees could be held incommunicado for up to 15 days. It was during this period — before their detentions were officially acknowledged and before detainees were placed under the jurisdiction of the special military tribunals established by Decree 50 and transferred from military or police custody to prison — that torture was most frequently reported. According to many detailed testimonies obtained by Amnesty International, prisoners were subjected to both physical and mental torture and ill-treatment to press them to sign extrajudicial statements which they had often not read, and sometimes signed while blindfold. Some prisoners were presented on Salvadorian television as they signed such statements, which the government then described as proof that they were guilty of the allegations against them.

The torture methods reported to Amnesty International suggested an increasing reliance on methods such as prolonged sleep deprivation, threats against relatives and the use of drugs, but also included beatings, electric shocks and the use of the "*capucha*" (hood impregnated with lime), and sexual threats and abuse, particularly of women prisoners. Amnesty International repeatedly appealed to President José Napoleon Duarte and other officials to investigate torture allegations and bring those responsible to justice.

Amnesty International also expressed concern that even after their detention had been acknowledged, detainees held under Decree 50 were not dealt with within the time limits established by the decree. At the close of 1986, many hundreds of political prisoners had been in detention for four or five years; an estimated 90 per cent had not been tried.

These and other abuses occurred in the context of continuing civil conflict in the country. Amnesty International also received reports that armed opposition groups were responsible for abuses including summary executions and kidnappings of government officials, business people and others they believed to be government spies. Amnesty International condemns the torture and execution of captives by anyone. The available information did not appear to confirm other charges that the opposition (and to a lesser extent the military) were using landmines against targeted groups of civilians.

A number of local human rights workers were arrested in an apparent effort to disrupt their work of collecting information on human rights abuses and their humanitarian assistance to displaced people in contested zones. Joaquín Antonio Cáceres Hernández, Press and Information Secretary and long-standing board member of the independent *Comisión de Derechos Humanos de El Salvador, no-gubernamental* (CDHES), non-governmental Human Rights Commission of El Salvador, was arrested in November 1985. Then in May and June 1986 a further eight people working with the CDHES and other Salvadorian human rights groups were arrested. At a series of government-organized news conferences one of the detainees stated that she had placed herself voluntarily in the hands of the authorities. She described the alleged infiltration of Salvadorian human rights groups by the armed opposition, and said that her information had led to the other arrests. She also made allegations, which she later withdrew, of links between foreign and local church and humanitarian assistance organizations, local human rights groups and the armed opposition. Amnesty International twice asked the government, in May and again in October, to assure the physical integrity of the human rights workers and to investigate allegations that some had been forced under torture to sign medical certificates that they had not been ill-treated. The organization also asked several international bodies, including the Inter-American Commission on Human Rights (IACHR) of the Organization of American States (OAS), to call on the Salvadorian authorities to release the human rights workers if they had been detained because of their human rights activities.

By the end of 1986 several of the human rights workers had been released, including María Teresa Tula de Canales of the *Co-madres*, Mothers' Committee. She was reportedly abducted on 6 May by men in plain clothes, and stabbed and raped before being abandoned two days later in a park in San Salvador. She was seized again on 28 May, once more by men in plain clothes. This time her detention was acknowledged by the Treasury Police. Freed on 23 September, reportedly on the personal orders of President Duarte, she told him in the presence of journalists who had been summoned to witness her release that she had been tortured in official custody. In June Amnesty International had asked for her to receive medical attention for the wounds suffered at the time of her first, unattributed abduction.

Amnesty International also appealed on behalf of a number of other church, refugee and relief workers reportedly detained and tortured because they had participated in discussions and public events to promote a peace dialogue in the country or because of their work with displaced people and those made homeless by the earthquake which struck the country in October.

In January Amnesty International called for inquiries into 52 separate incidents in which trade unionists had been arrested, tortured, had "disappeared" or had been killed, apparently because of their trade union activities. Among the victims were José Humberto Centeno Najarro and his sons José Vladimir and Jaime Ernesto, aged 21 and 18, who were arrested on 25 November 1985, allegedly in reprisal for their father's activities as leader of the Salvadorian telecommunications union. The brothers were still in custody at the end of 1986. In December Amnesty International renewed appeals for an inquiry into their sworn statements that they had been drugged and tortured to force them to sign confessions implicating them in the 1985 kidnapping of a government official.

Among the many other trade unionists on whose behalf Amnesty International appealed in 1986 were Febé Elizabeth Velásquez, who was arrested in July after addressing mass demonstrations in the capital on behalf of the trade union confederation which she represented, and four transport union workers arrested in March and April. Febé Velásquez was released four days after her arrest, reportedly after the personal intervention of President Duarte. In July Amnesty International sought assurances that the others, who were in Mariona prison and had reportedly been tortured during interrogation by the National Guard, would receive medical treatment.

Students and teachers continued to be arrested and detained. For example, Rufino Antonio Quesada, President of the *Asociación General de Estudiantes Universitarios Salvadoreños* (AGEUS), General Association of Salvadorian Students, was held briefly in March. He had been involved in the *Jornada por el diálogo y la Paz*, Day of Peace and Dialogue, held by students and professors of the University of El Salvador in December 1985.

Amnesty International also appealed in November on behalf of a number of peasants from San José Las Flores, Chalatenango, seized by soldiers of the first Infantry Brigade. They had spoken about their lives in a zone of conflict between the opposition and the Salvadorian military on tapes which had been confiscated from three foreign journalists arrested in September and forced to leave the country. The peasants were subsequently released.

Steps were announced during the year to improve judicial procedures, including setting up a forensic science laboratory and training programs for judicial personnel. However, despite fresh evidence uncovered by human rights groups in recent years, there was little progress in the official inquiries periodically promised by President Duarte into specific cases of human rights abuse. These cases included a number of mass killings of non-combatant civilians by the military, as well as individual "disappearances" and extrajudicial executions, among them the murder of Archbishop Oscar Romero in March 1980. In the two cases in which lower level security personnel were convicted of killings, both of which involved US citizens, efforts by US human rights groups to have the higher-ranking officials who they believed ordered the murders prosecuted were reportedly hampered by the authorities.

Investigations were announced, however, into the alleged involvement of senior military officials in a kidnapping ring. About 20 people were arrested in April on suspicion of involvement in the kidnappings, but as far as Amnesty International was aware no one was convicted. Three of those arrested died in suspicious circumstances (two of them in police custody) and some 15 others were released. One of the people initially detained had been accused of having organized the murders in January 1981 of two US labour advisers and the head of the Salvadorian Agrarian Reform Institute.

Amnesty International also continued to follow closely the situation of the many thousands of Salvadorians who in previous years had fled from army sweeps through their areas or from attacks upon their families to seek asylum abroad. Particularly in view of discussions about large-scale repatriation from Honduras, Amnesty International was concerned about reports that returned refugees were viewed by the Salvadorian authorities as a potential source of support for the opposition, and were therefore in danger. In November Amnesty International submitted to the UN High Commissioner for Refugees lists of Salvadorian refugees who had reportedly been detained or "disappeared" in El Salvador after repatriation, both voluntary and involuntary, from Honduras.

In view of its continuing concerns in the country, Amnesty International informed the government in August that it wanted to visit the country in December to discuss these matters. It received no definite response to its proposal until shortly before the delegation planned to leave for El Salvador, when it was informed that the

October earthquake had made the planned date "inconvenient". The Salvadorian authorities proposed March 1987 instead, but by the end of 1986 had not confirmed this new date.

Amnesty International also submitted information on its concerns to relevant international organizations including the UN special representative on El Salvador, its Working Group on Enforced or Involuntary Disappearances and its Special Rapporteurs on summary or arbitrary executions and on torture, and to the IACHR of the OAS. In its 1986 Annual Report, the IACHR found that, in El Salvador, threats to the right to life continued and that Decree 50 continued to have a negative effect on judicial guarantees for due process and prompt administration of justice. Resolution 41/157 passed by the UN General Assembly in December 1986 stated that despite the efforts of the government to reform the administration of justice, the judicial system in the country continued to be "notoriously" unsatisfactory, and serious and numerous violations of human rights continued to take place. The resolution committed the UN to keeping under consideration the human rights situation in the country.

Grenada

Amnesty International continued to monitor the trial of former members of the People's Revolutionary Government (PRG) and the People's Revolutionary Army (PRA), charged with the murder of former Prime Minister Maurice Bishop and others in 1983 (see *Amnesty International Report 1984* to *1986*). Fourteen of the 18 defendants were sentenced to death on 4 December. Amnesty International appealed for clemency and raised certain concerns about the fairness of the proceedings in the case.

In May Amnesty International sent an observer to part of the trial, which began in April after several adjournments. Shortly after the trial started, the defence lawyers withdrew from the case at the request of the defendants, who refused to recognize the jurisdiction of the court. In pre-trial motions the defence had challenged the legitimacy of the Grenada Supreme Court — the independent court system set up in 1979 by the PRG — by which the defendants were being tried. They argued that the reinstatement of the 1974 constitution required a return to the Eastern Caribbean judicial system (which, among other things, provided the right of final appeal to the Judicial Committee of the Privy Council in the United Kingdom, a right abolished by the PRG). The appeals court ruled that the constitution required Grenada's eventual return to this system but upheld the legitimacy of the Grenada Supreme Court for this trial.

On 2 May Amnesty International wrote to the Minister of Justice expressing concern about reports that the recently appointed Supreme Court Registrar, responsible for summoning jurors to the trial, had formerly been a member of the prosecution team in the case. Amnesty International also expressed concern about reports that some members of the jury pool had cheered when the judge informed the defence lawyers that they were liable to be cited for contempt of court during preliminary proceedings on 11 April and on other occasions also had shown themselves to have a less than impartial attitude towards the defendants. This had apparently not led to any juror being disqualified, although one alternate juror was later removed when it transpired that his son had been killed during the 1983 events. Amnesty International received no reply.

During the trial itself the defendants, who were unrepresented, entered pleas of not guilty to the charges, but refused to participate otherwise in the proceedings. Most of them were removed from the courtroom each day, after disrupting the proceedings by chanting. Most of the witness testimony for the prosecution was therefore given in the absence of the accused. Summaries of this testimony were read to the defendants by the trial judge but they declined to cross-examine the witnesses. After the prosecution had given its evidence, the defendants made unsworn statements to the court in which they denied the charges against them and alleged, among other things, that some of the statements used in evidence against them had been obtained by torture.

The jury returned its verdict on 4 December: 14 of the 18 defendants were convicted of murder and sentenced to death by hanging. They included former Deputy Prime Minister Bernard Coard, former Minister for Women's Affairs Phyllis Coard, former Army Commander Hudson Austin and former Ambassador to Cuba, Leon Cornwall. Three former soldiers found guilty of having carried out the shooting of Maurice Bishop and others were convicted of manslaughter and sentenced to prison terms ranging from 30 to 45 years. A fourth defendant, Raeburn Nelson, was acquitted on the direction of the judge. Fabien Gabriel, one of the 19 originally accused, had been granted a pardon at the beginning of the trial after agreeing to testify for the Crown.

Amnesty International wrote to the Governor General of Grenada on 16 December appealing for commutation of the death sentences. It noted that no executions had been carried out in Grenada for several years and said that a resumption of executions would be contrary to the spirit of international human rights standards, which encourage governments progressively to restrict the use of the death penalty with a view to its ultimate abolition. Amnesty International said it was still investigating other aspects of the case. An appeal against their convictions was pending at the end of 1986.

A total of 17 people were under sentence of death in Grenada at the end of the year.

Guatemala

During 1986 Amnesty International was concerned about instances of apparent "disappearances" and extra-judicial executions, although such reports were received on a lesser scale than in previous years. It was also concerned about the harassment and intimidation of those seeking clarification of past human rights violations. However, Amnesty International welcomed a number of legislative changes relevant to its human rights concerns instituted or promised by the country's first elected president in more than 20 years, Vinicio Cerezo Arévalo, who took office in January. Despite some improvement in the human rights situation, however, there was minimal progress in determining responsibility for the tens of thousands of cases of torture, "disappearance" and extrajudicial execution of people from all sectors of Guatemalan society which had occurred during the previous two decades of military government.

Under President Cerezo's predecessors, the perpetrators of such abuses were sometimes clearly identified as uniformed members of Guatemala's police and military forces. On other occasions abductions and killings were carried out by heavily armed men in plain clothes acting in the guise of "death squads". However, since the 1970s Amnesty International had examined hundreds of such cases and had concluded that the "death squads" were generally made up of regular police and military personnel, acting in plain clothes but under superior orders. Amnesty International had never received a substantive reply to its repeated appeals to the authorities to carry out investigations into the reported abuses in order to determine responsibility for them and bring the perpetrators to justice.

Amnesty International therefore wrote to President Cerezo shortly before his inauguration expressing its hopes that the protection and promotion of human rights would be an integral part of his program of government. Amnesty International submitted to the new President a copy of the memorandum summarizing its long-term concerns in Guatemala which it had sent to his predecessor, General Oscar Humberto Mejía Víctores, in December 1985. Amnesty International also submitted a series of recommendations which it felt the new government should implement to ensure respect for human rights in the country. The organization stressed its belief that in-depth investigations into how "disappearances" and extrajudicial executions had been planned and carried out were necessary in order to identify and modify the institutionalized structures and policies which had permitted these violations to take place on a massive scale for more than two decades.

In February an Amnesty International news release announced that it had put these recommendations to President Cerezo. It also explained Amnesty International's view of the general amnesty which had been announced by the outgoing military government on the eve of President Cerezo's inauguration. The measure, Decree 08-86, was one of an estimated 40 decrees, not all of them made public, passed by the outgoing military government in its final days in power. Under the decree it would not be possible to prosecute the perpetrators of "political crimes and related common crimes" committed between March 1982 (when General Efraín Ríos Montt came to power in a military coup) and 14 January 1986. Amnesty International does not oppose measures of magnanimity or clemency, provided that they do not pre-empt or obstruct judicial, administrative or other investigations to establish publicly the truth about what had occurred. Amnesty International was concerned, however, that the January 1986 amnesty law could encourage further human rights violations by giving the perpetrators of past crimes a sense that they could act with impunity.

In the first months of his administration supporters of President Cerezo's own Christian Democrat Party "disappeared" and were killed, apparently the victims of extrajudicial execution. For example, Christian Democrat Alfonso Jerónimo Pérez was killed by armed men in civilian dress as he returned home to Jocatán, Chiquimula, on 29 January. His assailants then cut off his hands, ears and head.

Trade unionists also were subjected to human rights violations during 1986 as they attempted to revive Guatemala's trade union movement, virtually obliterated by the wholesale repression of its leadership and members since the late 1970s. In February, for example, José Mercedes Sotz was seized on a Guatemala City street by heavily armed men who held him for several hours while they tried to intimidate him into giving up his activities with the *Sindicato Central de Trabajadores Municipales* (SCTM), Central Municipal Workers Union. In August Amnesty International called for investigations into the whereabouts of Jorge Herrera, a legal adviser to several Guatemalan trade union organizations and a former teacher at the School of Trade Union Studies at the *Universidad de San Carlos* (USAC), University of San Carlos, itself a long-term target of government repression. Jorge Herrera, who was abducted in the capital on 26 July and was still missing at the end of the year, was the fifth member of his family to have "disappeared" or been killed in recent years reportedly because of their trade union activities. Jorge Herrera's brother and sister-in-law were among 17 trade unionists who "disappeared" after being abducted in front of witnesses by approximately 50 armed soldiers while attending a trade union seminar in Escuintla in August 1980. In letters to President Cerezo in August 1986 Amnesty International again called attention to the cases of the trade unionists abducted from Escuintla. It said these "disappearances" were representative of cases where Amnesty International considered that sufficient information was already available to enable further inquiries to establish who was responsible and bring them to justice. Among other such cases to which Amnesty International drew special attention in 1986 were those of student Luís Fernando de la Roca Elías, who "disappeared" after being seized in September 1985 by kidnappers using cars subsequently traced to the Ministry of Justice and the Justo Rufino Barrios military barracks in Guatemala City; teacher Hugo de León Palacios, who was abducted in front of his students in Guatemala City in March 1984; and Ileana del Rosario Solares Castillo, who was detained in Guatemala City in September 1982 under the terms of Decree 46-82 of July 1982. She was seen in custody by another prisoner who was later freed, but her name was not included in the list of those released when Decree 46-82 was rescinded in 1983, and there was no further news of her whereabouts.

Amnesty International's letters to President Cerezo in August welcomed certain legislative developments in Guatemala, including the provision in its new constitution that the international conventions to which Guatemala was a party would in principle prevail over the country's own laws. Amnesty International also welcomed the country's new *amparo* and *habeas corpus* act, (Decree 1-86 of January 1986), and the provisions of the new constitution which called for the appointment of a *Procurador General de Derechos Humanos*, Human Rights Attorney, and for the establishment of a

Congressional human rights commission. Amnesty International also noted President Cerezo's announcement in February that he had disbanded the *Departamento de Investigaciones Técnicas* (DIT), Department of Technical Investigations, the intelligence division of the National Police which had repeatedly been named as responsible for "disappearances" and extrajudicial executions since its discredited predecessor, the *Cuerpo de Detectives*, Detective Corps, was itself disbanded under the administration of General Ríos Montt.

In November Amnesty International's delegation to the Organization of American States (OAS) General Assembly in Guatemala City met President Cerezo. The delegation expressed the organization's disappointment that no further details were yet available of the proceedings which he had announced for the trial of former DIT agents accused of human rights abuses of civilians. The organization was also disappointed that by the close of the year, the Human Rights Attorney had not yet been appointed and the structure and operating methods of the Congressional human rights commission remained unclear.

Amnesty International was also concerned that members of the *Grupo de Apoyo Mutuo por el Aparecimiento con Vida de Nuestros Familiares* (GAM), Mutual Support Group for the Appearance Alive of our Relatives, who had pressed for an alternative, independent commission to be established to inquire into the whereabouts of their missing relatives, had encountered threats and harassment. In May Amnesty International informed President Cerezo of its concern that GAM president Nineth Montenegro de García had been followed through Guatemala City by eight men in a jeep who pointed their guns at her. It recalled the still unresolved killings of two GAM leaders in 1985, and asked the government to guarantee the physical integrity of the group's members so that they could continue their legal activities to find their missing relatives. The government replied that it was investigating the allegations and that groups such as GAM, which it described as "in opposition to the government", were accorded the necessary protection by the government. In September Amnesty International again called upon the authorities to ensure the physical integrity of GAM members following reports that Nineth Montenegro de García had once again begun receiving threatening telephone calls, and had on several occasions been called a "terrorist" on Guatemalan television. At an army news conference on 17 September she was accused of impugning the honour and prestige of the army and GAM's activities were described as "dangerous". President Cerezo replied to Amnesty International that it was the relatives of the "disappeared" who had adopted a threatening posture by interrupting a military parade to call attention to their relatives' cases, and that the army communique had been misinterpreted. Amnesty International responded in a series of meetings with President Cerezo during his October tour of the USA and Europe that it considered that certain language used in the communique implied a threat to GAM. For example, it contained the passage: "If anything should happen to the GAM president or any of its members it was already anticipated by those who are their puppeteers and who conceived this Machiavellian plan." In December Basilio Tuíz Ramírez, who was associated with GAM, was abducted on the road between Panajachel and San Andrés, Sololá, by men carrying machetes and a Galil rifle believed by witnesses to be members of the army. He was still missing at the end of 1986.

On a number of occasions Amnesty International expressed to President Cerezo its view that any repatriation of Guatemalan refugees should take place only under the supervision of qualified international observers. Many thousands of refugees had fled from army attacks upon their areas to seek asylum in Mexico and elsewhere. Amnesty International considered it to be the responsibility of the Guatemalan authorities to ensure that such returned refugees were protected from human rights abuses at the hands of the Guatemalan police and military forces.

In the course of 1986 Amnesty International also raised its concerns in Guatemala with the UN special representative on Guatemala, its Working Group on Disappearances, its Special Rapporteurs on summary or arbitrary executions and on torture, the UNHCR and the Inter-American Commission on Human Rights (IACHR) of the Organization of American States. In its 1986 Annual Report, the IACHR found that in Guatemala reports of human rights violations had decreased under the new government, but noted that the phenomenon of "disappearance" had not ceased. It expressed its fears that the amnesty decree could hinder judicial efforts to investigate actions of recent years which had left a legacy of a "large number of persons abducted, illegally detained, tortured, assassinated, and 'disappeared'."

At its March session the UN Commission on Human Rights asked for a Special Representative to be appointed to continue the human rights investigations previously carried out by the special rapporteur it had named in 1983. The UN General Assembly decided to continue its examination of the human rights situation in the country.

Guyana

Amnesty International was concerned about reports of torture and ill-treatment of people held in police custody and about the use of the death penalty.

In February Amnesty International wrote to President Hoyte about the ill-treatment of three youths taken into police custody in December 1985. According to reports from relatives and other sources, Andrew Mayers, Subryan Mokeen (both 18) and Donald Morrison (aged 14) were arrested and taken to a New Amsterdam police station where they were beaten. Andrew Mayers is alleged to have been particularly badly treated: beaten on the head, stomach and groin and seen by relatives bleeding from the ears and mouth. The three were remanded in custody on murder charges and Andrew Mayers was reported to be detained in the infirmary of New Amsterdam Prison in late January 1986. In its letter, Amnesty International asked whether an investigation had been carried out and for the result of any inquiry. No reply had been received by the end of the year.

In June Amnesty International asked for information about reports that Anthony La Cruz, a 53-year-old Amerindian, had been tortured in police custody in January. According to his statement, during his 48-hour detention he was stripped and repeatedly beaten with wire and a five-foot piece of wood; police tied wire around his testicles and pulled him around the room; he was ordered to eat excrement out of a toilet; the police threatened to shoot him and placed a gun at his head which proved not to be loaded when the trigger was pulled. He spent the night lying on a table with his hands cuffed behind his back and was further beaten while thus restrained.

Amnesty International continued to be concerned about the use of the death penalty in Guyana. On 24 June Malcolm Daniels became the fifth person to be executed since hangings resumed in October 1985, after a 15-year period in which no one had been executed in Guyana (see *Amnesty International Report 1986*). Amnesty International expressed its regret at the executions. It believed there were 26 prisoners on death row at the end of 1986.

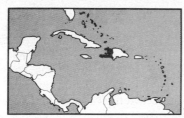

Haiti

Amnesty International was concerned about indiscriminate killings of demonstrators, widespread arbitrary arrests, torture and "disappearances" before the government of "President for Life" Jean-Claude Duvalier was overthrown on 7 February and replaced by a *Conseil national de gouvernement* (CNG), National Council of Government, composed of military officers and civilians. The new government took a number of measures with the declared aim of improving respect for human rights. However, with very few exceptions, it took no action to investigate the widespread human rights abuses which had taken place under previous governments, despite well-documented evidence in many cases of the involvement of members of the security forces. Amnesty International continued to be concerned after February about reports of the short-term detention of prisoners of conscience; the torture and ill-treatment of detainees; at least two "disappearances"; and about trials which did not conform to internationally recognized standards of fairness.

In the weeks before the overthrow of Jean-Claude Duvalier, protesters were indiscriminately killed by security forces and suspected opponents of the government were arbitrarily arrested, tortured or made to "disappear" in large numbers, against a background of generalized popular protest and demonstrations calling for an end to the Duvalier family's 29-year rule. Amnesty International appealed on behalf of a number of the victims, such as Gabriel Hérard and Jacques Emmanuel Bonheur, members of the *Parti démocrate chrétien haïtien* (PDCH), Haitian Christian Democrat Party, who were arrested by security forces at the end of December 1985, and Augustin Auguste, another PDCH member, who was arrested on 28 January by members of the *Volontaires de la sécurité nationale* (VSN), National Security Volunteers, commonly known as *tontons macoutes*. Gabriel Hérard was released on 8 February, but Jacques Emmanuel Bonheur and Augustin Auguste remained "disappeared".

After 7 February when the CNG, headed by former Army Chief of Staff Henri Namphy, took power, a number of measures aimed at improving respect for human rights were implemented. On 7 February, 26 political prisoners, most of whom had been held without charge or trial, were released from the National Penitentiary. It was announced that there were no political prisoners left in detention. On

13 February Amnesty International telexed the new government welcoming the releases of the political prisoners, among whom were a number of prisoners of conscience. However, Amnesty International was concerned that those arrested in previous years who had "disappeared" were not among those released. It urged the new government to initiate thorough and impartial investigations into the fate of the "disappeared" and to prevent recurrence of such violations and, wherever possible, to compensate the victims.

The new government also brought in laws relating to a number of freedoms, including freedom of the press, association and assembly, which were previously unknown or severely limited. Dozens of new civic associations were formed, some of which were concerned with the protection of human rights, for example the *Comité féminin de lutte contre la torture*, Women's Committee against Torture; the *Ligue des anciens prisonniers politiques haïtiens* (LAPPH), League of Former Haitian Political Prisoners, and the *Centre haïtien de défense des libertés publiques*, Haitian Centre for the Defence of Public Liberty. Trade unions were organized in many workplaces, political exiles were allowed to return, new newspapers and magazines started to circulate and television became accessible to political groups and new associations.

The CNG published a schedule of political reforms to culminate in a presidential election in February 1988. A Constituent Assembly was elected in October and a plebiscite on the new constitution was announced for February 1987. Other political measures taken by the CNG were the introduction of laws governing political parties and the press, which were passed in July. The failure of the CNG to bring an end to human rights abuses by the security forces was illustrated by the numerous killings carried out by army units as a means of crowd control. On 19 March five people were reportedly killed by an army unit in Martissant on the outskirts of Port-au-Prince. In another incident on 26 April, at least six people were killed and some 50 wounded after soldiers opened fire on an authorized and peaceful march of relatives of victims of human rights violations as it approached Fort Dimanche military barracks and prison in which hundreds of political prisoners had starved to death, been executed or "disappeared". Amnesty International appealed for an independent and impartial inquiry into the incident. The government announced that an inquiry would be carried out, but made it clear that it found the army's action a "normal reaction of enlisted soldiers . . . in the face of an attempted invasion by individuals openly encouraged by agitators". An Amnesty International delegate in Haiti met the Minister of Justice within days of the incident and conveyed Amnesty International's concerns. The delegate also expressed concern about continuing reports of ill-treatment of detainees, in particular at the Port-au-Prince police headquarters known as the *Recherches criminelles*. As far as Amnesty International was aware, the results of the announced government inquiry had not been made public by the end of 1986.

Amnesty International was not able to determine whether any of the prisoners still in detention at the end of 1986 were prisoners of conscience. In most cases the authorities did not bring the detainees before a judge or reveal the grounds for the detention. Amnesty International was, however, concerned about numerous short-term arrests of members of opposition political parties and associations, journalists, church workers and people involved in literacy campaigns, youth and other grassroots organizations. In April, according to the Haitian Centre for the Defence of Public Liberty, Pasteur Paul, a Baptist Minister, was held for eight days and beaten at the *Recherches criminelles* and then released without charge or explanation. Himler Laguerre, a member of the Association of Youth of the City of Aquin, was arrested by the army on 8 September and reportedly beaten in detention. He was released without charge on 8 October. Marie-Paule Jeune, a member of *Racine*, a grassroots organization, was taken to the *Casernes Dessalines* military barracks after being arrested at a rally on 18 October. She was beaten before being released, two days later. Jean Paul Duperval and José Sinaï, two members of the *Komite Inite Demokratik* (KID), Committee for Democratic Unity, and Jean Robert Laforêt, a journalist at Radio Cacique, were arrested on 17 October when the two KID members announced that they were going on hunger-strike to protest against the conditions in which the Constituent Assembly elections were to be held on 19 October. Jean Robert Laforêt was covering the story for the radio station. The three were reportedly taken to the *Casernes Dessalines*. The journalist was released the same day, the other two on 20 October. Many other people were arrested in other parts of the country, including Cap Haïtien. Préméus Jasmin, a literacy worker, was arrested on 7 October without a warrant, beaten and held for several days. As in the other cases mentioned, he was apparently arrested because of his political views.

Amnesty International was concerned that, with very few exceptions, no action was taken by the government or the courts to investigate the human rights abuses which took place before 7 February, in spite of the well-documented evidence in many cases of the involvement of named members of the security forces in abuses not only before but also after the CNG took power. The organization received reports of at least two "disappearances" following arrest by the security forces after February. Charlot Jacquelin was arrested on

19 September in Cité Soleil, a shanty town on the outskirts of Port-au-Prince. Two men, one in civilian clothes and one dressed in olive green (normally worn by the military), were said to have entered his home while police officers in blue uniforms (worn by the Port-au-Prince police) waited outside. Charlot Jacquelin was taken to the local police station at Cité Soleil, where shortly afterwards eight police officers arrived and took him away to an unknown destination. In response to appeals from Amnesty International, the Director of Judicial Affairs at the Ministry of Justice wrote on 21 October enclosing a communique issued by the headquarters of the Haitian armed forces on 30 September, which said that "the case of Charlot Jacquelin is unknown to the Port-au-Prince Police Headquarters". Charlot Jacquelin had been working as a literacy teacher on a church-run project.

In July an Amnesty International delegate visited Haiti to gather information about the trials of several members of the governments of François Duvalier and Jean-Claude Duvalier. The organization wished to assess the fairness of the proceedings and to obtain information brought out at the trial about the widespread human rights violations which occurred under those governments. The delegate attended the trial of Edouard C. Paul, former director of the *Office national d'alphabétisation et d'action communautaire* (ONAAC), National Office for Literacy and Community Action, charged in connection with the killing in March 1969 of Pierre Denis, a suspected Communist Party member. The jury found Edouard C. Paul guilty of complicity in the murder of Pierre Denis, and the judge sentenced him to three years' imprisonment. Amnesty International's delegate also studied the proceedings of the court martial of Colonel Samuel Jérémie, who was charged with beating, shooting and killing several demonstrators in Léogâne on 31 January 1986. On 30 May he was found guilty and sentenced to 15 years' hard labour. Another trial studied by the delegate was that of Luc Désir, close collaborator in security matters with both previous "Presidents-for-Life". The trial lasted 16 hours without interruption and ended at around 4.15 am on 6 July. Luc Désir was sentenced to death for the illegal arrest, torture and murder of three people suspected of being political opponents of François Duvalier. In the opinion of Amnesty International's delegate, the proceedings in the trials of Luc Désir and Edouard C. Paul were not marked by the solemnity and order required for a fair hearing. Furthermore, there were grounds for doubting the impartiality of the jury in the trial of Luc Désir: their questions revealed a bias against the defendant which was shared by the partisan crowd in the courtroom. These two trials were initiated by the victims' families. Amnesty International was concerned that there was no evidence that the government had actively helped the investigations by seeking government records or conducting interviews with police and army officers who might have had evidence to offer. Amnesty International urged the government to establish an independent commission of inquiry to investigate past human rights abuses, particularly since named members of the army allegedly involved in serious abuses were still in active service.

Amnesty International received reports of the continued use of torture and other cruel and inhuman treatment of both political and criminal suspects in prisons and other detention facilities. Wilnor Lapatrie, according to his own testimony, was arrested on 6 August by an army officer and two soldiers after he had been denounced as being a leader of the disbanded *tontons macoutes*. He was taken to a local police station where he was tied in the position known as the "*djak*" or "*pau d'arara*" (parrot perch) and repeatedly beaten with a stick. The following day he was transferred to Fort Dimanche where he remained for 11 days in a cell with no bed and with practically no food. Although he was injured by the beating, he was not given any medical treatment. He was released after he agreed to pay a fine.

However, the most frequent allegations of torture and other forms of ill-treatment concerned detainees held in the *Recherches criminelles*. For example, Benito Eddy, a member of the PDCH, alleged that he was arrested without warrant on 6 August and taken to the *Recherches criminelles* where he was beaten and kept in a small cell with 14 other prisoners, and where he remained for nine days before being released without charge. He said he saw three prisoners die, apparently as a consequence of lack of food and ill-treatment. Benito Eddy reportedly made a complaint to the Ministry of Justice, but Amnesty International was not aware of any inquiry being ordered, or of any general measures being taken to prevent ill-treatment of detainees.

Amnesty International submitted information to the Inter-American Commission on Human Rights and to the UN Working Group on Enforced or Involuntary Disappearances.

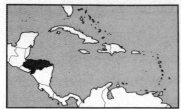

Honduras

All the long-term political prisoners known to Amnesty International were released in March under an amnesty granted by the incoming government of President José Azcona Hoyo. During 1986, however, there were reports of arbitrary detentions in rural areas of peasant organizers and trade unionists, most of whom were released on bail or without charge. The lack of effective judicial control over arrests and pre-trial detention and the frequently reported use of torture were continuing areas of concern. Amnesty International remained concerned about the failure of the government to take further steps to clarify the whereabouts or fate of prisoners who had "disappeared" under the previous governments of Policarpo Paz García and Roberto Suázo Córdoba, allegedly at the hands of a specialized military intelligence unit. Reports were received in May that irregular forces opposed to the Nicaraguan Government (known as *contras*), which operated from bases in Honduras with the knowledge of the Honduran authorities, had abducted Nicaraguan refugees, including children, from camps in Honduras, often apparently for the purpose of recruitment. Abuses were also reported in refugee camps housing Salvadorian refugees, including harassment and arbitrary detention of refugees by the Honduran army.

On 6 March 30 political prisoners went on indefinite hunger-strike demanding their release. Many had been held for several years without being formally tried and some had not had access to a defence lawyer. Among them were several prisoners on whose behalf Amnesty International had appealed in previous years. Ricardo de Jesús Ramírez and Gregorio Pinto Alvarado had been among a group of 19 people detained in 1984 and accused of belonging to a rural guerrilla group, the *Frente Popular Revolucionario Lorenzo Zelaya* (FPR). Ricardo de Jesús Ramírez and Gregorio Pinto Alvarado maintained that they had been forced to "confess" under torture. Reports of torture were also received in other cases, including that of Gustavo García España who was detained in July 1985 (see *Amnesty International Report 1986*). On 12 March Amnesty International sought assurances that the prisoners on hunger-strike would be given medical care and called for them to be promptly brought to trial or released. All the hunger-strikers were released at the end of March under an amnesty declared by the new President to mark his coming to office on 27 January.

Amnesty International continued to be concerned about reports of detentions without warrant, particularly of members of peasant organizations. In October the organization asked about the legal position of peasant leader Marco Danilo Guardado Nájera, detained on 29 July and held incommunicado for several days in the Fourth Infantry Battalion base in La Ceiba. He had recently been elected treasurer of the *Cooperativa Agroindustrial de la Palma Africana* (COAPALMA), the Agroindustrial African Palm Cooperative, an organization representing some 50 cooperatives of African palm producers in the Bajo Aguán region in northern Honduras. He was accused of sedition and disturbing the peace, and was transferred to prison in Trujillo to await trial. No reply was received to Amnesty International's inquiries on his behalf and the organization was investigating his case.

Another peasant leader detained was Benicio Flores, public relations secretary of the *Central Nacional de Trabajadores del Campo* (CNTC), the National Agricultural Workers' Union. He was arrested on 18 December in Tegucigalpa, by armed agents of the *Dirección Nacional de Investigaciones* (DNI), a plain clothes police unit. He had reportedly been involved in supporting a group of peasant farmers in Morazán, Yoro, in a land dispute. According to reports, the peasants had recovered over 260 acres of land which was also claimed by a local landowner and the army had tried to evict the peasants from the land. On 19 December Amnesty International sought assurances that Benicio Flores would not be ill-treated in custody and urged his immediate release unless he was to be brought before a competent court and charged. It was subsequently reported that he was released on bail on 22 December pending his trial on charges of robbery, usurpation of land, damage and death threats. Amnesty International continued to investigate the case.

A number of reports were received during 1986 of torture of detainees held incommunicado by police and military units. One was peasant leader Ovidio Betancourt Mairena, who was taken violently from his home in Tocoa, Colón, on 3 April by armed men in plain clothes, believed to be members of the DNI or a paramilitary group associated with the security forces. He was held for some hours, during which time he was reportedly blindfolded, beaten and threatened, his body pricked with a sharp instrument and a cord tied around his penis and pulled. He was finally abandoned in the countryside far from his home.

Other detentions took place in October in the context of counter-insurgency operations carried out in the north of Honduras where small guerrilla groups were said to be operating. Large numbers of people were reportedly detained, including human rights workers and trade union officials. On 24 October Amnesty International sought clarification of the situation of a number of these detainees. They included Pedro Alberto Luperón, a teacher and trade union official who also worked for the *Comité para la Defensa de los Derechos Humanos de Honduras* (CODEH), Honduran Committee for the Defence of Human Rights, in Tela; and Germán Aguirre, President of the local committee of CODEH in Tela. Both were released a few days after their detention. However, another man, Hermes Aguilar, who had been detained in Agua Blanca Sur, Yoro, on 16 October, died while in police custody in circumstances which have not been fully clarified by the authorities.

CODEH's national President, Dr Ramón Custodio López, was the victim of a series of attacks in September and October when attempts were made to fire-bomb his office in Tegucigalpa. In recent years CODEH has been an outspoken critic of the human rights performance of successive governments in Honduras. A week before the fire-bomb attacks, CODEH had publicized the existence of what it claimed was a death list containing the names of Dr Custodio and other public figures. According to CODEH, the list was compiled by a secret unit of the armed forces called Battalion 316, which it said acted on the orders of the highest levels of military command.

Reports which appeared in the Honduran press in August suggested operational links had existed in earlier years between units of the Honduran army and Nicaraguan irregular armed forces opposing the Nicaraguan Government based on Honduran territory, known as the *contras*. In an interview with an American journalist a former *contra* confessed to having participated in several killings, including that of student Eduardo Becerra Lanza, who "disappeared" in 1982. He claimed that he had formed part of a paramilitary group attached to a secret unit of the Honduran army known as the *Dirección de Investigaciones Especiales* (DIES). He said that following interrogation by the Honduran army, Eduardo Becerra Lanza and another student, Felix Martínez, were handed over to this group to be killed. The case of Eduardo Becerra Lanza was one of several under investigation by Amnesty International. At the time of his arrest on 1 August 1982 in Tegucigalpa, he was Secretary General of the *Federación de Estudiantes Universitarios de Honduras*, Federation of University Students of Honduras.

Another case of concern to Amnesty International, that of Angel Manfredo Velázquez Rodríguez, was under consideration by the Inter-American Commission on Human Rights (IACHR) of the Organization of American States. Angel Manfredo Velázquez, a student, was detained in Tegucigalpa on 12 September 1981. The IACHR considered that he had "disappeared" after detention and that the government had failed to clarify his fate, and referred the case to the Inter-American Court of Human Rights in April. Similar resolutions were made in the cases of Saúl Godínez Cruz, who "disappeared" in July 1982 and two Costa Rican citizens, Francisco Faíren Garbi and Yolanda Solís, who "disappeared" in Honduras in December 1981. Amnesty International continued to seek an official response to requests for clarification of the fate of Eduardo Lanza, Angel Manfredo Velázquez and a number of other "disappeared" prisoners.

Nicaraguan irregular opposition forces were allegedly responsible for the abduction from a refugee camp in Honduras of 18 Nicaraguan Sumo Indian refugees, many of them in their early teens, on 24 May. According to reports, the refugees were seized from their homes in the Sumo refugee settlement at Tapalwas in southern Honduras by members of the *contra* group the *Fuerza Democrática Nicaragüense* (FDN), Nicaraguan Democratic Force. Amnesty International called on the Honduran authorities to take immediate steps to locate them and to ensure their safety. Twelve of the refugees were later released after the Honduran armed forces established a commission to investigate the incident. One other was reported to have escaped earlier and five could not be traced.

Abuses against refugees in camps close to the border with El Salvador continued to be of concern to Amnesty International. In June two Salvadorian refugees from the Colomoncagua camps were detained by the Honduran army. One, David Palacios, aged 17, was epileptic and suffered from emotional problems. He was reportedly detained on 6 June when he left the camp without permission following an incident with other refugees. Claudia García, who had been suffering from gynaecological problems since the birth of her fourth child a year before, was detained while returning to the camp in an ambulance, after she had had an operation in a Tegucigalpa hospital. On 20 June Amnesty International asked where they were being held and why they had been arrested, and sought assurances that they would be humanely treated while in detention. They were released on 25 June on condition that they left the country.

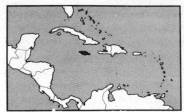

Jamaica

Amnesty International was concerned about the increased use of the death penalty in Jamaica. Fourteen prisoners were executed in 1986, all of them between June and December: this compares with nine executions in 1985 and eight in 1984 and brings to 52 the total number executed since 1980 when executions resumed after a four-year moratorium.

Amnesty International appealed for clemency on behalf of prisoners whose executions were imminent. Among these were Stanford Flowers and Winston Dixon, who were hanged after their third execution warrants were issued in November. They had been convicted in October 1981 of murdering a man in October 1980. The organization expressed concern about reports that new medical evidence put in question whether it had been shown beyond reasonable doubt at their trial that they had caused the death of the victim. In July Amnesty International brought to the attention of the Governor-General the UN Economic and Social Council Resolution 1984/50: Safeguards Guaranteeing Protection of the Rights of Those Facing the Death Penalty, which states that capital punishment may be imposed only when the guilt of the person charged is based upon clear and convincing evidence leaving no room for an alternative explanation of the facts.

In November Amnesty International wrote to the government about Albert Berry, who was reportedly aged only 16 when the murder was committed for which he was sentenced to death in January 1985. If this information is correct, the imposition of the death penalty contravened both Jamaican law and international treaties prohibiting death sentences on people aged under 18 at the time of the crime. Albert Berry had by then spent nearly two years on death row. Amnesty International expressed concern that the question of his age had apparently not been raised at his trial and requested an early review of his case. In his reply in December, the Minister of Justice informed Amnesty International that a review of the case had been set in motion.

There were believed to be over 170 prisoners under sentence of death at the end of 1986.

Mexico

Amnesty International's concerns included reports of political killings, torture, arbitrary arrest of political opponents and the use in evidence of confessions obtained under duress. Amnesty International was also concerned about "disappearances" in previous years which have never been satisfactorily clarified by the authorities. In the course of the year Amnesty International received detailed documents from the Mexican Government in response to its concerns.

On 14 May Amnesty International published *Mexico: Human Rights in Rural Areas — Exchange of Documents with the Mexican Government on Human Rights Violations in Oaxaca and Chiapas.* This included the text of a memorandum submitted on 22 November 1985 to the government of President Miguel de la Madrid Hurtado, and the Mexican Government's reply. The memorandum presented the conclusions of extended research by Amnesty International into human rights violations in the two southeastern states. On 15 May the Mexican Government expressed the view that its replies had not been taken into consideration sufficiently and on 6 October it provided updated information on the cases raised by Amnesty International.

One was that of Elpidio Vázquez Vázquez, killed in Villa de las Rosas, Chiapas, on 9 September 1979. According to an eye-witness who was wounded in the attack, the assailants arrived outside the home of another man, Eleazar Grajales, a local peasant leader, in a municipal truck and deliberately opened fire on him and his companions, killing Elpidio Vázquez. Two people, including the mayor of the town, were said to have been arrested on suspicion of involvement in the killing but later released. According to information provided by the Mexican Government on 6 January and included in Amnesty International's May report, the killing had not been officially reported, no suspects were identified and no investigation undertaken. The new information subsequently provided by the government corrected this; one of the assailants had been convicted and received a one-month prison sentence. The government also stated that the mayor had been charged with concealing the crime but that this charge had later been dropped. Another of the assailants, charged with the murder of Elpidio Vázquez, was never detained, despite an order for his arrest. Amnesty International replied on

31 December asking for more information about this and several other cases.

Amnesty International continued to receive reports of killings, detentions and torture in the states of Chiapas and Oaxaca, the majority in connection with land disputes. Violent evictions from farmland were reported in May in Chiapas. On 12 May eight people were reported killed and nine wounded when state security police entered the community of El Ambar, Jitotal, to evict the inhabitants. Seven other peasants were reported killed on the same day in Francisco Villa, Bochil, when houses were burned and peasants beaten. In some of the incidents, armed civilians were reported to have accompanied state security police. Numerous peasants were reportedly ill-treated during the evictions. Some of the communities affected maintained that they held legal land titles and others were negotiating their claims under an official state land-distribution program. Amnesty International appealed for a full, impartial inquiry into the killings.

On 31 December Amnesty International addressed the state government of Oaxaca about reported killings of Triqui Indians in the San Juan Copala area. Hilario Francisco Hernández was reportedly killed on 26 August, Manuel Martínez García and Juan Francisco Martínez on 8 September and Marcelino de Jesús López, Manuel Vázquez Martínez and Martinicio Martínez on 9 September. Amnesty International had been concerned for several years about reports of human rights violations, including killings, from this region in the context of land disputes. In the last five named cases troops were reported to have accompanied civilian gunmen in perpetrating the killings. Amnesty International called for an impartial investigation and for those responsible to be brought to justice.

Amnesty International adopted as prisoners of conscience seven men detained in Chiapas on 14 May. Some had taken part in a large demonstration by peasant farmers near Cintalapa for a higher price for their produce. After a large number of soldiers and police moved in, the demonstrators withdrew peacefully and, with the agreement of the state government, a delegation was named to go to the state capital to negotiate with officials. Twenty-nine people were arrested on the day of the protest, including the negotiators. Twenty-two were later released, but at the end of 1986 Jorge Enrique Hernández Aguilar, Manuel Hernández Gómez, Germán Jiménez Gómez, Jesús López Constantino, José Jacobo Nazar Morales and Julián Nazar Morales remained in Cerro Hueco prison being tried on charges including conspiracy, riotous assembly and terrorism. All seven later said they had been beaten and threatened to force them to confess to crimes they had not committed. Some of the 22 who were released said they had been forced to incriminate the seven and later withdrew their statements. Amnesty International believed that the seven had been accused of crimes because of their role in supporting peasant organizations.

During 1986 Amnesty International worked on behalf of 26 prisoners of conscience and possible prisoners of conscience in Chiapas, Guerrero, Oaxaca, San Luis Potosí and Veracruz. Zósimo Hernández Ramírez, a bilingual teacher of Nahua Indian origin, was detained in Huistipán, Ilamatlán, Veracruz, in June 1985. He had been an active supporter of peasants, almost all Nahua Indians, who had been involved in disputes with local landowning families over land which they claimed belonged to their community. He was transferred to Jalapa where he claimed he was tortured for six days to try to make him confess to crimes, including murder, of which he was innocent. In July 1985 he was transferred to Huayacocotl prison and committed for trial. Until December 1985 there was a legal dispute over where he should be held, ending with a decision by a state court that he should remain in Huayacocotl. During this time there was no progress in the trial proceedings against him. In April 1986 he was transferred without warning to the prison of Perote and a week later to Pacho Viejo, Coatepec. On 19 May he was sentenced to 18 years' imprisonment for murder, wounding and damage to property, and at the end of 1986 remained in prison awaiting the result of an appeal. Another Nahua Indian teacher whose case concerned Amnesty International was Guadalupe del Angel Antonia. At the time of his detention in May 1984 he was working as a primary school teacher in the community of Huesco, Tampacán, in the Huasteca region of the state of San Luis Potosí. The community had for several years been involved in a dispute with a landowning family over land claimed by the village, and he was active in support of the community. He was sentenced to seven years' imprisonment on charges including kidnapping, breaking and entering and wounding. Amnesty International believed both he and Zósimo Hernández may have been accused of criminal acts because of their non-violent activities in their communities, and continued to investigate their cases.

In May Amnesty International appealed on behalf of five prisoners from Huitzilan de Serdán, Puebla, and urged investigations into killings committed there. Those killed belonged to the *Unión Campesina Independiente* (UCI), Independent Peasant Union, which is affiliated to the *Coordinadora Nacional Plan de Ayala* (CNPA), the National Plan de Ayala Coordinating Body, an umbrella organization of independent peasant organizations. Since February 1984 a rival peasant organization known as *Antorcha Campesina*, Peasant Torch, was alleged to have been responsible for numerous killings in

Huitzilan de Serdán. In many of the incidents reported, state police officers were said to have accompanied *Antorcha Campesina* members. Juan Cabrera Pasión was shot dead in his home on 14 May 1984 in an incident reportedly involving 12 members of *Antorcha Campesina* accompanied by 10 uniformed state police agents. Manuel Peralta Cabañas and his 17-year-old son Martín Peralta Velázquez were killed on 22 April 1984, reportedly by four members of *Antorcha Campesina* accompanied by 12 uniformed state police agents. In both cases, formal depositions were made by eye-witnesses naming the civilians alleged responsible. On 6 October 1986 the Mexican Government sent Amnesty International information on these cases. It stated that inquiries had been opened on the basis of these depositions, but that the police investigation had produced no result in either case. The government also provided information on the five prisoners whose cases Amnesty International had raised. There were serious allegations of torture and of irregularities in the trials of these prisoners, who belonged to a peasant organization opposed to *Antorcha Campesina*. One of them, Martín Melchi Lira, a 23-year-old peasant farmer, had been arrested on 5 June 1985 and was awaiting sentence on charges of murder and robbery. The evidence against him appeared to consist of statements by three other prisoners, who all maintained that they had been tortured to force them to sign statements incriminating themselves and others, including Martín Melchi. The information provided by the government indicated that the charges had been dismissed, and at the end of 1986 Amnesty International was seeking confirmation of his release.

Amnesty International continued to work on the cases of 27 people who "disappeared" after arrest, and took up a further 24 such cases. All these "disappearances" took place between 1972 and 1983, but Amnesty International was concerned that the government had not provided a satisfactory explanation of the fate of the prisoners following their arrests. Many of the "disappearances" took place in the context of police and army intelligence operations against armed opposition organizations in the 1970s. The official information given to relatives in many cases was that the victim had been killed in an armed confrontation with the security forces, had gone into hiding, or had died as a result of conflict between rival guerrilla factions. Víctor Arias de la Cruz and Jorge Carrasco Gutiérrez were arrested in Guadalajara, Jalisco, on 28 February 1977. Neighbours who witnessed the arrest said that federal security police threw tear-gas bombs into the house they were in and the two gave themselves up, unhurt. On 1 March 1977 the Mexico City newspaper *Novedades* reported that they had been detained and had confessed to murder. Since then their families have been unable to ascertain their whereabouts or fate.

The authorities stated that both men escaped after the confrontation, and that Jorge Carrasco subsequently died from injuries received.

In January Mexico ratified the United Nations Convention against Torture and Other Cruel, Inhuman or Degrading Treatment or Punishment. In mid-June the Federal Law to Prevent and Punish Torture came into force. It obliged any authority aware of torture to report it immediately and prescribed up to 10 years' imprisonment for those in public office found guilty of torture. By the end of 1986 Amnesty International had received no information about trials or convictions under the law. Nevertheless, it continued to receive reports of torture of detainees. Juan Nicolás Hernández, a peasant farmer and leader of the *Organización Independiente de Pueblos Unidos de las Huastecas*, Independent Organization of the United Peoples of the Huastecas, a regional peasant organization, was arrested on 16 June in Huejutla, Hidalgo. He was reportedly taken into custody by armed men in plain clothes who identified themselves as federal judicial police officers, and later transferred to an army barracks. There he was reportedly left naked in a damp room for almost three days, then tortured while being interrogated; according to reports he was repeatedly beaten and kicked, liquid was forced up his nostrils, and when he lost consciousness, bottles of what he took to be urine were poured over his head. After several days of this treatment Juan Nicolás Hernández signed some documents, reportedly without knowing what they contained. On about 16 July he was handed over to the state judicial police. While in their custody his physical condition deteriorated sharply and he had an emergency operation in the civilian hospital. His relatives were only informed of his whereabouts in the last week of July. He was subsequently told that he was free to return home as soon as he was well enough to do so.

Amnesty International submitted information on Mexico to the UN Working Group on Enforced or Involuntary Disappearances and in August made an oral statement to this body.

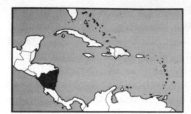

Nicaragua

Amnesty International was concerned about a pattern of short-term arrests of supporters of opposition parties and trade unions, some of whom the organization believed may have been prisoners of conscience. Such detentions occurred particularly in rural areas where irregular military forces opposed to the government known as the *contras* were active. Amnesty International also remained concerned about conditions of pre-trial custody for security-related detainees, who were often subjected to long periods of incommunicado detention before being released or allowed access to their families and lawyers. A number of reports alleging ill-treatment of detainees during pre-trial detention were received. Delays in the completion of interrogation and in the indictment or release of prisoners, particularly in rural areas, were reported. Restrictions on the right to fair trial arising from the use of self-incriminating evidence obtained under duress while prisoners were held incommunicado and summary trial procedures under the state of emergency also continued to be of concern.

Frequent reports of deliberate killings, abductions and torture of non-combatant civilians by the *contras* continued to be received. Amnesty International remained concerned that military assistance to these forces from the United States Government may have contributed directly to such practices, and twice asked that government what measures were being taken to ensure this was not the case.

In February Amnesty International published its report *Nicaragua: The Human Rights Record*, providing a summary of the organization's concerns since the overthrow of the government of Anastasio Somoza Debayle in July 1979. Many of the human rights violations of concern to Amnesty International had been reported in the context of armed conflict in remote rural areas, and of measures throughout the country to detect and punish people assisting the armed opposition forces. Most political prisoners detained since the imposition of the state of emergency in March 1982 were charged with involvement with armed opposition groups. The report expressed concern that the extraordinary powers accorded under the state of emergency to the *Dirección General de Seguridad del Estado* (DGSE), the State Security Service, the curtailment of *habeas corpus* in political cases, and the lack of access to prisoners in pre-trial detention centres, had facilitated the arbitrary detention and harassment of opposition party and trade union members. The report also criticized the system of special courts, *Tribunales Populares Anti-Somocistas*, established in April 1983 to deal with political cases under the Public Order Law, for failing to provide defendants with guarantees of a fair and impartial trial. The report noted that most prisoners believed to be prisoners of conscience were released before their cases came to trial or pardoned not long after their conviction by these courts. The organization received no response from the government to the concerns published in the report, which had been communicated in a letter to President Daniel Ortega before publication.

Some of the prisoners whose cases were discussed in the report were convicted or released in 1986. Julio Ramón Montes Martínez, a leader of the *Partido Social Cristiano* (PSC), Social Christian Party, who was arrested on 20 November 1984, was sentenced in January 1986 to nine years' imprisonment for counter-revolutionary activity, including the distribution of party literature attacking military conscription laws. Amnesty International made inquiries on his behalf as a possible prisoner of conscience. Among those released was journalist Luis Mora Sánchez, who had been detained on 15 June 1985 with Mauricio Membreno Gaitán, an official of the *Partido Social Demócrata*, Social Democratic Party, and charged with inciting a riot, following a demonstration during which a violent attack was alleged to have been made on police. Luis Mora was released in February and left the country in March. Mauricio Membreno Gaitán was sentenced to 11 years' imprisonment in February, reduced on appeal to eight years. Amnesty International believed there were doubts about the evidence of his participation in the violent incidents, and continued to investigate his case.

In September the Minister of the Interior stated that 3,910 prisoners were being held for offences committed under the Somoza government and for counter-revolutionary activities committed since its overthrow. At a news conference in July the Minister had put the number of prisoners in the first category (chiefly members of the Somoza National Guard) at 2,157, and in the second category at 1,802, of whom 777 had been convicted and 1,025 were awaiting trial. In June the National Assembly approved pardons for 308 prisoners serving sentences. Non-governmental sources reported an increase in the number of security related indictments during 1986, with the majority of detentions occurring in rural areas in which anti-government forces were active.

Many of those detained were members of legal opposition parties or party-affiliated trades unions, in particular the PSC, and the *Partido Liberal Independiente* (PLI), Independent Liberal Party. On 3 October Amnesty International informed the government of its concern about the continued detention of 16 members of the PLI reportedly arrested in May in the province of Nueva Segovia — among them Pedro Joaquín Ponce, José Castellón Rocha and Florinda Paniagua, all local party leaders — and about the arrest on 3 September of PLI Vice-President Bayardo Guzmán Martínez in Managua. It also expressed concern about the arrest on 29 August of Agustín Sánchez Narvaez, a leader of the *Central de Trabajadores de Nicaragua* (CTN), Nicaraguan Workers Confederation. The Foreign Ministry replied on 25 October that Bayardo Guzmán and Agustín Sánchez had been detained under the Public Order Law, and were released on 16 and 19 September respectively. No information was provided about the 16 PLI prisoners detained in May but a party source later informed Amnesty International that negotiations with the government had secured the release in July or August of Pedro Joaquín Ponce, Florinda Paniagua, and other local PLI leaders.

Amnesty International wrote in September to the Ministry of the Interior about the legal position of Dr Hugo Hernández Ochomogo, a doctor from Matíguas, Matagalpa, who was arrested by the DGSE on 20 February and held for trial. There were reports that he had been accused of giving medical assistance to wounded *contras* and of participating in fund-raising meetings on behalf of the *contras*. He denied both charges. No response was received to the letter and Amnesty International continued to investigate his case.

A number of reports and testimonies by released prisoners were received alleging ill-treatment of detainees held for interrogation by the DGSE, particularly in the major detention facility of El Chipote, in Managua. There were frequent complaints that detainees had been held for several days with very little or no food, forced to endure solitary confinement in cramped conditions without adequate lighting or ventilation, and subjected to treatment intended to disorient and weaken resistance, including sleep deprivation. Reports were also received of threats towards detainees or members of their families. After his release in February, Luis Mora Sánchez told journalists in Costa Rica that he had been kept handcuffed to the wall, naked and without food or drink for four days after his arrest on 29 April 1984. He also claimed to have been beaten and subjected to a mock execution. Mauricio Membreno Gaitán was also reported to have been kept handcuffed and fettered for four days after his arrest on 15 June 1985. Information received during 1986 reinforced the concern expressed in Amnesty International's February report about the treatment of detainees and the recommendations contained in that report that the authorities should impartially investigate all allegations of ill-treatment and introduce effective controls on the powers of arrest and detention exercised by the security police.

Amnesty International remained concerned about the death in

custody of Salomón Tellería Salinas, a member of the Social Christian Party from León. He was detained by DGSE officers on 6 December 1985 and taken to a detention centre in León known as Quinta Ye. He was reportedly moved from there to hospital on 12 February, where he died two days later. It was reported that while he was held in Quinta Ye, his detention was repeatedly denied, and that when a relative visited him in hospital a day before his death, his body was covered with bruises and other apparent signs of ill-treatment. In August Amnesty International wrote to the *Comisión Nacional de Promoción y Protección de los Derechos Humanos* (CNPPDH), the National Commission for the Promotion and Protection of Human Rights, a government supported body, having received reports that it had investigated the case. Amnesty International received no reply from the CNPPDH, and at the end of 1986 had received no further information as to whether an official inquiry had been opened into the case.

Reports of deliberate killings and summary executions of civilians, torture and kidnappings by the *contra* were received throughout 1986. The victims of killings and abductions included foreign volunteers working in government health and development projects in rural areas. In February and October Amnesty International wrote to the US Secretary of State, expressing concern at a pattern of such abuses by irregular forces under the political leadership of the *Unidad Nicaragüense Opositora* (UNO), the United Nicaraguan Opposition, which had in previous years received military assistance and training from agencies of the US Government. In June the US Congress voted to renew military assistance programs to these forces, including training, and to relax restrictions imposed by Congress in 1984 on the involvement in such programs of the Central Intelligence Agency (CIA). In its October letter to the Secretary of State, Amnesty International referred to a military manual, produced in 1983 by the CIA and distributed to the *Fuerza Democrática Nicaragüense* (FDN), Nicaraguan Democratic Force, which proposed the public "neutralization" of civilian local government officials, police and military personnel. Cases cited in the letter included the alleged torture and execution of Roman Catholic catechist Donato Mendoza by FDN forces on 25 March near Siuna, in the province of Northern Zelaya, and the killing of four Nicaraguan relief workers employed by the Evangelical Committee for Aid to Development (CEPAD) on 31 July in San José de Mula, Matagalpa province. The health clinic in which they worked was reportedly ransacked. The bodies of the four men were discovered, allegedly mutilated, by a search party a day after the attack on the clinic. Amnesty International asked the Secretary of State for information about the measures taken to ensure that the US Government assistance to these forces did not contribute to human rights abuses, including torture and summary executions. No reply had been received to either letter by the end of 1986.

Paraguay

Amnesty International's concerns included numerous arbitrary arrests and short-term detentions of students, journalists, peasants, trade unionists and opposition party activists, held in incommunicado detention under the state of siege. The organization was also concerned about judicial irregularities in the trials of political prisoners and the arrest and trial of several people under Law 209, which has frequently been used to prosecute people for the peaceful expression of their beliefs. A further concern was the torture and ill-treatment of political detainees and criminal suspects, and the death of a number of people while in the custody of security forces, who may have been the victims of extrajudicial execution.

During 1986 Amnesty International launched appeals on behalf of more than 150 individuals, the majority of whom were prisoners of conscience. Many were arrested during April and May in connection with a series of unprecedented anti-government demonstrations organized by trade unions, opposition parties and student organizations. Several peaceful protests were violently dispersed by the police, sometimes accompanied by armed civilians believed to be members of the *Guardia Urbana* (a militia force of the ruling Colorado Party).

Amnesty International received reports of numerous short-term arrests; the ill-treatment of detainees was common. On 27 April several people, including Paraguayan and foreign journalists, were reportedly beaten and then detained by police during a demonstration organized by the opposition *Partido Liberal Radical Auténtico* (PLRA), Authentic Liberal Radical Party. Police using tear gas, clubs and electric cattle prods dispersed approximately 1,000 members of the PLRA who were attempting to march peacefully to the Metropolitan Cathedral in support of the Roman Catholic church's call for "a national dialogue". Amnesty International issued urgent appeals on behalf of José Luís Simón, a Paraguayan journalist who was reportedly beaten by police with clubs during his arrest and then transferred to the *Departamento de Investigaciones de la Policía* (DIPC), Police Investigations Department, in Asunción, where he was held in incommunicado detention until his release without charge on 29 April. Also arrested were two journalists from the Federal Republic of Germany (FRG) and the press secretary of the FRG Embassy in Asunción who were held for several hours in the DIPC and alleged in a formal complaint that they had been ill-treated by the police. The state of siege in force in Asunción almost continuously since President Stroessner came to power in 1954 was renewed by the government every 90 days. Article 79 of the Constitution, which regulates the state of siege, was frequently invoked by the authorities to arrest political opponents "by order of the President" and to hold them for indefinite periods. Denial of the right to a fair trial and due process of law under state of siege powers of detention has been a long-standing Amnesty International concern.

In May Amnesty International appealed on behalf of Marcelino Corazón Medina, President of the *Comité de Coordinación de Productores Agrícolas*, Coordinating Committee for Agricultural Producers, who was arrested when a peaceful International Labour Day march organized by an independent trade union movement was violently broken up by police and armed civilians. He was reportedly beaten for several minutes by civilians armed with clubs before being arrested by police and taken to the DIPC, where he was held in incommunicado detention under Article 79 of the Constitution. He was transferred to the *Guardia de Seguridad*, a military barracks on the outskirts of Asunción, on 13 May and released without charge on 6 June.

Amnesty International also interceded on behalf of Alejandro Stumpfs, detained on 6 October and held in incommunicado detention under Article 79 of the Constitution in the *Guardia de Seguridad* until his release on 19 December. Alejandro Stumpfs is the second Vice-President of the *Movimiento Popular Colorado* (MOPOCO), the dissident wing of the ruling Colorado Party. He has been arrested several times in the past, and subjected to internal banishment.

Amnesty International continued to express its concern that legal proceedings against political detainees did not conform to internationally accepted standards for fair trials. Of particular concern was the undue delay in bringing detainees to trial.

In January Amnesty International sent a delegate to Paraguay to investigate reports of irregularities in the trial of Remigio Gimenez Gamarra, who had been on hunger-strike since 13 December 1985 to protest against his prolonged detention (see *Amnesty International*

Report 1986). He had been arrested in December 1978 and held in various detention centres under Article 79 of the Constitution until 1981, when he was formally charged with several offences allegedly committed between 1958 and 1960, including murder, armed robbery and being a leader of a subversive clandestine organization. Amnesty International's delegate met the criminal court judge in charge of the case and the President of the Supreme Court of Justice, explaining the organization's concerns in the trial including the extreme delay in judicial proceedings. Although, according to the Code of Criminal Procedures, the investigative stage of a trial should be completed within two months, in the case of Remigio Gimenez it lasted over seven years. Remigio Gimenez suspended his hunger-strike on 11 February; after receiving assurances from the authorities that legal proceedings would be expedited. In December 1986 he was sentenced to 30 years' imprisonment.

During the second half of 1986 there was a marked increase in the number of people arrested and charged under anti-subversive legislation, particularly Law 209 (In Defence of Public Peace and Liberty of Persons). Although by the end of the year the majority of those prosecuted under Law 209 had been granted conditional releases, at least two people considered by Amnesty International to be prisoners of conscience remained in prison while trial proceedings continued. One, Miguel Abdón Saguier, a lawyer and prominent member of the PLRA, was arrested on 13 September in the town of Ypacarai and transferred to Tacumbú National Prison, in Asunción. Dr Saguier was charged under Law 209 with sedition. At the trial the Prosecutor quoted remarks made by Dr Saguier about the right of people to rebel against oppression. Despite the court ruling that he should be in *libre comunicación* (free communication) in the prison, Dr Saguier was held in solitary confinement and visits were severely restricted.

Amnesty International also called for the immediate and unconditional release of Oscar Acosta, a journalist with *Radio Ñandutí*, who was arrested on 21 December after attending a church service for political prisoners. He was held in incommunicado detention in the DIPC and then transferred to Tacumbú National Prison and charged under Law 209. *Radio Ñandutí* is an independent broadcasting station and as a result of its outspoken journalism, its owner and staff have frequently suffered harassment and arbitrary arrest.

In October Amnesty International organized appeals on behalf of two trade union activists, Benjamín Livieres and Maria Herminia Feliciangeli, who were arrested without warrant in Asunción by armed plainclothes police. After several days in unacknowledged detention in the DIPC, they were transferred to regular prisons and formally charged under Law 209. Although the basis for the charges was not clear, Amnesty International believed that their arrest may have been related to their trade union activities in the newly formed *Agrupación Independiente de Trabajadores*, Independent Workers' Movement, which had reportedly been responsible for publicizing the deficient working conditions of shop workers in Asunción. Maria Herminia Feliciangeli and Benjamín Livieres were conditionally released on 17 and 30 December respectively.

Several of the public demonstrations which took place in 1986 were organized by the *Asociación de Médicos, Enfermeras y Empleados del Hospital de Clínicas* (AMEEHC), Doctors, Nurses and Staff Association of the Clínicas Hospital, the main public hospital in Asunción, in support of their demand for higher wages. The peaceful marches and meetings organized by the AMEEHC were often violently broken up by the police. Many of the hospital staff were detained for short periods and several staff representatives on the AMEEHC faced prosecution for alleged violation of Law 209. On 29 November Carlos Filizzola, President of the Clínicas Doctors' Association, was arrested in Asunción. After several days in incommunicado detention in police headquarters he was transferred to Tacumbú National Prison and charged with violation of Law 209. Dr Filizzola had previously been arrested on 2 May and held under the state of siege provisions until his release on 23 May, after the intervention on his behalf of the Archbishop of Asunción. More arrests followed in December. Among those detained were Elsa Mereles, President of the Clínicas Nurses' Association, and Héctor Lacognata, President of the *Central de Estudiantes de Medicina*, the medical students' union attached to the Clínicas Hospital. Although all the Clínicas staff were conditionally released by the end of 1986, legal proceedings against them had not been formally closed.

Amnesty International continued to receive reports of the torture of both political prisoners and criminal suspects in the custody of security forces. Many of the victims were peasants involved in land disputes who, during 1986, were increasingly subject to arbitrary arrest, ill-treatment or death.

In August Amnesty International appealed to the government to initiate an independent inquiry into the deaths of Francisco Martínez and Aurelio Silvero. The two were allegedly shot and killed by soldiers from the military base at Juan E. O'Leary, Alto Paraná Department, during an attempt to evict a group of 30 families from land they had occupied in Barrero 6, Alto Paraná Department. Later in the month a joint forces operation involving 300 military and police personnel returned to the community with a judicial eviction order. According to reports about 20 men were detained during the eviction.

They were reportedly beaten by members of the security forces in the presence of their families before being taken to a temporary military camp established on the disputed land. The detainees were tied to trees and beaten with clubs and sticks several times a day; from time to time water or dirt was thrown over them. While several of the peasants were released the following day, five remained tied to trees for at least four days before being transferred to Tacumbú National Prison and charged with trespass, land invasion, cattle theft and issuing death threats. Amnesty International expressed its concern about reports of torture and its belief that peasants involved in land disputes appeared to be denied the full protection of the law. Legal proceedings resulted in all five being released by November and the charges against them were reportedly dropped.

In July Amnesty International submitted information on its concerns in Paraguay to the UN under the confidential procedure for reviewing human rights violations (the so-called "1503 Procedure").

Peru

Amnesty International's concerns included the detention of prisoners of conscience on false charges of terrorism; long delays in trials of political detainees; evidence of torture and ill-treatment; and "disappearances" and extrajudicial executions by police, military and civil defence forces. There was a massacre of more than 150 prisoners following the quelling of revolts in three Lima area prisons on 18 and 19 June; some of the survivors were tortured; and evidence emerged that up to 60 other prisoners who were alleged by authorities to have died were secretly taken into the custody of the navy.

Members of the *Sendero Luminoso*, Shining Path, guerrilla group continued to carry out execution-style killings of captives in the emergency zones, and, for the first time, in Puno and Cusco departments (which were not under a state of emergency). Those killed included members of rural development teams and health workers, apparently solely for having cooperated with the government. Amnesty International condemns the killing of captives whether by governments or opposition groups.

Since 1981 all political prisoners, including prisoners of conscience, have been charged with terrorism. Most women political prisoners were held in the Chorrillos district of Lima, and in Lima's port of Callao. Men were held in Lurigancho Prison on Lima's outskirts, and in the island prison of El Frontón. Most Shining Path supporters were held in El Frontón, and in Lurigancho's Industrial Pavilion. Most of the other prisoners charged with terrorism were associated with legal opposition parties, labour organizations and peasant communities affiliated to the *Izquierda Unida* (IU), United Left coalition, and were held in Lurigancho's Pavilion 11B.

New legislation in May — Decree 24499 — required prisoners held on terrorism charges to be moved to a new top-security prison in Lima's Canto Grande area, and then many were to be dispersed to provincial prisons.

At the time of the prison revolts Lurigancho's Industrial Pavilion held 124 political prisoners, El Frontón's Blue Pavilion between 154 and 180, and Callao Women's Prison, "Santa Barbara" 72. On 18 June in coordinated actions prisoners in the three prisons took hostages and demanded protection from what they called an armed forces' plan of "genocide": they claimed the impending transfers to Canto Grande and provincial jails were part of a plot to isolate and kill them without witnesses. The revolts were over within 36 hours.

At "Santa Barbara", forces under air force command overpowered the prisoners, killing two. At Lurigancho's Industrial Pavilion, all 124 prisoners were killed, with more than 100 shot in the head by Republican Guards, soldiers and masked officers after they had surrendered; the killings were overseen by an army general.

On El Frontón, prisoners using firearms captured from their hostages killed three marines and wounded 20, while one hostage died in unknown circumstances. In the course of a 20-hour naval assault the cell block was partially demolished and many prisoners. died. Of at least 154 prisoners present, 35 were acknowledged to have survived. The authorities said the rest were buried under the ruins of the Blue Pavilion, and that the full death toll would be made known after the rubble was cleared. Naval forces subsequently prohibited access to the site, however, and by the end of 1986 no further official information had been made public on the identity of the dead and the missing, or even their number. The bodies of four prisoners were found by relatives in a Lima cemetery but the whereabouts of the others remained unknown.

Amnesty International later found evidence that up to 90 prisoners had surrendered at the Blue Pavilion on 19 June; that some were interrogated under torture and summarily executed on the island, while between 30 and 60 others were secretly removed from the island to the Callao navy base; and that marines had demolished the building after resistance had ceased. On 24 June Amnesty International urged the government to account for all the prisoners involved; to ensure the comprehensive investigation of any deaths; and to ensure that those responsible for the torture or murder of prisoners after surrender were prosecuted.

Government spokesmen stated that the bodies of the dead would be returned to their families, that the incidents would be investigated, and that abuses committed would be punished. However, bodies were not released to families but buried by the armed forces without notifying relatives and Decree 006-86-JUS of 19 June designated the prisons as "restricted military zones" closed to civilians. Although lower court judges sought to investigate the incidents the Supreme Court·ruled in August that investigations could be made only by the military courts.

On 24 June President García denounced the "annihilation" of prisoners after surrender at Lurigancho, and pledged to arrest and try those responsible. Some 45 Republican Guards were later transferred to Canto Grande pending a military court hearing. In November the highest military court, the *Consejo Supremo de Justicia Militar*, Supreme Council of Military Justice, dropped charges and ordered the release of all but the senior police officers involved. Amnesty International had no information on investigations into the incidents at El Frontón and "Santa Barbara".

An Amnesty International delegate went to Peru 10 days after the revolts to initiate investigations and make arrangements for a subsequent mission. A delegation visited Peru from 9 to 23 August, pursuing the prison incidents and other Amnesty International concerns. The delegation met government officials and members of the judiciary, the Attorney General's office and the General Staff of the Armed Forces Joint Command. Although unable to visit El Frontón, the delegates visited the new Canto Grande prison and had separate, private interviews with survivors from "Santa Barbara" and El Frontón prisons. The delegation also visited the departments of Ayacucho and Puno.

Amnesty International repeatedly addressed itself to the government over the prison incidents during 1986, stressing the organization's concern over the fate of the missing El Frontón prisoners, but their fate remained unknown.

In June 1986 an estimated 900 prisoners had been charged with terrorism, with some 500 of them in Lima area prisons. By the end of the year there were about 44 in Lurigancho's Pavilion 11B, many of them believed to be prisoners of conscience, while some 70 women and 90 men were held in Canto Grande prison.

Amnesty International worked on behalf of 46 individuals it

believed to be prisoners of conscience, or probable prisoners of conscience. They included students, trade unionists, peasant farmers and human rights workers. Some were released during 1986 after more than three years' imprisonment, when charges were dismissed. They included 11 peasant farmers detained in Tayacaja, Huancavelica in 1983 who were released in February 1986. Twelve others, detained in Cajabamba, Cajamarca in November 1982, were released in December 1986. Adopted prisoner of conscience José Pablo Aranda, also from Cajabamba, was among the prisoners killed in the June prison revolts.

Amnesty International continued to receive reports of widespread "disappearances", torture and extrajudicial executions in areas under states of emergency and military administration. Amnesty International called for inquiries into 16 cases of apparent extrajudicial execution in the Ayacucho region. Among the victims was Mamerto Huamani Chillcce, a municipal councillor in Huancapi, Victor Fajardo province. He was seized by troops on 27 April, beaten and dragged through the community behind a horse. His dumped body was found on 9 May. Victor Pariona Palomino and Alejandro Echaccaya were detained by troops from the Huancapi barracks on 28 April, and subsequently found dead, their bodies burned. Although civilian prosecutors investigated the cases, they were not empowered to question or charge military personnel, and the military apparently took no action against those responsible. Victims of "disappearance" included teachers and students at Ayacucho's university. Some of the "disappeared" whose cases were raised by Amnesty International and Ayacucho civilian authorities were released after more than two months in secret detention.

The Amnesty International delegation that visited Ayacucho in August met members of the judiciary and the public prosecutor's office, as well as the head of the political-military command. In the cities of Ayacucho and Huanta Amnesty International received scores of testimonies from witnesses of extrajudicial executions, torture, and arrests followed by "disappearance". Amnesty International raised some recent "disappearances" — where prisoners had been seen in custody at "Los Cabitos" command headquarters — with the Minister of Justice on 16 August.

On 5 September Amnesty International urged President García to intervene in the Ayacucho emergency zone. The organization stressed that judges and prosecutors had said that they had no access to prisoners in military establishments; that the military routinely and falsely denied that any prisoners were in detention; that the remedy of *habeas corpus* did not in practice exist; and that the judiciary's role in the protection of detainees had been reduced to forwarding written requests for information to the military command.

Amnesty International also expressed concern that in 1986 "disappearances" had been reported in new areas, with a series reported in Pasco department shortly after it was placed under a political-military command on 19 June. One victim was Teófilo Rimac Capcha, peasant community and United Left leader in the department, who was detained by an army patrol on 23 June and taken to the Carmen Chico army base near Cerro de Pasco. Several prisoners released in July testified to having seen him at the base and said he had been severely beaten. After widespread publicity an official communique acknowledged that Rimac Capcha had been in detention at Carmen Chico but said that he had "escaped". Amnesty International called for an independent inquiry.

Frequent reports were received of extrajudicial executions by government forces in apparent reprisal for guerrilla assaults on isolated communities. In one case, described by witnesses to Amnesty International delegates visiting Puno, seven agronomists working on state-run cooperatives were killed by Shining Path members on 18 June outside the town of Macarí. On 22 June army counter-insurgency forces raided Macarí. Tomás Quispe Urquizo — whose house was destroyed by troops — his wife, his children and Demetrio Quispe "disappeared" after arrest.

Amnesty International welcomed the efforts of the civilian judiciary and public prosecutors to document and investigate reports of "disappearance". The organization received a list prepared by the Ayacucho departmental public prosecutor of 172 cases of "disappeared detainees", 92 of which were unresolved, reported between 17 January and 4 December 1986 in that department. Amnesty International received information on 110 cases during 1986 which to its knowledge remained unresolved. It had received reports of approximately 1,700 unresolved "disappearances" since January 1983.

In several highly publicized cases in 1985 the Supreme Court awarded jurisdiction to the ordinary courts to try police and military personnel accused of mass killings (see *Amnesty International Report 1986*). However, rulings in 1986 supported military contentions that alleged human rights abuses could only be tried by military courts, on the grounds that they were carried out in the line of duty. In practice, to the knowledge of Amnesty International, military court investigations have rarely led to the trial and punishment of police and military personnel for offences related to counter-insurgency or anti-subversive measures. However, a draft law approved by the Senate on 11 December would exclude from military jurisdiction crimes "not related to service and, particularly, genocide, torture, secret arrest, forcible disappearance of persons". The draft law introduced a definition of forcible disappearance and secret arrest, to be punished by up to 25 years' imprisonment. The draft law was to be further considered in April 1987.

A National Council on Human Rights under the auspices of the Ministry of Justice was created on 6 September by presidential decree, bringing together representatives of key ministries, the Roman Catholic church and independent human rights organizations. The Peace Commission, which had been set up to review human rights observance and seek a peaceful end to political violence, was formally dissolved in September. Its members had resigned in late June after the prison incidents.

Amnesty International submitted information on its concerns in Peru to the relevant bodies of the UN and the Organization of American States.

Suriname

Amnesty International was concerned about reports that civilians had been killed by the army in circumstances suggesting that they may have been extrajudicially executed. The killings followed the outbreak of armed opposition to the government in July.

In July forces led by Ronny Brunswijk, a former army sergeant, began an armed campaign against the military government of Lieutenant Colonel Desi Bouterse, attacking a number of military targets and reportedly taking over parts of the country. The rebel forces operated mainly in eastern Suriname, an area populated by the ethnic group known as Bush Negroes, many of whom reportedly supported the rebel forces. The government imposed a state of emergency in this area on 1 December.

On 8 December Amnesty International expressed concern to the government about reports that between 13 and 18 unarmed civilians from the Bush Negro village of Moengotapoe in eastern Suriname had been killed by the Suriname army at the end of November. They were said to be mainly women and children and their bodies were said to have been riddled with bullets when they were found shortly after the army had left the village. In mid-December Amnesty

International received unconfirmed reports that at least 250 unarmed Bush Negroes had been killed by the army since July. It was alleged that government forces had attacked this group in reprisal for its support for Ronny Brunswijk's activities. In December government sources admitted that some civilians had been killed but denied that these were extrajudicial executions, stating that those killed were either involved in the fighting between the army and rebel forces, or were caught in cross-fire after having been warned to leave the area. Amnesty International was still investigating the killings at the end of 1986. By this time, several thousand Bush Negroes and members of other ethnic groups had fled from their homes in eastern Suriname and had temporarily settled in refugee camps in French Guiana.

More than a hundred people were reported to be detained in military prisons in or near the capital, Paramaribo, at the end of 1986 and Amnesty International was investigating reports that some had been tortured.

Amnesty International drew the attention of the UN Special Rapporteur on summary or arbitrary executions to the Moengotapoe killings.

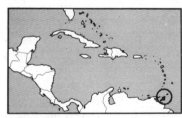

Trinidad and Tobago

Amnesty International continued to be concerned that approximately 25 prisoners were under sentence of death in Trinidad and that, in two cases, death sentences had been upheld despite evidence which cast doubt on the defendant's guilt. Amnesty International continued to monitor the cases of several prisoners under sentence of death who had exhausted all their legal appeals. No executions have been carried out since 1979.

The case of Kitson Branche, who was convicted in November 1972 of murdering a man in 1970, was the subject of appeals in Amnesty International's 25th anniversary campaign. Kitson Branche had spent 14 years on death row. New evidence in the form of an affidavit from a British pathologist was submitted to the Judicial Committee of the Privy Council in the United Kingdom in 1980. This cast doubt on the cause and time of the death of the victim, and suggested that he might have died of natural causes rather than strangulation. The Judicial Committee of the Privy Council refused to consider the new evidence on the grounds that it should have been presented at the time of the trial. There had been no further developments in Kitson Branche's case by the end of 1986.

Amnesty International also urged the authorities to grant clemency to Lalchan Nanan, who was convicted in 1977 of the murder of his wife and sentenced to death. He had exhausted all available legal appeals against his death sentence. In his appeal it was argued that the verdict of the jury which convicted him had not been unanimous, as required by the laws of Trinidad and Tobago for a conviction for murder. After the trial the foreman of the jury had informed the Registrar of the Supreme Court that he had misunderstood the word "unanimous", believing it to mean "majority". He reported that the jury had in fact been divided eight to four in their verdict. The Judicial Committee of the Privy Council did not accept this as grounds for granting Lalchan Nanan's appeal, which they rejected on 22 May 1986.

Amnesty International learned that Calvin Jeremy had his death sentence commuted to life imprisonment on 25 December 1985. Amnesty International had appealed for clemency on his behalf in June 1985.

The decision on the appeal in the case of Andy Thomas and Kirkland Paul, two other prisoners under sentence of death, was still pending at the end of 1986. Their lawyer's motion challenged the constitutionality of carrying out executions after so long a delay. Both men had been on death row since 1975 (see *Amnesty International Report 1986*).

United States of America

The death penalty continued to be Amnesty International's main concern. Eighteen prisoners were executed during the year, bringing to 68 the number executed since the death penalty was re-instated in the 1970s. A record 1,838 prisoners were on death row as of 20 December. Amnesty International also investigated a number of criminal trials in which it was alleged that the prosecutions were politically motivated, and there were complaints of ill-treatment of prisoners.

Ten of .the 18 executions during 1986 were in Texas. The others took place in Florida, Alabama, Georgia, North Carolina, South Carolina and Virginia. Amnesty International had appealed for clemency in every case where it learned that an execution was imminent.

James Terry Roach was executed by electrocution in South Carolina on 10 January for two murders committed when he was 17 and thus still a minor. He was sentenced to death despite a finding by the trial judge that he had acted under the domination of an older man (who was also executed), and was mentally retarded. A few weeks before the execution a doctor found that James Roach exhibited signs of a hereditary neurological illness, which his lawyer claimed cast doubt on his mental competence to be executed and might also have affected him at the time of the crime. However, an appeal on this and on grounds of his youth was turned down by the US Supreme Court. The state governor refused to grant clemency or a stay of execution pending the outcome of a complaint to the Inter-American Commission on Human Rights (see *Amnesty International Report 1986*). A decision by the Commission was still pending at the end of 1986.

A second juvenile offender, Jay Pinkerton, was executed in May 1986 in Texas. At least 32 other juvenile offenders were under sentence of death in 15 states at the end of the year.

On 4 June Amnesty International wrote to the Governor of Connecticut — one of only nine US states to prohibit death sentences on people under 18 at the time of the crime — expressing concern about a bill which would remove this restriction. The Governor replied that he had vetoed the bill.

David Funchess, a Vietnam War veteran convicted of killing two people during a robbery, was executed by electrocution in Florida on 22 April — despite evidence, which came to light only years after his 1975 conviction, that he was suffering from a severe mental disorder at the time of the offence. His trial lawyer had not been aware of his condition (Post-Traumatic Stress Disorder), the full extent of which was not revealed until his appeal lawyers interviewed his family and friends for the first time about his post-Vietnam War mental state. They testified that he had returned from Vietnam addicted to heroin, suffering from frequent "flashbacks" and nightmares and, among other things, had taken to sleeping in cars or in foxholes he had dug under the house. Appeals by his lawyers were denied.

Jerome Bowden, a mentally retarded black man, was executed by electrocution in Georgia on 24 June 1986 for the murder of a white woman 10 years earlier during a robbery. His execution came a day after a state-hired psychologist had conducted a three-hour intelligence test on him in prison and had found that his mental age of 12 was not low enough for him to be spared electrocution. Defence lawyers had no opportunity to challenge the findings. Jerome Bowden was convicted partly on the evidence of his own alleged confession and partly on the testimony of a co-defendant. It was not established which of the two had been the actual killer. The co-defendant was sentenced to life imprisonment at a separate trial.

On 19 September Amnesty International wrote to 12 US Senators about an amendment to a federal bill providing the death penalty for certain drug related offences, which had been passed by the House of Representatives. Amnesty International urged the Senate not to support the amendment, on the grounds that this would conflict with international human rights standards. The Senate subsequently voted against the death penalty provision in the bill.

In December Amnesty International wrote to Governor Anaya of New Mexico welcoming his commutation of the death sentences on the five prisoners on death row in the state on 28 November.

The US Supreme Court made a number of important rulings on the death penalty during 1986. In May the Court upheld the practice in most US death penalty states of excluding committed opponents of the death penalty from serving as jurors in capital trials. The ruling reversed a decision by a federal appeals court which had held that this practice was unconstitutional and that, in future, such people could be excluded only from the penalty phase of a capital trial.

In June, in the case of Florida prisoner Alvin Ford, the Supreme Court ruled for the first time that the constitution prohibited the execution of prisoners found to be insane. The ruling also held that Florida's statutory procedure for determining the mental competency of a condemned prisoner (which gave the final decision to the state governor) was inadequate. Alvin Ford remained on death row pending a re-evaluation of the Florida procedures.

In July the Supreme Court agreed to hear an appeal in a Georgia case in which it was alleged that the application of the death penalty there was discriminatory on grounds of race. The appeal, brought on behalf of black prisoner Warren McCleskey, cited a study which showed that killers of whites, especially black killers, were significantly more likely to receive death sentences than killers of blacks. Condemned prisoners in several states subsequently received stays of execution pending the ruling, which had not been given by the end of 1986.

The trial of 11 church workers belonging to the "sanctuary movement", who were charged with violating Immigration and Naturalization Service (INS) laws by helping undocumented Guatemalans and Salvadorians to enter and remain in the USA, ended in May. The defendants had offered assistance on religious and humanitarian grounds to those they believed to be genuine refugees whose lives would be in danger if they were returned to their countries of origin. They contended that they had been forced to take action because of the US Government's failure to grant political asylum to most Salvadorians and Guatemalans who had applied for it (see *Amnesty International Report 1986*). Eight of the defendants were convicted on 1 May on 12 counts of harbouring, transporting and conspiring to transport illegal aliens and were sentenced on 2 July to five years' probation. Three were acquitted. The charges carried maximum sentences of five years' imprisonment, and the convicted defendants risked resentencing if they violated their parole conditions by continuing to help undocumented aliens. Before the sentences were passed Amnesty International had written to their lawyer saying that it would adopt them as prisoners of conscience if they were sentenced to prison terms. Although Amnesty International did not dispute the right of the USA to enforce its immigration laws, it concluded that the defendants had been convicted of breaking laws which, in their current practice, directly facilitated human rights violations to which the organization was opposed.

In August, an Amnesty International delegate investigated the cases of several anti-nuclear protesters imprisoned for eight to 18 years for damaging nuclear silos. The delegate concluded that their cases did not fall within Amnesty International's mandate.

In September a Court of Appeals denied a motion for a new trial in the case of Leonard Peltier, a leading member of the American Indian Movement (AIM) convicted of murder in 1977. Concerned by apparent discrepancies in the ballistics testimony, which it believed

might have prejudiced the outcome of the trial, Amnesty Internationalal publicly stated in 1985 that the interests of justice would best be
served by granting him a new trial (see *Amnesty International Reports
1985* and *1986*). A motion by the defence for a rehearing of the case
by the full Court of Appeals was pending a ruling at the end of 1986.

In August nine members of the Yakima Indian tribe, convicted in
1983 of federal charges of illegally catching and selling fish, were
ordered into custody to serve prison terms of between two and five
years. At the end of 1986 Amnesty International was still seeking
information on prosecutions of non-Indians under the same legislation, in an attempt to establish whether or not the defendants had
been selectively prosecuted on account of their ethnic origin.

On 11 November Amnesty International wrote to the US Attorney
General, expressing concern about reports that a prisoner, Vinson
Harris, had died as a result of ill-treatment by prison guards. A North
Carolina coroner established that Vinson Harris had died of
asphyxiation after guards had tightly wrapped his head, neck and face
in bandages while he was being transported by bus to a federal prison
in March 1986. Before this, he had reportedly been beaten and
chained to a seat for asking to use the lavatory several times during
the journey. Amnesty International asked for a full inquiry to be
conducted into the incident, including investigation of the role played
by all officials who had witnessed it. On 23 December, the Director of
the Federal Bureau of Prisons replied saying that a federal Grand
Jury had indicted a prison guard on two charges of assault creating
serious bodily injury and violating the civil rights of an inmate.

On 30 December Amnesty International wrote to the Director of
the Federal Bureau of Prisons enclosing its observer's report on
federal district court hearings into a complaint brought by inmates of
the Penitentiary at Marion, Illinois. The lawsuit had examined,
among other things, allegations that inmates were beaten by guards
during the imposition of a "lockdown" in the prison in November
1983, following violent incidents in which two prison guards had been
killed by inmates. In August 1985 the magistrate found that there had
been no constitutional violation of the inmates' rights and dismissed
the allegations (see *Amnesty International Report 1986*). Amnesty
International's observer was unable to draw conclusions on the
substance of the allegations of brutality. However, he found serious
shortcomings in the measures taken to investigate the allegations.
The lawsuit initiated by the inmates themselves provided the only
independent means of reviewing the complaints. The federal court,
however, was limited to finding proof of specific violations of law or
constitutional rights and it was beyond its jurisdiction to examine
whether existing procedures or practices might have facilitated acts of

brutality, or to make recommendations to protect inmates. Amnesty International was concerned that there were a number of relevant circumstances which the court was unable to address, including the absence of the use of name tags by masked guards involved in the lockdown operation; the denial of access to lawyers in the immediate aftermath of the lockdown; the non-reporting by prison officials of the use of force, and the inadequacy of complaints procedures within the prison. Amnesty International recommended that the government set up an independent and impartial inquiry into the allegations of brutality, which would look into all the circumstances.

In February and October Amnesty International wrote to the authorities expressing concern that US military assistance to the irregular armed forces opposing the Government of Nicaragua (the *contras*) may have contributed directly to killings, abductions and torture by those forces (see *Nicaragua* entry).

Uruguay

Amnesty International's concerns continued to focus on the cases of Uruguayans who "disappeared" between 1973 and 1982, under the military government. In December a law was passed granting immunity from punishment to police and military personnel allegedly responsible for human rights violations committed during the period of military rule.

An Amnesty International delegation visited the capital, Montevideo, in March. The delegates met President Julio Maria Sanguinetti and government ministers to inquire about measures for the future protection of human rights, and to discuss the government's position on investigations into past human rights abuses. The delegates also met the President of the Supreme Court, members of parliament from the main political parties, representatives of human rights and lawyers' organizations, and relatives of the "disappeared". Amnesty International wrote to President Sanguinetti in July emphasizing the responsibilities incurred by new governments for measures to protect human rights in the future, to investigate human rights abuses, including "disappearances", committed under previous governments, and to bring those responsible to justice. The letter stated that Amnesty International did not oppose measures of magnanimity or clemency, provided that these did not pre-empt or obstruct judicial, administrative or other investigations to establish publicly the truth about what had occurred. The letter concluded by emphasizing the importance of a public condemnation of torture and the need to ensure that any future complaints of torture or ill-treatment of prisoners were thoroughly investigated and anyone found responsible swiftly brought to justice. Copies of the July letter were sent subsequently to parliamentary leaders of the opposition parties, and to the President of the Supreme Court. Extracts of it were published in the Uruguayan press in September.

A reply from President Sanguinetti was received in October which drew attention to the measures taken by his government to promote national reconciliation, including an amnesty for political prisoners. He pointed out that parliament had appointed commissions to investigate abuses committed under the previous government, and that these commissions had carried out their work without obstruction. He stated that delays in investigations by the courts were not the result of obstruction, but of jurisdictional disputes whose resolution by the Supreme Court was still awaited. President Sanguinetti outlined the arguments for an "unrestricted amnesty" for all military and police personnel accused of "crimes against the human person" during the military government. He affirmed his government's "absolute and unequivocal rejection of torture", and stated that complaints alleging violations of human rights since his government took office had been extremely few, and that all had been scrupulously investigated, without any firm evidence being found to support them.

In late August the government introduced to the Senate a draft law providing an amnesty for crimes committed by military or police officials between 1962 and March 1985 linked to the "war against subversion" and closing all investigations into them. The proposal was rejected on 29 September. An alternative opposition bill was also rejected. It would have provided for officials to be tried for violations of human rights committed between 1 March 1967 and 1 March 1985, but only in cases involving murder, serious wounding, rape and "disappearance", and provided that the cases had been filed with civilian courts before 22 September 1986. Finally, an opposition party proposal was approved which became law on 22 December. It granted exemption from punishment to all police and military personnel responsible for human rights violations committed before 1 March 1985 if such acts were carried out for political motives or in fulfilment of orders. The law required judges acting in such cases to seek a decision from the government as to whether the law was applicable or not, to be given within 30 days, and gave the government powers to order cases to be closed by the courts. In cases of "disappearances" already under investigation by the civilian courts, the law stated that the government would be responsible for instituting investigations and providing complainants with the results within 120 days.

Since the government of President Sanguinetti took office in March 1985, 38 cases involving "disappearances" under the military government had been filed with civilian courts, but judicial investigations had been deadlocked since August 1985 when the military courts contested the competence of the civilian courts (see *Amnesty International Report 1986*). In November 1986 the Supreme Court resolved the conflict of jurisdiction in a number of cases of human rights violations, confirming the jurisdiction of the civilian courts. They included the "disappearance" in September 1981 of Félix Sebastián Ortiz Piazoli (see *Amnesty International Report 1983*), and of trade union leaders Gerardo Gatti Antuña, León Duarte Luján and Hugo Méndez Donadio, who "disappeared" in 1976 after being held with 28 other Uruguayans in *Automotores Orletti*, a clandestine detention centre in Buenos Aires. Witnesses had identified Uruguayan military intelligence personnel as participants in their capture and interrogation.

Amnesty International was concerned about several aspects of the new law which was enacted only hours before military personnel were reportedly due to be summoned to testify before civilian courts. In particular, it was not clear what mechanism of appeal was available to plaintiffs in the event of their questioning the government's judgment as to the applicability of the law; what safeguards would be introduced to ensure that investigations to be conducted by the government into "disappearances" were conducted thoroughly and impartially; whether there was any provision for investigations to be continued if the 120 days envisaged by the law proved insufficient to enable the necessary information to be gathered; in the event that the investigations established that crimes had been committed, what legal remedies would be available to the relatives or their representatives, what provision had been made to compensate them and what steps would be taken to make the results of investigations public.

In October Uruguay ratified the UN Convention Against Torture and Other Cruel, Inhuman or Degrading Treatment or Punishment.

Venezuela

Amnesty International remained concerned about the long-term detention of civilian political prisoners being tried by military courts. During 1986 Amnesty International investigated allegations of arbitrary killings by police, mostly of ordinary criminal suspects, and cases of reported "disappearance". It was also concerned at evidence of inadequacies in the judicial and prison systems, which involved delays of several years in the trials of most prisoners, including some political prisoners, and prison conditions which sometimes amounted to cruel, inhuman or degrading treatment.

Fourteen civilian prisoners arrested between 1978 and 1982 who were being tried by military tribunals for politically motivated offences remained in detention without having been convicted. Their trials made little or no progress during 1986. Others whose cases were transferred to civilian courts after several years before military tribunals also remained in prison without verdicts being reached.

The Venezuelan press reported growing public concern about conditions in Venezuela's prisons. Amnesty International was concerned about reports of beatings and the arbitrary use of disciplinary measures such as punishment cells, deprivation of food and medical treatment, and physical punishment. In some prisons the overcrowding, lack of hygiene, deficient diet, frequent punishment and poor medical attention constituted a serious risk to the inmates' mental and physical health.

Amnesty International received a number of reports about individuals killed in incidents involving police officers, where witnesses or relatives maintained that the deaths had resulted from beatings or the unwarranted use of firearms. In at least one case the killings appeared to be politically motivated. Nine political activists were shot dead on 8 May, in a mountainous area of the state of Yaracuy. Official sources stated that the killings were the result of an armed confrontation with guerrillas. Other sources claimed that the victims had been unarmed and that some of them had been arrested before being shot. In response to public denunciations a parliamentary committee was asked to investigate the incident, but so far as was known, no information about its findings had been made public by the end of 1986.

In March human remains were discovered in wells in the state of

Zulia. This drew attention to the unresolved cases of dozens of individuals missing in this and other regions, some for several years, who had reportedly been arrested by police in connection with ordinary criminal offences before "disappearing". Four corpses were identified as those of men reportedly arrested by police in recent years. In another case three members of the state police were charged with the killing of Jorge Rogelio López Silva, a youth who "disappeared" following his arrest in Maracaibo on 13 November 1985. His family received information that his body was in one of the "death wells".

Among those who died during 1986 after being detained by police were César Montilla and Jorge Terán Carmona. César Montilla was arrested on 2 May during a police raid in Antímano. When he was released 13 days later he had broken ribs and other injuries, as a result of which he died in hospital shortly afterwards. According to reports Jorge Terán Carmona was severely beaten in front of his family when arrested at his home in Caracas by police on 23 March. He died on 11 April of internal injuries.

There were an estimated 200 to 300 complaints pending in the courts concerning deaths or "disappearances" believed by relatives to have resulted from unlawful police action. Many of the victims were reportedly detained by police and later shot, or died as a result of ill-treatment. Although in some cases officers had been convicted of the killings, little or no progress appeared to have been made in most judicial investigations.

Asia and the Pacific

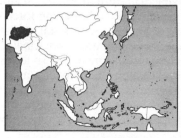

Afghanistan

Amnesty International was concerned about persistent reports of systematic torture and ill-treatment of prisoners in the custody of the *Khedamat-e Etela-at-e Dawlati* (KHAD), State Information Services, renamed the Ministry of State Security. Reports of extrajudicial executions by Soviet troops supported by Afghan military personnel continued to be of concern. Amnesty International was also concerned about the continued imprisonment of thousands of political prisoners, some of whom were prisoners of conscience. Political prisoners, many of whom were accused of active support for the armed opposition, were held without trial, or were imprisoned after political trials that did not conform to internationally recognized standards. Amnesty International continued to be concerned about the imposition of the death penalty, including its use in cases involving politically motivated violent crimes heard by special revolutionary courts without right of appeal.

In May Dr Najib was appointed General Secretary of the ruling People's Democratic Party of Afghanistan (PDPA) and on 20 November President Babrak Karmal resigned from the presidency of the Revolutionary Council.

Torture was a major concern of Amnesty International. On 9 September Amnesty International wrote to the President of the Revolutionary Council, expressing its concern about persistent allegations of torture. These allegations were described in detail in an Amnesty International report published on 19 November: *Afghanistan: Torture of Political Prisoners*, which marked the start of a worldwide campaign. It contained testimonies from former political prisoners who stated that they had been tortured by KHAD agents and quoted some former prisoners who said that Soviet personnel had been present when they were tortured. The report described widespread arrests of government officials, teachers, shopkeepers and students. Among them were people said to have been active in armed opposition groups as well as people who had not used or advocated violence. Prisoners were reported to have been most commonly tortured in KHAD interrogation centres in Kabul or in provincial cities, but Amnesty International also interviewed people who were tortured in prisons and at military posts. The torture was said to include beatings, electric shocks to sensitive parts of the body, being burnt with cigarettes and having hair torn from the scalp. Women prisoners reported not only being tortured but being forced to witness the torture of male prisoners. Many prisoners stated that Soviet personnel were present during torture and often participated in interrogations, but did not themselves torture prisoners. In a few cases Amnesty International received allegations that Soviet personnel were directly involved in applying torture themselves. The report pointed out that torture was prohibited by Afghanistan's constitution, as well as by international human rights instruments ratified by Afghanistan.

In its letters to President Karmal on 9 September and a subsequent letter to General Secretary Dr Najib of 24 November Amnesty International urged the government to implement recommendations for the prevention of torture. The organization urged it to issue clear public instructions that torture would not be tolerated. It also urged the government to ensure that relatives, lawyers and doctors had frequent access to detainees and that detainees would be brought promptly before a judicial authority to ensure that incommunicado detention did not become an opportunity for torture. It urged the government to establish an impartial body to investigate all complaints and reports of torture. Amnesty International also reminded the authorities that according to international standards, confessions or other evidence obtained under duress should not be invoked as evidence in legal proceedings.

In view of the allegations that Soviet personnel were sometimes present when prisoners were tortured or ill-treated, Amnesty International wrote on 9 September to the President of the USSR. It urged the Soviet Government to investigate the allegations of involvement of Soviet personnel in torture in Afghanistan. Amnesty International also called for Soviet personnel alleged to be involved in torture to be brought to trial.

As in previous years, fighting between Soviet and Afghan troops on the one side and armed opposition groups on the other continued throughout 1986. The conflict inhibited the collection of reliable information: direct communications with the victims of human rights violations within Amnesty International's mandate was extremely difficult. The government failed to respond to Amnesty International's repeated requests for information and the official, government-controlled Afghan news media provided little information of relevance to Amnesty International's concerns. International observers continued to face difficulties in obtaining access to the country. The special rapporteur appointed by the UN Commission on Human Rights in 1984 made yet another unsuccessful attempt in June to travel to Afghanistan. The International Committee of the Red Cross (ICRC) was able to visit Afghanistan to discuss future activities. However, according to its published reports, the ICRC was not able to visit prisons or prisoners during the year for protection purposes.

Amnesty International continued to receive allegations of extra-judicial executions in a number of Afghanistan's 29 provinces. For example, a total of 30 unarmed civilians were reported to have been killed by Soviet and Afghan military personnel on 23 March in a military operation in the villages of Bamba Koat, Sairum Qala and Omar Qala in the vicinity of Darra-e Noor valley in the Kuz Kunar district of Nangarhar province. The killings were reported to have been in reprisal for the killing of a Soviet military officer and some Afghan soldiers during earlier fighting between government forces and an armed opposition group in the nearby village of Khomargosh. According to the information available to Amnesty International, on 26 March, in a similar operation by Soviet and Afghan troops in the village of Suten, again in Darra-e Noor, a total of 66 unarmed villagers, among them children, were reportedly killed. Amnesty International received other allegations of reprisal killings of civilians by Soviet and Afghan military personnel. On 16 August, 42 men, women and children were alleged to have been killed in a military operation in Naqiabad in the Injil district south of Herat. Civilians were also reported to have been killed in Wardak, in Takhar and in Kandahar in three other similar incidents. At the end of 1986 Amnesty International was still trying to obtain further information about these reported killings.

Amnesty International continued to call for the unconditional release of Professor Habiburahman Halah, Professor Hassan Kakar, Shukrullah Kohgadai and Dr Osman Rustar who had been adopted as prisoners of conscience. They had been members of a discussion group at Kabul University seeking a peaceful solution to the armed conflict and were sentenced in 1983 to seven, eight, seven and 10 years' imprisonment respectively. They were held in Pul-e Charkhi prison, Kabul. Professor Kakar was suffering from varicose veins and his eyesight was poor and deteriorating. The authorities rejected Professor Kakar's request for a medical check-up. Amnesty International was unable to obtain further news of the other three prisoners.

Amnesty International continued to investigate the cases of 35 political prisoners who were said to be members of the *Afghan Mellat*, Afghan Social Democratic Party. They were arrested in 1983, reportedly tortured and sentenced to between five and 18 years' imprisonment in trials that Amnesty International believed did not conform to internationally established standards for a fair trial. Three of the prisoners were reported to have been released.

Amnesty International received reports from various sources of people being arrested and detained on political grounds but was unable to establish the exact number of these arrests. In November the government announced that the sentences passed on a number of male and female prisoners were to be remitted. On 18 December Amnesty International wrote to the Minister of Justice asking for details of this measure.

The number of death sentences announced by Kabul Radio in 1986, including those imposed *in absentia*, was eight, fewer than the 40 officially announced the previous year. Amnesty International believed these were only a proportion of the total number of death sentences which were imposed. The organization received information indicating that Dr Mohammad Younis Akbari, a nuclear physicist who had been sentenced to death on charges of subversion and counter-revolutionary activities in May 1984 (see *Amnesty International Report 1984* and *1985*), was still alive in late 1986. However, despite continued efforts throughout 1986 by Amnesty International to elicit a response from the government as to his fate, none was forthcoming.

Amnesty International continued to receive reports of torture and executions of Soviet and Afghan soldiers and of supporters of the government by opposition groups. Three militiamen were executed in February after a "trial" by opposition groups in Herat. In a television program shown by the British Broadcasting Corporation on 13 October Mohammad Juma, a member of an armed opposition group in Kandahar led by Abdul Latif, stated that as the chief executioner of the group he had beheaded many captured prisoners. The program also contained a sequence in which a captured prisoner was ill-treated by members of the opposition group. Amnesty International condemns as a matter of principle the torture or killing of prisoners under any circumstances, whether by government or non-government forces.

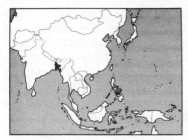

Bangladesh

Amnesty International was concerned about the short-term detention of hundreds of government opponents — including some prisoners of conscience — at times of parliamentary and presidential elections, when specific restrictions were imposed on political activities. Several prisoners arrested in connection with criminal offences were reported to have died as a result of torture. With mounting conflict in the Chittagong Hill Tracts there were increased reports of arbitrary arrests, torture and extrajudicial executions of non-combatant tribal people by military and paramilitary forces. Amnesty International was also concerned about the death penalty; among the prisoners executed was a youth aged only 16 at the time of the murder of which he was convicted.

Martial law, imposed in March 1982, remained in force until 10 November, although martial law courts were withdrawn after 22 March. The lifting of martial law followed parliament's adoption of the Constitution (Seventh Amendment) Act, also known as the Indemnity Bill. This provided for the full restoration of rights guaranteed in the Constitution, including fundamental rights such as freedom from arbitrary arrest and torture. It also validated all sentences passed by any martial law court, stating that they could "not be called into question before any court or tribunal".

Parliamentary elections were held on 7 May amid reports of widespread violence, which was mainly instigated by government supporters, and election rigging. Martial Law Regulation No. V of 1986, issued the previous week, prescribed up to seven years' imprisonment for anti-election publicity or participation in anti-election meetings or processions. The Bangladesh Nationalist Party (BNP), the opposition party led by Begum Khaleda Zia, wife of former President Zia-ur-Rahman, boycotted the elections. Among those arrested were several BNP leaders, who were detained under the Special Powers Act (SPA) for several days. Political activists were also reported to have been arrested in different parts of the country. Amnesty International appealed to President Ershad on 2 May for the release of all individuals detained for the non-violent exercise of their right to freedom of expression or peaceful assembly.

Amnesty International also appealed for the release of Golam Mohiuddin Ghous, executive director of the journal *Amader Kather* (Our Message), the owner of the press on which it was published, the publisher of *Shangbadik* (Journalist) and one of *Shangbadik*'s reporters. All four men were arrested on 15 May and placed under one-month detention orders under the SPA. The two journals had reportedly carried articles accusing the government of electoral fraud. All were released when the detention orders expired.

The presidential elections were held on 15 October, and were won by President Ershad. They were boycotted by the two main opposition party alliances, led by the Awami League (AL) and the BNP respectively. Criticism of the elections and anti-election activities were again made punishable under a martial law regulation by up to seven years' imprisonment. Dozens of political activists belonging to different opposition parties were reportedly arrested in the run-up to the elections, some for defying the ban on holding anti-election rallies. They were released; some after only a few days' detention, others some weeks later.

On various Islamic and national holidays prisoners were released. On 7 June the government freed 136 political prisoners. Among them were several whose cases had been taken up by Amnesty International, which had urged that they should be released or charged with a recognizable criminal offence. They included Jalal Ahmed, a leader of the student organization affiliated to the BNP, who had been held without trial for 15 months; Tipu Biswas, leader of the Communist League of Bangladesh; and Zahiruddin Swapan, prominent in the League's affiliated student organization, who had been charged, together with two others, with participating in an "unlawful assembly" the previous November. In August the authorities released a further 177 prisoners, including some who had been held under the SPA. It was unclear how many of these were political prisoners. In mid-December 203 prisoners were released. Among them were an unspecified number of SPA detainees, including, reportedly, political, trade union and student activists arrested for their opposition to martial law.

A new security force, the Presidential Security Force, was established in June to protect the President and other senior officials. It was given wide powers of arrest without warrant and authorized to use lethal force on anyone resisting arrest. Amnesty International was concerned that members of the force were granted immunity from prosecution, except when expressly ordered by the government.

In June Amnesty International published a *File on Torture* containing testimonies of torture from political prisoners arrested between February 1983 and mid-1985, who had been held incommunicado in the custody of the armed forces intelligence service, the Directorate General of Forces Intelligence (DGFI). The *File on Torture* also presented information about political prisoners and criminal suspects reportedly tortured in police stations. The testimonies alleged: persistent beatings with a wooden cane or "hunter", a whip-like instrument of plaited leather; being suspended from the ceiling by the arms; exposure to cold air fans for extended periods; and having the face covered by a cloth repeatedly soaked in water. Amnesty International also received reports that several prisoners arrested in connection with criminal offences died in 1986 as a result of police torture. It raised three such cases with the authorities. Two of the victims were said to be aged 17. The post-mortem on Mohammad Ashiqul Islam, a school student, noted that his death was caused by a brain haemorrhage and injuries "which are . . . homicidal in nature". An inquiry into his death was conducted by an army officer and a magistrate, and in July three police officers at the station where he had been held were dismissed. Three other police officers were suspended from duty in October, pending the outcome of a departmental inquiry into the death of Shafiqul Islam Arun, an apprentice, after he had been held for three days in a Dhaka police station. In December the Inspector General of Police was reported to have warned that a police officer found torturing a detainee would risk dismissal and could also be jailed. Amnesty International appealed for impartial judicial inquiries into complaints of police torture and for criminal proceedings to be instituted against any police personnel against whom there was evidence of involvement in torture.

In October Amnesty International published a report — *Bangladesh: Unlawful Killings and Torture in the Chittagong Hill Tracts* — which detailed extrajudicial killings and torture of non-combatant tribal people reportedly committed by military and paramilitary personnel. Many of the incidents described took place in the first half of 1986. Amnesty International acknowledged that the armed opposition group, the tribal *Shanti Bahini* (Peace Force) had killed non-tribal residents in the area and emphasized its condemnation of the execution of prisoners by anyone, including opposition groups. Among the reported extrajudicial killings by law enforcement personnel which Amnesty International described were killings attributed to the Bangladesh Rifles (BDR) on 18/19 May near the Indian border post at Silacherri. A group of some 200 tribal people were said to be approaching the border to cross into India, having left their villages following military operations in their locality in early May. They were reportedly apprehended by troops of the 31st battalion of the BDR, who were said to have surrounded them and made them walk into a narrow valley. In this restricted space, the soldiers are reported to have fired indiscriminately, killing an unknown number of unarmed people. The report also contained testimonies from tribal villagers describing being tortured during interrogation at army and BDR camps. Prisoners were reported to have been kept for several days in pits or trenches within the camps' perimeters and questioned about the whereabouts of *Shanti Bahini* units. The most frequently cited methods of torture were having hot water poured into the mouth and nostrils, being hung upside down and beaten and being burned with cigarettes. Amnesty International called upon the government to establish an impartial, independent commission of inquiry to investigate this and other reports of unlawful killings and torture by the security forces, and to publish its findings. At the end of 1986 the government sent Amnesty International a response to its report stating that all allegations of human rights abuse were investigated and appropriate action taken against those responsible. On 21 December Amnesty International replied, asking for specific information on the nature and findings of the inquiries the government said it had conducted. It also requested further details of three incidents in May during which people were reportedly killed unlawfully. Amnesty International also expressed concern about reports that following an attack on army personnel by *Shanti Bahini* forces in the area in mid-October, tribal people had been tortured during interrogation by military personnel at the sports stadium at Rangamati. Later in the month tribal men from a village in Khagrachari district, where *Shanti Bahini* units were understood to have been active, were reportedly beaten in Bet Chari army camp.

At least 10 people were sentenced to death by special martial law courts between January and March. Amnesty International learned of three executions during 1986, but it believed that the total number of death sentences and executions was probably higher. In July Amnesty International appealed for the commutation of the death sentences imposed on bank employees Mansur Hussain Khan and Abdur Rashid Mia, convicted by a special martial law court under martial law regulations of misappropriation of funds. This was the first case known to Amnesty International in which the death penalty was imposed for an offence other than murder or serious injury. The court reportedly sentenced them originally to 30 years' imprisonment and the administrative body that reviewed this verdict noted that these sentences could "not be disturbed". (Sentences imposed by military courts could not be submitted for judicial appeal.) However, President Ershad increased the sentences to the death penalty on 3 July. This was the second occasion known to Amnesty International on which President Ershad substituted a death penalty for a term of imprisonment imposed by a court. Amnesty International submitted information on these death sentences, as well as on the impending execution of Mohammad Selim, to the UN Special Rapporteur on summary or arbitrary executions. Mohammad Selim, aged 17 when executed for murder on 27 February, had also been tried by a military court.

In November Amnesty International appealed to the government not to introduce the death penalty for drug-related offences, as had been recommended by an official committee.

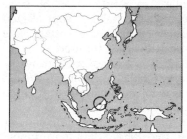

Brunei Darussalam

Amnesty International was concerned about the continued detention without trial of some 30 political prisoners, five of whom it had adopted as prisoners of conscience and for whose release it had appealed for many years. All five had been imprisoned for more than 22 years under Emergency Orders for their alleged involvement in an armed revolt in December 1962 led by the *Partai Rakyat Brunei*, Brunei People's Party. The Sultanate had been ruled under emergency laws since 1962.

In February the government approved registration of a second political party, the Brunei National United Party (BNUP), following the establishment of the Brunei National Democratic Party (BNDP) the previous year which was then the Sultanate's sole legal political organization.

Ten previously unacknowledged political detainees most of whom had been held since the mid-1970s were released during 1986, after taking an oath of loyalty to the Sultan. This brought the total number of releases to 24 since Brunei Darussalam became fully independent in January 1984.

Most of the prisoners about whom Amnesty International continued to be concerned were thought to have reached advanced years, and were believed to be held in virtual isolation. In October Amnesty International publicized their cases as "forgotten prisoners" when it appealed to the Sultan to release them, as it believed they continued to be held not for their involvement in the rebellion but as a general deterrent to political activity. No reasons were made public for the continued detention of these and other political prisoners.

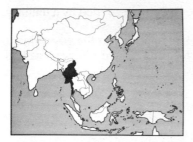

Burma

Amnesty International was concerned about continuing allegations of extrajudicial executions and torture of civilian political suspects, most of whom were of ethnic minority origin, by the Burmese armed forces in areas of armed rebellion in eastern Burma, particularly in Karen State. Suspects were reportedly detained without charge or trial, as were alleged members of Muslim or communist armed groups in the western state of Arakan, some of whom were allegedly also tortured.

In eastern Burma, combat continued between government forces and armed groups claiming to be fighting for the autonomy of various minorities, including the Karens, the Kayah and the Mons. It resulted in the flow of thousands of refugees to Thailand.

These refugees claimed there had been·numerous human rights abuses by the Burmese army since mid-1984, when government operations against insurgents in eastern Burma intensified. Amnesty International attempted to assess this information, which was consistent with earlier such allegations (see *Amnesty International Report 1986*). Among the allegations received in 1986 were that the army had killed or tortured civilian Karen villagers in custody, and shot civilian Karen villagers on sight while they were fleeing from their homes. According to the refugees, the victims were ill-treated and executed because they were suspected of involvement in the activities of the insurgent Karen National Union, or in some instances simply because they were Karen. Among the forms of torture they alleged were burning and mutilation of parts of the body and near-drowning and near-suffocation.

Refugees from Karen State also alleged that traders and porters of Karen or other ethnic minority origin continued to be extrajudicially executed while travelling through restricted areas. They were allegedly shot by army firing-squads on the grounds that their presence in the area was prohibited.

Amnesty International also learned that refugees from the Mon, Kayah and Shan States had made similar allegations. They too alleged that Burmese troops operating in these eastern parts of the country had in 1986 and earlier years committed human rights abuses.

In January Amnesty International publicly expressed its continuing concern about 18 Muslims from the western state of Arakan who had allegedly been tortured in late 1985 by security forces in order to extract "confessions". They were charged at the end of 1985 with treason and accused of involvement in armed opposition to the Buddhist-dominated central government (see *Amnesty International Report 1986*). Concerned that evidence produced by torture might be used against them, the organization again urged the government to investigate the allegations and ensure that these prisoners were being humanely treated. It also asked for assurances that they would be promptly tried. However, by the end of 1986 no news had been received that their trial had begun, and Amnesty International was unaware of any action taken by the government to look into allegations that they had been tortured.

In early September Amnesty International urged the government to allow four Arakanese Muslims arrested in August, apparently on suspicion of anti-government activities, access to relatives and legal counsel. They were reportedly detained incommunicado. The organization also appealed for them not to be held without charge or trial, but by the end of 1986 there was no news of any proceedings against them.

In mid-September Amnesty International expressed concern about reports that at least 14 Arakanese, most of whom were Buddhists, who had been arrested in June and July on suspicion of involvement in the armed activities of the insurgent Arakanese Communist Party, were being held without charge or trial in Rangoon, and about allegations that another person arrested with them, a lawyer named Soe Myint, had been tortured. It urged the government to investigate the torture allegations and to ensure that all those held were being well treated and would either be released or promptly charged and fairly tried. In early November the official press announced that 24 people had been charged in connection with alleged Arakanese Communist Party activities. They included Soe Myint and the 14 others about whom Amnesty International had expressed concern.

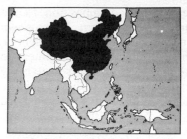

China

Amnesty International was concerned about the imprisonment of prisoners of conscience and the conditions under which they were held, and about the extensive use of the death penalty. It was also concerned about reports of torture and ill-treatment of criminal suspects in police custody.

In December the People's Republic of China signed the UN Convention against Torture and Other Cruel, Inhuman or Degrading Treatment or Punishment, a move welcomed by Amnesty International. This followed various official statements during the year that the government was committed to eradicating torture. In October Zhang Siqing, Deputy Chief Procurator, was reported to have stated: "The key task of procuratorial work for the next year will be the eradication of torture to extract confessions, illegal detention, dereliction of duty by police officers and accidents caused by negligence".

By the end of 1986 the organization had collected extensive reports published in the Chinese press during the previous two years which revealed many cases of torture and ill-treatment of criminal suspects in police custody. According to these accounts, torture often occurred when people were illegally detained, usually during the first few hours or days of detention. Some accounts concerned cases where torture had caused the death of the victims.

An example reported in September 1986 was the case of a village party secretary in Shaanxi province who was charged with illegally detaining 72 villagers whom he suspected of stealing part of his bicycle bell and ordering 17 of them to be tortured. In another case, a lawyer from Jinjiang county in southern Fujian province was arrested in May 1985, repeatedly poked with an electric baton and beaten for asking a police officer carrying out a "household registration" to produce his identity papers. The lawyer lodged complaints after being released and one public security officer responsible for his ill-treatment was arrested. On 19 September the *China Daily* reported that during the first half of 1986, "the number of cases [of illegal detention] nearly doubled over the same period last year, to 949, in which more than 140 people were reported to have been tortured". Allegations of ill-treatment of prisoners included beatings, poking with electric batons, use of tight handcuffs and suspension by the arms.

Amnesty International was also concerned at reports that some political prisoners had been held for long periods of time in solitary confinement. Wei Jingsheng, a prisoner of conscience detained since 1979 who was said to have suffered a nervous breakdown after several years in solitary confinement, was still reported to be in a poor physical and mental condition in early 1986. Despite repeated appeals by Amnesty International, the authorities did not make public any specific information about his condition or his place of detention, which remained unknown.

In May Amnesty International received reports that another prisoner of conscience, Xu Wenli (see *Amnesty International Report 1986*), had been confined since late 1985 in a windowless cell entered by a trap-door in the ceiling. It was further reported that he was being denied all visits, mail and access to newspapers or reading material, and that his food ration had been reduced. This treatment was said to be a punishment for the circulation abroad in October 1985 of a document he had written in prison on his arrest, detention and trial. Amnesty International published excerpts from this testimony in February. On 9 May Amnesty International asked the government to investigate Xu Wenli's treatment and to release him. But in September he was still reportedly held under the same harsh conditions and fears were expressed for his health.

Amnesty International was also concerned about the detention and health of several elderly Roman Catholic priests adopted by the organization as prisoners of conscience who were arrested during the 1950s for remaining loyal to the Vatican or expressing opposition to government measures to control religious affairs. Some were released in the late 1970s and rearrested in 1981. One of them, Francis Xavier Wang Chuhua, who had been imprisoned for 30 years, was reported in early 1986 to be suffering from tuberculosis, to have a cataract in one eye and to have lost his sight in the other. He had been transferred to a labour camp in Qinghai province in 1980 and had received a new sentence of seven years' imprisonment in 1981. Thomas You Guojie, a priest from Nancheng in Jiangzxi province serving a sentence of 10 years' imprisonment in a labour camp, was also reported to be in a poor state of health, suffering from high blood pressure.

Arrests of people believed to be prisoners of conscience were reported during the year. In April Zhang Xiaohui and Li Caian, two students from Beijing University's history department, were arrested, allegedly for distributing pamphlets criticizing the Chinese Communist Party and calling for the creation of a new political party called the "China Youth Party". According to unofficial sources, they had written a theoretical article criticizing Marxism and the leadership of the Communist Party, but had made no attempt to form a political party. A spokesman from the University foreign affairs office confirmed in May that they had been arrested for "counter-revolutionary activities". They were reportedly due to be tried at the end of June, but no confirmation had been received by the end of 1986. Both were reported to have participated in student demonstrations in Beijing in late 1985 and to have been kept under surveillance since then. The demonstrations, initially a protest against the flood of Japanese goods on the Chinese market, later extended to complaints about the students' living conditions, inflation and official corruption.

Student demonstrations on a larger scale took place throughout China in December 1986, when tens of thousands of students marched in a dozen major cities to demand democratic reforms and freedom of the press. Although the demonstrations were initially tolerated by the authorities, unauthorized demonstrations were later banned in several cities. Warnings were issued in the press against "elements hostile to socialism who were infiltrating the students to encourage protests". Wall-posters, banned since 1979, appeared in Beijing University in late December demanding democracy and an end to the one-party system. One wall-poster reportedly called for the release from prison of two Beijing students arrested in April.

Demonstrators were reportedly arrested during protests in Shanghai, Nanjing and Beijing and there were allegations of police brutality towards demonstrators temporarily detained. While it was officially denied that any students had been arrested, official reports indicated that at least six workers were arrested in Shanghai and Nanjing on charges ranging from disrupting public order and damaging property to spreading rumours during demonstrations, and one man, officially described as an "agitator", who had taken part in a demonstration by students at Beijing Teachers' University on 29 December, was arrested for "making statements that incited students".

Amnesty International also received reports from various sources about the arrests of groups of Catholics in Hebei province in May and June 1986. More than 40 Catholics were arrested around midnight on 29 May in Qiaozhai village, Gaocheng county, by truckloads of armed police coming from several counties. Among those arrested were elderly priests and nuns, and a large group of young seminarians and novice nuns who were training in a seminary established without official permission in Qiaozhai. Police were reported to have beaten them on the trucks when they started saying prayers and singing hymns. It was also alleged that several young novices were isolated from the others, each tied with her arms around a tree, stripped naked and insulted "with dirty language" for several hours. Most of those arrested were reported to have been released after interrogation but at least two priests, Father Liu Xilue and Father Gao, were reported to be still detained in July. In September Amnesty International called on the government to investigate the allegations of ill-treatment by police and to make public the results of its findings as well as the charges against those still detained. In October the Chinese Embassy in Australia stated in a letter that: "a handful of bad elements had grouped themselves into an illegal underground organization under the cover of Catholicism in Beiqiachai village of Gaocheng county, Hebei province. They were detained by the public security organ in Gaocheng county on 30 May this year. All these detainees were released soon after the examination. During the detention no one was ill-treated or insulted." No further information was available to Amnesty International about these arrests by the end of 1986.

Among other Catholics reported to have been arrested in June in Hebei were four seminarians who had gone to visit an elderly Bishop. No further news was received about them.

Amnesty International continued to appeal for the release of other prisoners of conscience, among them editors of unofficial journals who took part in the "democracy movement" and had been detained since 1981, and Tibetans arrested for advocating Tibetan nationalism. Among them was Geshe Lobsang Wangchuk, a monk and Buddhist scholar arrested in 1981 for writing leaflets on the history of independent Tibet. He reportedly refused to retract his statements about Tibet and was sentenced to 18 years' imprisonment in February 1984. Amnesty International was also investigating the cases of Tibetans reported to have been arrested since 1983 for their political activities, and learned of the release of several others detained for possessing or circulating information advocating Tibetan nationalism.

Fu Shenqi, the former editor of an unofficial journal in Shanghai imprisoned since 1981 for his association with other editors of unofficial journals, was reported to have been released on parole in July 1986, having served five years of his seven-year sentence. Amnesty International also learned of the release of two other prisoners of conscience who had been active in the "democracy movement".

The use of the death penalty for a wide range of offences remained a major concern. Legislation providing for accelerated procedures for trial, appeal and executions continued to be applied. During 1986 Amnesty International documented 257 death sentences, of which 180 were carried out shortly after sentencing. These figures (which are believed to represent only a fraction of the total number of executions and death sentences throughout the country) were higher than those recorded by Amnesty International in 1985.

Amnesty International continued to be concerned about the

humiliating treatment of condemned prisoners who were paraded through the streets, hands tied behind their backs, with placards hanging round their necks, or who were taken to sentencing rallies attended by thousands of people before being executed. Execution usually took place immediately after such rallies. In Beijing, 31 people aged between 19 and 35 were executed on 25 June after a public sentencing rally in Beijing's Capital Gymnasium. Seven of them were convicted of murder, three of rape and 21 of theft or robbery. In Henan province, 3,000 people attended a rally held on 14 July by the Huaihua Prefecture Intermediate People's Court to pronounce the death sentence on two people convicted of corruption. In Lasa, the capital of the Autonomous Region of Tibet, one man convicted of murder and stealing firearms was executed on 14 September after a rally in the City Stadium attended by some 10,000 people.

On 20 June the Minister of Public Security stated that the practice of parading condemned prisoners sentenced to death through the streets had stopped "some time ago". However, reports indicated that the practice had not stopped nationwide. In one case, a 24-year-old man was reported to have been paraded through the streets on 5 September before being executed in the Zhuhai Economic Zone.

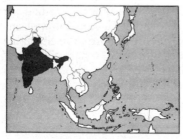

India

Amnesty International was concerned about the detention of hundreds of political detainees held without charge or trial under special "anti-terrorist" legislation or preventive detention laws. The organization was concerned that these laws lacked legal safeguards required by international human rights standards and that they allowed people to be detained for non-violently expressing their opinions. There were allegations from most Indian states of ill-treatment and torture of detainees and some detainees allegedly died as a result. Amnesty International was concerned that some alleged supporters of armed opposition groups were deliberately killed in "encounters" staged by the police, and that landless peasants were extrajudicially killed by police. The organization was also concerned about several executions.

Acts of political violence were reported from various states, including the Punjab, West Bengal, Bihar, Jammu and Kashmir and Andhra Pradesh. Armed groups in the Punjab demanding a separate Sikh state killed police, local officials and civilians. Reuters reported on 20 September that 480 political killings had taken place in the state between January and September. In West Bengal, supporters of the Gorkha National Liberation Front staged a violent campaign for a separate state, while in Andhra Pradesh some left-wing political groups advocating social and economic reform adopted violent methods.

Politically motivated arrests were reported from many Indian states. A number of those arrested were held in preventive detention under the National Security Act (NSA) which permits detainees to be held without charge or trial for up to one year (in the Punjab, two years). These periods of detention could be renewed indefinitely. Others were arrested under the 1985 Terrorist and Disruptive Activities Act. Amnesty International believed that the Act's provisions were so broad that people could be detained for non-violently expressing their political opinions (see *Amnesty International Report 1986*). Among the several hundred people reportedly arrested under the Act during 1986 were several whom Amnesty International considered prisoners of conscience. On 12 August the editor of the fortnightly publication, *Dalit Voice*, was arrested for publishing an article which the government alleged was seditious. He was released one week later without having been charged. The editor and printer of an Urdu weekly, *Nai Duniya*, were arrested under the Act on 5 November and detained for 15 days for publishing, a year earlier, an interview with an expatriate Sikh leader advocating a separate Sikh state. Another prisoner of conscience was a Sikkimese Buddhist and former leader of the Naya Sikkim Party, Captain Sonam Yongda, who was arrested on 6 January under the NSA for making a series of speeches, more than a year before his arrest, in which he allegedly criticized the incorporation of Sikkim into India and called on the Sikkimese to re-establish their lost rights. He was held without charge or trial and was reportedly suffering from recurring paralysis of the left side of the body.

In November Amnesty International wrote to the authorities about the continued detention, apparently under the NSA, of 379 Sikh detainees held in Jodhpur Jail, Rajasthan. They were among some 1,500 people arrested when the Indian army attacked and entered the Golden Temple, Amritsar, in June 1984. Amnesty International expressed concern that the detainees had apparently been held beyond the two-year legal maximum and that there could be some among them who had been arrested simply for having been present in the Golden Temple. Amnesty International also stated that if these detainees were tried under the Terrorist Affected Areas (Special Courts) Act, they might not be given a fair trial since the Act permitted procedures incompatible with Article 14 of the Internationalal Covenant on Civil and Political Rights, to which India is a party. The Act permitted special courts to try people on charges of "waging war": it was mandatory for special courts to sit *in camera*, courts could sit in jails and the identity of witnesses could be kept secret. The burden of proof was transferred from the prosecution to the defence, if the accused was in an area where firearms or explosives were used, or where the security forces were attacked or resisted. Appeals could be lodged only within 30 days of sentence. A special court was established in Jodhpur Jail which by August had, according to one report, started proceedings against these detainees, although no details had emerged by the end of 1986. All the detainees were reportedly charged with identical offences on the basis of cyclostyled "confessions" that they were members of the All India Sikh Students Federation or the *Dal Khalsa* (an outlawed Sikh organization). Sixty of the detainees in Jodhpur had been held in 1984 in Ladha Kothi Jail, Sangrur, Punjab, together with 30 others. An official commission established by the Punjab state government submitted a report in May which found evidence that the 90 detainees arrested at the Golden Temple in June 1984 had been tortured. The commission recommended compensation for the 90 detainees and disciplinary action against 22 police officers reportedly involved. Amnesty International was investigating the cases of the 379 Sikh detainees in Jodhpur, urging the government either to release them or to give them a fair trial under ordinary procedures of criminal law.

In December Amnesty International urged the release or fair trial without delay of Prakash Singh Badal, leader of the breakaway *Akali Dal* faction formed in May 1986, Gurcharan Singh Tohra, the newly elected President of the *Shiromani Gurdwara Prabandhak Committee* (SGPC), Temple Management Committee, and an estimated 200 members of the *Akali Dal (Badal)* faction and the All India Sikh Students Federation (AISSF). They were arrested and held without charge or trial under the provisions of the NSA in early December after 22 bus passengers, mostly Hindus, were killed in Hoshiarpur on 30 November 1986, an incident for which the Khalistan Liberation Force (the armed wing of the AISSF) had claimed responsibility. Subsequently parts of Punjab were declared "disturbed areas" and the state governor asked the army to assist the police and paramilitary forces. The new Director General of Police of the Punjab, appointed in March 1986, announced new police and paramilitary operations aimed at the elimination or arrest of leaders and members of armed

Sikh groups. Amnesty International received an increasing number of reports that some killings of Sikh activists in the state were the result of "fake encounters" staged by the police or paramilitary forces. According to these reports, the victims were deliberately killed, some after capture. Amnesty International was not able to investigate these reports but an official four-member committee, headed by a former judge, studied 35 "encounters" in the state and reported in February that almost all such cases in the Punjab were "fake encounters". On 25 June a magisterial inquiry found that the Border Security Force had been guilty of deliberate killings and recommended that charges of murder be brought against those responsible, but few inquiries into alleged extrajudicial killings were held. Extrajudicial killings were also reported from other parts of India, including West Bengal.

Of particular concern were reports from the state of Bihar where landless peasants increasingly opposed illegal land occupation or appropriation by local landowners. Left-wing political groups, some advocating peaceful change, as well as "Naxalites" (Maoist revolutionaries, some of whom resorted to violence), were also active in the state. Local landowners often employed criminals in private armies and operated in league with local police and politicians. One example of this was an incident in Arwal, Gaya district, where a dispute developed over a plot of government land which had been used by villagers but which was appropriated by a local landowner. In league with police and local authorities the landowner had peasant huts on the plot demolished. On 19 April police surrounded the Gandhi Library where a protest meeting organized by the left-wing group *Mazdoor Kisan Sanghash Samiti* (MKSS) was attended by over 500 people. Police opened fire and killed 23 men, women and children. The police claimed they fired at MKSS workers trying to attack the nearby police station with lethal weapons, but local witnesses, journalists and representatives of civil liberties bodies found no evidence of this. The Gaya District magistrate, visiting the spot one hour later, reportedly described the police firing as "unwarranted, unorganized and uncontrolled". There were widespread demands for a judicial investigation and in August 25,000 people were reportedly arrested to prevent demonstrations before the state assembly. The Bihar Government did not order an independent investigation but asked a member of the Board of Revenue to carry out an official inquiry. On 6 October he was reported to have found that the firing was not "fully justified" and that the police had used "excessive force". The Supreme Court was reported to have ordered the state government to grant compensation to the victims. By the end of 1986 it had not been paid and no action was known to have been taken against those responsible.

Deaths in police custody allegedly as a result of torture or shooting continued to be reported from many Indian states including Andhra Pradesh, Bihar, Union Territory of Delhi, Karnataka, Kerala, Madhya Pradesh, Maharashtra, Punjab, Rajasthan, Uttar Pradesh and West Bengal. In Andhra Pradesh, 11 such deaths were reported in the first nine months of the year, three of them during one week in September alone. In one case, a senior naval officer found seven wounds on the body of one of the victims, T. Muralidharan, who the police said had committed suicide in a police station. Amnesty International expressed concern about these deaths but welcomed the state government's decision to hold a judicial inquiry. The outcome of the investigations were not known at the end of 1986. Amnesty International also expressed concern about the deaths of several Sikhs in police custody in New Delhi. Among them was Daljit Singh who died on 24 January in the custody of the New Delhi police. The police stated that he died of high blood pressure, but Amnesty International received evidence that he died of torture. Suraj Singh died on 13 August in the Gandhi Nagar police station, Eastern Delhi. According to the police he hanged himself in the toilet, but relatives alleged he died of beatings in Shakarpur police station. Amnesty International asked for a judicial inquiry in these cases but was unaware of any being instituted. However, in December a magisterial inquiry found that the death of Dayal Singh in a Delhi police station had been the result of torture and recommended that four police officers be charged with murder. In several other such cases police officers were reported to have been charged with murder.

Reports of torture and ill-treatment by the police were received from nearly all Indian states. A number of the victims were members of the scheduled castes and scheduled tribes. For example, tribal leader Shankar Yadu Lokhande died in Narajangaon police station in March, according to the police by hanging, but according to members of the tribe, because of beatings in police custody. There were also repeated reports that tribal women had been raped by local police. In some cases the Central Bureau of Investigation investigated the allegations and was reported to have established that there was evidence of rape. In October the Supreme Court heard the report of a commission it had established which recorded statements by 584 people about rape by police of tribal women in Gujarat. The commission indicted local police and hospital doctors for covering up evidence of rape. In Jammu and Kashmir political prisoners complained of beatings in various jails, but most reported that torture took place during interrogation in police custody.

In 1986, as in previous years, dozens of people were sentenced to death, mainly for murder. In November the Minister for Home

Affairs stated that 35 people had been executed in the three years ending 1985. In April the Indian Supreme Court confirmed a stay of execution for Daya Singh — who had been arrested in 1965 and sentenced to·death for murder in 1978. The Supreme Court confirmed a previous ruling made in 1983 that a person sentenced to death may demand commutation as of right if the sentence has not been carried out within two years.

On 22 January three Sikhs — Satwant Singh, Kehar Singh and Balbir Singh — were sentenced to death on charges of murder and conspiracy to murder the late Prime Minister Indira Gandhi. The trial took place in Delhi's maximum security Tihar Jail. On 3 December the New Delhi High Court dismissed the appeals of the three men who said they would be appealing to the Supreme Court.

Throughout 1986 Amnesty International wrote to the Prime Minister and other government officials reiterating its proposal for an Amnesty International delegation to visit India to discuss the international protection of human rights as well as its human rights concerns in India. However, by the end of 1986 the government had failed to respond.

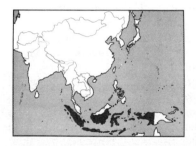

Indonesia and East Timor

Amnesty International was concerned about the imprisonment of hundreds of political detainees, including prisoners of conscience and possible prisoners of conscience, whom it believed may have been unfairly tried. The prisoners included Muslim activists and government critics in Java, suspected supporters of independence movements in Irian Jaya and East Timor, and people arrested in connection with a coup attempt in 1965, many of whom had been associated with the banned *Partai Komunis Indonesia* (PKI), Indonesian Communist Party. Amnesty International continued to receive reports of torture and ill-treatment of prisoners, often during interrogation immediately following arrest, and of extrajudicial executions, particularly in Irian Jaya. Amnesty International remained concerned about the use of the death penalty. Ten executions, of a Muslim activist and nine former PKI members, were carried out, and Amnesty International knew of 23 prisoners under sentence of death.

On 25 June Amnesty International published a report *Indonesia: Muslim Prisoners of Conscience* which documented the cases of over 100 prisoners detained after a violent demonstration in Tanjung Priok, Jakarta, in September 1984 (see *Amnesty International Report 1985* and *1986*). The report described in detail the cases of 15 prisoners of conscience detained for protesting about the government's handling of the Tanjung Priok incident or for criticizing government policies which they believed violated Islamic teachings. Many prisoners were reportedly ill-treated while held in incommunicado detention after their arrest. In a letter of 19 June to President Suharto, forwarding a copy of the report before publication, Amnesty International expressed concern that the trial of these prisoners might not have been fair. In many cases, the organization noted, access to counsel was limited, the time to prepare a defence was short and considered inadequate by defence lawyers, the right of the defence to call witnesses was restricted, and evidence alleged to have been obtained illegally was accepted in court.

At the end of 1986 Amnesty International was working on behalf of 14 Muslim activist prisoners of conscience, all of whom had been convicted of subversion under Presidential Decree 11/1963, the so-called anti-subversion law. The rights guaranteed to criminal suspects under the country's Criminal Procedure Code, such as limits on pre-trial detention, do not apply to people charged with subversion. Amnesty International urged the government to review the anti-subversion law with a view to similarly protecting the rights of people arrested and detained under it.

Sentences imposed on prisoners of conscience were often heavy. In January Lieutenant General Dharsono, who had signed an open letter calling for a fact-finding commission into the Tanjung Priok incident, was sentenced to 10 years' imprisonment, reduced on appeal in May to seven years. Other prisoners, however, had their sentences increased on appeal by the prosecution. Andi Sukisno, a Muslim student tried in Malang on subversion charges in 1985 (see *Amnesty International Report 1986*) and adopted as a prisoner of conscience in 1986, had his sentence raised from eight to 15 years on appeal to the East Java High Court. Another prisoner of conscience adopted during 1986 was Dr Oesmany Al Hamidy, a 72-year-old disabled professor at an Islamic college in Tanjung Priok. Arrested in September 1984, he was sentenced in March to eight years' imprisonment on subversion charges for having given sermons criticizing alleged official corruption and government policies, particularly a draft law which would require Muslim organizations to accept *Pancasila*, the state ideology, as their sole ideological foundation.

Dozens of Muslim activists accused of subversion were tried during 1986. Amnesty International was investigating the cases of 16 Muslim religious teachers and lecturers arrested in January in Solo, Karanganyar, Boyolali, Surakarta and Klaten in central Java, who were accused of attempting to set up an Islamic state in Indonesia. Their trials began in July. The defendants were members of a network of village-based groups, known as *Usroh*, which, they claimed, was designed to develop closer ties among Muslims through religious study. All 16 denied the charges against them, but all were convicted and sentenced to between five and 11 years' imprisonment. In October, Amnesty International requested detailed information on the charges against these prisoners from the Attorney General and local government officials. By the end of the year no response had been received, and available press reports gave no indication that any evidence was produced during their trials to show that they had used or advocated violence. The trials of other prisoners accused of involvement in *Usroh* groups in Yogyakarta, Karanganyar, Bantul and Brebes in central Java, were still in progress at the end of 1986.

Amnesty International continued to be concerned about reports that suspected supporters of the *Organisasi Papua Merdeka* (OPM), the Free Papua Movement, which had been waging an armed struggle since the mid 1960s to establish an independent state of West Papua in Irian Jaya, were being held without charge or trial in military detention centres in Sorong, Merauke and Jayapura. One prisoner, Nabot Wanma, was reported to have been held since June 1985 and to have been tortured (see *Amnesty International Report 1986*). At the end of 1986, he was reported to be still detained at the military police headquarters in Kloofkamp Bawah, Jayapura. In December Amnesty International wrote to the Minister of Justice expressing concern that these prisoners were not brought before judicial authorities after their arrest and given a fair trial within a reasonable time, in accordance with internationally recognized standards. Several trials of political prisoners in Irian Jaya were reported to have taken place during 1986, including those of seven out of 12 men deported from Papua New Guinea in October 1985 (see *Amnesty International Report 1986*).

In response to inquiries from Amnesty International about the possibility of sending observers to attend trials of political prisoners in Java, Irian Jaya and East Timor, the government stated in December that their attendance at court proceedings would constitute interference in its internal affairs and would not be tolerated.

Amnesty International continued to be concerned about approximately 100 prisoners still in detention after having been convicted of involvement in an attempted coup in 1965. It continued to appeal for the release of three prisoners who it believed had been accused of involvement solely because of their non-violent activities in the PKI and associated organizations. One was Pudjo Prasetio, who had been a full-time worker for the PKI in Bali. He had been arrested in 1967 but was only brought to trial in 1979, when he was sentenced to life imprisonment. He was held in Grobogan prison, Bali.

In other cases there were prolonged delays in appeal hearings. In October Amnesty International highlighted the case of a "forgotten" prisoner of conscience, Manan Effendi bin Tjokrohardjo, vice-chairman of the PKI for East Kalimantan, who had been arrested in October 1965, a few days after the coup attempt, and sentenced to death in 1967. He lodged an immediate appeal against his sentence, but it was not heard by the high court until April 1982, over 14 years later. The high court stated that it had only received the relevant papers from the district court in January 1982 and then commuted the sentence to life imprisonment.

Torture and ill-treatment by both military and police personnel continued to be reported. In July Amnesty International appealed for an investigation into the death in custody in Jakarta of Muhammad Djabir on 25 January. The day before his death he had told his nephew that he was being beaten to force him to make a statement accusing a former cabinet minister, Haji Mohammad Sanusi, of plotting to assassinate the President. His family claimed to have seen marks of torture on him both when they visited him in prison and when his body was returned to them after his death. Amnesty International was also concerned at reports of the deaths of a number of detainees held for alleged criminal offences in police stations, where their relatives believed they died as a result of ill-treatment. In September it appealed for independent investigations into five such deaths in police custody between June and August.

Amnesty International made public in September reports of the ill-treatment of a number of people who had been briefly detained on suspicion of supporting independence for the South Moluccas. About 30 people were reported to have been arrested following the raising of a South Moluccan flag between Partu and Haria on Saparua island on 25 April. All these detainees were released by the end of May, but many claimed to have been beaten and ill-treated.

Amnesty International was concerned about reports that Indonesian security forces had carried out extrajudicial executions during 1986 in the areas of Kiwirok, Merauke, Sarmi and Paniai in Irian Jaya. Amnesty International urged the Minister of Justice in December to investigate reports that Yunus Firtar, Roby Tanjau and Wilhemus Inday had been killed in custody by members of the Indonesian military.

Reports of torture, arbitrary arrest and unfair trials of political prisoners suspected of supporting the *Frente Revolucionaria de Timor Leste Independente* (Fretilin) continued to be received from the Indonesian-occupied territory of East Timor. People arrested and interrogated by the Indonesian security forces in district and sub-district military commands, such as those in Baucau and Lospalos, appeared to be especially at risk. Amnesty International was also concerned about the fairness of trials of political prisoners in East Timor. Amnesty International learned of 10 further trials which took place in 1986, bringing the total number of prisoners tried to well over 200 since they began in December 1983. As all of the defendants pleaded guilty and none lodged an appeal, Amnesty International was concerned that the trials may not have been fair. The defendants reportedly had no choice of counsel other than a government-appointed defence team.

More than 600 people continued to be held without charge or trial on Atauro island off the coast of East Timor. Although the Indonesian Government referred to these people as "temporarily displaced persons", Amnesty International was concerned that they were being forced to stay on the island as part of a policy to break up suspected Fretilin support networks.

In a statement of its concerns in East Timor before the UN Special Committee on Decolonization on 15 August, Amnesty International noted the failure of the Indonesian Government to conduct investigations into reports of extrajudicial executions or "disappearances" reportedly carried out in previous years by military personnel. Amnesty International stated that it believed the absence of such investigations by the Indonesian authorities increased the likelihood that such grave violations could occur again.

Amnesty International was concerned about the increased use of the death penalty during 1986. Ten executions, all involving political prisoners, were confirmed by the government. On 12 September Maman Kusmayadi, a Muslim activist was executed. He had been convicted of involvement in the storming of a police station in Bandung in 1981, allegedly to obtain weapons for the establishment of an Islamic state. On 2 October Amnesty International wrote to President Suharto expressing concern about the execution and outlining the reasons for its unconditional opposition to the death penalty.

In October the government announced that nine former members of the PKI had been executed in the last week of September and first week of October, on the anniversary of the coup attempt in 1965. All of them had been held under sentence of death for over 15 years. They had all been tried by special military courts which allowed them no right of appeal to a higher court, in contravention of international standards.

Amnesty International repeatedly appealed for the commutation of all outstanding death sentences. The organization learned of two death sentences imposed during 1986, both for murder. Among those under sentence of death at the end of 1986 were 16 prisoners convicted of involvement in the 1965 coup attempt, three Muslim activists, and seven prisoners convicted of ordinary criminal offences. In November Amnesty International renewed its appeals for the abolition of the death penalty.

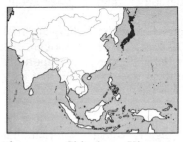

Japan

Amnesty International was concerned about the use of the death penalty. It wrote to the government expressing concern about two executions. The names of the prisoners executed were not disclosed but Amnesty International believed that they were Shigeharu Kimura and Reiichi Tokunaga, who had been convicted of murder and robbery in December 1975 in the same trial. They were reportedly executed on 20 May. Amnesty International continued to urge the government to commute all death sentences. At the end of 1986, some 74 prisoners were known to be under sentence of death; they had all been convicted of murder, five of them of politically motivated murders. At least 23 had had their sentences upheld by the Supreme Court and eight had been under sentence of death for between 10 and 36 years. Several had filed appeals for retrial. On 30 May the Shizuoka District Court ordered the retrial of Masao Akahori who had been sentenced to death in May 1958. The court questioned the validity of his confession and other evidence against him.

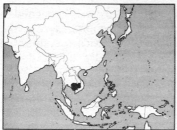

Kampuchea (Cambodia)

Amnesty International was concerned about human rights violations by the People's Republic of Kampuchea (PRK) authorities who administered most of the country's territory and population with the support of Viet Nam. Several thousand prisoners were held without trial, among them some prisoners of conscience. Amnesty International was also concerned about reports of torture, about unfair trials of political prisoners and about the death penalty. Amnesty International was concerned, too, about human rights violations by the UN-recognized Democratic Kampuchea (DK) authorities, whose three Coalition Government partners continued to wage war within the country and to administer camps along the Thailand-Kampuchea border.

Amnesty International believed that almost all of the several thousand political prisoners held by the PRK authorities were imprisoned without charge or trial, and that among them were some prisoners of conscience. Reports of arbitrary arrest and detention continued. As in previous years, political suspects were reportedly tortured during interrogation and held incommunicado in shackles in dark and dirty cells. Amnesty International received reports that former political opponents of the government, officially termed "misled people", who surrendered to the authorities during 1986, were restricted to camps and held without charge or trial for unspecified periods of "re-education". Only one political trial was officially reported during the year. One of the 10 defendants, all of whom were convicted, was sentenced to death and Amnesty International was concerned that the convicted men may not have been allowed adequate opportunities to defend themselves.

Information obtained by Amnesty International during 1986 corroborated reports that people arrested in previous years for suspected involvement with DK or other opposition activities had been the victims of human rights abuses. The organization received dozens of first-hand testimonies from former political prisoners and over a hundred reports about other individual political prisoners, 88 of whom were believed to be still imprisoned in 1986. These reports contained consistent allegations of torture being inflicted between 1979 and 1985. The organization also interviewed several former PRK police officers and government officials, who told it that in past years political prisoners had been tortured by their colleagues or Vietnamese advisory "experts" working with them. Torture of

Kampuchean political prisoners by Vietnamese "experts" assigned to PRK detention centres was alleged in several reports, as was the presence of Vietnamese personnel when PRK officials committed torture. Twelve political prisoners were allegedly killed during interrogation or died as a result of torture between 1979 and 1985, and over 30 others reportedly died in prison in that period due to inadequate medical treatment for injuries caused by torture, untreated diseases, or lack of food.

Severe beatings, whippings and other assaults were the forms of torture most commonly reported to Amnesty International. Also frequently reported were near-suffocation, usually by putting a plastic bag over the victim's head, near-drowning, sometimes using irritant liquids such as soapy water or fish-sauce, and electric shocks. Other reported tortures included being held in covered petrol drums and subjected to continuous loud noises, being burned with powdered limestone or heated instruments and being buried alive.

Amnesty International had the names of more than 400 of the several thousand political prisoners whom it thought were held without charge or trial in the PRK in 1986, including the names of several prisoners of conscience, but relatives had expressed fears that disclosing prisoners' names could put them at risk. The list included people believed to be imprisoned in detention centres in 14 of the PRK's 20 provinces and municipalities. Most of them were in national, provincial or municipal centres administered by the PRK authorities, but several were in centres run exclusively by Vietnamese personnel.

Although the PRK news media provided fewer statistics about political arrests in 1986 than in previous years, they did reveal that 19 people were arrested on political grounds throughout the country during one week in January, and seven in Kampung Thom province during the first quarter of the year. Statements emphasizing the importance of carrying out political arrests were broadcast by the official radio to the security forces. For example, it broadcast a March "circular", signed by Secretary General Heng Samrin of the ruling Revolutionary People's Party of Kampuchea, which called on the PRK authorities "firmly to implement . . . security plans for [the] year by fulfill[ing] additional plans to take turns sweeping up all kinds of enemy forces" and in particular "carry[ing] out well the task of unmasking hidden enemy elements". An editorial in July in the party journal *Pracheachun* similarly stressed that it was "imperative" to "vigorously stimulate . . . security measures to mop up . . . enemy elements hidden among the people".

Amnesty International received detailed reports of several people arrested during 1986 accused of opposition political activities. Three people were reportedly arrested in Siem Reap-Utdar Meanchey province, and one in the capital, Phnum Penh, all during the second quarter of the year. One was a low-ranking PRK police official, one a member of the Islamic Cham minority, one a health professional and one a small trader. They were reportedly detained without charge or trial and tortured during interrogation. Among the tortures allegedly inflicted on them were electric shocks and near-drowning. They were also alleged to have been held in dark cells, and two to have been shackled for long periods. The organization also received reports of two other political arrests, one of a low-ranking ministerial employee in Phnum Penh and another of a health professional in Kandal province.

In May Amnesty International wrote to the Chairperson of the PRK Council of Ministers, Hun Sen. It expressed its concern about reports of torture and ill-treatment of political prisoners imprisoned without charge or trial in the PRK. While regretting the lack of any response to the correspondence it had addressed to PRK authorities during 1985 (see *Amnesty International Report 1986*), Amnesty International requested permission to visit the PRK to discuss its concerns. In its September *Newsletter*, the organization publicized reports of torture in the PRK. At the same time, the organization again wrote to Chairman Hun Sen, requesting his comments on the reports, and in particular any information on safeguards against torture.

Amnesty International continued to be concerned about allegations that some of the 4,414 former political opponents who the PRK news media said had voluntarily surrendered to the authorities during the first 11 months of 1986 were held without charge or trial in "re-education" camps. In its May letter to Chairperson Hun Sen, the organization expressed concern at the lack of legal safeguards against the indefinite arbitrary restriction of such people, who were officially described as "misled" people who had "repented".

In October 1986 the PRK news media announced that 10 people accused of being DK-affiliated "counter-revolutionaries" who had committed acts of armed sabotage against the PRK had been tried in the province of Kampung Speu. This was the first known publicly announced political trial in the PRK since December 1983, and the first in the PRK's history to result in a publicized death sentence on a political prisoner in custody. Amnesty International called for commutation of the death sentence passed on Chea Saran and reiterated its concern that political suspects in the PRK might not receive fair trials.

Amnesty International was concerned about reports of human rights abuses by the three parties which formed the DK, which administered several hundred thousand Kampucheans. The organization received reports that some partners to the coalition had committed extrajudicial executions of political and criminal suspects; that they had held political prisoners, including prisoners of conscience, without charge or trial; that they had severely ill-treated political prisoners; and that they had systematically raped Vietnamese and other refugee women in military custody.

The organization received reports of three prison camps run by one coalition partner, the *Partie* of Democratic Kampuchea (PDK), the President of which was Khieu Samphan. Their prisoners were said to include political suspects held without charge or trial because of alleged "liberalism", some of whom were believed to be prisoners of conscience. Political prisoners suspected of serious offences are reportedly often shackled. In addition, the PDK news media claimed with some frequency during 1986 that its armed forces operating in the interior had killed non-combatants during offensive operations, and it appeared from these official accounts that the reported victims might in some instances have been executed in custody.

The organization also received reports of two prisons run by another coalition party, the Khmer People's National Liberation Front (KPNLF). They were said to be administered by KPNLF personnel who disputed the political authority of its original President, Son Sann. The prisoners reportedly included people suspected of espionage and of supporting Son Sann against his rivals. Political prisoners held in one of these prisons were allegedly put in dark cells, shackled and severely beaten. Amnesty International also received reports that KPNLF personnel — both those opposed to Son Sann and his supporters — had shot and beaten to death political and criminal suspects. In addition, it received reports that anti-Son Sann KPNLF troops had repeatedly raped Vietnamese and other refugee women taken into custody at their Chamkar Kor base camp, and that some of the victims had died as a result. The organization outlined these concerns in a meeting with Son Sann, the Prime Minister of the DK coalition government, in November.

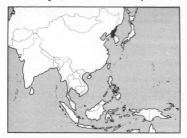

Korea (Democratic People's Republic of)

As in previous years, Amnesty International's work on the Democratic People's Republic of Korea (DPRK) continued to be seriously hampered by the lack of information emerging from the country. The authorities disclosed no information about arrests, trials or imprisonment for political offences, or the death penalty, except occasionally to announce that people allegedly entering the DPRK for espionage purposes had been arrested. However, a range of sources continued to allege that the rights of freedom of expression and association, guaranteed under the International Covenant on Civil and Political Rights to which the DPRK acceded in 1981, were strictly curtailed. According to these reports, individuals who criticized the President or his policies were liable to punishment by imprisonment or "corrective labour".

Amnesty International continued to receive reports that there were substantial numbers of political prisoners. Some were believed to be held in penal institutions, but others were reportedly sentenced to terms of "corrective labour" which could be served at a person's normal workplace (working for part or no wages) or at other designated places. These reportedly included mountainous areas in the northeast of the country where prisoners were set to work in agriculture or mining and where conditions were said to be very harsh.

Amnesty International was concerned about two Japanese nationals detained in the DPRK since November 1983. Isamu Beniko and Yoshio Kuriura were the captain and chief engineer of a refrigeration ship which sailed regularly between Nampo in the DPRK and Osaka in Japan. They were detained after Min Hong Kyu, a young North Korean army sergeant, hid on their ship and reached Japan in late October 1983. The DPRK authorities alleged that they were involved in espionage, and said that they would be released in exchange for the defector, who remained in Japan.

Although some prisoners were detained without trial, others were apparently brought to trial, in some cases at the scene of the alleged offence. Amnesty International was unable to ascertain whether defendants were afforded rights of defence and appeal.

The penal code provides the death penalty for a range of political and criminal offences. Amnesty International believed that death sentences were imposed and executions carried out, although details were not available.

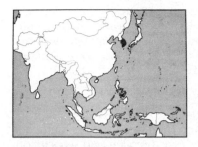

Korea (Republic of)

Amnesty International was concerned about a marked increase in the number of prisoners of conscience who faced long terms of imprisonment for alleged pro-communist activities, were detained for short periods or were placed under house arrest. Twenty-five prisoners of conscience arrested between 1971 and 1982 remained imprisoned. Reports of the ill-treatment and torture of prisoners continued to be received, including reports of three deaths in custody reportedly as a result of ill-treatment. Two students were sentenced to death for anti-government activities and espionage and 13 people convicted of criminal offences were executed.

On 11 June Amnesty International published *South Korea, Violations of Human Rights*. This report described the cases of 25 prisoners of conscience arrested between 1971 and 1982 who were convicted under the National Security Law of pro-communist activities or espionage for North Korea. Two remained in detention under the Public Security Law after completing their sentences because they refused to sign a statement that they had been "converted" to "anti-communism". The report also described the use of other laws to detain prisoners of conscience for shorter periods, such as the Law on Assemblies and Demonstrations, the Minor Offences Punishment Act and Article 104(2) of the Code of Criminal Procedure on "insulting and slandering the state". Analyzing several political cases, it pointed out frequent procedural irregularities such as arrests without warrant and prolonged pre-trial incommunicado detention and the use of confessions allegedly obtained under torture as evidence. Prisoners' testimonies of torture were reproduced and conditions conducive to ill-treatment and torture of prisoners identified. The report also described the use of the death penalty. It was submitted in the form of a memorandum to the South Korean Government in August 1985. The government told Amnesty International's visiting delegates in November that it was committed to protecting human rights but did not reply to the specific points in the memorandum. On 10 June Prime Minister Lho Shin-young told the National Assembly that his government would try to stop human rights abuses but that it could not be sure of preventing "acts of atrocity" at "grassroots level".

According to official statistics over 3,400 people were charged with political offences in 1986, many more than in 1985. Over 80 per cent were students; the others were workers, clergymen, Buddhist monks, members of political organizations, journalists, teachers and politicians. Some 1,500 were still in detention at the end of 1986. The rest were released with a warning or served sentences of up to 29 days in police custody under the Minor Offences Punishment Act. The majority of those held for longer periods were charged either under the Law on Assemblies and Demonstrations with participation in illegal demonstrations (which usually carried sentences of 18 months to three years' imprisonment) or under the National Security Law with pro-communist activities (which usually carried sentences of five or seven years). Student protests often involved violence, and Amnesty International was not able to establish in most cases whether the individual students arrested had used or advocated violence.

Between January and June several hundred people, mostly students, were arrested for calling for a revision of the constitution to allow presidential elections by direct suffrage instead of by an electoral college. From 12 to 24 February over 100 members of the Council for the Promotion of Democracy (CPD), a body chaired jointly by opposition leaders Kim Dae-jung and Kim Young-sam, and supporters of the opposition New Korea Democratic Party (NKDP) were briefly detained or placed under house arrest in Seoul and other cities to prevent a petition campaign demanding direct presidential elections. Amnesty International called for the release of all those who had peacefully called for constitutional revision.

On 3 May violent clashes between police and demonstrators in Inchon prevented a rally organized by the NKDP from taking place. Five student and dissident organizations were accused of having organized the violence to foment a popular uprising and overthrow the government. The NKDP stated that the violence had been started by agents provocateurs. The dissident organizations accused were part of *Mintongnyon*, the United Minjung Movement for Democracy and Unification (UMMDU), an umbrella organization of 23 dissident groups. Its Chairman, Reverend Moon Ik-kwan, previously adopted as a prisoner of conscience on three occasions, was arrested on 21 May, the day after he spoke at a rally at Seoul National University, during which a student burned himself to death in an act of protest against the government. The Reverend Moon Ik-kwan was charged with inciting campus unrest and with having ordered UMMDU members to prepare anti-government leaflets for the rally in Inchon on 3 May which, the authorities said, contributed to the rioting. On 4 November the Reverend Moon Ik-kwan, who had boycotted his trial, was sentenced to three years' imprisonment. Amnesty International again adopted him as a prisoner of conscience.

Throughout 1986 people were arrested for possessing books the authorities considered subversive. Among them were 12 people connected with three unlicensed publication groups in Seoul who were arrested on 25 March. Nine of them, including Koh Kyung-dae, Kim Sang-bok and Kang Woo-keun, were sentenced to up to four years' imprisonment under the National Security Law for "giving ideological support to radical students". Amnesty International sought details of the books they had published and believed that they might be prisoners of conscience.

Following the appearance on university campuses of wall-posters allegedly reproducing North Korean propaganda in mid-October, the government announced that it would act against all dissident groups it regarded as pro-communist and radical. At least 130 people were subsequently arrested and charged under the National Security Law with pro-communist activities. Among them were several prisoners of conscience for whose release Amnesty International campaigned. Yu Sung-hwan, an opposition member of the National Assembly, was arrested on 17 October for distributing the text of a speech before the Assembly in which he said that the government should stress Korean unification rather than anti-communism. Sagong Jun and Sohn Man-ho were arrested for giving him publications he reportedly used to draft his speech. On 8 November Han Kwang-ok, spokesperson of the CPD, was arrested for distributing a press statement questioning the authorities' claim that the students involved in a protest at Konkuk University between 28 and 31 October were communists. Between 10 and 15 December three journalists were arrested for publishing in *Mal* (The Word), an underground publication, specific government instructions to the media on the reporting of certain news items, including items about political arrests and torture.

Amnesty International urged the authorities to carry out impartial and thorough investigations into reports of torture and ill-treatment of prisoners and reiterated its recommendations for measures to prevent such abuses. Koh Kyung-dae, Kim Sang-bok and Kang Woo-keun, who were arrested on 25 March for publishing books the authorities considered subversive, were held incommunicado at the Anti-Communist Bureau of the National Police in Namyoung-dong, Seoul, for up to a week. They were reportedly beaten, and one of them subjected to electric shocks. On 13 April Hong Jung-sun, a television drama writer, was reportedly beaten by officers of the Agency for National Security Planning who suspected him of hiding a dissident wanted by the police. Several members of the Seoul Federation of Labour Movement were reportedly held for a week at the Songpa military security centre, south of Seoul, in May. One of them, Kim Min-su, was reportedly beaten, twice subjected to electric shocks, and forced five times to drink water to which chilli had been added. The others also claimed that they had been tortured.

Chang Mi-kyong, a factory worker and union activist, filed a complaint against the police in which she claimed to have been beaten and given electric shocks after her arrest in late April for distributing leaflets demanding a pay increase. Wide publicity was given to the case of Kwon In-suk, a student expelled from university because of her political activities. She was arrested on 4 June for using false identification papers in order to obtain work in a factory. She claimed that during the three days of her interrogation in Puchon police station she was beaten and sexually abused for refusing to give information on former students wanted by the police. The prosecution authorities which investigated her complaint against a police officer found that she had been subjected to physical and verbal abuse but concluded that her claims of sexual abuse were a "fabrication". The police officer was dismissed but no charges were brought against him. A group of 166 lawyers, supported by the Korean Federation of Bar Associations, challenged the prosecution authorities' conclusions but on 2 November the Seoul High Court turned down their application. Paik Ki-wan, a leader of the UMMDU, was arrested on 7 November for making a speech on 19 July in which he accused the government of covering up the sexual abuse of Kwon In-suk. Amnesty International called for his release and was particularly concerned about his health which had been poor since he was tortured in 1979.

In four separate trials, eight people were acquitted of murder or other criminal offences after the courts found that their convictions were based on false confessions obtained under torture. Amnesty International urged the authorities to investigate 18 incidents which occurred between March and October in 10 different prisons where prisoners were reportedly ill-treated after they protested about their conditions of detention. Amnesty International received reports that the prisoners were beaten, confined to punishment cells too small for them to lie down, and that some, who were on hunger-strike, were brutally forcibly fed.

The authorities did not reply to Amnesty International's requests for information about the outcome of their investigations into three deaths in detention. Chang Yi-kee died in late March and Kang

Ho-keun on 25 April, reportedly after being beaten when they objected to political indoctrination during their military training. Shin Ho-su was found dead in a cave in Chollanamdo eight days after he had been taken away by officers of the Anti-Communist Bureau of Inchon on 11 July. People who saw his body reported that his arms were tied behind his back and that there were bruises on his ankles and wrists, and challenged the official announcement that he had committed suicide.

Amnesty International urged the authorities to commute the death sentences on Yang Dong-hwa and Kim Song-man who were convicted on 20 January 1986 of anti-government activities and espionage for North Korea. The Supreme Court confirmed their sentences on 23 September. They had reportedly been tortured when held incommunicado in July and August 1985. Amnesty International also appealed for the commutation of the death sentence on Kim Song-chol for a series of offences including murder and robbery, which was upheld by the Supreme Court on 25 February. Amnesty International expressed its concern to the authorities about the execution on 26 and 27 May of 13 people convicted of criminal offences.

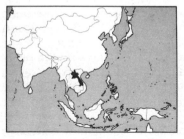

Laos

Amnesty International continued to be concerned about the detention and physical restriction of several thousand people without charge or trial, among them many prisoners of conscience. They had not been allowed to return home since being taken into custody for "re-education" at the time of a change in government in 1975. Amnesty International was also concerned about reports of the imprisonment without charge or trial of people accused of involvement in armed opposition activities or "espionage". It was concerned about allegations that some people held on political grounds had been subjected to torture or ill-treatment during interrogation or had been punished by being shackled, sometimes while being kept in dark cells. Another allegation of concern was that Laotian troops had extrajudicially killed 35 Laotian refugees in Thailand.

Thousands of people continued to be held for "re-education" in remote parts of at least seven provinces: Houa Phanh, Xieng

Khouang, Khammouan, Savannakhet, Salavan, Xekong and Attapeu. Most of them were restricted to camps where they did forced labour, including road construction, logging and clerical work. Some were restricted to agricultural settlements growing crops such as rice, coffee and sugar cane. Others were restricted to small towns where they worked in factories, as artisans, or in minor administrative posts for the local government. According to information Amnesty International received from people currently and formerly held for "re-education", from their relatives and from foreigners who had talked to them, they remained where they were involuntarily. Amnesty International believed that most were held not because of any offences they might have committed before 1975, but on account of the authorities' suspicions that they were opposed to the policies and practices of the current government. It considered that many of them could be prisoners of conscience. People held for "re-education" whom Amnesty International had adopted as prisoners of conscience included Khamkhing Souvanlasy, a former educationalist and secretary general of the Unesco National Commission for Laos; Samlith Ratsaphong, a former official in the pre-1975 Ministry of Information and a journalist, and Pane Rassavong, a former economic planner. The first two were restricted to Sop Pan camp and Pane Rassavong was held in Xamtai camp, both in Houa Phanh province. Amnesty International called for the government to release all prisoners of conscience held for "re-education", and to release any other people held for "re-education" if they were not to be promptly charged with criminal offences and fairly tried.

Amnesty International had appealed in April 1985 on behalf of more than 2,600 named individuals reportedly held for "re-education". During 1986 Amnesty International received reports that about 260 of them were released in 1985 or 1986, and also learned the names of nearly 200 people previously held for "re-education" who had been released before 1985. Most of those released had been held in Houa Phanh province in northeast Laos. Among them were the prisoner of conscience Khamtan Khanhalikham, a meteorologist who had been restricted to the province's Xamtai camp, and Kamseng Vorasane, a former police official. Amnesty International had appealed on their behalf for many years. Two people, former low-ranking army officers, were released in mid-1986 from Attapeu province in the southeast. Bansisomphonevong had been restricted to Samakhixay town, and Sonexay had been restricted to a camp known as Katamtok. They were among 180 former low-ranking military and civil service personnel held for "re-education" without charge or trial in Attapeu province on whose behalf Amnesty International had been appealing since April.

Some people released from "re-education" were given official documents issued by the Ministry of the Interior, copies of which Amnesty International was able to examine. Called "Authorization for Leaving to Be a Citizen", the documents had a space for the reason why the individual had been "liberated" (*potpoy*), and stated that the holder was "authorized to go to make a living . . . at home".

The organization interviewed several people who had been arrested after attempting to "jump" (*ton*) "re-education" without such documents and had been returned to restriction or imprisoned without charge or trial. According to their accounts and other reports, escaped detainees who had been rearrested had in recent years been imprisoned in jails in Sop Hao in Houa Phanh province, in Xai Settha and Xamkhe in Vientiane municipality, in Nong Pat in Vientiane province, in Keng Khan, Xepon, Phabang and Ban Dong in Savannakhet province, in Xanxay, Done Makkheua (Boeung Vay) and Samakhixai in Attapeu province, in Pakxe and Pakxong in Champassak province and in a secluded place near the Vietnamese border in Xekong province. Amnesty International received reports that in recent years, including 1986, people who were imprisoned after attempting to escape from "re-education" had been held in shackles for prolonged periods, sometimes in dark underground cells.

The organization also interviewed several people who had been imprisoned without charge or trial for allegedly supporting the armed opposition activities of "national salvation" (*kouxat*) groups, "spying" or "making trouble" in "re-education". They reported that they and people arrested on suspicion of organizing escape attempts had been tortured with electric shocks and severe beatings in recent years in Nong Pat, Samakhixai and Xamkhe prisons, and had also been shackled and in some instances held in dark cells.

In July Amnesty International wrote to Kaysone Phomvihane, Chairperson of the Laotian Council of Ministers, and other government officials about allegations that in June government armed forces had killed 35 Laotian refugees, including 11 women and 18 children, at a settlement near the border in northern Thailand. It received information suggesting that the killings may have been punishment for having left Laos and for suspected involvement in armed opposition activities. The organization called on the government to initiate a full investigation into the allegations. In response, the government provided Amnesty International with an official statement denying responsibility for the incident.

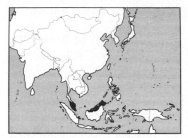

Malaysia

Amnesty International continued to be concerned about the long-term detention without charge or trial of about 30 prisoners, including a number of prisoners of conscience under the Internal Security Act (ISA), and about the increased use of the death penalty, mostly for offences related to drugs and firearms. It was also concerned about the extension of provisions under the Dangerous Drugs Act to introduce mandatory caning for minor offences. An Amnesty International delegation visited Malaysia during March 1986 to investigate information relating to the detention of political prisoners under the ISA.

Under Section 8 of the ISA people considered by the authorities to represent a threat to national security may be detained without charge or trial for renewable two-year periods. At the beginning of 1986 Amnesty International knew of approximately 80 such prisoners, most of them accused of being members of the banned Communist Party of Malaya (CPM). Some of these detainees had been held for more than 10 years. There is no opportunity for them to challenge their detention in court. Among the prisoners of conscience for whose release Amnesty International has appealed for many years were Wong Yong Huat and Loo Ming Leong, both held without trial since 1972. At least 14 prisoners who had been held since the mid-1970s were released during 1986. According to the government three people were arrested under this legislation during 1986.

Among those held under the ISA for whose release Amnesty International worked were members of the Islamic opposition party *Parti Islam se Malaysia* (PAS). Abu Bakar Bin Chik and Haji Suhaimi Said were released during 1986, having been detained since July 1984 and March 1985 (see *Amnesty International Report 1985* and *1986*). However, both men were released under ISA restriction orders which limited their freedom of movement and association. Amnesty International was also concerned about the detention without charge or trial under the ISA of 36 followers of the Islamic teacher Ibrahim Mahmud. Together with 123 others who were later released, they had been arrested in connection with the "Memali incident" in November 1985 when 18 people, including the teacher, died in violent clashes between Muslim activists and the police. The 36 had originally been arrested under the Emergency Ordinance, and in January 1986 they were served with two-year detention orders under the ISA. They were released in June, two months before Malaysia's general elections, by order of the

Head of State on the grounds that they no longer posed a threat to national security.

Those still detained under the ISA were believed to be held at the Kamunting Detention Centre in Taiping, the Police Rehabilitation Centre in Mukim Batu near Kuala Lumpur, and the Special Branch Detention Centre in Johore Bahru.

Amnesty International was concerned about the increasing use of the death penalty. At least 15 people were executed during the year, and at least 48 sentenced to death. In all cases the organization appealed to the government to commute the death sentences imposed, and expressed its regret at the executions that took place. Thirty-five of the death sentences were imposed following convictions for drug trafficking. Those executed were mostly Malaysian nationals but included three foreigners — two Australians and an Indonesian — who were hanged in July and August despite widespread appeals for clemency. This brought the number of people executed for drug trafficking offences since 1975, when the death penalty was introduced for such offences, to 47. A further 139 people had already been convicted and were awaiting the outcome of their appeals.

According to Malaysia's National Security Council, at least 590 suspected drug traffickers were arrested during the year under Section 39(B) of the Dangerous Drugs Act (1952), as amended in 1983. Conviction for trafficking carries a mandatory death penalty and the possession of 15 grams of heroin, 200 grams of cannabis or 1,000 grams of opium is considered sufficient evidence of trafficking. Amnesty International was also concerned about a new amendment to the Dangerous Drugs Act introduced in December which imposed stiffer penalties for minor drug offences, including mandatory caning of between six and 10 strokes, which Amnesty International considers cruel, inhuman and degrading punishment, in addition to a jail sentence.

At least nine people were sentenced to death during the year for the illegal possession of firearms under Section 57 of the ISA, which carries a mandatory death sentence. This brought the number of people convicted under this section of the ISA and awaiting the outcome of their appeals to 83. At least 31 people convicted under Section 57 of the ISA have been executed since 1975. Among them was Sim Kie Chon who was executed in March, after two stays of execution (see *Amnesty International Report 1986*).

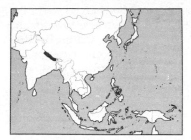

Nepal

Amnesty International was concerned about short-term detentions of people who participated in peaceful political activities or expressed criticism of the government and the "non-party" political system. Dozens of other political prisoners, some of whom had been held for over 18 months, remained in jail without formal charge or trial under the Public Security Act (PSA), although about 100 PSA detainees were released. A small number of Christians were arrested on charges of propagating their beliefs and trying to convert others to the Christian faith. Amnesty International received reports of torture of criminal suspects in police custody and of ill-treatment of political prisoners in a Kathmandu jail.

Under the constitution, introduced in 1962, political parties are officially prohibited, but in recent years political parties have continued to organize. During 1986 some political meetings were disrupted and those present taken briefly into custody. Politically active students were also arrested for holding meetings and demonstrations or for possessing allegedly seditious literature. In mid-July several people collecting signatures on a petition calling for the release of political prisoners were arrested, some of whom were still in jail at the end of 1986.

At the time of the elections to the *Rastriya Panchayat* (National Assembly), held on 12 May, several candidates and their supporters were reportedly arrested because during the election campaign they had made or distributed political statements deemed objectionable or anti-constitutional. One of them, Govinda Nath Upreti, was later charged under the Treason (Crime and Punishment) Act with accusing members of the Royal Family of responsibility for electoral malpractice. Under the Act, anyone convicted of fomenting "hatred, malice or contempt" towards the Royal Family may be sentenced to three years' imprisonment. For such offences, the Zonal Commissioner acts as both prosecuting authority and judge, a provision contravening internationally recognized legal standards.

A few other political prisoners, including people likely to be prisoners of conscience, were also arrested and charged under the Treason (Crime and Punishment) Act. They included several journalists. In November Amnesty International appealed for the release of Keshav Raj Pindali, the 71-year-old editor of *Saptahik Bimarsha* (Weekly Thought), and Rup Chand Bista, a member of the

Rastriya Panchayat, both of whom were reportedly charged under the Act. They were accused of spreading hatred and malice towards the king following the publication of a satirical poem written by Rup Chand Bista in *Saptahik Bimarsha* during the election campaign.

The majority of political prisoners, including prisoners of conscience, were held without formal charge or trial under the PSA. PSA detainees are served with nine-monthly detention orders, renewable up to a maximum of three years. The orders may not be challenged in court and the only means of review is through an Advisory Board, appointed at the government's discretion and restricted to making recommendations. During the first half of 1986 most of the prisoners held under the PSA in connection with the teachers' demonstrations and *satyagraha* (civil disobedience movement) of 1985 (see *Amnesty International Report 1986*) were released. One exception was Bishnu Bahadur Manandhar, a communist leader who had been arrested on 4 June 1985 during the *satyagraha*. In August Amnesty International wrote to the newly-elected Prime Minister, Marich Man Singh Shrestha, expressing concern that under the provisions of the PSA detainees could be held arbitrarily, without charge or trial, on executive orders. The letter also raised a number of cases from among the dozens of prisoners detained under the PSA, including that of Bishnu Bahadur Manandhar. Amnesty International urged that these prisoners should be released unconditionally if no criminal charges were to be brought against them.

Of the 100 or more prisoners still held in January 1986 in connection with the 1985 bombings some remained in incommunicado police custody in Kathmandu, most of them reportedly at the District Police Office at Hanuman Dhoka. During the first four months of the year they were gradually transferred to various jails where other prisoners arrested during the bombing campaign were already held. All these prisoners were understood to have been arrested under the Destructive Crimes (Special Control and Punishment) Act 1985, which allows suspects to be held in police custody for up to 180 days. In late 1985 and early 1986, the special court established under the Act ordered the release on bail of at least some of the prisoners, but before their release they were served with further detention orders under the PSA. Many of them were eventually released in June and early October. Among those remaining in detention were Dr Jitendra Mahaseth and Mahadev Shah, both in Nakhu Jail, Kathmandu. In late October the trial of some 100 people charged with involvement in the bombings began before the special court in closed session.

Amnesty International was also investigating the alleged "disappearance" of at least three people arrested at the time of the bomb explosions. One was Dr Laxmi Narayan Jha, a medical practitioner in Janakpur. Arrested in late June 1985, he was kept in police custody in Janakpur for some two weeks before being transferred to Kathmandu. He was initially reported to be held there in the District Police Office. In response to a *habeas corpus* petition filed by his family in the Supreme Court, police officials denied that he was in their custody. His whereabouts remained unknown at the end of 1986.

Among the other detainees held under the PSA and released during 1986 were seven prisoners held beyond the expiry of sentences imposed for politically motivated criminal offences: six were freed in June, and Radha Krishna Mainali, whom the Supreme Court had ordered to be released in January 1985 before it was made known that he was held under the PSA, was freed in December.

The Nepalese Constitution prohibits efforts to convert any person from one religious faith to another. The penal code provides for three years' imprisonment for propagating religious faiths so as "to disrupt the traditional religion of the Hindu community", and six years for conversion. The sentence for any person who is converted is up to one year. Several Christians were arrested on charges of seeking conversions and two Muslims for propagating their faith. On 5 April a priest and two nuns, all Indian nationals, together with several Nepalese Christians, were arrested by the police in the eastern part of the country and charged with seeking conversions. They were reportedly beaten in police custody and forced to sign confessions they had not read. They were released on bail 12 days later. Other Christians who were prosecuted and sentenced were also granted bail while awaiting trial and pending appeal after conviction.

During 1986 Amnesty International received reports that prisoners arrested for criminal offences had been tortured in police custody. One prisoner is reported to have died as a result of police torture in November 1985 in Rajbiraj, Sagarmatha Zone. Chaudhry was reportedly beaten and had a wooden stick pressed against his throat to stop him breathing. The local police reportedly stated that he committed suicide by hanging himself. The doctor who conducted the post-mortem found that Chaudhry's body showed bruising on the neck and chest and substantial swelling on the front of the neck. Four police officers were subsequently tried in connection with the death. One was convicted of the offence and three were acquitted. The doctor responsible for the post-mortem report was understood to have been dismissed from government service in January, for "involvement in politics". In July some political prisoners held at the Central Jail, Kathmandu were reportedly beaten by prison warders. They also complained of being held for several days in handcuffs and in solitary confinement.

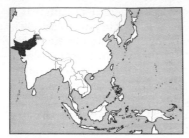

Pakistan

Amnesty International was concerned about the arrests of hundreds of opposition party members who were jailed for short periods for participating in non-violent political activities. Dozens of members of the Ahmadiyya community were arrested for defying the ban on practising their faith. Several long-term prisoners of conscience were released during 1986, but political prisoners convicted under the previous martial law administration remained without judicial redress. They had been sentenced by military courts after trials which Amnesty International considered unfair. Reports of extrajudicial executions, particularly in Sind province, and of torture by the police were investigated by the organization. Dozens of floggings were imposed by the courts, and several death sentences, although the frequency of such punishments was less than in previous years.

Martial law was lifted on 30 December 1985. Military courts were abolished and constitutional rights suspended since 1977, such as freedom of speech and freedom of assembly, were restored. The High Courts could again hear petitions invoking fundamental rights. However, before the lifting of martial law, the constitution had been amended to provide an absolute indemnity for all acts under the martial law regulations. This was intended to prevent prisoners sentenced by military courts from challenging the legality of their convictions.

Among the prisoners of conscience released during 1986 were Rasul Bux Palejo, Fazil Rahu and Dr Hasan Zafar Arif (see *Amnesty International Report 1986*), who had been held without trial under detention orders for five and a half years, two and a half years and one and a half years respectively. Other prisoners of conscience were freed at the end of their prison sentences. They included the peasant leader Jam Saqi who had been in jail since December 1978, and student activists Sher Mohammad Mangrio and Imdad Hussain Chandio who had been in jail for over five years. Amnesty International continued to appeal for the release of Ahmad Kamal Warsi and Ghulam Shabbir Shar, arrested in July 1980, who were serving seven-year sentences imposed by a military court in 1985. They had been convicted of sedition for possessing "anti-state literature" and other charges relating to their non-violent political activities.

The alliance opposition of more than a dozen political parties, the

Movement for the Restoration of Democracy (MRD), which had boycotted national elections held under martial law in 1985, continued to call for new elections. Huge public gatherings were held in the weeks following the return in April of Benazir Bhutto, the leader of the Pakistan People's Party (PPP), the largest party in the MRD. In defiance of a government ban on rallies on Independence Day, 14 August, the MRD continued to organize demonstrations in Lahore and Karachi. Amnesty International was concerned that hundreds of MRD leaders and activists had been arrested in the days preceding the planned demonstrations and were held for some weeks without trial under the Maintenance of Public Order Ordinance (MPO). Benazir Bhutto was arrested following her attempt to address a public meeting in Karachi on 14 August. Further demonstrations, to protest at these arrests, were held during the remainder of August and early September, and many hundreds of people were arrested. Some of these demonstrations, particularly in Sind province, resulted in violent clashes with the police. Benazir Bhutto was released on 8 September and by the end of the month all the prisoners held under the MPO were freed.

During September and October leaders of the Sindhi-Baluch-Pakhtoon Front (SBPF), which advocates a confederal structure for Pakistan, toured Sind province to promote their party's program. In early November, several were arrested under the MPO. Mumtaz Ali Bhutto, the party's convenor, was arrested on the grounds that his speeches had "aimed at disrupting the territorial integrity of the country . . . creating commotion and disturbing public tranquillity . . ." Another 10 leaders of the SBPF were arrested and reportedly charged with sedition. Amnesty International asked the Sind authorities for the reasons for their arrest and expressed concern that their detention might have violated their right to freedom of expression.

Members of the Ahmadiyya community continued to face arrest and up to three years' imprisonment for calling themselves Muslims or using Muslim practices in worship (see *Amnesty International Report 1985* and *1986*). In Mardan, more than 15 Ahmadis were arrested and charged. They included two brothers, shop proprietors, who were arrested because the cash receipt pad used in their shop was inscribed with a Muslim epithet, "In the name of God the Benificent, the Merciful". They were each sentenced to five years' imprisonment, charged under two sections of the Pakistan Penal Code (PPC). On the morning of 17 August, the Muslim festival of *Eid*, over 100 Ahmadis who had gathered at the community's place of worship in Mardan were taken into police custody after which their place of worship was demolished by a group of local people. All were released late the same night, except for four prominent members of the community who were charged under Section 298 of the PPC. Similar arrests took place in Karachi, Quetta and other parts of the country. Those convicted were sentenced to between one and 10 years' imprisonment. While awaiting trial or appeal hearings, these prisoners were released on bail.

Amnesty International continued to appeal for the retrial of over 100 political prisoners charged with criminal conspiracy and sedition and sentenced to long periods of imprisonment by military courts during martial law. They had been sentenced in closed trials, with no right of appeal. Amnesty International believed their trials failed to conform to international standards of fairness and was concerned that they still had no form of judicial redress. Amnesty International called for them to be retried before an ordinary court in which all minimum legal safeguards for a fair trial were guaranteed. In spite of the constitutional ban on challenging convictions by military courts, some prisoners filed petitions before the high courts, arguing that the military courts which had convicted them were constituted in contravention of military law, or that their arrest and interrogation had been unlawful. No progress had been made by the end of the year. In late 1986 the Minister for Justice and Parliamentary Affairs repeatedly stated that the government was considering a proposal to grant the right of appeal to these prisoners but no further details had been announced by the end of the year.

Allegations of extrajudicial executions by law enforcement personnel were investigated by Amnesty International. In Lahore, two men were shot dead on 18 September after a curfew had been imposed during clashes between Sunni and Shi'a Muslims. According to the authorities, the men had been shot by law enforcement personnel as they damaged a Shi'a mosque. But local residents claimed they had been summarily killed as they were eating lunch in a house near the mosque. Amnesty International called for a judicial inquiry to be held into these deaths.

Amnesty International also received complaints that some unarmed villagers from rural areas of Sind province, where the anti-government protests in August had been most widespread, had been arbitrarily killed by police or paramilitary personnel in settlements where the authorities stated that criminals were sheltering. For example, Amnesty International received allegations that in the village of Ahmed Khan Brihmani, near Dadu, an elderly man named Chatto Khan was summarily killed by law enforcement personnel on 23 August. Units from the paramilitary Indus Rangers and local police were said to have ordered all the houses to be evacuated, and, finding him inside one of them reportedly dragged him out and shot him at close range. Amnesty International was seeking further details about this and other alleged arbitrary killings in Sind. No official inquiries were known to have been initiated into these deaths.

Throughout the country, torture of criminal suspects in police custody was reported. Some political prisoners were also allegedly tortured, apparently to intimidate them. Allah Dino, from the village of Tando Mohammad Khan, was arrested in late August by police after he had filed a petition to a local court complaining that his brother had been unlawfully killed during a demonstration held by the PPP on 5 July. Allah Dino was kept in police custody for 15 days and reportedly beaten on the soles of his feet and his back, and hung upside down. He was reportedly then forced to make his thumb impression on a paper he could not read, authorizing the withdrawal of his petition. In Lahore, Qamar Anjum, a student activist in a faction of the Muslim League belonging to the MRD, was arrested on 25 August after addressing a public meeting. According to his bail petition both his feet were injured "due to physical torture by the police" and he needed five days' hospital treatment.

Sentences of flogging continued to be imposed, mainly for drug-related offences or violation of Islamic ordinances concerning sexual offences.

Amnesty International continued to appeal for the total abolition of the use of bar fetters and shackles on prisoners. During the year a few political prisoners and a much larger number of prisoners held on criminal charges, had been kept in fetters for varying periods, in violation of international standards for the treatment of prisoners.

Large numbers of prisoners reportedly remained under sentence of death, although the precise number was not known. According to the official figures published by the Jail Reforms Committee, established by the government in 1983 to review the prison system, there were 2,105 prisoners under sentence of death in December 1984, including those awaiting appeal. Death sentences continued to be imposed in criminal cases. In Punjab province, more than 40 prisoners were executed between July 1985 and June 1986. Some prisoners previously sentenced to death by military courts challenged their convictions in the high courts and were granted interim orders staying execution. Among these was Javed Iqbal, who was convicted of murder five days before the lifting of martial law. According to the petition filed on his behalf, Javed Iqbal was already in jail at the time the murder was allegedly committed, and an entry in the jail register apparently confirmed this. The cases of four prisoners sentenced to death by military courts in verdicts announced after the lifting of martial law were submitted by Amnesty International to the UN Special Rapporteur on summary or arbitrary executions.

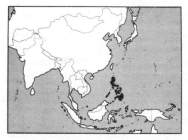

Philippines

Before Corazon Aquino assumed the presidency on 25 February, Amnesty International had been concerned about the indefinite detention of prisoners of conscience and possible prisoners of conscience under emergency legislation which the government of President Ferdinand Marcos had retained from the martial law period (1972 to 1981). The organization had also been concerned about widespread reports that members of the Armed Forces of the Philippines and paramilitary groups under their command had tortured political prisoners and had been responsible for "disappearances" and extrajudicial executions of opposition figures and suspected supporters of the New People's Army (NPA), the armed wing of the Communist Party of the Philippines. Amnesty International had also been concerned about the continued imposition of death sentences, although no judicial executions had been carried out since 1976.

Reports of human rights violations increased during the campaign preceding the presidential election on 7 February. Amid accusations of electoral fraud, the National Assembly declared President Marcos the winner on 14 February. Corazon Aquino, his opponent, also claimed victory and called for a campaign of civil disobedience. On 22 February Acting Chief of Staff of the Armed Forces Fidel Ramos and Minister of National Defence Juan Ponce Enrile withdrew support from Ferdinand Marcos, and over the next four days tens of thousands of people went into the streets in support of Corazon Aquino and the rebel officers. On 25 February Corazon Aquino was sworn in as President and Ferdinand Marcos fled into exile.

The new government came to power with a stated commitment to the protection of human rights. On 27 February President Aquino announced that all political prisoners would be released. With Executive Order No. 1, she restored the writ of *habeas corpus*, and with Executive Order No. 8 of 18 March, she established a Presidential Committee on Human Rights (PCHR) chaired by former Senator Jose W. Diokno. The PCHR was given a mandate to investigate complaints of past and current human rights abuses and to propose safeguards to ensure that violations did not take place in the future. On 28 February and 25 March Amnesty International wrote to President Aquino welcoming the initiatives her government had taken towards the protection of human rights.

An Amnesty International mission visited the Philippines in May to hold talks with the President and other officials of the new government and with representatives of non-governmental organizations about the protection of human rights. Based on those discussions Amnesty International sent a memorandum to the Philippines Government in July which outlined further safeguards for consideration by the government to ensure fair trials for political prisoners, eliminate torture, "disappearances" and extrajudicial executions and abolish the death penalty. Many of these measures were already under consideration by the government and by the end of 1986 a number of them had been implemented. The government ratified two important international human rights standards, the UN Convention against Torture and the International Covenant on Civil and Political Rights, in June and October respectively, and a revised Bill of Rights was included in the draft of a new constitution, prepared by a Constitutional Commission in October, which specifically prohibited torture and abolished the death penalty. A PCHR proposal which went into effect in July as Memorandum Order No. 20 required the study of human rights to be included as an "integral and indispensable" part of the education and training of all police, military and other arresting and investigating personnel. In November President Aquino repealed Presidential Decrees 1877 and 1877-A, which under the previous government had authorized the detention without recourse to the courts of people suspected of national security offences.

Reports of human rights violations received by Amnesty International during 1986 were far fewer than in previous years. By the close of 1986 Amnesty International was not aware of any prisoners of conscience still in detention. As a result of President Aquino's directive of 27 February, over 500 political prisoners held under Presidential Commitment Orders or Preventive Detention Actions (see *Amnesty International Report 1986*) were released, among them 23 prisoners of conscience on whose behalf Amnesty International had been working. However, over 100 other prisoners whose detention may have been politically motivated but who were charged with criminal offences reportedly remained in prison at the end of 1986. A Presidential Committee on Political Prisoners/Detainees chaired by the Minister of Justice was established to review their cases, and by the end of August the Committee had developed procedures under which such prisoners could apply for pardon. By the end of the year, 90 cases had been reviewed and 15 prisoners had been recommended for pardon.

Amnesty International continued to work during 1986 on behalf of six people who "disappeared" under the government of President Marcos. These included Father Rudy Romano, a priest who "disappeared" in Cebu City in July 1985, and John Seva and Emilio Togonon, organizers for the National Federation of Sugar Workers who "disappeared" in Bacolod, Negros after a rally they helped to organize in March 1985. Amnesty International transmitted to the PCHR its concerns about these men and about two who "disappeared" after the change in government, Ernesto Delantes and Anastacio Magsulit, both of Negros. At the end of 1986 Ernesto Delantes, who reportedly "disappeared" on 7 March after having been arrested by soldiers of the 7th Infantry Battalion in Kabankalan, Negros, was still missing; Anastacio Magsulit, however, who was reported to have "disappeared" on 31 May, after having been abducted by uniformed personnel from the 7th Infantry Battalion and Civilian Home Defense Forces (CHDF) in Tapi, Kabankalan, was returned to his family in July.

Amnesty International continued to be concerned about reports of extrajudicial execution of suspected supporters of the NPA and of people active in organizations alleged to be linked to the National Democratic Front (NDF). In its memorandum to the Government of the Philippines in July Amnesty International stated that international human rights standards required that all reports of possible extrajudicial executions and "disappearances" should be impartially and effectively investigated. In this regard, in December representatives of the organization discussed with the Minister of Justice the investigation into the November killing of trade union leader Rolando Olalia by people reportedly linked to the military. The Minister said that the Ministry of Justice was committed to strengthening the National Bureau of Investigation so that all reports of such killings could be effectively investigated.

Amnesty International also received reports of abuses by the NPA including torture and killing of suspected informants, landowners and local officials. Amnesty International as a matter of principle condemns the torture or execution of prisoners by anyone, including opposition groups.

In December Amnesty International representatives met the Minister of Justice and members of the PCHR to discuss the remaining political detainees and procedures for investigating reported violations. They also met representatives of human rights organizations, local government officials and regional military commanders to discuss specific cases of reported violations in northern Luzon, Bicol and Panay as well as the human rights situation in those regions more generally.

More than 400 prisoners were under sentence of death at the end of 1986. In July Amnesty International sent a memorandum recommending abolition of the death penalty to the Minister of Justice for transmission to the Constitutional Commission. In a letter to the Minister in November Amnesty International welcomed the inclusion in the draft bill of Rights of a section abolishing the death penalty. Under the draft bill, the death penalty would be abolished "unless for compelling reasons involving heinous crimes the Congress hereafter provides for it."

Singapore

Amnesty International continued to appeal for the release of one prisoner of conscience who had been detained without trial for 20 years. It was also concerned about the use of the death penalty, which was mandatory for drugs offences.

Chia Thye Poh, a former member of parliament representing the opposition *Barisan Socialis*, Socialist Front, had been detained since October 1966 under the Internal Security Act (ISA) which provided for indefinite detention without judicial review at the discretion of the Minister for Home Affairs. Chia Thye Poh had never been charged, although in May 1985 the government alleged that he was a member of the outlawed Communist Party of Malaya (CPM) who had been instructed to penetrate the *Barisan Socialis* in order to destabilize the government. The authorities persistently demanded what amounted to a confession of guilt in exchange for his release. On 28 October the Foreign Minister stated that Chia Thye Poh would be released if he gave "a simple undertaking to renounce the use of force to overthrow the Government" and that "alternatively [he can] go to any country willing to accept him". Amnesty International believed that Chia Thye Poh was imprisoned because of his non-violent political activities and appealed again for his unconditional release in its "Prisoner of the Month" campaign in September.

Amnesty International learned of one execution, in January, of a labourer for drug trafficking, and of the imposition of the death sentence on a Malaysian, Tan Sek Cheong, who was convicted of drug trafficking in May. The organization appealed for the sentence to be commuted. Under the Misuse of Drugs Act (1973) as amended in 1975, possession of, and unauthorized traffic in over 15 grams of heroin or fixed amounts of other drugs incurred a mandatory death penalty. At least 20 prisoners convicted of drug offences had been executed since 1975. Three other prisoners, including two women convicted in 1981 for the ritual murder of two children, were still awaiting the outcome of their appeals against the death sentence.

Amnesty International also remained concerned about the routine imposition of mandatory canings of three to 12 strokes for a wide variety of offences ranging from rape to a second conviction for putting up posters without permission, on the grounds that it constitutes cruel, inhuman or degrading punishment.

On 1 August parliament adopted amendments to the Newspaper and Printing Presses Act (1974), empowering the Minister for Communications and Information to curtail the distribution of foreign periodicals without actually banning them. Anyone illegally selling or distributing copies of a restricted publication became liable to a prison term of up to two years and a fine of up to S$10,000 (US$4,680). A leading international weekly was declared a restricted publication and had its circulation immediately curtailed. In September parliament passed amendments to the Parliament (Privilege, Immunities and Powers) Act (1962), giving parliament the power to suspend any member of parliament's immunity from civil proceedings for statements made in the house and to imprison a member for the remainder of the current session in addition to imposing a fine of up to S$50,000 if found guilty of dishonourable conduct, abuse of privilege or contempt. Amnesty International was monitoring the application of both amendments to the law.

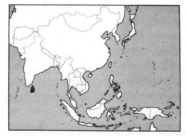

Sri Lanka

Arbitrary killings of hundreds of Tamil civilians, often in reprisal for attacks by armed Tamil groups, continued to be reported as armed conflict between such groups and government forces intensified. A major concern was the "disappearance" of well over 300 young Tamil men during the last three years; a number of them were feared to have died as a result of secret shootings in army or police custody or as a result of torture, which was widespread. Thousands of political suspects were arrested under the Prevention of Terrorism Act (PTA) and Emergency Regulations. Many were held for several years without trial, often after long periods of incommunicado detention. The majority were Tamils, but increasing numbers were Sinhalese suspected of links with armed Tamil groups or involvement in alleged attempts to overthrow the government. Amnesty International was also concerned about courts trying political suspects under special PTA procedures with changed rules of evidence.

Armed Tamil groups seeking a separate Tamil state in the north and east of the country increased their activities, particularly in eastern Sri Lanka, killing hundreds of security forces personnel in combat. They abducted and killed dozens of alleged "informers" and several Tamil civilians, including some political leaders. Armed Tamil groups also acknowledged responsibility for killing unarmed Sinhalese civilians in the capital Colombo and in villages in eastern Sri Lanka; some of these killings were said to be in reprisal for widespread extrajudicial killings of Tamil civilians by the army, Special Task Force (STF) of the police and the paramilitary "home guards" in the north and east. In its communications to the government during 1986 Amnesty International stressed that, as a matter of principle, it condemned the torture or execution of prisoners by anyone, including armed opposition groups. It emphasized, however, that such acts of violence could never justify the security forces themselves resorting to torture, extrajudicial killings and "disappearances", practices then widely reported throughout Sri Lanka.

Amnesty International received hundreds of reports that people taken away by members of the security forces "disappeared"; officials subsequently denied knowledge of their arrest or whereabouts or stated that they had been released. On 10 September Amnesty International launched a campaign and published a report, *"Disappearances" in Sri Lanka*, the text of which had previously been presented to the President and the Minister of National Security with a request for comments. Amnesty International urged the government to explain what had happened to 272 people reported to have "disappeared" between June 1983 and April 1986. All but one of the "disappeared" were Tamil. Many were farmers, labourers and fishermen, often from poor families. Others were students and civil servants and one was a Roman Catholic priest, Father Mary Bastian, who was killed, according to witnesses, by soldiers on 5 January 1985. His death was initially reported in an Information Department press release two days later, but was subsequently officially denied. Amnesty International said that it had evidence in all these cases that the "disappeared" had been taken away by members of the army, air force or, in the Eastern Province, by the STF. In a few instances, members of the paramilitary "home guards" were allegedly responsible. The "disappeared" were reportedly taken to camps and police stations in Amparai, Batticaloa, Jaffna, Mannar, Trincomalee and Vavuniya districts. In one case, eye-witnesses reported that at least 28 young men were taken away from Naipattimunai and other villages in the Kalmunai area in the Amparai district on 17 May 1985 by STF personnel. There was evidence that the STF shot and killed them and disposed of their bodies in secret, but the government repeatedly denied that they had been arrested or shot, although it failed to explain what had happened to them. Paul Nallanayagam, President of the Kalmunai Citizens Committee, who had made on-the-spot investigations, was arrested the day after he had spoken to journalists about the incident and was charged with spreading rumours or false statements (see *Amnesty International Report 1986*). During his trial, which took place between March and July and ended in his acquittal, the High Court judge found that the evidence which was produced "cast a serious doubt on the prosecution case that no arrests took place at Naipattimunai by the STF officials on 17 May 1985".

In its report, Amnesty International called on the government to establish speedy and independent investigations into the whereabouts of the "disappeared" and to inform their relatives immediately. It also recommended that the government set up a regularly updated central register of arrests to which lawyers, relatives and the courts could have immediate access and that security personnel found responsible for "disappearances" should be prosecuted. By the end of 1986, 72 more "disappearances" had been reported to Amnesty International.

On 25 September the government stated that the report was "one-sided and ignored counter-affidavits the government had filed with the United Nations". However, despite four urgent requests by Amnesty International to the Minister of National Security in September and October, the government failed to make available the information it had given the UN and Amnesty International was therefore unable to comment publicly on it. The Chairman of the official Media Centre suggested that Amnesty International should bring cases of "disappearances" before the Sri Lankan courts so that the government could cross-examine witnesses. In response, Amnesty International emphasized that it was the government's responsibility to investigate and clarify "disappearances", a duty the UN had also underlined. Amnesty International said witnesses risked repercussions if their testimonies implicated security forces personnel in "disappearances". It urged the government to invite the UN Working Group on Enforced or Involuntary Disappearances to visit Sri Lanka but by the end of 1986 it had not visited the country nor had the International Committee of the Red Cross been given permission to carry out protection activities there. In December the government reportedly asked an official body to maintain a register of missing persons but Amnesty International received no reply to its request for information on this. Amnesty International's various requests to the President and Minister of National Security to visit Sri Lanka to discuss its concerns also received no response.

By the end of 1986, Amnesty International had been able to clarify only three "disappearances": two people had been found to be imprisoned in Welikada prison, Colombo, awaiting trial, and a third had been released from Boosa Army Camp after seven months' unacknowledged detention. The UN Working Group on Disappearances had considered 326 cases by the end of 1986; despite a government response on 212 cases, the Working Group said only five had been resolved and the fate and whereabouts of 321 people remained unclear.

There were continuing reports, particularly from eastern Sri Lanka, that unarmed Tamils had been shot dead deliberately in reprisal for attacks by Tamil separatist groups on security forces personnel and civilians. In a report released in April on extrajudicial killings in Sri Lanka from September 1985 to March 1986, Amnesty International described in detail 10 such incidents. The organization had dozens of eye-witness accounts describing how Tamil men were taken out of their houses to be shot, often within sight of their relatives. Although some inquests were held, Amnesty International recommended that the government order an independent body to investigate alleged extrajudicial killings to determine criminal responsibility. Officials often stated that Tamil civilians were killed "during a shoot-out" or by armed Tamil groups, but in many cases Amnesty International had evidence that they were in fact victims of extrajudicial killings by the security forces. One example was the killing of Brother M. Wenceslaus on 20 June at the Tholakatty Monastery, Jaffna. The next day, the government announced that he had been killed by "Tamil terrorists". However, three witnesses testified during an inquest that they saw between 10 and 50 soldiers going towards the shed where Brother Wenceslaus was working and then heard a gun shot. One witness testified that he saw soldiers speak to Brother Wenceslaus and hit him before hearing the fatal shot. The inquest returned a verdict of homicide. Amnesty International was not aware of any action by the police to identify those responsible in this and many similar cases of alleged extrajudicial executions by security forces personnel, hundreds of which were reported during 1986.

Thousands of suspects, mainly Tamils but also Sinhalese, were arrested and held without trial under the PTA. Some were released within weeks of arrest but others were kept in prolonged detention. Many of these were initially held incommunicado, often for periods exceeding the legal maximum of 18 months. Many were then held under Emergency Regulations permitting indefinite detention without trial. Thousands were transferred to prisons or camps in the south. At the end of 1986 over 2,500 people were officially reported to be detained in Boosa Army Camp, the largest camp in the south. Among the detainees were seven women and a 14-year-old girl.

An increasing number of arrests in the south of both Tamils and Sinhalese were reported. By the end of 1986 over 400 Sinhalese were estimated to be detained under the PTA and Emergency Regulations, among them Pulsara Liyanage, a lecturer at Kelaniya University arrested on 1 November. She was one of 60 people described by officials as "Sinhala extremists, believed to have links with northern terrorist groups". They included members of left-wing groups, among them the *Janatha Vimukti Peramuna Nava Pravanathayaya* (JVP NP), New Tendency, and the *Sama Jawadi Janatha Viyaparaya* (SJV), Socialist People's Movement. They had not been charged or tried by the end of 1986. Among the others arrested were students detained for putting up posters opposing government policies.

Of the estimated 100 Tamils of Indian origin arrested between 1983 and September 1986, 60 were still detained at the end of 1986 in Welikada Prison, Colombo and Bogambara Prison, Kandy. Of these, 22 had been held for nearly two years without charge or trial and were among over 200 Tamil detainees held under the PTA whose cases had been taken up by Amnesty International for investigation. Most claimed they had been tortured.

Over 100 Tamil detainees were reportedly tried under the PTA on charges of failing to give information to the police about the activities of armed Tamil groups or of creating hatred amongst communities. They were given prison sentences ranging from several weeks to five years. Amnesty International was concerned that many of them were reportedly convicted on the basis of "confessions" allegedly obtained under torture by the police or army. Statements made to the police are normally not admissable as evidence in the courts, but the PTA permits such statements and places the burden on the accused to prove that statements were made under duress.

Amnesty International continued to receive allegations of torture at various police stations and army camps. Released prisoners stated that they had been beaten, often on the soles of the feet, hung upside down, forced to inhale burning chilli fumes and burnt with cigarettes.

Female detainees said they had been beaten, had had police batons forced into their vaginas and had been raped. Torture was also reported from Boosa Army Camp where prisoners were reportedly held in unhygienic conditions without medical treatment. Detainees were reportedly beaten with pipes, sometimes resulting in broken limbs, had chilli powder applied to sensitive parts of the body, and both male and female detainees complained of sexual abuse.

Amnesty International continued to oppose the deportation of Tamils to Sri Lanka by other governments. Several Tamils were detained, apparently for short periods, on arrival in Colombo after being returned against their will from France, Switzerland and Australia where they had sought political asylum.

On 16 October a Dutch national, Cornelius Stephanus Vanderhulst, was sentenced to death for attempting to smuggle heroin. No executions have been carried out since the present government assumed office in 1977.

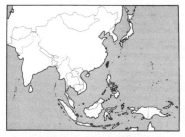

Taiwan

Amnesty International continued to appeal for the release of 19 prisoners of conscience arrested between 1975 and 1980 and to urge the retrial of some 70 prisoners, most of whom were arrested in the 1970s and were convicted of sedition after military trials which Amnesty International considered unfair. During 1986, 27 political prisoners were released, including one prisoner of conscience. Amnesty International received reports of torture and ill-treatment of criminal prisoners and of several deaths in custody. Seven people convicted of murder were executed.

On 10 October Amnesty International wrote to President Chiang Ching-kuo welcoming his announcement on 7 October that his government would soon lift martial law, in force in Taiwan since 1949, and end the practice of trying civilians by military courts. Amnesty International believed that the procedures of military courts which tried civilians for sedition and serious criminal offences carrying the death penalty contravened international standards of fair trial. Amnesty International was concerned because suspects tried under the Military Trial Law were denied access to lawyers for up to four months until their indictment, military trials were sometimes held in closed sessions and, in practice, military courts were not entirely independent from the government.

Amnesty International was concerned about the reported ill-health of two prisoners of conscience, Chen Ming-chong and Yang Chin-hai. The authorities supplied Amnesty International with information on their medical condition and treatment. In July Amnesty International wrote to the government acknowledging that Chen Ming-chong and Yang Chin-hai had been given medical treatment but expressing concern at their continued ill-health and urging their immediate release. Chen Ming-chong had a history of illness including a peptic ulcer. He had previously been arrested in the 1950s and spent 10 years in prison for allegedly belonging to a communist organization. He was rearrested in July 1976 and sentenced to 15 years' imprisonment for allegedly plotting an armed communist rebellion. However, to Amnesty International's knowledge, the only evidence that Chen Ming-chong had planned to smuggle arms into Taiwan consisted of "confessions" by himself and his co-defendant, reportedly extracted under torture. He was also said to have assisted an opposition member of the Legislative *Yuan* (Assembly) during his election campaign in December 1975 and to have been involved in a project to set up an opposition party. Yang Chin-hai, a businessman and the president of the Kaohsiung District Chamber of Commerce, had assisted opposition candidates in local and national elections. He supported Yen Ming-sheng in the December 1975 elections to the Legislative *Yuan* and was arrested with him in May 1976. Both men had been involved in a project to set up an opposition party. Yang Chin-hai and Yen Ming-sheng were convicted of planning to overthrow the government by distributing "subversive literature" and planning acts of sabotage. They were sentenced to life imprisonment and 12 years respectively. The evidence against them was contained in confessions which they said had been obtained under torture. Yang Chin-hai was suffering from a chronic peptic ulcer and a lung complaint.

Amnesty International also called for the release of Yu Hsin-min, a taxi driver, who was arrested on 17 April 1985 for "making propaganda for the communists". He was sentenced to three years' reformatory education. Yu Hsin-min, who was born on mainland China and went to Taiwan in 1949, was reportedly convicted for listening to radio broadcasts from the People's Republic of China and talking about them.

Among the political prisoners released during 1986 was Chen Chu, the assistant manager of the Kaohsiung branch of *Formosa* magazine and a long-time political and human rights activist, who Amnesty International adopted as a prisoner of conscience after her arrest in

1979. She was released on parole on 4 February after serving half her 12-year sentence for sedition. Twenty-six other prisoners convicted of sedition were released on parole on 4 February and 30 October. They had been arrested in the 1970s under the Statute for the Punishment of Sedition and given sentences of between 10 years and life imprisonment. Amnesty International had made inquiries about 20 of them. Although it had few details on their cases it believed that they might be prisoners of conscience and had urged the authorities to review their cases.

A visit to Taiwan requested by Amnesty International did not take place. In October 1985 Amnesty International delegates had been denied entry visas to visit Taiwan to discuss human rights concerns with the government and others. A visit by a doctor to investigate the condition of four prisoners of conscience whose health was of concern to Amnesty International had also been refused. Subsequently, the authorities stated that they would welcome a visit but required that all meetings be arranged by themselves or by the Chinese Association for Human Rights, a condition which Amnesty International would not accept.

Amnesty International received several reports of torture and ill-treatment of criminal suspects and convicts in custody. It also received reports that four people had died in custody as a result of torture and ill-treatment. Among them were Huang Nan-hsing, who died on 18 April in Taliao prison in Kaohsiung and whose body was covered with bruises according to an initial coroner's report and Chiang Kai-chieh who died on 15 August at the Hsichi police station, whose body was also said to be covered with bruises. The detailed conclusions of the authorities' investigations into these cases and two other cases of deaths in custody were not known to Amnesty International. In another case, a police officer from the Sanchung police branch in Taipei was charged with assaulting Hsu Chin-yuan in early April. The results of the trial were not known to Amnesty International.

Amnesty International expressed its concern to the authorities about the execution of seven people convicted of murder by civilian courts.

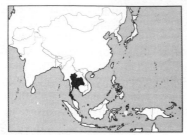

Thailand

Amnesty International continued to be concerned about the imprisonment of people convicted of "lese majesty" because they had expressed political opinions on matters involving the Royal Family. It was also concerned about the prolonged detention without charge or trial of political prisoners, and about trial procedures for political prisoners which did not always meet international standards. There were allegations of arbitrary killing, torture or ill-treatment of Kampuchean refugees by the military and allegations that a number of criminal prisoners were deliberately killed while trying to escape. Five death sentences were reportedly carried out during 1986 and at least 26 people were sentenced to death.

In January three prisoners of conscience convicted of "lese majesty" — Samaan Khongsuphon, Thawan Saengkaanjanaanon and Phongtheep Manuuphiphatphong — were pardoned by King Bhumibol Adulyadej (see *Amnesty International Report 1984*). Rattana Uttaphan, another prisoner of conscience convicted of "lese majesty", was released in May, but a fifth, Anan Seenaakhan, remained in prison. Phromneet Baanthip, whose conviction of "lese majesty" the organization continued to investigate, also remained in prison (see *Amnesty International Report 1986*). In a letter to the King in December, Amnesty International urged him to release Sanan Wongsuthii who had been sentenced to five years' imprisonment on charges of "lese majesty" in November, and to drop the charges of "lese majesty" against Wiira Musikaphong, Secretary General of the Democrat Party and a member of parliament. These charges arose from speeches he made during the parliamentary election campaign in July.

Amnesty International continued to be concerned that people arrested for alleged "communistic activities" could be held without charge or trial for up to 480 days (see *Amnesty International Report 1986*). Some of the 25 people reportedly arrested for "communistic activities" during 1986 were still being held without charge at the end of the year.

The organization wrote to Prime Minister General Prem Tinsulananonda reiterating its concern that people tried for political offences under martial law were denied the right to appeal, and expressed concern at the delays in concluding the trials of some political suspects.

Amnesty International also wrote to the Prime Minister in May about reports that three Kampuchean refugees had been tortured by members of the armed forces' Task Force 80. The three had been tortured while held incommunicado in a prison inside Khao I Dang refugee camp on suspicion of involvement in armed attacks on the camp by Kampuchean "bandits". The organization urged the government to investigate and prosecute those found responsible. Amnesty International also urged that the three either be released or charged and tried, and that they be granted full access to lawyers and representatives of the UN High Commissioner for Refugees. In response, Squadron Leader Prasong Soonsiri, then Secretary General of the Thai National Security Council, denied the allegations and called on Amnesty International to re-examine its information, while indicating that formal charges would be brought against the three men. In June an Amnesty International delegation visited Thailand and met the three men at a civilian prison to which they had been transferred under court remand. On the basis of their evidence Amnesty International concluded that they had been tortured by being burned with a hot flat iron, as well as by other methods. Amnesty International urged that they be allowed proper medical treatment and the opportunity to seek asylum abroad. During the delegation's visit, the three met legal counsel for the first time. They were subsequently tried for armed robbery but in December the court decided to drop the case for lack of evidence. The authorities then allowed them to resettle abroad.

When Amnesty International published its findings in July confirming the torture, Squadron Leader Prasong publicly stated that Amnesty International had received information about the case from two unnamed Amnesty International members in Thailand. He reportedly accused them of having been associated with the Communist Party and suggested that they might be arrested. Amnesty International denied that it had received any information from its members in Thailand, and stated that the organization would be deeply concerned if any retaliatory measures were taken against anyone for allegedly providing information. No arrests took place.

During 1986 Amnesty International also received allegations that other Kampucheans had been beaten and forced into cesspools at the Thai military camp of Kamput. In November a man held in custody by Task Force 80 at Khao I Dang camp was allegedly deliberately shot after attempting to escape from detention in the camp prison.

Amnesty International expressed concern at reports that two criminal inmates at Sakon Nakhorn provincial prison were killed by security authorities to whom they had surrendered following an attempted escape. Six other prisoners, held in Chonburii and

Nakhorn Siithammaraat provincial prisons and in Baang Khwaang central prison in Bangkok, were allegedly killed by prison officials during 1986 to punish them for trying to escape.

Amnesty International urged the government not to execute 13 prisoners whom the organization was able to identify by name, who were sentenced to death during 1986 for murder and heroin trafficking. In December the sentence on Surachai sae Daan was commuted to life imprisonment by the King. In a letter welcoming this, the organization urged him to commute all other death sentences also. Five prisoners sentenced in previous years were executed in 1986.

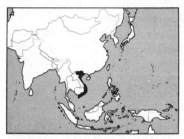

Viet Nam

Amnesty International's predominant concern remained the detention without trial for "re-education" of thousands of individuals held on account of their positions in the armed forces or the civilian administration of the former Republic of Viet Nam. Several dozen political prisoners were arrested in more recent years; they too were mostly held in detention without charge or trial. The organization believed many of them to be prisoners of conscience. Amnesty International continued to be concerned about the use of the death penalty and about reports of ill-treatment and deaths in custody of political prisoners.

The organization's research into compulsory "re-education" was hampered considerably, as in previous years, by the strict censorship and control over information exercised by the government. Amnesty International was unable to ascertain precisely how many of the individuals taken into custody in 1975 or 1976 remained in "re-education" camps in 1986. However, it received reports suggesting that a large number of prisoners had been released in recent years, while others had merely been transferred to other camps. A figure given by the government in May, stating that the number of such detainees had been reduced to some 6,000, could not be confirmed and Amnesty International continued to receive various estimates claiming the number was considerably higher. Most of these detainees were held in "re-education" camps in the southern delta, and a significant number of camps in northern Viet Nam had been closed in recent years. Conditions in the southern camps were said to have improved somewhat, with family visits allowed by the authorities on a more regular basis. Detainees were also allowed to receive some food from their relatives to supplement the generally meagre camp rations, as well as specialized medicines which the camps were unable to provide. Other reports continued to emphasize that detainees were frequently denied any contact with their families. "Re-education" continued to consist largely of compulsory manual labour, with sporadic self-criticism sessions at the end of the working day or on special occasions designated by the camp superintendent. Amnesty International continued to make repeated representations to the government to release these prisoners unconditionally, or to charge and try them without further delay, in accordance with the International Covenant on Civil and Political Rights, to which Viet Nam acceded in 1982. A letter to the government in October reiterated this concern and welcomed the government's announcement in August that it would release a number of prisoners from "re-education", including the sick and elderly, war invalids and those whose families were facing economic difficulties. No details of any such releases were, however, made public before the end of 1986.

Amnesty International continued to work for the release of a number of individual adopted prisoners of conscience who had not been part of the previous administration but who were believed to have been arrested for expressing opinions deemed contrary to those of the post-1975 administration. Among them were a number of writers, journalists, artists, intellectuals of various professions and members of various non-communist political parties. For example, Professor Phan Ngo, a teacher and author, Truong Van Quynh, a doctor, and Nguyen Dinh Luong, a teacher, had all been members of the *Viet Nam Quoc Dân Dang*, Viet Nam Nationalist Party, which was banned by the new authorities after April 1975. Also arrested in 1975 and 1976 were the journalists Nguyen Viet Khanh, Le Van Tien, Le Khai Trach and Truong Vi Tri. Lawyers Nguyen Thanh Long, Do Trong Nguyen, Pham Kim Qui and Vu Ngoc Truy were arrested soon after the cessation of hostilities in 1975, along with doctors Ly Trung Dung and Nguyen Dan Que. As far as Amnesty International was aware, they were all still held in "re-education" camps at the end of 1986.

Amnesty International continued to appeal for the release of several Buddhist, Catholic and Protestant religious figures arrested in recent years for dissenting from government efforts to control activities in the religious, literary and cultural spheres. Among these prisoners of conscience held without trial were the monks Thich Nguyen Giac, Thich Nhu Minh, Thich Duc Nhuan, and Thich Tri Sieu, all of whom were reportedly held in Chi Hoa Prison in Ho Chi

Minh City throughout 1986. Among the Catholic clergy still in detention were Fathers Thadeus Nguyen Van Ly and Paul Trinh Cong Trong, as well as the Jesuit Superior Joseph Nguyen Cong Doan, and Joseph Le Thanh Que. The Protestant pastor, Ho Hieu Ha, of the Tran Cao Van Church in Ho Chi Minh City also remained in detention. He was arrested in December 1983 when the authorities confiscated the church compound and informed him that it had been requisitioned for the exclusive use of the government.

Amnesty International was also concerned about reports that two prominent Buddhist monks, Thich Quang Do and Thich Huyen Quang, were still living under surveillance, in virtual isolation and confined to their home villages. Monseigneur Nguyen Kim Dien, Roman Catholic Archbishop of Huê, was similarly restricted. He was placed under house arrest, and contact with his diocese made virtually impossible, after the arrest in late 1985 of two nuns, Truong Thi Ly and Truong Thi Nong, who had been delivering his correspondence from Huê to Ho Chi Minh City. The nuns were subsequently accused by the authorities of espionage under Article 74 of the new penal code, but were not tried. Amnesty International considered them to be prisoners of conscience.

Amnesty International received reports in October that some of Viet Nam's foremost writers and novelists, among whom were Doan Quoc Sy, Hoang Hai Thuy and Duong Hung Cuong, were about to be tried in Ho Chi Minh City for writing, reciting and circulating uncensored literature allegedly used "to spread counter-revolutionary propaganda inciting rebellion and antagonism against the govern- ment". The writer Nguyen Hoat reportedly died in custody in July. They were all arrested in May 1984.

During 1986 Amnesty International continued to receive reports from former detainees of deliberate ill-treatment and torture in several "re-education" camps in previous years. For example, detainees who infringed camp regulations, often in minor ways, were, according to these reports, held in prolonged solitary confinement, shackled and deprived of food for long periods.

Amnesty International was also concerned about reports that Vietnamese personnel had been involved in the torture of Kam- puchean political prisoners in the People's Republic of Kampuchea. Amnesty International communicated its concern to Pham Van Dong, Chairperson of the Council of Ministers, in September but no reply was received in 1986.

Amnesty International repeatedly appealed to the government to commute the death sentences passed on Chu Van Tan, Ngo Van Truong and Phan Anh Tuan between June and August by the People's Tribunal in Ho Chi Minh City. Phan Anh Tuan was

convicted of armed robbery; Chu Van Tan and Ngo Van Truong
were convicted of attempting to overthrow the government. These
and about 20 other offences, ranging from especially serious
economic crimes to murder, were made punishable by death under
the new Code of Criminal Law which came into force in January. No
executions, however, came to the attention of Amnesty International
during 1986.

The Pacific

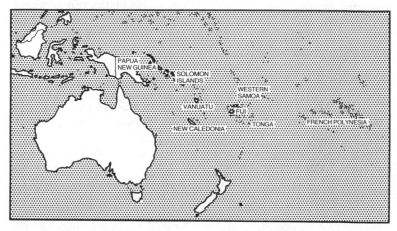

Amnesty International delegates met government officials in several
countries and territories in the Pacific region during 1986 to introduce
Amnesty International and to discuss safeguards for the protection of
human rights.

In February two Amnesty International delegates met government
officials and representatives of non-governmental organizations in
Papua New Guinea to discuss the organization's concerns about
refugees from the Indonesian province of Irian Jaya. Amnesty
International had been concerned that some refugees might be
forcibly repatriated to Indonesia, where they would be at risk of
torture. The Papua New Guinea Government, however, assured the
delegates that no refugees would be returned against their will and, as
far as Amnesty International was aware, none were. Aben Pagawak,
one of 12 refugees returned to Irian Jaya in October 1985 and then
imprisoned and reportedly tortured there, had escaped and returned

to Papua New Guinea. In June Amnesty International heard that he might be deported again following a conviction for illegal entry. Amnesty International appealed to the government not to deport Aben Pagawak as it believed he might be tortured after being returned. The Justice Minister, in a letter dated 27 June, assured Amnesty International that neither Aben Pagawak nor anyone else with refugee status would be forcibly returned to a country where they risked human rights abuse. In July Amnesty International wrote to the Justice Minister welcoming both these assurances and the announcement that Papua New Guinea had ratified the Convention and Protocol relating to the Status of Refugees.

In August and September, an Amnesty International delegate visited Vanuatu, New Caledonia, the Solomon Islands, Tonga, Fiji, Western Samoa and French Polynesia to introduce Amnesty International and to discuss safeguards for the protection of human rights with government officials and representatives of non-governmental organizations.

Although Amnesty International had no major concerns in the Pacific countries, its representative raised the issue of the retention of capital and corporal punishment in Fiji and Tonga. In November and December Amnesty International wrote to the director of the Fiji Law Reform Commission and the Prime Minister of Fiji urging the total abolition of the death penalty, which was retained only for extraordinary crimes such as treason and genocide. No executions had ever taken place under these laws. It also urged the Fiji Commission to review the provisions in the Penal Code relating to flogging which could be imposed for 33 offences, and to recommend an end to all such corporal punishments as Amnesty International believed that they constituted cruel, inhuman or degrading treatment. In December Amnesty International wrote to the Prime Minister of Tonga urging the government to abolish the death penalty. The last executions in Tonga were carried out in September 1982 when three men were hanged for murder.

Amnesty International also wrote to the governments of Vanuatu, the Solomon Islands, Fiji, Tonga and Western Samoa in December urging them to ratify international instruments for the protection of human rights such as the International Covenant on Civil and Political Rights, the Convention against Torture and Other Cruel, Inhuman or Degrading Treatment or Punishment and the International Covenant on Economic, Social and Cultural Rights. The Solomon Islands has ratified the International Covenant on Economic, Social and Cultural Rights.

Amnesty International's concerns in New Caledonia are described under the entry on France.

Europe

Albania

Amnesty International was concerned about the existence and application of legislation severely restricting certain human rights. It could not assess accurately the number of prisoners of conscience, because of official censorship and restrictions on freedom of movement. The organization was also concerned about inadequate legal safeguards for political detainees, harsh prison conditions and allegations of ill-treatment of detainees. It did not learn of any death sentences or executions (such information was not made public), but remained concerned about the number of offences for which the death penalty could be imposed.

On 13 January a "general pardon" effected the release of the following categories of political prisoners: those serving sentences of up to six years' imprisonment for "anti-state agitation and propaganda" or "flight from the state" (recidivists excluded); female political prisoners serving sentences of up to 20 years' imprisonment; all political prisoners under 18 years old; and political prisoners with a year or less of their sentences left to serve. Other political prisoners had the remainder of their sentences reduced by a quarter. No official figures were published about the number of prisoners benefiting from the pardon. From unofficial sources Amnesty International learned of two political prisoners who had been released. Amnesty International's information indicated that a large proportion of political prisoners were serving prison sentences of 10 years or more and that most were adult men; it therefore seemed likely that the chief effect of the pardon on political prisoners was to shorten their sentences rather than to bring about their release.

Amnesty International noted that the pardon decree confirmed that since the previous pardon in November 1982 people had continued to be imprisoned on charges of engaging in "anti-state agitation and propaganda" under Article 55 of the criminal code. The great majority of prisoners about whom Amnesty International received information in recent years were convicted under this article for criticizing economic or political conditions in the country or under Article 47, paragraph 11 ("flight from the state"). Amnesty International learned of further such cases in 1986. They included a group of men from Vlore who were said to have been sentenced in 1985 to prison terms of between 16 and 25 years for "anti-state agitation and propaganda" and a worker from Kavaje serving a 25-year prison sentence for attempting to leave the country illegally.

Since 1967, when Albania was officially declared "the first atheist state in the world", all organized or public forms of religious worship have been illegal. In that year religious buildings were closed and all religious communities, Muslim and Christian, were deprived of legal status and their functionaries prohibited from exercising their offices. In the following years Amnesty International received various reports of clergy being imprisoned or interned (usually on collective farms). In 1986 refugees stated that Father Pjeter Meshkalla, an 80-year-old Jesuit, had been arrested in Guri i Zi, near Shkoder, after he had celebrated mass in a private house. Former political prisoners who had known Father Meshkalla in prison had in previous years informed Amnesty International that the priest was first imprisoned for 10 years in the 1950s. In the 1960s he was imprisoned for a further 15 years and was said to have been released in the early 1980s. Amnesty International was not able to find out what happened to Father Meshkalla after his most recent arrest.

Official hostility to religious belief and to former clergy was reflected in an article published in March in the monthly *Rruga e Partise* (The Party's Road). Referring to "former clergy" and "declassed elements dissatisfied with the people's government", it said that "Experience has shown that religious propaganda or religious rites practised by these elements are simply a mask for their hostile political aims and intentions." The writer said that such people were punished according to their degree of guilt, "from unmasking them in social courts, down to, and including, penal prosecution". At the same time he denied that people were persecuted for their religious convictions.

Amnesty International also learned of people who had been interned. This punishment can be imposed under the criminal code for up to five years as a supplementary penalty, or administratively for unspecified periods, on people officially thought to represent a danger to the country's social system and on "members of the family of fugitives living inside or outside the state". This punishment was reportedly imposed on six members of the Popa family from Durres in 1968, apparently in retaliation for political offences allegedly committed by their relatives. In December 1985 they left the collective farm without official permission and took refuge in the Italian Embassy in Tiranë. The authorities refused to let them leave the country and they were still in the embassy at the end of 1986.

Amnesty International continued to be concerned about inadequate legal safeguards for political prisoners during investigation and trial proceedings, in particular the absence of provisions entitling them to visits from relatives and legal aid during investigation. Political prisoners were almost always denied legal aid at their trials.

Former political prisoners have told Amnesty International that during investigation they were held in small, dark, basement cells, and often obliged to sleep on the cement floor or on boards with blankets but no mattress. They complained that they were given little to eat and were interrogated at night and deprived of sleep. Most alleged that they were beaten during investigation.

Prison conditions for political prisoners were regularly described as very harsh, with poor food, hygiene and medical care. Political prisoners reportedly continued to be held in Burrel prison, but others formerly held in Spac labour camp were said to have been moved to another site near Tuc in Puke district where, as at Spac, they mined pyrites. Yet other political prisoners formerly held in Ballsh were said to have been transferred for a period to Zejmen in Lezhe district.

Austria

During 1986 Amnesty International received allegations that people held in police custody during 1985 had been ill-treated. Amnesty International urged the authorities to investigate the allegations in two cases, those of Kurt Schwarz and Herbert Matejka, who both alleged that they had been beaten and given electric shocks. The authorities replied that an inquiry had established that Kurt Schwarz' claims were unfounded, but they gave no details of the investigation. Amnesty International wrote back requesting this information but received no reply by the end of the year. The other prisoner, Herbert Matejka, escaped shortly after his arrest in August 1985 and fled to the Netherlands where he was rearrested. While in detention there he was examined by a psychiatrist who stated that Herbert Matejka's account of his treatment was coherent, that his emotions were consistent with such an experience and that there were no indications that his story was the result of delusions. The Austrian authorities replied to Amnesty International saying that the times at which Herbert Matejka said he had been ill-treated were not consistent with their records, but they did not comment in detail on the substance of the allegations. Herbert Matejka was extradited to Austria but escaped again from custody on 24 September 1986.

Bulgaria

Amnesty International was concerned about large numbers of ethnic Turks who remained detained following a campaign of enforced assimilation of the ethnic Turkish minority and believed that many of them might be prisoners of conscience. It was also concerned about reports of torture of ethnic Turks. The organization worked for the release of a number of other prisoners of conscience. It learned of one death sentence and 17 executions.

In April Amnesty International published *Bulgaria: Imprisonment of Ethnic Turks*, a report detailing its concerns about human rights abuses during the enforced assimilation of the ethnic Turkish minority. Despite strict censorship Amnesty International had obtained the names of over 250 ethnic Turks reportedly arrested between December 1984 and March 1985 when, according to the authorities, the entire minority — estimated to number 900,000 or 10 per cent of the population — "spontaneously" and "voluntarily" renounced their Islamic names for Bulgarian ones. Amnesty International also received reports that ethnic Turks had been killed by the security forces.

In press reports following Amnesty International's publication the Bulgarian authorities consistently denied both the existence of the minority and all allegations of human rights abuses or violence during the campaign. On 24 September Amnesty International wrote to the authorities pointing out major inconsistencies between its findings and those reported in the official Bulgarian media. On 10 October a Bulgarian Embassy official in the Federal Republic of Germany admitted to an Amnesty International delegation that during a demonstration against the campaign in Ivaylovgrad three people had been killed.

During 1986 Amnesty International worked for the release of a number of ethnic Turkish prisoners of conscience arrested during the assimilation campaign. For example, Halim Pasadzhov, from Sofia, was a journalist for the bilingual publication *New Light*. After the campaign began, the use of Turkish was banned and the publication was available only in Bulgarian. He was arrested in January 1985 after refusing to change his name "voluntarily", released after two months but rearrested in May 1985 for his continued opposition to the assimilation policy. He was charged with espionage after notes taken of foreign radio broadcasts were found in his home. He was allegedly subjected to torture, including *falange* — beating on the soles of the feet — during detention.

Amnesty International continued to receive reports of the imprisonment of ethnic Turks for following the Islamic custom of having their sons circumcised. For example, Kalbiye Saadettinova from Kitnitsa village near Kardzhali was reportedly arrested for having her two sons circumcised. To Amnesty International's knowledge she was still being held in detention in Sliven prison at the end of 1986.

Amnesty International investigated a large number of cases of ethnic Turks whom it believed might be prisoners of conscience. In view of reports of violent conflict between security forces and ethnic Turks during the assimilation campaign, the organization requested further details on the cases from the authorities. For example, in April Amnesty International took up for investigation the case of Omer Mustafov Kochandzhiev, a school teacher from Dolni Voden. He was arrested in 1985 with his wife, who was later released. Amnesty International received reports that Omer Mustafov Kochandzhiev was detained in Belene — a prison camp on an island in the Danube where large numbers of ethnic Turks arrested during the campaign were reportedly detained — and that his wife and two sons were banished for three years to a village in Blagoevgrad district. Amnesty International believed that they were banished under the People's Militia Law, which allows internal banishment for up to three years and other restrictions on freedom of movement to be imposed administratively, that is without trial, on certain categories of people. These restrictions, which can be indefinitely renewed, have reportedly been imposed on many ethnic Turkish families who protested at the assimilation campaign.

These restrictions have also been imposed on released prisoners of conscience and in Amnesty International's view can themselves constitute a form of detention. For example, Hristo Kulichev, pastor of the First Congregational Church in Sofia, was sentenced in May 1985 to eight months' imprisonment. He had refused to stand down as pastor when a government-approved pastor was appointed despite the wishes of the congregation (see *Amnesty International Report 1986*). After his release in September 1985 he was banished under the People's Militia Law to Nozharevo, a village in northeast Bulgaria, for continuing his religious activities. He had to report twice daily to the authorities and his wife was allowed to visit him only once a month. These restrictions were such that Amnesty International considered them a form of detention and adopted him again as a prisoner of conscience.

Amnesty International continued to work for the release of other prisoners of conscience imprisoned for reasons unconnected with the assimilation campaign. One such prisoner of conscience was Kostadin Angelov Kalmakov who protested against the imprisonment of conscientious objectors (see *Amnesty International Report 1986*). He was sentenced to four years' imprisonment in 1982 for "anti-state propaganda" under Article 108 of the criminal code to which was added a further year from a previous suspended sentence imposed for complaining in the course of conversation about the food situation.

However, due to official censorship, Amnesty International believed that the cases which came to its notice during 1986 represented only a portion of the total. Former prisoners of conscience have estimated that immediately before the assimilation campaign, at the end of 1984, there were about 250 political prisoners in Stara Zagora prison, where at that time most political prisoners were held. The majority had been convicted of attempting to leave the country without permission. The constitution does not guarantee freedom of movement and only rarely are citizens who seek to emigrate permitted to do so. Those who attempt to leave the country without permission may be punished by up to five years' imprisonment under Article 279 of the criminal code, or up to six years if the offence is repeated. Amnesty International believed that the numbers of such people convicted did not substantially change in 1986.

Amnesty International learned of one death sentence and 17 executions, in each case for offences involving loss of life.

The organization submitted information about its concerns under the UN procedure for confidentially reviewing communications about human rights violations (the so-called "1503 procedure"). During 1986 Bulgaria ratified the UN Convention Against Torture.

Czechoslovakia

Amnesty International's main concerns were the continuing imprisonment of prisoners of conscience, the ill-treatment of some prisoners of conscience and the use of the death penalty. At the end of 1986, there were 33 prisoners who had been adopted as prisoners of conscience or whose cases were being investigated by Amnesty International, although the total number of prisoners of conscience was believed to be higher. Amnesty International also learned of many people who were given suspended sentences, charged without being remanded in custody or harassed for peacefully attempting to exercise human rights.

Amnesty International remained concerned at the imprisonment of prisoners of conscience under laws explicitly restricting the non-violent exercise of human rights. In June, it called upon the authorities to bring these laws and their application into line with their obligations as a party to the International Covenant on Civil and Political Rights and to release prisoners of conscience held under such legislation. In September Amnesty International appealed for the release of 17 prisoners of conscience detained for the peaceful exercise of the right to freedom of expression. These included Herman Chromy, a clerk from Melnik and a signatory of the unofficial Czechoslovak human rights document, Charter 77. He was sentenced to two years' imprisonment for "subversion" under Article 98 of the penal code. Herman Chromy was detained on 9 April following a house-search and charged with the lesser crime of "incitement" (Article 100). He was accused of making "anti-socialist" statements at work, distributing unauthorized literature and writing an open letter to the President criticizing Czechoslovak and Soviet officials. At his trial on 25 July before the Regional Court in Prague he was additionally accused of listening to *Voice of America* broadcasts. Amnesty International was concerned about irregularities in the interrogation and trial procedures. Some witnesses maintained that they were threatened by their interrogators and subjected to questioning for up to eight hours without meal breaks. Other witnesses were unable to substantiate their assertions that he had made "anti-socialist" statements. Herman Chromy denied that he was the author of the incriminating letter and although the charge was not proved by the court of first instance, the Supreme Court of the CSR ruled at his appeal hearing on 9 October that this letter be included in the charges against him.

Also convicted of "subversion" (Article 98) was Jaroslav Svestka, a woodcutter. He was accused of sending a letter to a friend in the Federal Republic of Germany which contained comments on George Orwell's novel *1984* and made comparisons with the contemporary situation in Czechoslovakia. He was initially charged with the lesser crime of "damaging the interests of the Republic abroad" (Article 112). On 28 April the Regional Court in Ceske Budejovice sentenced him to two years' imprisonment to be followed by three years of protective surveillance. In August the sentence was reduced to one year's imprisonment and the sentence of protective surveillance was quashed.

The possession of works by George Orwell was included in evidence against Eduard Vacek, an electrician from Teplice. He was sentenced to one year's imprisonment by the District Court in Teplice on 3 June for "hooliganism" (Article 202). A copy of George Orwell's *Animal Farm* found during a search of his home was considered to be "faulty" by the court, as it compared human society to that of animals. Eduard Vacek was also accused of writing and distributing texts between October 1983 and January 1986 which were considered to be "ironic parodies of society and contrary to socialist morality".

Amnesty International investigated the cases of Karel Srp, Josef Skalnik, Tomas Krivanek, Vladimir Kouril, Cestmir Hunat, Milos Drda and Vlastimil Drda who were remanded in custody by the Prague City procurator at the beginning of September. They were charged under Article 118 with "unauthorized business enterprise". The trial was due to take place in late December and Amnesty International sent an observer to Prague. However, formal defects in the indictment caused it to be postponed and the trial had not been rescheduled by the end of 1986. Milos Drda and Josef Skalnik were released from detention on grounds of ill-health, although the charge against them remained, but the procurator objected to the recommended release of three others who were also in poor health. All seven men were committee members of the Jazz Section of the Musicians' Union, which the authorities had tried to dissolve because of its unofficial cultural activities.

Active Christians continued to be arrested for unofficial religious activities and many received suspended sentences. Michal Mrtvy, an electrician from Olomouc, was sentenced on 29 October to 13 months' imprisonment, suspended for three years. He was convicted of "incitement" and "obstructing the State supervision of churches and religious bodies". However, the procurator appealed against the verdict and he was kept in detention pending appeal. At the end of 1986 he was still in prison. The trial court considered the distribution of copies of a religious text and the possession of duplicating equipment and of other religious literature to be in breach of Article 178 of the penal code: "obstructing the State supervision of churches and religious bodies". The court defined the text, "Revival of the Interest in Religion" by Erika Kadlecova, as "ideologically faulty but not of anti-state nature", and considered the duplication of 250 copies as "preparation to incitement" (Article 100).

Reports reaching Amnesty International indicated that many prisoners of conscience were held in conditions of inadequate hygiene, medical care and nourishment. There were also complaints that prisoners of conscience were singled out for particularly harsh punishments for failing to meet excessively high work norms and for minor infringements of prison rules. Punishments included reduced food rations and confinement in special punishment cells. In particular, Amnesty International was concerned about the mental and physical health of Jiri Wolf, a prisoner of conscience serving a six-year prison sentence in Valdice prison (see *Amnesty International Report 1984*). He had reportedly been given frequent administrative punishments and subjected to threats by the prison staff and fellow prisoners. He was suffering from severe depression as well as from chest pains and deteriorating vision. Amnesty International was also concerned about the health of Walter Kania, another prisoner of conscience in the same prison. Since 1980 he had suffered from angina and a liver complaint as well as from two heart attacks. He was reported to be receiving inadequate medical treatment and to be under physical and psychological stress.

Amnesty International learned of one execution for murder and the imposition of three death sentences in 1986 and appealed to the authorities against the retention and use of the death penalty.

Finland

Amnesty International was concerned about the imprisonment of conscientious objectors to military service. It was also concerned about procedures for asylum-seekers which could result in their being returned to countries where they would risk becoming prisoners of conscience, being tortured or executed.

In 1986 Amnesty International adopted three conscientious objectors to military service as prisoners of conscience. Their applications for alternative civilian service were rejected and they were given nine-month prison sentences by the courts. Under the legislation then in force a person could object to military service only on "profound conscientious grounds based on religious or ethical convictions". From January 1987 new legislation allows those who request it to perform alternative service. Lassi Tapio Kurittu applied on three separate occasions for permission to carry out alternative civilian service, but was ordered instead to present himself for unarmed military service. When he refused, he was sentenced to nine months' imprisonment. He began his prison sentence on 4 February, was pardoned by the President on 21 February, and released. Raul Otso Mannola also refused to do unarmed military service after his application for alternative civilian service was turned down. He began his nine-month prison sentence on 11 November 1985. In June Amnesty International took up the case of Niilo Markus Louhivouri, who was sentenced in December 1984 to nine months' imprisonment. The sentence was upheld by the Court of Appeal. The Minister of Justice replied in August that Niilo Louhivouri had the right to make a new application if he wished. However, he began his sentence on 10 November.

Amnesty International has been concerned for many years that the procedures for individuals seeking asylum in Finland did not guarantee that they would not be sent back to countries where they would face becoming prisoners of conscience, or being tortured or executed. In particular, Amnesty International was concerned about people who were forcibly returned to the USSR where they were subsequently held as prisoners of conscience. The organization sent two delegates to Finland in June to meet government officials and representatives of non-governmental organizations in order to obtain further information about the legal position and official practice. At the end of 1986 Amnesty International was finalizing a submission to the government on its findings.

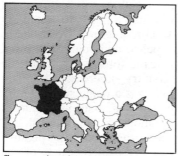

France

Amnesty International's principal concerns were the forcible return of refugees who might face torture or ill-treatment in their country of origin; the imprisonment of conscientious objectors to military service and the progress of judicial inquiries into the violent deaths of political figures in the overseas territory of New Caledonia.

The new government elected in March 1986 announced its intention to reform the laws relating to the fight against crime, delinquency and terrorism. A new law was passed in September tightening the conditions of residence and access by foreigners to France. This aspect of the projected legal reforms was of concern to Amnesty International when taken together with ministerial statements forecasting a change in French policy towards political refugees.

France has traditionally been unwilling to expel Spanish citizens of Basque origin when they claimed to be political refugees. On 19 July José Varona López, a Basque refugee, was expelled by administrative order under the procedure of "absolute urgency" (*"urgence absolue"*) on the grounds that the French authorities considered his expulsion "an urgent necessity for the security of the State or the safety of the public". He was not accused of any offence at that time in either France or Spain. On 20 July the French Foreign Minister stated that there might be further expulsions and that José Varona López was not a political refugee. On 23 July another Basque refugee was expelled under the same procedure. Both were handed over to the Spanish police, arrested and held incommunicado under the anti-terrorist law. On 25 July Amnesty International wrote to the Prime Minister about these two expellees who were, in its opinion, in danger of torture or ill-treatment. Subsequently, Amnesty International received reports from Madrid that following interrogation both men had alleged in court that they had been tortured. (See *Spain* entry.) On 1 August Amnesty International raised these reports with the government and urged it to review its policy. The letter referred to Article 3 of the UN Convention Against Torture, which was ratified by France on 18 February 1986, which states that a person must not be expelled to another state where there are substantial grounds for believing that he or she would be in danger of being subjected to torture. However, expulsions of Basques to Spain continued, with many of them making substantive allegations of torture and ill-treatment. The French Prime Minister replied to Amnesty International on 21 August citing the legal requirements that had to be fulfilled before a person could be expelled and pointing out that this procedure could only be used when the foreigner was not the subject of legal proceedings in another country; otherwise extradition was required. He emphasized that Spain was a democratic country which had accepted its human rights obligations under international law but did not comment on the allegations of ill-treatment.

Amnesty International was equally concerned about the possible extradition of Basque political refugees to Spain, because of the danger of torture and ill-treatment. In July José María Bereciartua was detained pending a decision as to whether France would agree to his extradition on charges of murder and related crimes. He had lived in France since 1973 as an officially recognized political refugee under the terms of the 1951 Geneva Convention. This status was withdrawn in 1979 because the French authorities considered that the altered political situation in Spain meant that he no longer required protection. However, he successfully appealed against this decision and his status as an officially recognized political refugee was restored in July 1984. On 2 December Amnesty International wrote to the Government asking it to obtain procedural guarantees from the Spanish Government before coming to any decision on extradition, ensuring that José María Bereciartua would not be tortured.

On 9 September the Minister Delegate for Security in the Ministry of the Interior declared that, in his view, the regulations protecting political refugee status in France no longer applied to nationals of any state within the European Community.

A new law on conditions of entry and residency in France was promulgated in September 1986. This retained the powers of expulsion by administrative order but widened its application to include all those whose presence, in the view of the authorities, "constitutes a particularly serious threat to public order".

By the end of 1986, 26 Basques had been expelled from France to Spain and a further six were the subject of extradition requests by the Government of Spain. Decisions on these extraditions were still pending at the end of 1986 and all six remained in detention.

Amnesty International adopted five conscientious objectors to military service as prisoners of conscience and continued to work for the release from prison of two others. Bruno Poirier had informed the Ministry of Defence that he was opposed to any kind of armed service because of his non-violent beliefs but that he was not opposed to doing alternative civilian service. His application was rejected because it was incorrectly worded. His new application was not accepted because it was sent after the statutory time limit. In March he was given a one-month suspended sentence by the tribunal of Bordeaux for refusal to obey, and was also sentenced to 160 hours of community work. Immediately after completing this sentence he was rearrested by the military authorities and spent a total of 40 days in isolation for refusing to wear military uniform. In June the Court of Appeal sentenced him to 15 months' imprisonment for refusing to respond to call-up orders and he was in prison at the end of 1986.

There were several outbreaks of violence in the French overseas territory of New Caledonia between groups led by the Kanak Socialist Nationalist Liberation Front (FLNKS), advocating full independence, and anti-independence groups. In September an investigating magistrate of the court in Noumea ruled that there were no grounds for the prosecution of eight men charged with killing 10 Kanak men, among them two brothers of the FLNKS leader, Jean-Marie Tjibaou, in Hienghene in December 1984. The eight men did not deny their involvement in the killings but the judge ruled that they had acted in self-defence. On 23 October Amnesty International wrote to the Minister of Justice expressing concern that the judge might not have examined all the available evidence and that failure to carry out a thorough and impartial investigation into these killings might give the impression that the government condoned them. The Attorney General and the plaintiffs (*partie civile*) appealed against the ruling. On 20 November the Appeal Court quashed it and ordered seven people to stand trial. The Minister of Justice informed Amnesty International of this decision on 5 December. Amnesty International was concerned about the length of time taken by the courts to investigate the violent deaths of political activists. A judicial investigation was opened in January 1985 into the killings earlier that month by marksmen of the *Groupe d'intervention de la gendarmerie nationale* (GIGN), Intervention Group of the National Police, of two FLNKS activists, Eloi Machoro and Marcel Nonnaro (see *Amnesty International Report 1986* and *Errata*). The court had still not reached a conclusion by the end of 1986. Furthermore, there was no apparent progress in the judicial investigation into the killing in 1981 of Pierre Declercq, leader of the pro-independence party, *Union calédonienne,* Caledonian Union.

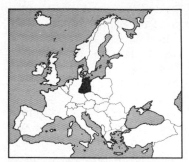

German Democratic Republic

As in previous years Amnesty International's main concern was the imprisonment of prisoners of conscience. The majority were would-be emigrants imprisoned either for trying to leave the country without permission or for their attempts to seek permission. The organization was also concerned that, along with other political prisoners, they were denied the right to a public trial. Many of them were convicted under laws directly restricting the exercise of basic human rights.

The right to leave one's country is severely restricted for GDR citizens below the age of retirement. To leave the country for any purpose, except for visits to other Warsaw Pact countries, requires special permission which is very difficult to obtain. Those caught leaving without permission faced up to eight years' imprisonment for "illegal crossing of the border" (Article 213 of the penal code), while those who persisted in their efforts to obtain permission risked arrest and imprisonment under a number of articles of the penal code which explicitly circumscribe the right to freedom of expression.

Some of those who persisted in their efforts to persuade government authorities to grant them exit visas were prosecuted for "impeding the activity of public bodies" under Article 214 of the penal code. Among them was Klaus-Dieter Ernst, a scaffolding-constructor, who was arrested on 28 July 1986 after applying repeatedly but without success for permission to emigrate. This was his third imprisonment for political reasons. In 1965 he was sentenced to one year's imprisonment for attempting to leave the country without permission and in 1971 he was sentenced to 18 months' imprisonment for "slandering the state".

A number of would-be emigrants, whose applications to emigrate had been repeatedly rejected, turned to foreign organizations and individuals in the hope that support or publicity abroad would improve their chances of emigration. Some of these were prosecuted and imprisoned for "treasonable passing on of information" (Article 99 of the penal code), "treasonable activity as an agent" (Article 100), or "taking up illegal contacts" (Article 219). These laws proscribe sending information out of the country and making contacts with foreign organizations and individuals if the activity is considered to be contrary to the interests of the GDR. None of them concern passing on secret information, which is covered by Article 97 of the penal code (espionage). Among those arrested were Mike Wolf and Dirk Braumann from Berlin (GDR). After repeated attempts to obtain permission to emigrate the two informed a friend in West Berlin of their wish to emigrate. They were arrested on 25 February 1986 and tried on 13 June. Each was sentenced to two and a half years' imprisonment for "treasonable passing on of information". Mike Wolf was released on 15 October.

Amnesty International sent a delegate to observe the trial but he was refused admission to the court on the grounds that the procurator had applied for the trial to be held behind closed doors. Amnesty International's delegate then asked if he might attend the trial until the court had taken a decision on this, and if he could be admitted to the pronouncement of the judgment following the trial. He was informed that this was only permitted for GDR citizens. According to GDR law, the pronouncement of the judgment must be public, even when the trial is held *in camera*. International law also stipulates that trials and especially judgments should be public. In neither case is the "public" specified to mean only citizens of the country concerned. Amnesty International's delegate noted that no notice of trials taking place that day was displayed at the entrance of the court building, calling into question whether ordinary GDR citizens are able to attend those parts of the trial which must by law be public.

During 1986 all political cases which Amnesty International was able to research were tried behind closed doors. Released prisoners reported to the organization that their families were not present even for the pronouncement of the judgment. They also reported that they were not allowed to mention their cases to relatives during visits. Prisoners' families therefore received only minimal information about the reasons for the imprisonment. If the families attempted to pass on the little information they had to organizations or individuals abroad they themselves risked prosecution under the laws restricting sending information out of the country.

Amnesty International considers that the lack of possibilities for any public scrutiny of political trials seriously jeopardized the prisoner's right to a fair trial. Lack of information about political trials made it impossible in many instances to assess whether the people concerned were prisoners of conscience. The organization also believes that because of the secrecy surrounding them, many cases of political imprisonment did not come to its attention. During 1986 Amnesty International worked on behalf of about 160 prisoners of conscience in the GDR but believed the total number to be much higher.

Among other prisoners of conscience adopted by the organization were two men from Jena who were charged with "public vilifi-cation" (Article 220 of the penal code), apparently for criticizing elections to the People's Chamber held in June. Andreas Richter was accused of writing the following slogan on the wall of a house: "Those who have the vote suffer, those who do not vote still suffer". Lars Matzke displayed on the door of his flat a collage he had made about the elections. Andreas Richter was sentenced to two years' imprison-ment on 4 September. Lars Matzke was sentenced later in the year to eight months' imprisonment.

As in previous years many political prisoners were released before completing their sentences and permitted to emigrate to the Federal Republic of Germany (FRG) in exchange for payment by the FRG Government. According to FRG Government sources the number released in this way in 1986 was expected to be somewhat less than the 2,500 who were released in 1985.

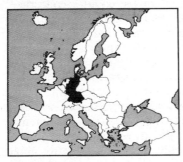

Germany, Federal Republic of

As in previous years, Amnesty In-ternational's main concerns were the imprisonment of conscientious objectors to military service, issues relating to the exercise of the right to freedom of expression, and alle-gations of ill-treatment of prisoners.

Although the right to conscientious objection to military service is guaranteed in the constitution, some people who apply for conscien-tious objector status are turned down. If they are subsequently imprisoned Amnesty International adopts them as prisoners of conscience if it believes their applications were based on grounds of conscience. The only such prisoner known to Amnesty International during 1986 was Siegfried Schierle, whose application for conscien-tious objector status had been rejected because it was considered to be politically motivated. He was tried on 4 April 1986 and sentenced to six months' imprisonment for "desertion" and "refusal to obey orders". He started serving his sentence on 28 October and was released on probation on 27 December.

Although Amnesty International did not adopt total objectors, that is those who refused to do both military and alternative service, as prisoners of conscience, the organization was concerned that some total objectors were apparently punished, not only for refusing to do any form of national service, but also for the non-violent expression of their beliefs. Among them was Christoph Bausenwein who had initially applied for and received recognition as a conscientious objector to military service. However, while doing alternative service he came to the conclusion that it was not genuinely outside the country's military and defence system. He consequently refused to do the remaining four months of alternative service. He wrote a book explaining his views which was published in 1984. Christoph Bausenwein was subsequently sentenced to a total of 16 months' imprisonment for deserting his duties. On appeal the Higher Regional Court upheld the sentence, stating in its judgment of 19 June 1985 that he had not changed his views and that "on the contrary, in publishing his book on total objectors he made himself a spokesman and example for total objectors. Because of the exceptional stubbornness of the accused, which is liable to undermine the discipline necessary in civilian service, a severe sentence must be imposed in order to have some effect and to deter potential imitators." The judgment did not claim that the book itself contravened the law. Christoph Bausenwein started to serve his sentence on 15 January 1986. During the year Amnesty International sent a series of letters to the Minister of Justice of Bavaria expressing concern that he had been given a longer prison sentence than normal for refusing to do alternative service, apparently because he had publicized his views on total objection.

Amnesty International received reports of beatings in Rheinbach prison in Nordrhein-Westfalen, including an allegation that on one occasion a doctor had to be called in to stitch up a prisoner's head following ill-treatment by prison staff. This had been the subject of investigation by the local procuracy, which had dismissed the allegations as unfounded. In a letter to the prisoner's lawyer justifying the decision the procuracy stated that the reliability of the prisoner's evidence was questionable since he had been convicted of crimes involving violence and deception. In a letter to the procuracy dated 5 December Amnesty International pointed out that in cases of alleged ill-treatment of prisoners there were frequently no eye-witnesses other than the prisoner and the prison staff involved, and that in view of the vulnerability of prisoners it was a matter for concern that their evidence was discounted on the grounds of crimes previously committed.

During 1986 the organization also intervened with the authorities on the issue of the isolation of politically motivated prisoners. Amnesty International was concerned about two aspects in particular: the fact that prisoners suspected of terrorist crimes were initially detained under special provisions expressly forbidding contact with other prisoners, and the lack of medical monitoring of politically motivated prisoners in isolation. The latter was caused by the prisoners' refusal to be examined by prison doctors and the authorities' refusal to give prisoners access to doctors of their own choice. Amnesty International believes that prisoners should have the right to consult doctors outside the prison system. In February the organization wrote to the authorities detailing its concerns.

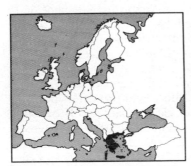

Greece

Amnesty International continued to be concerned about the imprisonment of large numbers of Jehovah's Witnesses for refusing to perform military service (see *Amnesty International Report 1986*) and about allegations of torture and ill-treatment of prisoners. Amnesty International wrote to the Prime Minister, Andreas Papandreou, on 22 August expressing concern about the imprisonment of conscientious objectors. The letter pointed out that the option of four years' unarmed military service was not a satisfactory alternative. It was twice as long as armed military service and Amnesty International believed that alternative service should be separate from the military system and of comparable length. The only reply received was a standard letter which did not address the substance of Amnesty International's concerns. At the end of 1986 Amnesty International knew of 234 Jehovah's Witnesses imprisoned for conscientious objection to military service. All were adopted as prisoners of conscience.

On 27 May 1986 an appeal court in Athens ruled that three Protestant Christian evangelical missionaries, Costas Macris, Don Stephens and Alan Williams, were not guilty of "proselytism" (see *Amnesty International Report 1986*). This charge had been brought against them after they gave a 16-year-old Greek youth a Bible and talked to him about religion. The court was reported as saying that there was nothing illegal in their evangelizing methods and that their message did not differ from that of the Greek Orthodox Church.

Throughout 1986 Amnesty International received allegations of torture and ill-treatment of prisoners and detainees by prison guards and police officers. The organization wrote to the Minister of Justice on 23 December about the alleged torture and ill-treatment of prisoners in Alicarnassos Prison on Crete, Kerkyra High Security Prison on Corfu and Eptapyrgion Prison. It also referred to cases of people ill-treated in police custody, including four young Englishmen interviewed by Amnesty International following their release from prison. They alleged that they had been ill-treated on 30 July and 1 August at Theologos Police Station and Kavalla Police Station on the island of Thassos. They said they were beaten, punched, kicked and slapped repeatedly by police officers and kept without food or water for 21 hours.

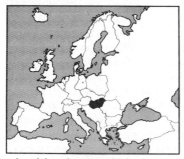

Hungary

Amnesty International was concerned about prisoners of conscience. Some were conscientious objectors to military service, others had helped people attempting to exercise their right to freedom of movement. The organization was also concerned that people were detained for short periods, harassed and, in one case, allegedly confined to a psychiatric hospital for exercising their right to freedom of expression. Amnesty International learned of the imposition of one death sentence.

Military service is compulsory in Hungary and the law does not provide for alternative civilian service outside the military system. Article 336 of the criminal code allows the courts to impose sentences of up to five years' imprisonment (five to 15 years in time of war) on those who refuse military service. Since 1977 members of some small Christian sects, including the Nazarenes and the Jehovah's Witnesses, have been allowed to do unarmed military service, but the authorities have refused to extend this to Roman Catholics. According to reports received by Amnesty International, in 1986 there were approximately 150 conscientious objectors serving sentences in Baracska prison where conscientious objectors are generally held. Most were Jehovah's Witnesses who had refused to do any form of military service, including unarmed military service.

Amnesty International could not obtain details on most of these prisoners but it worked for the release of nine Roman Catholic conscientious objectors, who, according to Amnesty International's information, belonged to small, pacifist, "basic communities" which advocate strict adherence to the teachings of the Bible. Three were adopted during 1986, including Joszef Peller, from Sopron. He was arrested in August and sentenced in October by the Budapest Military Court to three years' imprisonment under Article 336. He was allegedly ill-treated in pre-trial detention.

Ferenc Fulemule, a resident of Switzerland, was sentenced to six months' imprisonment by the Gyor/Sopron county court during 1986 for attempting to smuggle his cousin, a citizen of Czechoslovakia, out of Hungary to Austria. Similarly, Jan-Peter Büsching, previously a citizen of the German Democratic Republic (GDR) who had emigrated to the Federal Republic of Germany in December 1985, was arrested on 9 August while attempting to smuggle a friend, a GDR citizen, out of Hungary to Austria. Jan-Peter Büsching was subsequently sentenced to 10 months' imprisonment. Amnesty International believes that the people they had been trying to help were returned to Czechoslovakia and the GDR respectively, where they faced imprisonment of up to five or eight years for attempting to leave their countries illegally. On 23 October Amnesty International wrote to the Hungarian authorities pointing out that by returning such people they were party to the imprisonment of individuals for exercising their right to leave their country, albeit via a second country. Amnesty International regards as prisoners of conscience people imprisoned for trying to leave their own country for reasons of conscience, and likewise those imprisoned for trying to help them to do this. Ferenc Fulemule and Jan-Peter Büsching were adopted as prisoners of conscience.

Under Article 269 of the criminal code people convicted of acts liable to incite hatred of Hungary's constitutional order or allies, or national, racial or religious hatred, may be imprisoned for up to two years. If convicted of deliberate intent to incite, they face imprisonment of between one and five years under Article 148. If the offence is committed before a "large public" or by members of a group the punishment may be increased to up to three years' imprisonment under Article 269 and two to eight years under Article 148. Amnesty International believes that most people imprisoned for political offences were charged with "incitement" under these two articles.

On 15 March police broke up an unofficial peaceful procession of four to five hundred people commemorating the anniversary of the Hungarian revolution of 1848. Eleven people were arrested and others allegedly beaten by police. Tibor Pakh, a former prisoner of conscience (see *Amnesty International Report 1983*), was reportedly detained for the entire day to prevent him taking part in the procession. Olga Dioszegi was arrested and briefly detained earlier that day for collecting money during another demonstration. She was raising money to help pay a fine imposed on Jeno Nagy for unofficial publishing. Several people were sentenced, some repeatedly, during 1986 to fines of up to 10,000 forints (US$228) or 40 days' imprisonment for such activities.

Laszlo Rusai, a teacher from Hatvan, was arrested on 20 October after hanging a poster from his window commemorating the 30th anniversary of the Hungarian revolution of 1956. He was reportedly taken to the neurological department of the Bugat Pal hospital in Gyongos. On 23 October he was transferred to a restricted ward in the Visonta mental hospital where he was forcibly confined until his release on 11 November. Laszlo Rusai had been active in opposition circles and with unofficial publications. In 1985 he had been reportedly detained for 39 days, beaten by the police, and given a police warning for "violating the community" on account of his activities. As a result of this he had required psychiatric treatment. To Amnesty International's knowledge he had never been violent and this was the only psychiatric treatment he had previously undergone. Before his arrest he was reportedly in good health, physically and mentally.

Amnesty International learned of one death sentence, imposed on Ladislav Ambruz, a Czech citizen, for murder and rape. In July the Hungarian authorities stated in a report submitted to the Human Rights Committee, set up under the International Covenant on Civil and Political Rights, that in the preceding 10 years there had been 25 executions.

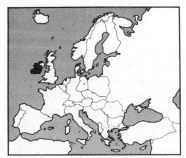

Ireland

Amnesty International continued to be concerned about the death penalty. The last execution took place in 1954. In 1986 the death sentence was commuted in the cases of four prisoners convicted of the murder of police officers (*gardai*). Thomas Eccles, Patrick McPhillips and Brian McShane were due to be hanged on 26 February, but their sentences were commuted to 40 years' imprisonment without remission on 21 February. They had been convicted of the murder of a detective. The sentence on Noel Callan, convicted of murdering a police officer during a robbery, was commuted on 29 May also to 40 years' imprisonment.

In March Amnesty International wrote to the Minister for Justice urging the government to abolish the death penalty for all offences. The organization pointed out that on 17 January the European Parliament had adopted a resolution requesting the Republic of Ireland to sign the sixth Protocol of the European Convention on Human Rights on the abolition of the death penalty in peacetime. Apart from the United Kingdom, Ireland was the only member of the European Community which had not signed the Protocol.

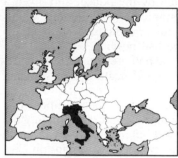

Italy

Amnesty International continued to be concerned about the excessive duration of judicial procedures in political cases, a long-standing concern of the organization. It investigated reports of torture and ill-treatment in police stations and *carabinieri* barracks and followed several judicial inquiries set up during 1986 to investigate allegations of torture or ill-treatment in previous years. Amnesty International increased its work for the release of conscientious objectors to military service.

In August Amnesty International published a paper entitled " '7 *April' Trial — Italy: Amnesty International's Concerns Regarding a Fair Trial Within a Reasonable Time"*. This was a summary of the main developments in the trial of 71 alleged members of the revolutionary left wing groups *Potere Operaia*, Workers' Power, and *Autonomia Operaia*, Workers' Autonomy. The first arrests were in April 1979, and the court hearing in Rome ended in 1984 (see successive *Amnesty International Reports* from 1980). The paper concluded that the Italian authorities had breached European and international standards relating to fair trial within a reasonable time, and made four main criticisms of the conduct of the proceedings.

Three of these criticisms related to the duration of the preventive detention of the defendants, 12 of whom had spent over five years in prison before judgment was given. Special public order legislation was introduced after the defendants' arrests. Amnesty International concluded that this legislation had been applied retroactively to prolong the already excessive period of preventive detention. Secondly, it found that the legal limits of preventive detention had been evaded. New arrest warrants had been issued shortly before the legal limits were reached, so that defendants could still be kept in prison if the court wished. Thirdly, the authorities did not, in Amnesty International's view, observe the ruling laid down by the European Court of Human Rights in relation to Article 5(3) of the European Convention proclaiming the right to fair trial or release. This states that there should be "special diligence in the conduct of the prosecution" in cases in which defendants are detained. In the "7 April" trial there was a delay of over 15 months during which no judicial activities relevant to the trial took place. During this whole period the main defendants were kept in prison.

The fourth of Amnesty International's main concerns was that a key witness for the prosecution had fled the country with the aid of the authorities, and therefore the court was not able to subject him to examination. Carlo Fioroni had been released from prison in 1982 after serving seven years of a 27-year prison sentence for kidnapping and murder. He gave highly incriminating evidence against the defendants in the secrecy of the trial's initial, investigative stage, after which he was helped by the authorities to leave the country before he could be questioned at the court hearing. Although the court expressed indignation that he was not available for examination it agreed to the prosecution's request for the information he had provided in the investigative stage to be accepted as evidence.

After publication of the paper, Amnesty International called on the authorities to take these criticisms into account in their approach to the forthcoming appeal. Defendants were sentenced to prison terms of up to life imprisonment, totalling over 500 years, on charges which included founding or belonging to an "armed band" and "subversive association". They were released provisionally, either on health grounds or because they had been held in preventive detention for as long as the law permits. The appeal hearing was expected to take place in Rome early in 1987.

In January verdicts were reached by the court in the Paduan section of the "7 April" trial, in which there were 141 defendants (see *Amnesty International Report 1986*). In contrast to the judgment in Rome, the court in Padua concluded that *Autonomia Operaia* was not an armed band, and it acquitted those who had been charged solely in relation to their alleged membership of the group.

Of the 47 people who were fully acquitted in Padua, three had earlier been convicted in Rome of founding an "armed band" and "subversive association". In Padua they were charged separately by the prosecuting judge with possession of arms. The investigating judge refused to accept the new charge because in his view it should have been heard in the earlier trial in Rome, and there was no fresh evidence to substantiate it. His decision was overturned by the Appeal Court of Venice and the three defendants were committed for trial. They were acquitted.

On 9 March 1985 one of the defendants in the Padua trial, Pietro Greco, a mathematics teacher who had earlier fled to France to escape imprisonment, was shot dead by a secret service agent in Trieste. He was not armed. Amnesty International monitored the subsequent judicial inquiry because of allegations that his killing had been deliberate, and that he had not, as police claimed, resisted arrest. On 24 October 1986 the Court of Assizes of Trieste sentenced Nunzio Maurizio Romano, an agent of the secret service (SISDE), and Maurizio Bensa, a member of the special anti-terrorist unit DIGOS, to eight months' imprisonment each for taking excessive but unpremeditated action in legitimate defence. Two other police officers were acquitted.

On 5 December Amnesty International wrote to Aldo Vezzia, Procurator General of Naples, about allegations of torture and ill-treatment of detainees in police stations and *carabinieri* barracks. About 30 such cases had been submitted to the procurator's office by various Neapolitan lawyers who stated that they were concerned by an increase in the use of torture and ill-treatment in order to extract confessions. In its letter Amnesty International described three cases. One detainee alleged that he had been beaten and had had a broom handle inserted into his anus; another that he had suffered extensive burns from cigarette ends and the third that the police had trampled on his hands with their boots.

The judicial inquiry into the death in police custody in Palermo of Salvatore Marino in August 1985 (see *Amnesty International Report 1986*) ended in October with the commital for trial in Caltanissetta of 12 police officials and four *carabinieri*. They were charged with taking part in involuntary homicide. The inquiry established that Salvatore Marino had died as a result of beating and ill-treatment.

During 1986 Amnesty International adopted as prisoners of conscience 17 conscientious objectors to military service. Among them were 13 Jehovah's Witnesses who had gone together to a military barracks in Viterbo in September to declare their refusal, on religious grounds, to carry out military service, although they said they were "not against the state and its institutions". The Jehovah's Witnesses were all sentenced to one year's imprisonment by a military tribunal in Rome and sent to the military prison of Forte Boccea.

Malta

Amnesty International continued to receive allegations that people held in police custody had been ill-treated. On 3 January and 17 February the organization wrote to the Minister of Justice and Parliamentary Affairs providing details on two cases in which ill-treatment was alleged and asking if any investigation had taken place. The organization had written in July 1985 about five other cases (see *Amnesty International Report 1986*). All seven prisoners alleged being ill-treated at various times between 1980 and 1985. In May Amnesty International received a detailed reply from the Minister, which addressed the seven specific cases. In the case of Wilfred Cardona the police denied using violence, but claimed that during interrogation Cardona banged his head against a table in a fit of desperation which was attributed to family problems. In four cases the Minister said that investigation would not be appropriate as legal proceedings were still continuing. In one case — that of Leonard Debono, found dead in 1980 — the Minister said that no progress had been made in the inquiries. Referring to the acquittal in 1985 of Anthony Mifsud by a jury, the Minister said that "they felt they could not rely on the statement he had made to the police" but that "I do not regard the evidence . . . as justifying any further investigation".

Norway

Amnesty International continued to be concerned about the imprisonment of conscientious objectors to military service. In Norway an objector's application for alternative service is assessed by the Minister of Justice on the basis of whether the person's conviction is profound and based on purely pacifist principles. On 31 January Amnesty International wrote to the Minister of Justice about Ulf Alstad, who began a 45-day prison sentence on 8 January for refusal of military service, his second period of imprisonment. On 22 July the organization urged the release of prisoner of conscience Stein Roar Kringeland, who began his 90-day sentence on 10 June. The court of Trondheim acknowledged that his refusal to carry out military service was based on firm and sincere conviction. However, it upheld the view of the Ministry of Justice that his application did not express principles that were purely pacifist. Amnesty International also urged the authorities to review their current practice. The organization wrote again on 14 October to the Minister of Justice asking for the release of Vidar Aas, who was imprisoned in September for 90 days for refusing to do military service.

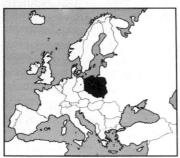

Poland

Amnesty International was concerned about the arrest and detention of hundreds of prisoners of conscience and welcomed the release of almost all of them under a wide-ranging amnesty. The organization received allegations that some political prisoners were ill-treated and that others were denied the right to choose their own legal representatives. It was also concerned about legislation which endangered the right to a fair trial and about short-term detentions of people for the non-violent exercise of their right to freedom of expression. Amnesty International was also concerned about the death penalty.

According to official figures there were 159 political prisoners in March. By July Amnesty International believed that there were over 250 political prisoners, most of whom had been arrested since the limited act of clemency announced in November 1985 (see *Amnesty International Report 1986*). The majority were detained because of their involvement in underground activities of the banned trade union Solidarity or in the production and distribution of unauthorized literature and were considered by Amnesty International to be prisoners of conscience.

Zbigniew Bujak was the chairperson of Solidarity in Warsaw and a founder member of the Provisional Coordinating Committee (TKK) — the underground Solidarity leadership formed after the declaration of martial law in December 1981. He was arrested on 31 May after being in hiding since martial law was imposed. He was charged with preparing to overthrow the state under Article 128 of the penal code. Arrested on the same day were Ewa Kulik, reportedly an organizer of the underground press in Warsaw, who had also been in hiding since martial law was imposed, and Konrad Bielinski, who had escaped from a martial law internment camp in 1982 and joined the TKK in Warsaw. Julita and Tomasz Mirkowicz, at whose apartment Zbigniew Bujak was arrested, were arrested on 18 August, the day after their return from the USA. Also arrested in connection with Zbigniew Bujak's arrest were: Alicja Komorowska and Zbigniew Lewicki who reportedly possessed keys to the apartment; and Julita Mirkowicz's father, a senior Foreign Ministry official. All were released in September under the amnesty.

Amnesty International took up the cases of Zbigniew Bogacz and four others from Katowice. They were sentenced on 9 April by the Mikolow regional court to between one and a half and three and a half years' imprisonment for producing and distributing leaflets calling for a 15-minute strike. They were also released under the terms of the amnesty.

On 17 July the *Sejm* (Parliament) approved an amnesty law which came into effect on 23 July. The law enabled courts and procurators to order releases before 15 September. Political prisoners excluded from the amnesty were those convicted of: high treason; participation in a conspiracy against the Polish People's Republic; espionage; sabotage and activity detrimental to the socialized economy; preparations for high treason or conspiracy; membership of an association detrimental to the Polish People's Republic or of an underground or criminal organization; so-called "small economic sabotage"; and recidivists. The Public Prosecutor could ask the Supreme Court to release those prisoners whose offences fell outside the scope of amnesty law. Additionally, those people who had not been charged by 17 July with committing a crime against the state or public order could benefit from the law if by 31 December they voluntarily reported and confessed to the authorities, or to a Polish diplomatic or consular mission abroad.

On 12 September the authorities announced that all political prisoners except those charged with terrorism, espionage, sabotage or giving away state secrets would be released under the terms of the amnesty. On 15 September it was announced that 225 political prisoners had been released.

Not included in the amnesty were some people imprisoned for refusing to do military service on conscientious grounds, for example Wojciech Jankowski and Jaroslaw Nakielski, both members of the "Freedom and Peace" movement (RWP) which demands an alternative to military service. Wojciech Jankowski was sentenced on 23 December 1985 to three and a half years' imprisonment for refusing to do military service (see *Amnesty International Report 1986*). Jaroslaw Nakielski was arrested on 15 April for "persistently refusing to serve in the army". He was reportedly transferred to a psychiatric hospital from which he escaped. He was rearrested on 15 September while on his way to report to the authorities so as to benefit from the amnesty. Amnesty International adopted both as prisoners of conscience. They were both released by early November. Another RWP member, Ryszard Bonowski, was arrested on 26 July for refusing to do military service. He remained in detention until his trial on 1 October when he was sentenced to two years' imprisonment suspended for three years.

Amnesty International also received reports stating that there were up to 300 Jehovah's Witnesses serving prison sentences in 1986 for refusing to do military service. The organization was able to obtain details on only four of these prisoners who were all adopted as prisoners of conscience: Zenon Katulski, Jan Plitt and Bronislaw Kreft, were sentenced to three and a half years, two and a half and two and a half years' imprisonment respectively in December 1985; Tadeusz Gorczynski was sentenced to two and a half years in early 1986. To Amnesty International's knowledge all four were still in detention at the end of 1986.

The organization appealed on behalf of Leszek Moczulski, leader of the Confederation for an Independent Poland (KPN) (see *Amnesty International Report 1986*), who was sentenced to four years' imprisonment on 22 April. He was reportedly denied adequate medical treatment after suffering heart attacks in detention on the night of 1/2 July and again on 27 August. He was released, along with other KPN members, in September under the amnesty. Among the other prisoners of conscience released under the amnesty were senior Solidarity activists Wladyslaw Frasyniuk and Bogdan Lis; Jan Kostecki of the Szczecin Committee in the Defence of the Rule of Law, imprisoned on 23 May after his appeal was turned down (see *Amnesty International Report 1986*); and Marek Adamkiewicz whose imprisonment in 1984 had led to the formation of the RWP (see *Amnesty International Report 1986*).

Amnesty International received numerous reports that detainees and convicted prisoners of conscience were ill-treated. It appealed on behalf of Wladyslaw Frasyniuk (see *Amnesty International Report 1986*) who was allegedly severely beaten by warders in Lubsko prison on 26 March after refusing to cooperate with the prison authorities when they tried to move him by force into solitary confinement. Before the beating, the prisoner with whom Wladyslaw Frasyniuk shared his cell was taken out and the cells nearby were emptied. According to reports, a group of 30 warders then entered and systematically beat Wladyslaw Frasyniuk with their fists and kicked him in the stomach and back. He was then put into solitary confinement for a month.

Amnesty International received reports that some political detainees due to be tried in military courts were denied the right to choose their own legal representatives. Solidarity activists Tadeusz Jedynak and Bogdan Borusewicz, arrested in June 1985 and 11 January 1986 respectively, were reportedly refused lawyers of their choice. Both were charged with "preparation to overthrow the state by force" under Article 128 in connection with Article 123 of the penal code, but were released in September under the terms of the amnesty.

On 24 October the *Sejm* passed legislation introducing new offences into the Code of Petty Offences. These included participation in "actions designed to foster public disquiet", unauthorized publishing activities and banned organizations "if the range of the deed or its effect are not extensive". Previously, such offences had usually been prosecuted under Article 282a of the penal code which carried prison sentences of up to three years' imprisonment. The new legislation transferred such cases to misdemeanour courts which could impose a maximum sentence of three months' imprisonment or a fine of 50,000 zlotys (US$250) and where an "accelerated procedure" was applied. Under this "accelerated procedure" an investigation is conducted by the police alone (without involving the Public Prosecutor's Office) and has to be completed within 48 hours. A trial is held at the end of the 48 hours at which the police stand in for the Public Prosecutor and the case is heard by a single judge. An appeal against sentence can be lodged. Because of the speed of the procedure, Amnesty International was concerned that there would be insufficient time for defendants to prepare a defence. For example, on 11 November Daniel Korona, a student, was detained after leaflets calling for the commemoration of Poland's independence in 1918 had been thrown out of a window in Warsaw. On 12 November he was sentenced to a fine of 50,000 zl under Article 52a of the misdemeanour code for distributing an illegal publication, a charge he denied. Reportedly, the only prosecution witness at the hearing told the tribunal that he had intuitively sensed that Daniel Korona had thrown the leaflets because he acted suspiciously when leaving the building. The defence lawyer was reportedly refused access to the case file and was also initially refused entry into the tribunal.

Another example of the use of the "accelerated procedure" followed the arrest in Warsaw on 15 June of Joanna Wierzbicka-

Rusiecka and five others in connection with the production of an unauthorized publication. At their first hearing the following day they reportedly had no defence counsel other than a lawyer who happened to be in court on another matter, who refused to act for them owing to unfamiliarity with the case and the number of defendants involved. On 23 June, by which time they did have defence counsel, they were sentenced to between 12 and 18 months' imprisonment. Amnesty International was also concerned about allegations that some of the defendants were ill-treated by the police following arrest. They were all released under the amnesty.

After the amnesty Amnesty International continued to receive reports of people being arrested and detained for short periods for attempting to exercise their right to non-violent freedom of expression. At least 22 people in Warsaw and Krakow alone were detained and fined by misdemeanour courts for participating in peaceful demonstrations on 11 November marking the anniversary of Poland's independence after the First World War. In December Francisek Kocik and Stanislaw Szyba were among those detained and fined. Some people also had their cars confiscated by misdemeanour courts for transporting unofficial publications.

Amnesty International learned of the imposition of seven death sentences and of two executions, in each case for murder.

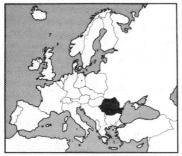

Romania

Amnesty International worked for the release of prisoners of conscience imprisoned for the non-violent exercise of their right to freedom of expression and for attempting to leave the country. The organization received allegations that political prisoners had been ill-treated in detention and denied access to family and legal representatives for long periods.

During 1986 Amnesty International learned of a number of prisoners convicted in previous years under Article 166 of the criminal code. This covers "propaganda against the Socialist State" and carries a sentence of five to 15 years' imprisonment. Ion Bugan was arrested in March 1983 after driving his car through the centre of Bucharest displaying a picture of Nicolae Ceausescu, the President and leader of the ruling Romanian Communist Party, under which he had written the caption "We don't want you, hangman". He was sentenced to 10 years' imprisonment under Article 166 and adopted as a prisoner of conscience. Another prisoner of conscience was Gheorghe Nastasescu, a building worker from Iasi, who was sentenced in 1982 to nine years' imprisonment under Article 166 because he made a speech and handed out leaflets in Bucharest calling on the populace to demonstrate their dissatisfaction with President Ceausescu.

On 2 June an amnesty was granted by presidential decree. People sentenced to up to five years' imprisonment or corrective labour were pardoned and released, sentences of between five and eight years were reduced by one third; those between eight and 10 years by a fifth. Excluded from the amnesty were people sentenced for murder or other violent crimes which resulted in death, robbery, illegal abortion, rape, "crimes against social property with serious or particularly serious consequences", bribery, intimidation, the use of force and escaping from prison. Amnesty International welcomed the release of 13 adopted prisoners of conscience under this amnesty. It also welcomed the release on 18 April of Radu Filipescu, sentenced to 10 years' imprisonment in 1983, and Dorel Catarama, whose 10-year prison sentence imposed in 1982 had been raised to 14 years on appeal. Amnesty International had adopted both as prisoners of conscience (see *Amnesty International Report 1985*).

However, some prisoners of conscience were not released despite the amnesty. For example, Laszlo Buzas and Erno Borbely, both members of the ethnic Hungarian minority, were arrested in 1982 and each sentenced to six years' imprisonment for "propaganda against the Socialist State" under Article 166 of the criminal code. They were reportedly accused of having sent abroad the text of an anti-Hungarian leaflet which they alleged had been produced and distributed with the aid of the Romanian authorities (see *Amnesty International Report 1984*). Adalbert (Bela) Pal, also a member of the Hungarian minority, was sentenced in August 1983 to six years' imprisonment under Article 166 after complaining of corruption within the ruling Romanian Communist Party and protesting at the lack of opportunities for ethnic Hungarians to be educated in Hungarian (see *Amnesty International Report 1985*). All three remained imprisoned despite the amnesty and a previous similar amnesty in 1984. Amnesty International was particularly concerned about the continued imprisonment of Adalbert Pal as it learned that he suffered from Huntington's Chorea, which was diagnosed before his arrest, and that his health had seriously deteriorated during his detention. Between May and October his wife was refused permission to visit him. He was released on 21 December, before the expiry of his sentence, but the other two were still imprisoned at the end of 1986.

The right to emigrate is severely restricted. Although a certain number of Romanians leave the country legally each year, Amnesty International knows of many people who have repeatedly been refused permission to emigrate. A Romanian citizen who applies to emigrate runs the risk of harassment, loss of work or demotion, and, in some cases, imprisonment. Those who attempt, or make preparations for, unauthorized border crossings face prosecution under Article 245 of the criminal code which allows for prison sentences of six months to three years. Dan Chitila was arrested in June by the Yugoslav authorities after having crossed illegally into Yugoslavia from Romania. On 26 July he was returned to Romania and subsequently convicted under Article 245. Eugen Brecheci was reportedly arrested on 2 August after discussing with two friends the possibility of fleeing the country. Amnesty International sought details of the charges against him from the Romanian authorities. It believed he may have been charged under Article 245. Both men were subsequently released.

Individuals are also imprisoned under decree 153/1970 for the non-violent exercise of their human rights on charges of "parasitical" or "anarchic" conduct. This provides for summary trial without the right to legal defence and prescribes sentences of up to six months' imprisonment or "corrective labour without deprivation of liberty". For example, Florin Rusu, a teacher, was reportedly arrested in June and sentenced to four months' imprisonment for "parasitism". He had previously served a similar sentence for "parasitism" in 1984. On both occasions he had reportedly been refused employment by the state, the sole employer, because of his political activities for the National Peasant Party — one of Romania's leading political parties before it was banned by the authorities in 1948.

Amnesty International believes that some detainees have been tried on false criminal charges for exercising their right to freedom of expression. For example, Ioan Ruta was demoted from his job as head of a Bucharest factory when his wife defected to the USA and was granted political asylum there. He complained in writing to the authorities about this demotion and was arrested on 27 February. He suffered a heart attack and contracted hepatitis in pre-trial detention and was denied access to his family and legal representation until early June, shortly before his trial began. On 6 November he was sentenced to seven years' imprisonment for accepting bribes in exchange for granting employment. He denied the charges and stated that the real reason for his arrest was his refusal, despite repeated requests from the authorities, to divorce his wife after her defection. One of the prosecution witnesses reportedly retracted his evidence in court, saying that his original statements were made under duress. Amnesty International sought further details of the charges and evidence produced.

Amnesty International continued to receive allegations of ill-treatment of political detainees. Gigi Mocanu was arrested in early May on charges of possessing foreign currency. The real reason for his arrest may have been because he had made a cassette recording of events concerning the detention of his brother Emil Mocanu, a prisoner of conscience arrested in September 1984 for helping another brother flee from Romania. Following his arrest Emil Mocanu was allegedly beaten by officials, as was Gigi Mocanu, who was reportedly beaten on the soles of his feet with iron bars. Emil Mocanu and Gigi Mocanu were released in March and July respectively.

Amnesty International did not learn of any death sentences imposed or carried out during 1986.

Spain

Torture and ill-treatment of detainees held incommunicado under the anti-terrorist law continued to be Amnesty International's main concern. Many of the allegations of torture and ill-treatment were made by Basques arrested in Spain after being expelled from France. Judicial proceedings were in progress in connection with allegations of torture involving many members of the security forces; in a prominent trial, three Civil Guard officers were convicted of torturing detainees. In another case the security forces refused to comply with the order of the court conducting a judicial investigation into allegations of torture. Amnesty International adopted an imprisoned conscientious objector to military service as a prisoner of conscience for the first time since the introduction of new legislation on conscientious objection in December 1984.

Amnesty International considered that the widespread use of incommunicado detention under the anti-terrorist law facilitated the torture and ill-treatment of detainees. The Minister of the Interior declared in an official statement on 17 September that 1,026 people had been held incommunicado under this law since its introduction on 26 December 1984. In the first seven months of 1986, 295 people were held incommunicado; only 30 per cent of these detainees were brought before a court. According to this statement, 90 per cent of the arrests related to *Euskadi Ta Askatasuna* (ETA), the armed Basque group, which was allegedly responsible for 34 killings in this period.

In December the government announced that it intended to allow certain articles of the anti-terrorist law to expire in January 1987 but the exceptional powers given to the police to hold detainees incommunicado for up to 10 days were to remain. Amnesty International noted no improvements in safeguards, such as improving access to legal assistance; removing procedural restrictions in the exercise of *habeas corpus* under the anti-terrorist law; or increasing the effectiveness of judicial supervision or medical examination of detainees.

Amnesty International continued to receive allegations of torture and ill-treatment. In July, for the first time, such allegations were made by Basques expelled from France under a new policy of the French Government. The first two Basques arrived on 19 and 22 July and were immediately arrested under the anti-terrorist law. They were held incommunicado in the *Dirección General de Seguridad* (DGS), General Security Headquarters, in Madrid. After interrogation both men were charged with belonging to an armed band and transferred to Carabanchel prison. According to reports received by Amnesty International, both men made complaints to the court about their treatment. In particular, José Varona López alleged that he had been hit on the head with a telephone directory, hooded and beaten while tied down. The forensic surgeon attached to the court described in writing injuries to his wrists, feet and legs which appeared consistent with his allegations. On 30 July Amnesty International asked the Minister of the Interior to investigate these allegations. No reply was received. A further 24 Basques were expelled from France to Spain in 1986 and numerous allegations of torture and ill-treatment were made. In all these cases, the expellees were handed over directly to the police at the frontier, transferred to Madrid and held incommunicado under the anti-terrorist law.

Juan Ramón Ruiz de Gauna was handed over to the Spanish police on 30 July. He alleged that he was beaten during his transfer from the border to Madrid and his interrogation in the DGS, where he spent a night chained by the neck to a radiator. He received two medical examinations and was transferred to Carabanchel prison on 2 August where a prison doctor issued a certificate recording injuries consistent with his allegations. In the case of Augustín Azkarate Intxaurrondo, expelled to Spain from France on 15 October, the judge of the Central Court in Madrid asked for him to be admitted to hospital after he had spent six days incommunicado in the DGS. The prisoner alleged that he had been severely beaten and given electric shocks in the police headquarters in San Sebastian before being transferred to Madrid where he was again beaten and had his head forcibly held under water.

On 29 December Amnesty International wrote to the Minister of the Interior giving details of further allegations of torture and ill-treatment made by Basque refugees.

The President of the *Asociación Pro Derechos Humanos*, Association for Human Rights, stated when presenting the Association's annual report at the end of the year that 25 members of the police and Civil Guard had been convicted for acts of torture, ill-treatment or injuries to prisoners in 1986. An estimated 150 further trials on such charges were pending.

The Provincial Court of San Sebastian, in an important decision of 23 November, convicted three members of the Civil Guard of torturing three brothers – José María, Lucio and Victor Olarra — in 1983 (see *Amnesty International Report 1984, 1985* and *1986*). One was sentenced to six months' imprisonment and three years' suspension from service, and the other two to four months' imprisonment and two years' suspension each. A fourth Civil Guard was acquitted. The court also recognized that a fourth detainee had been injured but concluded that it could not establish how this had occurred. The judges found that José María Olarra had been tied to a plank allowing his head to be forced into a bucket of water. All three brothers were kicked, punched and beaten.

On 17 September the Minister of the Interior publicly announced that he had ordered Civil Guards to disregard the order of a court in Bilbao which was investigating allegations of torture. Ninety officers had been requested by the investigating judge to attend an identity parade. The Minister stated that the Minister of Justice had been consulted and the decision was made with the full support of the President of the Government. However, the officers did participate in the identity parades after an appeal against the order had been dismissed by the court.

Amnesty International appealed for the release of Francesc Alexandrí Muchart, a conscientious objector to military service whose application for conscientious objector status was rejected because it was presented after the date stipulated for his induction into the army. Such applications are inadmissible under the provisions of the 1984 law on conscientious objection. Amnesty

International has criticized this and other major features of the law (see *Amnesty International Report 1986*). Francesc Alexandrí was imprisoned in a military barracks in May pending trial on charges of desertion and refusal to perform military service. On 10 December, following a 26-day hunger-strike, he was transferred to his home where he remained under house arrest at the end of 1986.

Switzerland

Amnesty International was concerned about the imprisonment of conscientious objectors to military service and the return to Sri Lanka of members of the Tamil minority, reportedly against their will.

Regular periods of military service are compulsory for men aged between 20 and 50 and there is no alternative civilian service. There is limited access to unarmed military service for conscripts who can prove that the use of arms would result in "a severe conflict of conscience" on religious or ethical grounds. Article 81 of the Military Penal Code allows military tribunals to sentence people refusing military service to up to three years' imprisonment although, in practice, sentences rarely exceed one year. If a tribunal recognizes an individual's "severe conflict of conscience" on religious or ethical grounds, a sentence of up to six months' imprisonment may be passed. This is normally served in the form of *arrêts répressifs*, a system of imprisonment allowing prescribed work during the daytime outside the place of detention or, more exceptionally, in the form of "semi-detention", allowing the objector to continue normal or approved employment during the day. In 1985 the Federal Military Department conducted a public consultation on the possibility of "decriminalizing" certain categories of conscientious objection to military service (see *Amnesty International Report 1986*). On 2 July 1986 the Federal Council instructed the Federal Military Department to draw up a draft law for parliament's consideration, taking into account the findings of the consultation.

Amnesty International worked on the cases of 45 people sentenced to imprisonment of three to 12 months for refusing armed military service. A number of these cases were still under investigation by Amnesty International at the end of 1986 to determine whether they were prisoners of conscience. Among those adopted as prisoners of

conscience were conscientious objectors who had applied unsuccessfully for unarmed military service and objectors who had refused all
forms of military service but had expressed their willingness to
perform an alternative civilian service.

On 10 October Amnesty International telexed the head of the
Federal Department of Justice and Police urging that members of the
Sri Lankan Tamil minority should not be returned against their will to
Sri Lanka, in view of continued widespread arbitrary arrests, torture,
extrajudicial killings and "disappearances" there. During 1986
Amnesty International received reports that 18 Tamils had been
returned by Switzerland. However, on 16 October the Delegate for
Refugees of the Federal Department of Justice and Police announced
that the authorities were not at that time considering repatriating all
Tamils whose requests for asylum had been rejected since the
situation in the north and east of Sri Lanka was "precarious". Tamil
cases would be examined individually before a decision to return
anyone was made. In the view of the Delegate, some 40 asylum
seekers could be returned in view of the experience of previous
returned Tamils and because "they had relations in the quieter
regions of the island". The repatriation of Tamils convicted of
offences relating to drugs would continue.

During 1986 Switzerland ratified the UN Convention against
Torture.

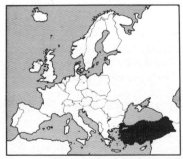

Turkey

Amnesty International was concerned about the continued imprisonment of prisoners of conscience,
torture and ill-treatment of prisoners and the imposition of the death
penalty. After a study of trials of
political prisoners by military courts
the organization concluded that
these courts did not give political prisoners fair trials.

At the end of 1986 martial law was still in force in five of Turkey's
67 provinces and a state of emergency existed in a further eight
provinces. The exact number of prisoners of conscience was not
known, but at the beginning of the year there were approximately
15,500 political prisoners, of whom several hundred were recognized
as prisoners of conscience by Amnesty International. During 1986
many of these were released as a result of an amendment to the Law

on the Execution of Sentences which came into force on 19 March. The amendment increased the remission of sentences for some criminal and political prisoners. A number of defendants in political trials were also released conditionally while their trials continued.

Prisoners of conscience adopted by Amnesty International included members of political parties and groups, writers, journalists, publishers, academics, members of the Kurdish ethnic minority and people imprisoned for their religious activities.

Members of political parties and groups were usually imprisoned under Article 141 of the penal code, which prohibits membership of "illegal organizations". They included members of the illegal Turkish Communist Party (TKP) and of other left-wing parties which had been legal until they were banned after the 1980 military coup. Trials of members of the Turkish Workers' Party (TIP) continued in Istanbul military courts. In April the retrial of 47 TIP members was reported to have been postponed until June, but no further reports appeared. The trial of another 168 members which started in May 1984 was still in progress at the end of 1986. Amnesty International did not know whether any of the defendants were in prison. Five members of the Turkish Workers' and Peasants' Party (TIKP) remained in prison at the end of 1986. Legal proceedings continued in various parts of Turkey against members of the Turkish Socialist Workers' Party (TSIP). Amnesty International knew of six defendants who were still in prison at the end of 1986 serving sentences relating to previous convictions. Another TSIP member was rearrested in November. (See *Amnesty International Report 1985* and *1986* for all the above cases.)

Four members of the Turkish Communist Party-Union (TKP-B) were arrested and charged under Article 141 with planning to distribute political leaflets disguised as sweets at a trade union rally on 22 February in Izmir. Their trial ended in November when they were sentenced to between four and six years' imprisonment. The trials of other TKP-B members continued, but the total number of TKP-B members in prison at the end of the year was not known.

In February and March the 12 remaining imprisoned defendants in the Turkish Peace Association (TPA) case were released. The two trials of TPA members were combined and in November the Military Prosecutor asked for sentences of between five and 15 years for 37 defendants and acquittal for 28. Four defendants had their cases set aside. Two defendants, Orhan Apaydin and Ismail Hakki Öztorun, died during the year. The trial was still continuing at the end of 1986 (see *Amnesty International Report 1983* to *1986*).

The trial of the 1,477 leaders, officials and advisers of the Confederation of Progressive Trade Unions (DISK) which had been running for five years, ended in Istanbul on 23 December. Two hundred and sixty four defendants received prison sentences of between five and a half and 10 years; 1,169 were acquitted and the remainder either had their cases set aside for separate trial or dropped. All those convicted were also sentenced to periods of internal exile and banned from public service for life. Defence and prosecution have appealed against the verdict. DISK and 28 of its 30 affiliated trade unions were dissolved.

Journalists, writers and publishers continued to be prosecuted under Article 142 of the penal code which prohibits making "communist propaganda". Hüseyin Kivanç, a publisher, was detained on 13 May. His trial had opened 10 years earlier. On 23 October he was acquitted in one case. The three other cases against him were combined. The trial continued at the end of the year.

On 12 November Halil Berktay, a political scientist, Cenan Biçakçi, a trade unionist, and Ali Kalan, a lawyer, were also arrested under Article 142. They had participated in a meeting organized by the journal *Saçak* in Ankara on 26 July. The Public Prosecutor issued arrest warrants on the grounds that the discussion had violated Article 142. The three men remained in prison awaiting trial at the end of 1986.

Many Kurds remained in prison. Some were charged with or convicted of violent offences; others imprisoned on account of their non-violent political or cultural activities were adopted by Amnesty International as prisoners of conscience. Among these were Mehdi Zana, former Mayor of Diyarbakir, and Recep Maraşli, a publisher, who remained in Diyarbakir Military Prison (see *Amnesty International Report 1984, 1985* and *1986*). The hearing of Mehdi Zana's appeal against his 24-year sentence passed in October 1983 was scheduled for 25 November but was adjourned until 1987.

Amnesty International adopted as prisoners of conscience several Muslim activists who were convicted under Article 163 of the penal code which prohibits attempts to adapt "the basic social, economic, political or judicial orders of the State to religious principles or beliefs". Among them was Osman Coşkun, an imam who was sentenced to seven years and three months' imprisonment in November for his non-violent religious activities in Muslim communities in the Federal Republic of Germany, where he lived from 1980 until his return to Turkey in March 1986. Other people imprisoned under Article 163 included writers and journalists. Emine Şenlikoglu, writer and chief editor of the periodical *Mektup* remained in prison serving a sentence of six years three months for a book she wrote (see *Amnesty International Report 1986*).

In June the Plenary of the Courts of Appeal quashed the sentences reimposed on 23 Jehovah's Witnesses by the Ankara State Security Court in 1985 (see *Amnesty International Report 1985* and *1986*). The Plenary stated that "every Turkish citizen has the right to freedom of faith and conscience, the choice of faith and religious practice" and ruled that Jehovah's Witnesses should not, therefore, be prosecuted under Article 163.

On 15 December Amnesty International wrote again to Prime Minister Turgut Özal about three Greek Cypriots — Andreas Hatjiloizou, Andreas Costas Kassapis and Leontios Leontious — taken prisoner by the Turkish armed forces during the hostilities in Cyprus in 1974 and missing since then (see *Amnesty International Report 1974* to *1981*, and *1986*). No response had been received to earlier letters calling for an investigation into the whereabouts of the three men, who were among many Greek Cypriots taken prisoner and missing since 1974.

Political cases continued to be heard by military courts even in those provinces no longer under martial law. In October Amnesty International published a report, *Unfair Trial of Political Prisoners in Turkey*. Since the introduction of martial law in December 1978 more than 48,000 political prisoners had been sentenced to imprisonment or death after unfair trials. The report concluded that the military courts were not independent from the executive authorities either in law or in practice; that lawyers defending political prisoners had been prevented from adequately representing their clients; that detainees charged with political offences had been subjected to excessively long trials and periods of pre-trial detention; and that military courts had repeatedly failed to investigate defendants' allegations that statements had been extracted under torture. On 13 April the newspaper *Cumhuriyet* reported that Military Court No. 1 of Diyarbakir province had ruled that an admission of guilt by a defendant could be considered as evidence even if it had been obtained by illegal means.

Allegations of torture of both political and criminal prisoners continued. These related to both those held in incommunicado detention in police stations and prisoners in military and civilian prisons. Among the allegations of torture received was that of Servet Ziya Çorakli, a member of TKP-B. He was detained in Izmir on 21 February and charged with planning the distribution of political leaflets at a trade union rally on 22 February. In April Amnesty International heard that he had been repeatedly tortured during detention and was severely injured. He had been admitted to a military hospital several times.

In November Amnesty International issued a document *Turkey: Torture and Ill-Treatment of Detainees and Prisoners* which stated that Amnesty International had not observed any fundamental changes in the attitude or the practice of the police or prison officials relating to the torture of detainees and prisoners during the previous 12 months. The document provided detailed information about alleged torture during 1985 and 1986, including statements from former prisoners who had been interviewed by Amnesty International. The organization knew of eight deaths which occurred either in custody or shortly after release between January and July 1986, alleged to be the result of ill-treatment during interrogation.

In December, following student protests and hunger-strikes, Amnesty International received details of students who had been detained and tortured. Among them were Sedat Karaduman and Salih Turan, students at Ankara University. They were detained on 26 November and held for 11 and 15 days respectively, during which time Salih Turan had to receive hospital treatment. Yilmaz Onay, a theatre director and writer who was also detained in Ankara from 22 to 25 December, told a press conference that he had been stripped naked, given electric shocks and hosed with ice-cold water during his interrogation by police. He gave journalists a copy of a medical report which he stated confirmed that his body bore the signs of torture.

In April 1986 an Istanbul military court sentenced three policemen to prison terms of 10 years eight months for causing the death under torture of Mustafa Hayrullahoglu in November 1982, two days after he had been detained. Amnesty International had urged the authorities to investigate the cause of death (see *Amnesty International Report 1984*).

A memorandum submitted to the authorities in February dealt with Amnesty International's concerns about Iranian refugees who could face torture, execution or imprisonment as prisoners of conscience if returned to Iran. The memorandum included a series of recommendations and requests for clarification. The organization welcomed the willingness expressed by officials to investigate its reports of *refoulement* (forcible return) and the stated policy of the authorities that any Iranian who feared persecution in Iran would not be returned there. However, the organization continued to receive reports of *refoulement* and of Iranians seeking asylum in Turkey being turned back at the border before their cases could be evaluated by competent officials. In one border incident on 2 January, four Iranians were shot dead by Turkish border guards. In response to Amnesty International's appeal for information the authorities said that the four were among a group entering Turkey illegally. They had been fired on by guards after disobeying an order to stop. A fifth person was wounded and later resettled in a third country. In October Amnesty International learned of several Iranians being expelled. The organization asked for urgent consideration to be given to reviewing the procedures for dealing with Iranian refugees to protect them against the possibility of *refoulement*. The authorities replied that the cases referred to were under investigation and assured Amnesty International that genuine refugees were not returned to Iran.

However, an article in the Iranian newspaper *Keyhan*, published in Tehran on 29 November, reported that six people it described as members of the Kurdish political parties, *Komaleh* and the Kurdish Democratic Party, had been arrested in Turkey and handed over to the Iranian police. On 22 December Amnesty International asked the Turkish authorities about the six men, who could face torture or execution in Iran because of their suspected political activities.

Although no executions took place during 1986, 134 death sentences were reported in the Turkish press. The number of people under sentence of death at the end of 1986 was estimated to be several hundred. One hundred and twenty-four death sentences were awaiting ratification by the Turkish Grand National Assembly (TBMM). Amnesty International continued to appeal against executions and for the total abolition of the death penalty.

Union of Soviet Socialist Republics

Amnesty International observed no improvement in the harsh and arbitrary treatment of prisoners of conscience in 1986. Although it learned of fewer political arrests, Amnesty International was disturbed that the Soviet authorities continued to imprison many citizens whose conscience had led them to dissent peacefully from official policies, and to apply compulsory psychiatric measures to others. There was no reduction in the number of capital offences: at least eight people were executed and Amnesty International learned of a further 17 sentenced to death.

During 1986 Amnesty International worked on behalf of more than 530 individuals whom it knew or suspected to be prisoners of conscience, but official censorship and restrictions on freedom of movement, which limited the flow of information, made it probable that the real total was much higher.

In statements to audiences abroad Soviet representatives dwelt at length on human rights. In July the Soviet Committee for European Security and Cooperation marked the 11th anniversary of the signing of the Helsinki accords by announcing a plan to set up a commission which would "inform Soviet citizens of their rights". Amnesty International wrote to the committee's chairman asking which rights the new body would seek to promote; who would compose it, and how they would be appointed. It also asked if the commission would try to redress abuses of human rights and to raise petitions on behalf of individual complainants with the appropriate authorities. No reply had been received by the end of 1986.

In an interview with the French newspaper *L'Humanité* in April, Mikhail Gorbachov, the General Secretary of the Communist Party of the Soviet Union, maintained that there were no political prisoners in the USSR, but acknowledged that over 200 prisoners were serving sentences for "anti-state crimes". Amnesty International wrote to him in November asking for clarification of his remarks. It pointed out that of the 28 laws that prohibit "anti-state crimes", Soviet courts had habitually applied three to punish individuals solely for expressing their conscientiously held beliefs, or for trying to leave the country without permission. The organization enclosed a sample of over 140 cases and asked for a list of the 200 for comparison.

At least 12 prisoners of conscience were unconditionally released in 1986, either before their sentences had expired or from indefinite confinement. They included Academician Andrey Sakharov, who had been exiled to Gorky without charge or trial since 1980, and his wife Yelena Bonner, the Moscow Helsinki monitor. Most of the 12 were apparently pardoned. In its letter to Mikhail Gorbachov, Amnesty International welcomed the releases but repeated its call for an amnesty for all Soviet prisoners of conscience. It also renewed its request to meet representatives of the Soviet Government to discuss its concerns.

The Soviet news media gave unusually frank coverage to social and political issues during 1986 in what was described as a campaign for *glasnost* — "openness". Several legal problems were debated and Amnesty International welcomed the proposal of certain innovations by high-ranking officials of the USSR Supreme Court and the Ministry of Justice of the USSR. One such was that crime statistics should be published regularly for the first time since 1934 — a step Amnesty International had urged so that, for example, informed and public reassessment of the use of the death penalty could take place. Another proposal was that prisoners be permitted to see a lawyer when the investigation of their case began, rather than only when it was completed. If this proposal were to be implemented Amnesty

International believed it might make for fairer trials and could help protect prisoners from ill-treatment before trial.

Amnesty International had repeatedly expressed concern that current procedure made prisoners in investigation prisons particularly easy targets for abuse (see *Amnesty International Report 1986*). They could be held incommunicado for as long as nine months while their cases were being investigated and during that time they did not have to be produced before a judge or a procurator as a safeguard against ill-treatment. In March Amnesty International appealed for an urgent inquiry into the treatment of Dr Vladimir Lifshits, a Jewish mathematician who required 10 days' hospital treatment for concussion and a broken nose following a beating by criminals in Leningrad investigation prison. News of his injuries emerged only after he saw a lawyer. Officials had not allowed his wife to see him, nor even notified her of his transfer to hospital. To Amnesty International's knowledge no steps were taken to investigate the beating or punish those responsible. Dr Lifshits was later sentenced to three years' imprisonment in connection with his efforts to emigrate. Other allegations of beatings by officials, or by prisoners acting with apparent official consent, reached Amnesty International from psychiatric hospitals, prisons and corrective labour colonies. Amnesty International knew of no investigations into these allegations.

Conditions in the prisons and colonies of the corrective labour system where most prisoners of conscience were held remained consistently poor. Prisoners were kept on monotonous, meagre rations with only rudimentary medical care, and had to meet excessively high work targets, often involving heavy physical labour. Failure to meet these targets and other infractions of the rules incurred administrative penalties ranging from cancellation of visits and letters to transfer to harsher conditions. In Amnesty International's experience prisoners of conscience incurred the most severe of these penalties very quickly, and although they were legally entitled to appeal against their treatment in uncensored letters to the Procurator — who was responsible for seeing that their legal rights were observed — their appeals were invariably rejected.

The experience of Anatoly Marchenko was a case in point. He was sentenced in 1981 to 10 years' imprisonment and five years' internal exile for "anti-Soviet agitation and propaganda" after he had sent abroad memoirs of a previous imprisonment. From 1983 he repeatedly complained to the procuracy that officials had handcuffed him and beaten him unconscious in strict regime corrective labour colony Perm 35 (see *Amnesty International Report 1985*). His complaints were ignored. Instead labour colony officials punished him by cancelling his visits, placing him for long spells in solitary confinement with reduced rations, and initiating his transfer to Chistopol prison, the country's harshest corrective labour institution. In December Anatoly Marchenko died after an unsuccessful hunger-strike in which he had appealed for the prosecution of the officials he said had beaten him, and for a visit from his wife, whom he had not seen since 1984. Amnesty International had repeatedly appealed on his behalf. In August Mark Morozov, another long-standing prisoner of conscience, died in Chistopol prison after a long illness.

Against this background Amnesty International remained disturbed by the terms of the law against "malicious disobedience" whose introduction was described in the *Amnesty International Report 1984*. It carries up to five years' imprisonment and empowers directors of prisons and corrective labour colonies to prosecute prisoners who have incurred repeated administrative penalties. In 1986 Soviet commentators sharply criticized the way courts had convicted criminal prisoners of "malicious disobedience" even though in many instances the administrative penalties had been illegally imposed in the first place. Amnesty International feared that in cases involving prisoners of conscience the risk of wrongful prosecution was even higher. At least another eight prisoners of conscience were convicted of "malicious disobedience" in 1986, some only days before they completed previous sentences. From their trial documents Amnesty International found officials had punished them for activities which it considered were the legitimate exercise of human rights, such as wearing a cross, or requesting a Bible. Amnesty International welcomed the acquittal by judicial review of Vladimir Poresh, Tatyana Osipova and Samuil Epshtein, previously convicted on this charge.

Soviet citizens were still at risk if they exercised their freedom of conscience in ways that did not conform to official policy and in 1986 at least 150 people were prosecuted for doing so. No one was acquitted of a political or religious offence to Amnesty International's knowledge, but the courts passed more probationary and deferred sentences than usual.

Despite official moves towards *glasnost*, individuals who communicated uncensored information on controversial topics faced imprisonment under laws restricting freedom of expression. Sentences of up to 10 years' imprisonment and five years' internal exile were passed on at least 11 people for "anti-Soviet agitation and propaganda". One was a Georgian dentist, Immanuil Tvaladze, who was convicted in June of compiling an unofficial record of a major trial in Tbilisi in 1984 in which four alleged hijackers were sentenced to death. (An account of the public protests that greeted their sentences appeared in

Amnesty International Report 1985.) Another 30 individuals received sentences of up to three years' imprisonment on the less serious charge of "circulating anti-Soviet slander". They were mostly religious believers convicted of distributing or printing Bibles and prayer books produced on home-made presses.

Religious believers remained the largest single category of prisoners of conscience in 1986. Around 40 Baptists who had refused on principle to submit to the state's restrictions on religious freedom were imprisoned for up to 10 years under the laws against "anti-social religious activity" and "violating the laws separating church and state", and several Jehovah's Witnesses, Pentecostalists and Hare Krishna devotees were also imprisoned on these charges. Some who stood trial in 1986 had served previous sentences spanning 20 years for activities such as teaching religion to children, or writing theological texts. In November Amnesty International published information on Rudolf Klassen, a Baptist preacher from Kazakhstan with a history of 17 years' imprisonment, who was released in August.

Soviet law offers no alternative to military service, and eight young men whose religious beliefs prevented them from bearing arms or swearing the military oath were imprisoned for up to three years for "evading regular call to active military service". Several would-be emigrants were also imprisoned on this charge after refusing call-up because they feared it would give them a security classification and further delay their emigration. In December Amnesty International produced a paper on *Imprisoned Conscientious Objectors in the USSR* drawing on the cases of 42 Jews, ethnic Germans, Baptists, Jehovah's Witnesses, Pentecostalists and others imprisoned on such charges since 1980.

By the end of 1986 Amnesty International believed that at least 44 prisoners of conscience were still being held against their will for indefinite periods in psychiatric institutions. Some had already been confined for over 15 years, under close supervision in special psychiatric hospitals, where isolation from relatives and friends made them especially vulnerable to ill-treatment with drugs or beatings. In December Amnesty International distributed a letter that had emerged from Alma-Ata special psychiatric hospital which illustrated these risks. It had been written in 1984 by Nizametdin Akhmetov, a worker from Bashkiria. Although Amnesty International believed he was still confined as a prisoner of conscience, it did not know what had happened to him since. During the year the authorities continued to use compulsory psychiatric measures to deter or punish acts of non-violent dissent. Nineteen individuals were confined on these grounds — most of them supporters of an unofficial peace group in Moscow, who were arrested going to or from the group's public events. Several of the 19 were said to have received forcible treatment with powerful drugs that gave them acute physical discomfort, and a number were still confined at the end of 1986.

The USSR retained 18 capital offences in peacetime and in May amended the law against bribe-taking by officials to increase the circumstances in which it was punishable by death. In 1986 the maximum sentence for prisoners whose death sentences had been commuted was raised from 15 to 20 years. Although Amnesty International interpreted this as encouragement to officials to reduce death sentences, it learned of no commutations in 1986. Eight executions and 17 death sentences were announced in the official press, but because of official secrecy the real total was probably higher than reported. Amnesty International appealed for clemency in each case.

In view of allegations that Soviet military personnel in Afghanistan were sometimes present during the torture of detainees, Amnesty International wrote to the Soviet President in September urging investigation of the allegations (see *Afghanistan* entry).

United Kingdom

Amnesty International was concerned about the inadequacy of investigations into fatal shootings by the security forces in Northern Ireland. It continued to be concerned about judicial procedures and about allegations of ill-treatment of prisoners in Northern Ireland. Amnesty International was also concerned about the detention pending deportation of Amanullah Khan, a Kashmiri leader in Britain, whom it believed might be a prisoner of conscience, and about allegations of ill-treatment of prisoners in Britain.

Over the years Amnesty International has been concerned about incidents in Northern Ireland in which members of the security forces shot people dead in circumstances that gave rise to allegations that these killings were planned. Amnesty International wrote to the government on 5 August expressing concern at the government's failure to deal adequately with issues raised by a series of incidents since 1982 in which unarmed individuals were shot dead by security forces (see *Amnesty International Report 1986*). The organization reiterated its call for the government to set up an independent judicial inquiry into these issues and said that a series of trials arising from the killings, in which police officers had been charged with murder, had established that senior police officers had made efforts to conceal important evidence. Similar allegations were made in connection with an inquiry into police conduct related to the killings headed by a senior British police officer, John Stalker, who was removed from duty before his report had been completed. Amnesty International said that the allegations in connection with the Stalker inquiry made the need for an independent judicial inquiry even more pressing. The government replied on 1 September restating its opposition to setting up such an inquiry because it believed the existing investigative procedures and laws were adequate (see *Amnesty International Report 1986*). On 30 September Amnesty International made public its concerns. On 16 December it accepted an invitation from the Minister of State for Northern Ireland to meet government officials in the following year to discuss its concerns. By the end of 1986, the first of three parts of a report about the above-mentioned killings had been submitted to the Chief Constable of Northern Ireland by another senior British police officer, who took over the external inquiry from John Stalker in June 1986.

Amnesty International was concerned about judicial procedures in the special "Diplock Courts" in Northern Ireland in which cases of alleged terrorism are heard without a jury. In particular, the organization monitored those cases in which uncorroborated evidence from alleged former accomplices, commonly known as "supergrasses", formed the sole basis of the prosecution's evidence. Four appeal hearings took place in 1986, in each of which most of the convictions under appeal were quashed. In July 1986, 18 people who had been sentenced in August 1983 on the basis of evidence given by Christopher Black, a former Irish Republican Army (IRA) member, had their convictions quashed. In exchange for giving evidence, Christopher Black had been granted immunity from prosecution. The Appeal Court judges decided that he had not been a completely honest or reliable witness. In the same month, the Appeal Court quashed a further two convictions based on the evidence of another IRA informer, Kevin McGrady. In November the convictions of eight people, some of whom had been in custody for over four years, were quashed, after the judges ruled that the IRA informer, Robert Quigley, was an "evasive, devious, inventive and lying witness". He too had been given immunity from prosecution. Amnesty International delegates observed the appeal hearing of 27 people convicted on the basis of evidence given by former Irish National Liberation Army (INLA) member Harry Kirkpatrick. In December, 24 of the 27 people had their convictions quashed. The judgment described Harry Kirkpatrick as a "dangerously flawed witness" whose evidence could not be relied on to sustain the convictions where there was no corroboration. In October the Director of Public Prosecutions dropped the charges against some 20 people who had been accused on the basis of testimony by a former IRA member, Angela Whoriskey.

Amnesty International continued to investigate allegations of ill-treatment of suspects detained under the anti-terrorist legislation in Castlereagh and Gough Barracks interrogation centres. Former detainees alleged that during interrogation they had been hit, kicked and threatened with violence against themselves and their families. The organization also received reports of ill-treatment of prisoners in Crumlin Road and Magilligan prisons.

Amnesty International investigated allegations that strip-searches of women prisoners in Armagh Prison, Northern Ireland, in recent years had not been carried out solely for security purposes, but with the deliberate intention of degrading or humiliating the women. As part of its investigation, the organization wrote to the government on 23 February seeking clarification of the circumstances in which a number of strip-searches had taken place in Armagh Prison. Amnesty International believes that strip-searching constitutes ill-treatment when it is carried out with the deliberate intention of humiliating or degrading prisoners. Furthermore, the organization considers that the practice of strip-searching, given its nature, is open to abuse and should be used only where strictly necessary. The government replied on 24 March stating that strip-searching was a routine, necessary security measure, and that there was no question of the searches being used to degrade or humiliate prisoners. In November the organization wrote again to the government to say that its concern had not been alleviated and to urge the government to reconsider its policy on strip-searching.

Amnesty International was concerned about the detention pending deportation of Amanullah Khan, a Kashmiri leader who had lived in Britain since 1977. The organization had monitored his case since his arrest in September 1985, when he was charged with possessing chemicals in order to make explosives. In September 1986 he was acquitted, but was immediately detained once again pending his deportation to Pakistan on unspecified grounds of national security. On 22 October 1986 Amnesty International wrote to the government stating that it believed that Amanullah Khan might be a prisoner of conscience, detained for his non-violent political activities in the United Kingdom in support of the independence of Kashmir. The organization asked the government to make public its reasons for deciding to detain and deport him. On 13 November Amanullah Khan made representations to a government-appointed advisory panel, which has no binding powers. During the hearing he was not entitled to legal representation. On 17 and 19 November Amnesty International again appealed to the government for more detailed information. It pointed out in particular that the government's statement of the reasons for deportation contained information which it claimed linked him with violent activities but which Amanullah Khan said confused his own organization with another. On 16 December Amnesty International telexed the government to express disappointment at not receiving any replies to its letters. However, Amanullah Khan had been deported to Pakistan the previous day.

In recent years, a considerable volume of new evidence and information has come to light in connection with the convictions and life sentences of 10 people for bombings of pubs in Birmingham, Guildford and Woolwich in 1975. The 10 persistently claimed that their signed confessions had been extracted by physical ill-treatment and threats of violence, while they were being held incommunicado. In December the organization requested the government to review the cases urgently with a view to establishing whether the prisoners had been fairly convicted.

Amnesty International received allegations that Ella O'Dwyer and Martina Anderson, two remand prisoners in Brixton prison, London were being strip-searched not primarily for security reasons but in order to degrade and humiliate them. On 29 May the organization wrote to the Home Secretary expressing concern at reports that they had been strip-searched more often than necessary given the strict security conditions under which they were being held. On 25 June the government replied that strip-searches were only undertaken where the interests of security required that they should be, and refuted any suggestion that they had been carried out in a manner calculated to harass, humiliate or degrade the women concerned.

The report of a government-established inquiry into the interrogation of eight servicemen by the UK military police in Cyprus in 1984 was published in May 1986 (see *Amnesty International Report 1986*). It concluded that none of the servicemen had been subjected to cruel, inhuman or degrading treatment. However, the report also concluded that they had been, for part of the time, unlawfully held in custody during their interrogation and had been subjected to pressures, including isolation and repeated lengthy interviews, that were likely to render their statements unreliable. The government decided to compensate them financially for their periods of unlawful detention. By the end of 1986 no disciplinary proceedings had been brought against the military police.

Yugoslavia

Amnesty International was concerned about the imprisonment of prisoners of conscience; during 1986 it worked on the cases of 249 individuals whom it knew or suspected to be prisoners of conscience, but it believed that the actual total was considerably greater. It was concerned that many political prisoners were denied a fair trial and that, in Kosovo in particular, courts had apparently relied heavily on evidence obtained under pressure. The organization received a number of allegations that political prisoners had been ill-treated during investigation proceedings and it continued to be concerned about conditions in some prisons where political prisoners were serving their sentences. During 1986 Amnesty International continued to call for the release of two prisoners of conscience, Radomir Veljkovic and Milisav Zivanovic, forcibly detained in the psychiatric section of Belgrade Prison Hospital since 1973 and 1976 respectively; in June Milisav Zivanovic was released. Amnesty International learned of four death sentences. To its knowledge, no executions were reported.

According to official statistics, in 1986, 466 people were charged with political crimes, of whom 258 were ethnic Albanians. Seventy-three people were indicted for so-called "verbal crimes" under Article 133 of the criminal code dealing with "hostile propaganda". During 1986 Amnesty International learned of some 50 trials involving over 180 people in which the accused were convicted of political crimes, most frequently under Article 133 and Article 136 ("association for hostile activity") of the criminal code.

The situation in Kosovo province continued to be grave, with tension between the majority, ethnic Albanians, and the Serbian and Montenegrin minorities, who publicly protested that the failure of the authorities to safeguard them from attacks and pressures from Albanians was responsible for their continued emigration from the province. According to official statistics 1,400 people, almost all ethnic Albanians, were charged with political crimes in Kosovo between 1981 and mid-1986 and a further 6,500 were summarily sentenced for minor political offences. Between April and July 1986 more than 120 ethnic Albanians were sentenced in a series of group trials in Kosovo. They were generally convicted of membership of illegal nationalist groups, such as the Marxist-Leninists of Kosovo (MLK) or the Movement for a Socialist Albanian Republic in

Yugoslavia (LRSSHJ). They were mostly accused of having demanded that Kosovo should cease to be part of the Republic of Serbia and be itself given republic status, or of having called for the creation of an Albanian republic within Yugoslavia, composed of Kosovo and other regions with large ethnic Albanian communities, with a view to the eventual unification of this republic with Albania. They were generally found guilty of reading and distributing illegal nationalist literature, writing "hostile slogans", or, in some cases, of having contacts with political emigres. There were also cases in which the accused were charged with having amassed arms and planned acts of violence, although press reports generally gave few details of the supporting evidence and it was noticeable that defence counsel frequently asked for the charge to be changed to one of "hostile propaganda". Among prisoners of conscience adopted by Amnesty International were Sahit Berisha and five co-defendants sentenced in Pec in June to prison terms of between seven months and five years. Sahit Berisha and two other unemployed men in their twenties were convicted of being members of LRSSHJ. At their trial they denied this; in its written decision the only evidence cited by the court in support of its finding was statements made by the defendants during investigation proceedings, which they had subsequently retracted, saying they had been induced to make them under threats and pressure from state security officers. Four other defendants were found guilty of "hostile propaganda" for having possessed, read or given to another person to read, illegal nationalist literature. Amnesty International sought further information in connection with one of these.

Despite public pressure to reformulate Article 133 ("hostile propaganda") in such a way as to prevent its use to penalize the non-violent exercise of the right to freedom of expression, it was not amended. The abuses to which its formulation led were, in Amnesty International's view, illustrated by the conviction in Tuzla of Jovan Nikolic, a retired art teacher, Obren Jovic, a dentist, and Bogdan Antic, a doctor. The charges against them arose out of conversations they were alleged to have had with friends and colleagues, in which they criticized Yugoslavia's political and economic system, claimed that Serbs were discriminated against in Bosnia-Hercegovina, and denigrated other Yugoslav peoples, in particular Muslims. The defendants denied the charges and witnesses retracted their previous testimony or altered it, several alleging that they had given their original statements after being threatened by police. There was also no proof of counter-revolutionary intent on the part of the defendants, a necessary element of the offence. However, they were found guilty under Article 133, as well as under Article 157 ("damaging the reputation of the state" — for having allegedly ridiculed the late President Tito). Obren Jovic and Jovan Nikolic were sentenced to five and a half and five years' imprisonment respectively in March. Bogdan Antic, who because of ill-health was tried separately in November, was sentenced to four years' imprisonment. Unlike the other two, he remained at liberty pending appeal.

Amnesty International also adopted Halil Mehtic, a Muslim imam sentenced to three years' imprisonment in Zenica in April under Article 134 for "inciting national, racial and religious hatred". The charges were based on statements he allegedly made in sermons and during religious classes in which he supposedly preached the moral superiority of Muslims over Serbs and Croats and urged Muslims not to associate with or marry people of other faiths. Halil Mehtic produced witnesses who said that he had not made the statements of which he was accused, as well as other evidence testifying to his lack of religious or national prejudice. The same day, a court in Banja Luka (also in Bosnia-Hercegovina) sentenced a Roman Catholic priest, Father Filip Lukenda, also under Article 134, to four years' imprisonment, on similar charges. In November his sentence was reduced to two and a half years on appeal. Amnesty International sought further information about his trial.

The issue of conscientious objection to military service became the subject of public discussion after the Socialist Youth Alliance of Slovenia in October proposed alternative civilian service for conscientious objectors. Outside Slovenia this proposal generally met with official censure. Amnesty International adopted Ivan Cecko, a Jehovah's Witness from Slovenia who was sentenced in October to five years' imprisonment by Belgrade Military Court for refusing military service on religious grounds. It was his third sentence for this offence and he had already spent seven years in prison. He was released in December when the Supreme Military Court, following an appeal, ordered his retrial.

Detailed information that Amnesty International obtained on a number of political trials reinforced its earlier concerns about the fairness of trials for political detainees. Amnesty International was, for instance, concerned at the tendency of courts to rely heavily on testimony obtained during investigation proceedings, even when this was retracted in court on the grounds that it had been obtained under pressure and threat. Amnesty International also noted the frequent reluctance of courts to examine witnesses or other proposed evidence for the defence, thus heavily weighting the case in favour of the prosecution. There were also complaints that defence counsel were impeded in their work in various ways, such as by being denied private consultations with their clients and adequate access to records of investigation proceedings.

Amnesty International learned of allegations made by a number of ethnic Albanian political prisoners that they had been ill-treated during pre-trial proceedings. In September the organization urged the authorities to investigate allegations that Peter Ivezaj, an ethnic Albanian living in the USA with dual US and Yugoslav citizenship, had been ill-treated after his arrest on 19 August while visiting relatives in Montenegro. On 8 October he was sentenced to seven years' imprisonment in Titograd on charges of belonging to an emigre organization, the American-Albanian Student Association, in Detroit and of having taken part in anti-Yugoslav demonstrations in several US cities. His arrest and trial aroused protest in the USA and two days after his conviction he was released and allowed to return home. He subsequently stated that after arrest he was for three days denied food and was on three occasions beaten, kicked and punched by prison guards. At another trial (in Pristina in June), involving 23 ethnic Albanians said to be members of MLK, one of the accused, Kadri Raka, a minor, said that he had been forced to confess falsely to planning to place explosives in buildings by state security officers. Amnesty International's concerns about the treatment of political detainees in Kosovo were further aggravated by allegations that Male Morina, an ethnic Albanian student, had committed suicide in Pec on 11 December, a month after his arrest. It was alleged that he killed himself in a state of severe depression induced by the ill-treatment he suffered.

Amnesty International did not receive any information which would suggest that the harsh conditions in certain prisons where political prisoners were held had improved (see *Amnesty International Report 1986*). In March Dobroslav Paraga, a former prisoner of conscience (see *Amnesty International Report 1981*), sued the Croatian Secretariat for Justice for permanent damage to his health resulting from prison conditions and ill-treatment in detention from 1980 to 1984.

Amnesty International learned of three death sentences imposed for murder. It appealed to the State Presidency to commute the death sentence on Andrija Artukovic for war crimes after it had been confirmed by the Federal Court; the organization explained its unconditional opposition to the death penalty. Amnesty International did not learn of any executions.

The Middle East and North Africa

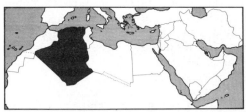

Algeria

Amnesty International was concerned about the continued imprisonment of prisoners of conscience; the arrest of human rights activists; trial proceedings which did not conform to internationally recognized standards for fair trial; allegations of torture and ill-treatment during detention; allegations of deaths in custody as a result of torture; and the death penalty.

During 1986 Amnesty International appealed for the immediate and unconditional release of 22 prisoners of conscience, sentenced to terms of between six months' and three years' imprisonment by the State Security Court in Medea in December 1985. The charges against them included membership of two unauthorized associations, the Algerian League of Human Rights and the *Association des fils des martyrs*, Sons of the Martyrs. In March Amnesty International replied to the Algerian Minister of Justice's letter of December 1985 (see *Amnesty International Report 1986*) repeating its reasons for considering them to be prisoners of conscience, stating that the prisoners had been convicted for exercising non-violently their fundamental rights to freedom of expression and association. Amnesty International learned of the release of 11 of these prisoners. A twelfth, Fettouma Ouzegane, remained in detention after completing her sentence. She was convicted of contempt of court in another trial. Among those released was Maître Ali Yahia Abdennour, President and founding member of the Algerian League of Human Rights.

In November Amnesty International received reports that a large number of people had been arrested following demonstrations in Constantine and Setif during November and that four people had died during the events in Constantine. Amnesty International wrote to the authorities about trials in which 186 of those arrested were sentenced to between two and eight years' imprisonment, reportedly for public order offences. Amnesty International requested details of the charges against them, the legal position of those still untried, and details of the trial proceedings, following reports that a large number of those tried had been denied the right to defence lawyers. Amnesty International also asked whether the reported deaths had occurred, and if so, for details of the circumstances surrounding them.

In December Amnesty International telexed the authorities about the reported re-arrest on 15 December of Maître Ali Yahia Abdennour. Amnesty International asked for the reasons for his arrest, his place of detention and what his legal position was. Amnesty International urged his immediate release if he were not to be charged with a criminal offence.

In December Amnesty International submitted to the authorities its report on the trial before the State Security Court in Medea in December 1985 of 40 people on charges including conspiracy against the security of the state, forming an armed gang and possession of arms. Amnesty International was concerned that the defendants had been kept in *garde à vue* (incommunicado) detention in police or military security custody longer than the legal maximum period. Most of the defendants alleged that they were subjected to torture and other forms of ill-treatment during interrogation, and that confessions invoked as evidence in court had been extracted under torture or the threat of torture. It appeared that the pre-trial investigation before the *juge d'instruction* (investigating judge) was mostly carried out in the absence of defence lawyers, and that not all of the defendants were informed of their rights, including the right to be assisted by defence lawyers, nor immediately informed of the charges against them. The majority of the defence lawyers were appointed by the court at the opening of the trial and therefore had little knowledge of the case. The court refused the defence request to postpone the trial for a few days in order to prepare a defence. The prosecution appeared to be based principally on statements by the defendants made during interrogation by the police or military security. No witnesses were called by the prosecution. Amnesty International asked to be informed of any inquiries into the allegations of torture and, if none had been undertaken, urged impartial and public investigations. It also stated that if the allegations were confirmed, a public retrial or an independent judicial review of the verdict and the sentences should be ordered; the victims should be compensated and those found responsible should be brought to justice.

In November Amnesty International asked the authorities for details of the circumstances of two reported deaths in detention and one reported death after release from police custody. According to Amnesty International's information, Abdelwahab Abderrahman was called for questioning by police in mid-July, kept in secret detention at the Central Commissariat in Oran, and his body later returned to his family. The police reportedly stated that he had died in a car accident. Mustapha Arris was arrested by security police in late September and returned to his home suffering from serious injuries. He died in Oran Hospital soon afterwards. Salem Lamali, reportedly detained without charge since October 1983 in Berrouaghia Prison, is believed to have died between 15 and 20 September following an operation.

Amnesty International learned of five executions carried out during 1986 and of five death sentences passed on individuals convicted of murder. Amnesty International appealed to the authorities in all cases, expressing the organization's unconditional opposition to the death penalty and urging that all death sentences be commuted.

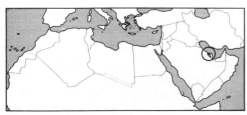

Bahrain

Reports of two deaths in custody, allegedly as a result of torture, reached Amnesty International during 1986. The organization was also concerned by reports of torture and ill-treatment of convicted political prisoners and of detainees held without charge for interrogation. Information allegedly òbtained through torture was admitted and used as evidence in a political trial. The organization was concerned about the continuing imprisonment of political prisoners who were possibly prisoners of conscience, and about reports of detention without charge or trial of political opponents of the government.

Throughout 1986 Amnesty International called on the government to set up impartial inquiries into all allegations of torture and to ensure that torture did not occur. Specifically, Amnesty International urged that a limit be placed on incommunicado detention, and that detainees be permitted access to lawyers and to relatives shortly after arrest and at regular intervals afterwards. The organization also urged the authorities to ratify human rights instruments outlawing torture.

On 9 September Amnesty International expressed concern about the reported death in custody of Radhi Mahdi Ibrahim, one of a group of 73 people involved in an alleged coup attempt in 1981, who had been sentenced to 15 years' imprisonment. He reportedly died in Al Jaw prison as a result of torture or ill-treatment and insufficient medical care. On 22 September concern was again expressed following the death in Al Qala' prison, Manama, of Dr Hashim Ismail Al Alawi, reportedly as a result of torture. Dr Al Alawi was detained in late August, reportedly for being in possession of leaflets criticizing the government.

Amnesty International repeatedly raised the case of five men reportedly tortured in Al Qala' prison while held in incommunicado detention between June and October 1985. The five — Fahd Jabbar Al Mudahaki, Abderrahim Abderrahim As-Sa'iy, Qasim Ahmad Al Hillal, Abdullah Hussein Al'Iysa and Radi Mahdi As-Samak — were apparently charged under Article 159 of the criminal code with membership of an illegal organization. Amnesty International received reports that the case against them was based solely on confessions obtained through torture. Amnesty International sought information about the procedures followed in this case, and details of the court, but no reply was received. On 1 September the organization made public its concern.

At the end of 1986 Amnesty International was continuing to investigate the cases of 13 possible prisoners of conscience. They were detained for between five and 10 years, some without charge or trial (see *Amnesty International Report 1985*). The organization learned of the release of Radi Makki Al Jabal, and was still trying to confirm reports that Nader Abu Drees and Mirza Muhammad Ali Fardan had also been released.

On 20 August Amnesty International wrote to the Minister of the Interior seeking information about some 15 people who had been detained since July because of their political views. On 24 November it wrote again about reports that some 30 political prisoners were held in Al Qala' prison without charge or trial. The organization called for detainees held solely for their non-violent political views to be released, and any others to be given a fair and prompt trial. It also sought assurances that the detainees were not being ill-treated.

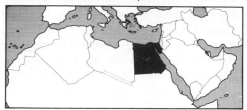

Egypt

Amnesty International's concerns included the short-term detention of hundreds of political prisoners, some of whom were prisoners of conscience, under state of emergency legislation; the detention of other individuals because of their religious or political beliefs; torture; and the use of the death penalty.

Amnesty International was concerned that state of emergency legislation appeared to be used to silence criticism of the government or to limit freedom of religious expression, and that prisoners of conscience were held without charge or trial under its provisions. The organization's concern was increased by evidence that certain individuals were arrested repeatedly. Amnesty International has frequently expressed its concern that this legislation contains insufficient safeguards to ensure that violations of the International Covenant on Civil and Political Rights, to which Egypt is a party, do not occur; particularly with regard to freedom of expression and the right to be charged and tried within a reasonable period of time. In May, the Egyptian parliament voted to extend the state of emergency for a further two years.

Hundreds of members and supporters of various Islamic groups were detained without charge or trial under state of emergency legislation, some of whom might have been prisoners of conscience. In March Amnesty International wrote to the authorities expressing its concern about the detention of 15 students from Minya University, for allegedly producing and distributing unauthorized leaflets and magazines. In May Amnesty International sought further information about the arrest and detention of 55 men, including the prominent religious leader Dr Omar Abdul Rahman, following clashes with security forces at a religious meeting in Aswan on 30 April. Amnesty International received further reports of the arrests of large numbers of Islamic activists throughout 1986 from all parts of the country, as well as allegations that some of these detainees had been tortured or ill-treated. Some defendants in cases referred for trial involving Islamic groups were tried in (Emergency) Supreme State Security Courts before a military tribunal, instead of the usual tribunal of civilian judges. Other detainees held under state of emergency legislation included members of various non-orthodox religious groups. Amnesty International believed that these detainees might have been prisoners of conscience.

During 1986 Amnesty International learned of many arrests in connection with trade union activity. On 7, 8 and 9 February over 300 arrests were reported in the industrial town of Mahalla Al Kubra in connection with a strike by textile workers. Amnesty International asked the authorities for the reason for these arrests, and called for those detained solely for taking part in non-violent trade union activity to be released. After two weeks, 33 were still in detention, but they were all released without charge in April.

A rail strike on 9 July led to the arrest of hundreds of railworkers in Cairo. Forty-five of them were still in detention in October and 37 of the 45 were charged and referred for trial before an (Emergency) Supreme State Security Court under Article 374 of the penal code which forbids strikes by workers in the public sector. The court released all the railworkers in late October, but their trial was still continuing at the end of 1986.

In December Amnesty International sought further information about the detention of 44 alleged members of a secret communist organization, *At-Tiyar Ath-Thawri*, The Revolutionary Tendency, detained in Cairo for reportedly producing and distributing publications critical of government policy.

A number of individuals were detained apparently because of their conversion from Islam to Christianity. Six members of the Coptic Evangelical Church were arrested between January and May, apparently because of their decision to convert to the Christian faith. The six were released from detention in July, but charges under Article 98 of the penal code, concerning attempting to divide national unity, were not dropped. Two Moroccan and two Tunisian Christians were detained in Alexandria in similar circumstances on 24 April. The four were deported to France in October after six months' imprisonment without formal charge.

On 24 May the verdict in two cases relating to the banned Egyptian Communist Party was announced. In the first, 12 people were convicted of producing and possessing publications undermining the basic principles of the constitution, the political system, and society. They were sentenced to between one and three years' imprisonment. In the second, related, case 22 people were convicted, but their sentences of one to three years had to be ratified by President Mubarak before coming into force. Of the 12 convicted in the first case, nine were imprisoned, the remaining three having escaped arrest. Amnesty International believed them to be prisoners of conscience, held for their non-violent opposition to government policies. Two people received prison sentences in both cases, which were to run consecutively.

In June Egypt acceded to the UN Convention against Torture and Other Cruel, Inhuman or Degrading Treatment or Punishment.

Amnesty International wrote to the authorities welcoming this step, and seeking information about procedures and results of investigations into allegations of torture since October 1981. No reply was received.

In September Amnesty International wrote to the government expressing its concern about reports that defendants in cases involving certain Islamic groups had been tortured. The letter named 43 members and supporters of Islamic groups detained for allegedly taking part in attacks on cinemas, video tape shops, and shops selling alcohol, and for alleged anti-government activities, who had reportedly been tortured in Tora Prison. The torture methods described to Amnesty International included: electric shocks, cigarettes being extinguished on the skin, beating with sticks and whips, and forcible insertion of objects into the anus. Official forensic medical reports stated that in some cases the physical scarring was consistent with the alleged method and timing of torture. Amnesty International called for all allegations of torture to be impartially investigated, and asked what measures had been taken to ensure that torture did not occur in Egypt's prisons. No reply was received.

Amnesty International noted reports that approximately 40 members of the security police had been charged in connection with allegations of torture made by defendants in the mass trials of alleged members of the *Al Jihad* organization, who were arrested in 1981. The first hearing in this trial before South Cairo Criminal Court took place on 23 December 1986, and further hearings were scheduled for February 1987. Other members of the security forces were reportedly under investigation in connection with allegations of torture.

The organization was concerned by the death in a prison hospital of Suleiman Khater on 7 January. He had been sentenced to life imprisonment in December 1985 for the murder of seven Israeli civilians at the Egypt/Israel border in the Sinai Desert. Official reports that he had committed suicide were widely questioned, and Amnesty International called for a public inquiry into the circumstances surrounding his death.

Amnesty International recorded 14 death sentences in 1986; 12 for drug-related offences and two for murder. In each case Amnesty International sought commutation of the death sentences. Three executions were recorded by the organization in the course of the year; all the victims had been convicted of murder.

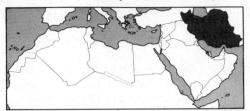

Iran

In 1986 Amnesty International recorded 115 executions for political and criminal offences, but believed the actual figure was much higher; political prisoners were sentenced in unfair trials held *in camera* with no access to a lawyer or right of appeal; and an unknown number of people believed to be prisoners of conscience continued to be incarcerated. Reports of torture and ill-treatment of political detainees continued to be received, and the organization recorded a number of cases of stoning to death, amputation of fingers, mutilation and flogging, carried out as forms of judicial punishment.

In a memorandum to the government dated 8 August, Amnesty International examined provisions of Iran's Islamic Penal Code in the light of international human rights standards, including the International Covenant on Civil and Political Rights (ICCPR), to which Iran is a party, and submitted a series of 10 related recommendations. Amnesty International pointed out that many punishments provided for in the penal code, such as stoning to death, crucifixion, mutilation, amputation and flogging, constituted cruel, inhuman or degrading treatment. Amnesty International recommended that they be replaced by other more humane punishments, consistent with international standards for the treatment and punishment of offenders. Other recommendations included a review of the use of confessions as a primary method of proof, which Amnesty International feared encouraged the use of torture or ill-treatment during interrogation, and of legislation which could be used to incarcerate prisoners of conscience. Amnesty International was particularly concerned that there appeared to be no legal limit to incommunicado detention, and urged a review of the penal procedural code to ensure the protection of detainees from torture, and the right to a fair and prompt trial. Amnesty International stated that it wished to contribute to the discussion in Iran before the final approval of the Islamic Penal Code of Iran, which had initially been approved for a five-year trial period and was to undergo a process of assessment before it was finally approved.

A second memorandum, dated 20 November, was sent to the authorities explaining Amnesty International's concerns in Iran: the incarceration of prisoners of conscience; the practice of arbitrary arrest and detention on political grounds; unfair trials of political prisoners; the use of torture and ill-treatment; and the application of the death penalty and other judicial punishments constituting torture or cruel, inhuman or degrading treatment. Amnesty International again made a series of recommendations to the Iranian authorities to improve respect for human rights.

Amnesty International sought comments on the two memoranda and proposed that they should be the basis for discussions between the organization and the government. It was ready to send a delegation to Tehran specifically for this purpose. Amnesty International requested a response by 31 December but none was received.

During 1986 Amnesty International recorded 115 executions, some of which were carried out in public. The organization did not believe that this figure represented the actual number of executions, which was probably considerably higher. Nevertheless, the figure was substantially lower than those recorded in previous years. Amnesty International continued throughout 1986 to appeal for an end to executions and for the death penalty to be replaced by alternative punishments. In most cases, as in previous years, Amnesty International did not learn about death sentences until after execution had taken place. However, in some political and criminal cases in which news of death sentences reached the organization before execution took place, Amnesty International appealed for their commutation. Among those executed during 1986 were members of various political groups and organizations, as well as three members of the Baha'i faith. Since the early 1980s most executions of suspected opposition activists have not been officially announced, and the majority of the executions recorded have been reportedly for criminal offences such as murder and drug trafficking. However, Amnesty International has received reports that some of those executed in recent years ostensibly for such criminal offences were in fact punished for their political activities. Most executions in Iran were by hanging or firing-squad but Amnesty International learned of six men and two women who were executed by stoning to death. They had been convicted on charges which included adultery, organizing prostitution and murder. Several other sentences of stoning were recorded but it was not known if they were carried out.

Amnesty International learned of hundreds of political arrests during 1986. Reports of releases of political prisoners or reductions in their sentences also reached the organization. Thousands of political prisoners were believed to be held but, as in previous years, Amnesty International was not able to estimate their number, nor how many were prisoners of conscience. Amnesty International's memorandum of 20 November called for the immediate and unconditional release of all prisoners of conscience, and for an end to arbitrary arrest and detention on political grounds. Amnesty International was concerned that some prisoners who had completed their prison sentences nevertheless remained incarcerated.

In July a number of leading members of the medical profession and doctors throughout the country were arrested after a strike in protest against government measures to close down the elected governing body of their professional association, and to introduce a parliamentary bill which would significantly reduce the association's autonomy. Some of those arrested were elderly and in poor health. Amnesty International called for the immediate release of the arrested doctors who, it believed, had been detained as a result of their non-violent opposition to changes within their professional association. Most were released shortly afterwards, but several former board members, including the Secretary General, were sentenced to terms of internal exile of between 12 and 18 months. Other political arrests included those of suspected members of opposition organizations.

Amnesty International remained concerned about the conduct of political trials, which appeared to be summary and provided no right of appeal. Virtually all political cases were heard by Islamic Revolutionary Courts. Amnesty International believed that the regulations governing these courts did not guarantee a fair trial and that, in practice, even the safeguards provided by the regulations were not adhered to. The organization was particularly concerned that political detainees had no access at any stage of the judicial process to a defence lawyer and that trial proceedings were held *in camera*. Many political defendants were not told in advance what the charges against them were, and were not allowed to present evidence in their defence, such as calling witnesses. Amnesty International considered that such procedures fell far short of internationally accepted standards for fair trial, including those set down in Article 14 of the ICCPR. Amnesty International's memorandum and recommendations to the government set out the minimum standards for a fair trial, to include, among other things, the right to a defence lawyer of the detainee's own choosing and the right to appeal against conviction and sentence.

Amnesty International continued to receive reports of physical and psychological torture of political detainees in prisons and detention centres throughout the country despite the constitutional provision forbidding such practices. The organization had received hundreds of reports of torture and ill-treatment over recent years. The detail in these reports, their number and their consistency made it clear that torture had been widespread, and that in some prisons and detention centres it had been routinely practised. Torture took place, according to Amnesty International's information, immediately after arrest and during incommunicado detention. Torture was usually inflicted on prisoners in order to extract confessions about political activities, and names of political activists. Another motive for torture was to induce prisoners to renounce their political or religious beliefs and sometimes to appear on television denouncing their former views. The methods most commonly reported to Amnesty International were beating, whipping and being suspended for long periods by the arms or wrists.

Amnesty International was concerned about the continued use of punishments such as flogging for a wide range of offences, and amputation of fingers for repeated acts of theft. Some floggings were carried out immediately after sentencing, with no possibility of appeal against verdict or sentence. Amnesty International recorded 11 cases of judicially imposed amputation in 1985 and the first half of 1986. In May a convicted thief had four fingers of his right hand severed by a special machine, in front of reporters, legal officials and prisoners, in Mashad. Amnesty International also recorded a number of cases in which prisoners were flogged before being executed. Amnesty International's memorandum urged a prompt and thorough review of the training of law enforcement officials, proposed detailed measures to safeguard detainees from torture or ill-treatment, in particular limits to incommunicado detention, and called for an independent investigation into all allegations of such treatment with a view to compensating the victims and bringing those responsible to justice.

In February Amnesty International submitted a written statement to the 42nd session of the UN Commission on Human Rights. The statement summarized the organization's concerns and called on the Iranian authorities to comply with international human rights standards to which they were committed. In March the commission voted to extend for a further year the mandate of the Special Representative to monitor the human rights situation in Iran.

On 4 December the UN General Assembly adopted Resolution 41/159, noting the interim report submitted by the newly appointed Special Representative of the Commission on Human Rights on the human rights siguation in Iran. The report expressed concern over the specific and detailed allegations of violations of human rights and urged the Government of Iran to uphold the rights in the ICCPR. The resolution urged the government to allow the Special Representative to visit the country, and concluded with a decision to continue to examine the human rights situation in Iran at the 42nd session of the General Assembly.

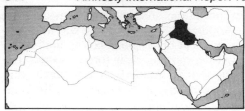

Iraq

Amnesty International's concerns continued to be the widespread arbitrary arrest and detention of hundreds of political prisoners, including possible prisoners of conscience; the long-term detention of political prisoners without trial, or after summary trials; the routine use of torture by the security forces; "disappearances"; the increase in the number of capital offences and the large number of judicial and extrajudicial executions, including executions for political offences.

An amnesty was declared in April for certain prisoners sentenced by civil and military courts. Enacted by Revolutionary Command Council (RCC) Resolution No. 387, it did not extend to prisoners convicted of murder, adultery, espionage, drug offences and those sentenced to death. Amnesty International was unable to verify how many prisoners were released. In September an amnesty was declared for army deserters who had given themselves up to the authorities between 28 July and 6 August (RCC Resolution No. 675).

Among the hundreds who continued to be detained in 1986 were members of prohibited political parties; other suspected government opponents or critics; army deserters and draft resisters refusing to fight in the war against Iran; student demonstrators; and relatives of such people arrested as hostages in lieu of suspects sought by the government.

As in previous years Amnesty International received reports of widespread arbitrary arrests of suspected government opponents and innocent civilians, as well as allegations of torture and deliberate killings by government forces. The organization raised these concerns in a speech to the United Nations Commission on Human Rights on 11 March. It referred to the "disappearance" of about 300 Kurdish children arrested in Sulaimaniya between late September and mid-October 1985 (see *Amnesty International Report 1986*). On 20 January the organization had appealed urgently for official clarification of the reasons for their detention, calling for the release of all children held because of the political activities of their parents or relatives. It also called for an investigation into reports that some of the children had been tortured, and that three of them had died in custody as a result. Their bodies were allegedly found in the streets on the outskirts of Sulaimaniya, their clothes bloodstained and their bodies bearing signs of torture. Amnesty International reiterated its concerns in a letter dated 19 February to President Saddam Hussain.

On 25 April, the government responded by stating that it had "found such allegations totally false". Amnesty International also referred to reports of the killing of some 300 people in Sulaimaniya and Arbil in October 1985, and the arrest of hundreds of others whose fate and whereabouts were unknown (see *Amnesty International Report 1986*). The organization had sent urgent appeals in December of that year, and reiterated its concerns in its letter of 19 February 1986. In August Amnesty International received a response from Iraq's Ambassador to the United Kingdom in which he stated that ". . . the allegations were pure fabrication clothed with a figure and a venue to make them appear credible."

In late March and early April a large number of civilians, including students, were reported to have been arrested in Arbil, in northern Iraq, following an assassination attempt in March on the Governor of Arbil by Kurdish opposition forces. Fifteen students were subsequently executed (see below), and the others "disappeared". In July Amnesty International urged the authorities to release all those detained during these events unless they were to be charged. No response was received.

Amnesty International continued to be concerned about the routine torture and ill-treatment of detainees in the custody of the security forces. The victims included political prisoners tortured to force them to sign "confessions" or to renounce their political affiliations. Over the years the government had denied allegations of torture even when supported by detailed medical evidence. It had also failed to show that such allegations were ever investigated or that any perpetrators were brought to justice.

Some detainees were reported to have died as a result of torture, such as Tayar Salim Muhammad, an 18-year-old student and member of the banned Kurdistan Democratic Party (KDP). He was detained in October 1985 and was reported to have died under torture in July. Amnesty International called for an investigation into his death and into reports of the torture of two other KDP members before their execution in November. The bodies of Mahdi Ibrahim Muhammad and 'Abed Taha Ibrahim were returned to their families on 8 November; their fingernails had reportedly been extracted and their eyes gouged out.

Amnesty International appealed to the authorities on numerous occasions following reports of the execution of large numbers of people. The organization received reports that hundreds were executed during 1986 but it had insufficient information to ascertain the precise number. Among those executed were said to be army deserters, members of banned political parties, suspected government opponents and students. Many of them were said to have been executed without trial or after summary trials by the Revolutionary Court with procedures which fell short of international standards. A number of people convicted of criminal offences were also executed during 1986.

On 3 January Amnesty International appealed to the government following reports of the execution of nine members of the banned Kurdistan Socialist Party-Iraq (KSP-I) in August and November 1985, as well as the execution in November 1985 of a KDP member. The government stated that in all three cases they were ". . . executed for their crimes including carrying out sabotage activities using explosives and weapons against the peace and security of innocent citizens. [They] were granted a fair trial where all judicial and legal measures were fully respected according to the Iraqi constitution and the laws in force, including the right to have court-appointed lawyers defending them." The government did not respond to the organization's additional appeals for an investigation into reports of the execution of large numbers of political prisoners and army deserters in Abu Ghraib and Mosul prisons in November 1985 (see *Amnesty International Report 1986*). On 13 February appeals were sent following reports of the execution of four KDP members and two students from the Technical Secondary School in Sulaimaniya in December 1985 and January 1986. No response was received. In December further appeals were sent following reports of the execution of five KSP-I members in August in Abu Ghraib prison and seven KDP members between August and November. Earlier in the year, nine other KDP members were reportedly executed in Mosul, Kirkuk and Baghdad. In its appeals, Amnesty International expressed fears for the lives of 16 other KSP-I members detained in Abu Ghraib prison who were said to be facing the death penalty.

Amnesty International also appealed on behalf of a number of people sentenced to death for criminal offences. On 27 May it appealed on behalf of a number of Egyptian workers sentenced to death for forging travel documents. On 3 June the organization learned that the death sentences passed on 10 Egyptians had been commuted. On 22 August Amnesty International received a letter from the Ministry of Foreign Affairs, stating that the 10 Egyptians were among a larger group arrested on charges of forging passports, residence cards and official stamps. The defendants had also been charged with smuggling currency abroad and economic sabotage. They were tried by a Revolutionary Court.

In October Amnesty International appealed to the authorities following the execution of seven Iraqis on charges of economic corruption. The seven, among them 'Abd al-Mun'im Hassan 'Alwan, under-secretary at the Ministry of Oil in Baghdad, were allegedly involved in facilitating contracts for foreign companies in return for bribes. Neither the trial nor the executions were public. The death sentences were passed on 19 August and ratified by presidential decree on 31 August. In a letter to Amnesty International dated 11 November, Iraq's Ambassador to the USA stated that the executions ". . . took place in accordance with the penal code of Iraq [and] were carried out with full respect for the due process of law."

Amnesty International remained concerned about the continued enactment of legislation increasing the number of capital offences. On 4 November Article 225 of the penal code was amended by RCC Resolution No. 840. The amendment prescribes the death penalty for publicly insulting the President of the Republic or deputy, the Revolutionary Command Council, the Arab Socialist Ba'th Party, the National Assembly or the government with the intent of mobilizing public opinion against the authorities.

In July Amnesty International appealed following reports that 21 people had been killed in northern Iraq, whom the organization believed might have been extrajudicially executed. Fifteen of them were students from secondary schools and the University of Salah al-Din who were reportedly arrested and summarily executed in public in Arbil between 27 March and 3 April. In another incident, six detainees were reportedly summarily executed in public outside Sulaimaniya Central prison on 9 April. The victims, sympathizers with the banned Patriotic Union of Kurdistan (PUK), were all said to be under 18. No response was received to the organization's appeals.

In late February Amnesty International appealed to the authorities following reports that two Iraqi students expelled from France on 19 February had been detained upon arrival in Iraq. Fawzi Hamza al-Ruba'i and Muhammad Hassan Khair al-Din had reportedly said they were afraid of returning to Iraq. Amnesty International requested details of their legal status and whereabouts and sought assurances that their safety would be guaranteed and that they would be permitted access to a lawyer and relatives. The organization also asked whether reports that one of them had been executed were true. On 4 March Amnesty International welcomed assurances from the Iraqi authorities that neither men had been executed. However, it remained concerned that they were detained and risked facing the death penalty. They allegedly belonged to *al-Da'wa al-Islamiyya*, Islamic Call, membership of which is a capital offence in Iraq. The organization urged the government to make known their whereabouts and the reasons for their arrest and continued detention. On 27 February Amnesty International also called upon the French Government to clarify the procedures followed which led to the involuntary expulsions, and urged it to obtain assurances from the

Iraqi Government that the physical safety of the two men would be guaranteed. The French Government informed Amnesty International on 11 March that France's Ambassador to Iraq had visited the two men on 9 March and was able to confirm that they were both in good health. Fawzi Hamza al-Ruba'i and Muhammad Hassan Khair al-Din were pardoned by President Saddam Hussain on 13 March and released on 22 March. This was confirmed in a letter to Amnesty International on 1 August. Following their release, the two men announced on Iraqi television that they had "repented" of their past activities. They returned to France on 26 September.

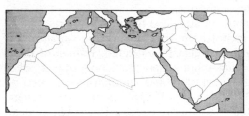

Israel and the Occupied Territories

Amnesty International's concerns were the imprisonment of prisoners of conscience and people who might be prisoners of conscience, and the continued use of administrative detention and restriction. Amnesty International received allegations of ill-treatment and torture of detainees in Israel and the Occupied Territories and in the border zone of South Lebanon where Israeli military forces maintained a presence. It was concerned about the inadequacy of safeguards to prevent ill-treatment and torture and about deficiencies in the complaints machinery for investigating allegations.

During 1986 Amnesty International adopted three prisoners of conscience, who were later released, and investigated the cases of 36 possible prisoners of conscience, 20 of whom were released. Six of the 39 were convicted of membership of an illegal organization or of incitement, one was a conscientious objector, 14 were under restriction orders and 18 were in administrative detention.

Amnesty International called for the unconditional release of Naftali Orner, a reservist in the Israeli Defence Forces (IDF), who was sentenced in September to 19 days' imprisonment for refusing to serve in the West Bank for reasons of conscience. Amnesty International was also concerned about three women who served between 12 and 40 days in prison in August, September and October after leaving their units and seeking exemption from military service on grounds of conscience developed after they had been conscripted. Amnesty International wrote to the Minister of Defence on 4 November and called for them to be granted exemption on grounds of conscience. It later learned that all three had been exempted on grounds of "unsuitability". All the conscientious objectors taken up by Amnesty International objected to doing military service only in particular areas. Amnesty International understood that a number of other conscientious objectors to military service and to serving in the Occupied Territories did receive exemption and were not imprisoned.

Amnesty International expressed concern to the authorities about two people it believed might be prisoners of conscience. Said Muhammad Al Ayla, from Gaza, was sentenced in February to nine months' imprisonment and two and a half years' suspended on charges of incitement, under Article 7(a) of Military Order (MO) 62. During a strike in support of security detainees in Ashkelon prison he had instructed someone to distribute leaflets denouncing the state of Israel. 'Alammudin Abu Ziad, from Majdal Shams in the Golan Heights, was sentenced in September to six months' imprisonment under the Law of Sedition (Section 133 of the Israeli penal code). He was charged with singing anti-Israeli, ·pro-Syrian songs during a demonstration in February 1985, which marked the anniversary of a protest strike against the annexation of the Golan Heights.

Amnesty International continued to investigate a number of cases of people imprisoned after being accused of membership of (or association with) various factions of the Palestine Liberation Organization (PLO). Some were convicted by the courts, others held in administrative detention. Amnesty International sought to determine the nature of the prisoners' involvement in these organizations and their activities, and the precise accusations and evidence against them. In each of the cases taken up by Amnesty International for investigation the organization had no evidence that the individual had personally used or advocated violence. In correspondence with Amnesty International the authorities maintained that membership of or active support for such organizations in itself amounted to advocating or contributing to the violence perpetrated by them. However, Amnesty International took into account the facts that there were in effect no legal political parties in the Occupied Territories and that the specific activities of these individuals had, as far as was known to Amnesty International, been peaceful. Amnesty International believed that each case had to be examined on its merits to determine whether an individual's association with a banned organization involved advocacy of violence.

Administrative measures were used to detain people for up to six months without giving full reasons (see *Amnesty International Report 1986*). Amnesty International received the names of 144 people administratively detained during 1986. They were mainly students and trade unionists and 107 of them had been released by the end of the year. Amnesty International considers that administrative detention is open to abuse and that many administrative detainees might have been prisoners of conscience. The Attorney General wrote to Amnesty International on 26 January that administrative detention was a preventive measure "generally invoked only in special circumstances and where there is corroborating evidence from two or more sources that the individual is engaged in illegal acts that involve direct danger to state security and to the lives of innocent people." However, details of detainees' activities and past convictions provided by the authorities did not always convince Amnesty International that these detainees had used or advocated violence. Amnesty International was also concerned that detainees were not given the full and precise reasons for their detention orders. The Attorney General's letter said that administrative detention was used only when "normal judicial procedures cannot be followed because of the danger to the lives of witnesses or because secret sources of information cannot be revealed in open court." Amnesty International replied on 30 July, saying that while it was in no position to assess the validity of this claim, it was concerned that this argument was used in almost all cases. It said that as a result, people were imprisoned on the basis of anonymous testimony. Furthermore, although administrative detention was subject to judicial review after 48 hours and at three months, and there was a right to appeal to the Israeli High Court, such safeguards were insufficient if detainees were never given the evidence against them and could not therefore challenge the grounds for their detention.

On 6 November Amnesty International telexed the Minister of Defence about Akram Haniyah, editor of the Jerusalem newspaper *Al Sha'ab* who had been detained pending deportation to Jordan on suspicion of being a PLO activist and a conduit for PLO funds and instructions. Amnesty International believed he might have been a prisoner of conscience and called for him to be formally charged and tried or released immediately, and not deported to Jordan or any other country where he might face imprisonment on account of his non-violent political beliefs. Akram Haniyah was deported to Algeria via Switzerland on 28 December.

The use of restriction orders (formally termed special supervision orders), which had been largely replaced in 1985 by administrative detention, was renewed. Amnesty International received the names of 66 people, mostly students and trade unionists, who during 1986 were restricted to their home towns or villages. Majid al Labadi, a trade unionist from Al Bireh, spent one year under a restriction order imposed in October 1984 confining him to his home town, then six months in administrative detention. In July 1986 he was served with another six-month restriction order. According to the authorities he was a leading activist in the Democratic Front for the Liberation of Palestine (DFLP — a faction of the PLO which had been involved in acts of violence) and had previous convictions for recruiting others to the organization. Amnesty International expressed concern that he had been restricted and detained for over two years without full reasons being given when it had not been shown that he had used or advocated violence.

During September Amnesty International publicized the case of Adnan Mansour Ghanem, who alleged he was tortured during interrogation in Gaza prison between 22 December 1985 and 21 January 1986. In May 1985 he was released after spending 17 and a half years in prison for armed infiltration into the Occupied Territories, and was rearrested in December on suspicion of renewed activity in the PLO. He alleged that he was hooded and handcuffed during prolonged periods of enforced standing and kneeling, subjected to near-suffocation, sleep deprivation, prolonged ice-cold showers, humiliation and threats and beatings all over the body which caused wounds and bruises to the face and head. Amnesty International was concerned about the apparent failure of safeguards to protect him from ill-treatment: he was denied access to his lawyer for 35 days, and to his family for six weeks. Despite his complaints at three court hearings, the judge ordered a medical examination only at the third hearing; and, although the judge sought assurances from the police that the interrogation was over, Adnan Mansour Ghanem alleged that his interrogation continued on his return to prison. Neither Amnesty International nor the defence lawyer were able to discover how often he saw a doctor during his detention in Gaza prison. A representative of the International Committee of the Red Cross (ICRC) visited him on 6 and 20 January. The ICRC has access to security detainees in the Occupied Territories from the fourteenth day of detention. Amnesty International considered that, while ICRC access to prisoners was an important safeguard, it was not sufficient to give full protection to detainees from ill-treatment. Amnesty International wrote to the authorities in January and in June urging an independent inquiry into this case and later learned that an investigation was being carried out.

During 1986 Amnesty International appealed to the authorities to investigate complaints of ill-treatment made by seven other security suspects who were detained in Jenin and Nablus prisons on the West

Bank, in Moscobiya detention centre in Jerusalem and in Acre police station in Israel. They alleged that the ill-treatment included beatings, prolonged hooding and enforced standing, solitary confinement and lengthy subjection to cold air and showers.

Amnesty International continued to receive reports that detainees held in Khiam prison in the border zone of South Lebanon by the South Lebanon Army (SLA) were ill-treated and tortured, sometimes, it was alleged, under the supervision of members of the IDF or the Israeli General Security Service. In September Amnesty International appealed to the Israeli authorities and to the leader of the SLA for an inquiry into these allegations (see *Lebanon* entry).

On 26 February Amnesty International wrote to the Minister of Defence about reports that dozens of villagers from Shakra in the security zone, who had been detained and interrogated by members of the IDF on 20 February, had been ill-treated and tortured by members of the SLA who were assisting the IDF. The IDF was seeking information about two Israeli soldiers who had been abducted in South Lebanon. According to journalists who subsequently spoke to some of those released, the detainees were beaten with wooden batons, burnt with cigarette ends and lighters and subjected to electric shocks. Five were hospitalized after their release. Amnesty International said that it appreciated the Israeli authorities' concern for the two soldiers but that this could not justify the use of ill-treatment and torture. Amnesty International also said that the fact that it was the SLA and not the IDF who physically ill-treated the detainees did not exonerate the Israeli authorities from responsibility. Amnesty International called for an inquiry to be carried out, the findings made public and any members of the IDF found to have ordered or tolerated such treatment duly prosecuted.

In May three former members of the General Security Service (GSS) alleged that two Palestinians who had hijacked a bus in April 1984 had been deliberately killed in the custody of the GSS, and that the Prime Minister had ordered the killings and a subsequent cover-up. At the time, officials had said that the two died during the storming of the bus, but press photographs showed them alive after capture by the army. A 1985 commission of inquiry found that the two Palestinians had been beaten to death during interrogation, but was unable to determine who was responsible. It recommended that an army commander should be tried, but an internal disciplinary court found that he had used "reasonable force" and cleared him of direct responsibility for the deaths (see *Amnesty International Report 1986*). In June Amnesty International urged an investigation into the new allegations. Following a police investigation, the Attorney General's office published its findings on 30 December. It found no evidence linking the Prime Minister to the incident, but criticized the political leadership for trying to avoid an investigation on grounds of national security. The members of the GSS implicated had earlier received pre-indictment presidential pardons.

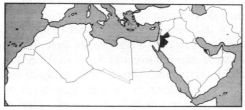

Jordan

Amnesty International continued to be concerned about the detention of prisoners of conscience and possible prisoners of conscience and about trials of political prisoners by the Martial Law Court which fell below international standards for fair trial. The organization was also concerned about reports of torture or ill-treatment of prisoners and about the death penalty.

During 1986 Amnesty International worked for the release of four prisoners of conscience and investigated the cases of 25 possible prisoners of conscience. One of the prisoners of conscience adopted by the organization was Jamil al-Nimri, a pharmacist arrested in May 1985 and sentenced in April 1986 to three years' imprisonment for membership of an illegal organization. Another was Yusuf Hamid, a student arrested in November 1980 and sentenced to 10 years' imprisonment for membership of an illegal communist organization. The two other prisoners of conscience, Samih Khalil and Suleiman Suwais (see *Amnesty International Report 1986*), were released on 25 May and 17 February respectively. Suleiman Suwais had been detained without charge for almost four months in the General Intelligence Building in Amman.

Amnesty International learned during 1986 of the release of 10 of the 25 prisoners whose cases it had been investigating. Among those still held at the end of 1986 was Mahmud 'Uwaydah, alleged to be a prominent member of the Islamic Liberation Party, who had been detained without trial in al-Mahatta Central Prison since September 1982. Also held were alleged members of the Jordanian Communist Party and other banned organizations. A large number of political prisoners were transferred on 3 September to al-Jafr Prison, in the southern desert, following protests at restrictive regulations introduced in August in al-Mahatta Central Prison.

Amnesty International learned of nine trials before the Martial Law Court of people charged with membership of illegal political organizations. In each case the defendants were convicted and sentenced to prison terms. The organization continued to be concerned about the fairness of the proceedings before the court and about the lack of any right of appeal against its sentences. It investigated the cases of prisoners convicted by the Martial Law Court, and adopted some as prisoners of conscience.

Martial law has been in force since 1967. In 1986 a pattern of arrest and short-term detention without charge of political prisoners under emergency legislation continued. The arrests were mostly carried out by the *Da'irat al-Mukhabarat al-'Amma*, General Intelligence Department, and detained political suspects were usually held in the General Intelligence Department headquarters in Amman for a few weeks to a few months and interrogated. Some were held incommunicado. Those who were to be detained for longer periods or brought to trial were usually transferred to ordinary prisons. During 1986 Amnesty International learned of 53 people arrested on political grounds by the General Intelligence Department, 42 of whom were released before the end of the year without having been charged. They included 22 alleged members of the Jordanian Communist Party, outlawed since 1953, who were held between 17 May and 4 September in Jweidah Prison near Amman. Amnesty International expressed concern that they may have been prisoners of conscience, and also inquired about the physical condition of a number of them. It received assurances from the authorities that they had access to medical attention.

Further reports of torture or ill-treatment reached Amnesty International during 1986. Durgham Jiryis Halasa, a trade unionist from Karak, was reportedly tortured while held incommunicado for a number of weeks in the General Intelligence Department headquarters in Amman following his arrest on 16 May. Amnesty International appealed on his behalf, and he was released on 4 September. When security forces dispersed students demonstrating within the campus of Yarmuk University at Irbid on 15 May a number of students were killed and others were reportedly beaten while being taken to detention centres. Amnesty International expressed concern about the deaths and Prime Minister Zaid al-Rifai replied stating that three students had died because "of the pressure of the crowd. The students fell and they were trampled upon by their fellow students. They did not die at the hands of the police." In another action by security forces on 6 August within al-Mahatta Central Prison, apparently aimed at confiscating prisoners' belongings, a number of prisoners were reportedly beaten.

During 1986 Amnesty International recorded four executions, all for murder, and the passing of death sentences *in absentia* on three people convicted of selling land in the Israeli occupied West Bank to Israelis. The organization conveyed its concern about the apparent increase in the rate of executions in 1985; in their reply the Jordanian authorities expressed their belief in the use of the death penalty as a deterrent and as a fit punishment for certain crimes. Amnesty International continued to reiterate its position on the death penalty and expressed regret at the executions.

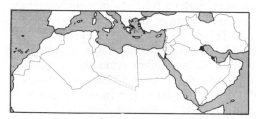

Kuwait

Amnesty International was concerned during 1986 about trials before the State Security Court of political prisoners, some of whom might be prisoners of conscience. The organization received allegations of torture or ill-treatment of detainees and was concerned about the use of the death penalty.

Amnesty International learned of six trials before the State Security Court during 1986, all held *in camera*. Kamil Husayn 'Ali Dashti and 'Abd al-Rahman Muhammad 'Ali Fakhru were convicted of having written leaflets which the authorities said called for the overthrow of the government. Their cases were investigated by the organization as possible prisoners of conscience. Kamil Husayn 'Ali Dashti was sentenced in November 1985 to five years' imprisonment (see *Amnesty International Report 1986*). Army Major 'Abd al-Rahman Muhammad 'Ali Fakhru was sentenced in April 1986 to 10 years' imprisonment. Also among those sentenced to imprisonment by the State Security Court were 'Abd al-'Aziz 'Ali Karim, found guilty in April of planning to blow up a water plant in Doha and sentenced to 15 years' imprisonment, and 'Ala' Muhammad Reda al-Atrash, an Iraqi national sentenced to death in November on charges of involvement in an attempt on the life of the Amir in May 1985. In all these cases Amnesty International was concerned about the secrecy of the proceedings and about the lack of any right to appeal against the court's verdicts.

Allegations of torture or ill-treatment by the State Security Intelligence Agency were received by Amnesty International during 1986. Most reports concerned foreign nationals who were detained for short periods and subsequently deported. Alleged methods included beatings and having hot water thrown on the head. Detainees were also reportedly threatened with being sent to countries where they risked human rights abuse. In December 1985 and February 1986 Amnesty International expressed concern about reports that nine people were tortured following their arrest in March 1985 and that eight others had died under torture between March and November 1985 (see *Amnesty International Report 1986*). The organization urged the authorities to investigate the reports, and, if they were verified, to bring to justice those found responsible. No reply was received.

Two prisoners, both convicted of murder and sentenced to death, were known to have been executed in 1986. Nadi Abu al-Hamad 'Uthman, an Egyptian national sentenced in 1983, was executed in January, and Ranja Suwami Tobal, an Indian national sentenced in 1984, was executed in March. The organization had appealed for their sentences to be commuted. In November Amnesty International sought clarification of reports that Turki Muhammad Nasir, a Saudi national sentenced to death in April for murder, may have been insane at the time of the crime. He was reported to have committed suicide in the prison hospital where he had been undergoing psychiatric treatment shortly after having been sentenced to death. In December Amnesty International appealed to the Amir to commute the death sentence passed on 'Ala' Muhammad Reda al-Atrash and all other outstanding death sentences.

A bill introducing the death penalty for crimes against aviation safety was submitted in March by the government to the National Assembly for approval. Amnesty International appealed to the government and members of the National Assembly not to adopt it.

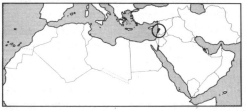

Lebanon

Amnesty International's concerns in 1986 were the widespread arbitrary arrest and detention without trial of political detainees; abductions and "disappearances"; ill-treatment and torture of prisoners and extrajudicial executions of prisoners.

Amnesty International was concerned about human rights violations committed in Lebanon by the forces of the Government of Lebanon, which appeared to be no longer in effective control of any part of the country, by the Government of Syria, whose forces controlled the eastern and northern regions of the country, and were deployed in West Beirut and by the Government of Israel. Amnesty

International was also concerned about human rights abuses committed by the four main militias controlling territory, namely: the Lebanese Forces (LF), a coalition of Christian militias which controlled East Beirut and the region to the north as far as Barbara; Amal, a mainly Shi'a Muslim-based militia which controlled West Beirut, the area surrounding the Palestinian refugee camps in South Beirut, and parts of south Lebanon; the Progressive Socialist Party (PSP), a mainly Druze party which administered the Shouf mountains and assisted Amal in controlling West Beirut; and the South Lebanon Army (SLA), a mainly Christian militia, which since June 1985 had assisted the Israeli Defence Forces (IDF) in controlling the "security zone" along the south Lebanon border. Amnesty International also received numerous reports of abductions of Lebanese and foreign nationals and ill-treatment and killings of captives by many other militias, including *Hizbollah* and the Islamic Jihad. Amnesty International as a matter of principle condemns the execution and torture of prisoners by anyone including opposition groups. However, Amnesty International considers that governments, as the originators and guarantors of international human rights standards, bear responsibility for their implementation. The organization believed that the four main militias had governmental attributes, such as effective control of territory, and therefore had the means and the responsibility to protect human rights.

Amnesty International continued to receive reports that all four militias arrested and detained political opponents, members of rival factions held as hostages and members of their own militia held for disciplinary reasons. Amnesty International was concerned that detainees were denied their rights to a normal legal process, and to regular access to their families, and were not allowed the protection of the International Committee of the Red Cross (ICRC). Amnesty International was concerned that many had "disappeared" and that families often faced difficulties in establishing the whereabouts of their relatives.

The Lebanese Forces were reported to be holding at least 100 people at the end of 1986 in various detention centres in Qarantina in East Beirut, in Byblos, Amshit, Adonis and Qattara. On 15 January Samir Geagea overthrew Elie Hobeika as leader of the LF. Following this and other clashes between rival Christian factions, hundreds of suspected opponents of Samir Geagea were arrested. Most were held for short periods. The Fifth Brigade of the Lebanese Army stationed in East Beirut, which fought alongside the LF against Elie Hobeika, was also reported to have carried out arrests during 1986 and to have handed over detainees to the LF. On 24 April, 33 Muslim detainees who had reportedly been held by the LF as hostages were released.

They included Lebanese Shi'ites, Sunnis and Druze, as well as two Syrians and two Egyptians. Two of them had been "missing" for 11 years. Although the LF declared that they were no longer holding any prisoners, other sources, including the released prisoners, claimed that there were other detainees. Amnesty International took up for investigation the cases of three Lebanese Muslims from Sidon who were reported to have been arrested by the LF but who were not among those released in April. Fadi El Habbel was reported to have been arrested between Beirut and Tripoli in February 1983; Fadi and Khalid Shehadeh, two brothers, were reported to have been arrested near Sidon in March 1984. Former detainees had reported seeing two of them in Qarantina prison within the past year. Amnesty International appealed to the leader of the LF asking for the reasons for their continued detention, urging that they be allowed to confront any charges against them, and arguing that they should not be held solely on the grounds of their political opinions, allegiances or ethnic origins. In December Amnesty International received a letter from Karim Pakradouni, Vice-President of the Executive Committee of the LF, who said that they had released all detainees in their prisons on 15 January, when Samir Geagea took over as leader of the LF, and that the two brothers were not in prison on that date. Amnesty International was continuing its investigations.

Amnesty International continued to be concerned about the detention by Amal militiamen of hundreds of Palestinians, members of the Sunni-based Murabitun militia (which in 1985 was defeated by Amal for control of West Beirut), members of the Lebanese Communist Party, members of the SLA and Amal deserters. At any one time there were reportedly several hundred prisoners in captivity, most of whom were held for short periods. Amnesty International received numerous reports from a variety of sources of young Palestinian men being arbitrarily arrested at Amal checkpoints near the Palestinian refugee camps in Beirut and south Lebanon, at Amal roadblocks on the Sidon to Beirut coastal road and on the road to Beirut International Airport. Large numbers were arrested during periods of armed hostilities, which broke out frequently during 1986, between Amal and the Palestinians in the camps in Beirut and south Lebanon. Those arrested at such times were usually taken to Burj al Murr prison in Beirut. Some Palestinian detainees, allegedly leading members of the Palestine Liberation Organization (PLO), were reported to have been handed over to the Syrian forces and held in Anjar in the Beka'a valley or in Damascus in Syria. The mainly Shi'a Sixth Brigade of the Lebanese Army, which was stationed in West Beirut and fought alongside Amal, also made arrests and held detainees.

The PSP were believed to be holding up to 100 detainees, including Christians held as hostages, and members of the PSP held for disciplinary reasons, but Amnesty International could not verify individual cases.

Amnesty International continued to be concerned about detainees held by the SLA in Khiam prison in south Lebanon. In July Amnesty International received the names of over 220 people who were reported by former detainees to be held by the SLA in Khiam at that time. Among them were teenagers, women and old men. Amnesty International believed that there were between 100 and 200 held at any one time in Khiam, mostly Lebanese suspected of carrying out military operations against the SLA or the Israeli Defence Forces.

In August Amnesty International appealed to the Syrian Government on behalf of over 30 Lebanese arrested by Syrian forces in Tripoli between February and June and transferred to Damascus for interrogation. Some were reportedly tortured. (See *Syria* entry.)

Amnesty International received many allegations of ill-treatment and torture from former detainees held by Amal, the LF and the SLA. The widespread practice of incommunicado detention and the absence of any safeguards meant that all detainees held by the militias were at risk. Families often faced difficulties in discovering a detainee's whereabouts and obtaining permission to visit. The ICRC was allowed access to only a few of the detainees held by the militias: to some of those held by the LF and by Amal. In July it resumed visits, after more than two years, to PSP-held prisoners but was not permitted access to SLA-held prisoners in Khiam.

Reports of torture and ill-treatment of detainees held by Amal continued. Many of these reports concerned Palestinians arrested at Amal checkpoints, who were beaten before being released. Palestinian combatants and suspected combatants arrested during hostilities were reportedly taken to Burj al Murr for interrogation. One former detainee interviewed by Amnesty International, who had been arrested in June and taken to Burj al Murr, said that during interrogation he was hung from the ceiling by his feet and beaten with a thick stick, and forced into a metal chair and given electric shocks. Amnesty International received similar allegations from other sources. In December, following reports of the arrest of hundreds of Palestinians in Beirut and south Lebanon and of the ill-treatment of detainees, including teenagers, Amnesty International sent appeals to Nabih Berri, the leader of Amal (who was also Minister of Justice in the Lebanese Government). The organization urged him to ensure that detainees were held in accordance with internationally accepted standards, that no one was held in prolonged incommunicado detention and that all detainees had immediate access to an independent humanitarian organization such as the ICRC, and that no one was ill-treated or tortured or executed. In November Amnesty International made a similar appeal on behalf of an Israeli airman who was shot down in south Lebanon on 16 October and whom Amal claimed to be holding. Amnesty International received no reply to either appeal.

During the first half of 1986 Amnesty International received allegations that detainees held by the SLA were tortured in Khiam prison, and that this sometimes took place in the presence of, or under the supervision of, members of the IDF or the Israeli Security Service. Amnesty International interviewed one former detainee arrested in early 1986 who said that for most of a week he was hooded with a thick black canvas bag and had his hands tied behind his back. According to his account he was kicked all over his body, punched and beaten with electric cable, stripped, soaked with water and subjected to electric shocks to all parts of his body, including the testicles. He said that on three separate occasions he was suspended for several hours by his wrists, which were handcuffed together from a crossbar, with his toes barely touching the ground. In September Amnesty International appealed to General Lahad, head of the SLA, and to the Israeli Minister of Defence, urging a public and impartial inquiry into these allegations, and access to the prison by the ICRC. General Lahad told journalists in June that no visits would be allowed until the whereabouts of three SLA soldiers, who had been kidnapped by the pro-Iranian armed group *Hizbollah*, were disclosed. The Israeli Attorney General in a letter of 21 December said that "while Israel does have good relations with the South Lebanon Army, it is in no position to dictate to them how to cope with the grave threat they face".

Amnesty International also received reports of detainees held by the LF being ill-treated and tortured, but was unable to obtain detailed information.

In late December Amnesty International received reports that over 200 people had been killed by Syrian troops and Syrian-backed militia in Tripoli (see *Syria* entry).

Three people sentenced to death by a Lebanese criminal court for murder had their sentences commuted to imprisonment. Several others sentenced to death in 1982 and 1983 were believed to be still in prison (see *Amnesty International Report 1986*).

Amal summarily and publicly executed three people by firing-squad during 1986: one on 8 July accused of committing four murders, and two others, on 30 July and 30 November, accused of planting bombs in cars. Amnesty International called on the leader of Amal to take steps to prevent any further executions. Amnesty

International received numerous reports that Palestinians, and others, arbitrarily arrested by Amal militiamen at roadblocks or outside the refugee camps had been killed on the spot.

The LF was also reported to have carried out summary executions of political opponents. Following an attempt by the former leader of the LF, Elie Hobeika, to overthrow Samir Geagea on 27 September, about 250 supporters of Elie Hobeika were reported to have been arrested and to have "disappeared". On 10 October, 67 bodies were discovered in a common grave near Jounieh. Later 30 bodies were recovered from the sea. Although their identities were never publicized, they were believed to have been among those arrested earlier by the LF. Amnesty International learned the names of 50 of the people reportedly arrested in September whose fate remained unknown and sought further information about them.

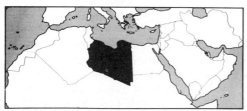

Libya

Amnesty International was concerned about renewed official calls for the "physical liquidation" of political opponents of the government, some of whom were in detention. It was also concerned about the continued detention of 75 prisoners of conscience. Some political prisoners were reportedly detained without trial, after being acquitted by the courts or after the expiry of their sentences. Reports of torture were received and the organization learned of one execution.

The General People's Congress, which held its annual ordinary session between 25 February and 3 March 1986, did not call for the "physical liquidation" of government opponents in its final resolutions, as it had in previous years. There were also statements in January and March by Major 'Abd al-Salam Jallud suggesting that the policy was no longer in use. However, other official calls for the "physical liquidation" of political opponents were renewed during 1986. In a speech broadcast by Tripoli television on 14 January, Colonel Mu'ammar Gaddafi reportedly referred to "Libyan Muslim Brothers . . . Libyan Ba'thists, Libyan monarchists, runaway entrepreneurs and middlemen, and drop-out students". He reportedly stated: "They collaborate with American intelligence against their own country! . . . hence we call them stray dogs. If we find them abroad we kill them, if they come here we throw them in the streets, we treat them as dogs." In an apparent reference to attempts on the life of Libyan opponents in Egypt (see *Amnesty International Report 1985* and *1986*) Colonel Gaddafi reportedly stated in June that: "Those Libyans who went to Egypt — went to liquidate Libyans . . . We continue with this and this is the resolution of the Libyan people." (Radio Tripoli, 11 June 1986). Further calls for the pursuit and elimination of "enemies of the Libyan people" and of "traitors" were issued in March and May by the Basic People's Congresses of New Benghazi and Bayda Central. An official radio station announced on 18 May that "Egyptian revolutionary forces and Arab masses in the Great Jamahiriya" had called for the "physical liquidation" of detained members of an Egyptian "spy ring". At the end of October several Basic People's Congresses from all over the country sent messages to Colonel Gaddafi urging the "physical liquidation" of a group of prisoners referred to in the Libyan news media as the "group of the enemies of God". One of these prisoners, Ahmad Muhammad al-Fallah, reportedly made a confession on Libyan television on 15 October. He apparently said that the group had received orders from United States intelligence agencies to assassinate Libyan "revolutionary elements" and "friends of the Libyan people who help them to be strong militarily". Amnesty International appealed to the Libyan authorities not to execute the prisoners. Information received by Amnesty International from the Libyan authorities in December indicated that eight of these prisoners had not been executed and were going to be brought to trial.

Muhammad 'Ashur, a former Libyan diplomat resident abroad, was assassinated in 1986, possibly in implementation of the policy of "physical liquidation". He was reportedly found shot dead in East Berlin on 3 March.

Amnesty International continued to work for the release of 75 prisoners of conscience and received reports that two of them had been executed in 1983. 'Abdullah Bilqasim al-Misalati and Salih 'Ali al-Zaruq Nawwal, who were arrested in 1973, were serving life sentences until April 1983 when they were retried and sentenced to death for membership of the Islamic Liberation Party (see *Amnesty International Report 1984*). Amnesty International was seeking clarification of the fate of the two prisoners. Among the other prisoners of conscience known to Amnesty International were people arrested in 1973 for membership of a Marxist political organization, students arrested in 1976 for opposing government interference in student affairs, and 16 writers and journalists arrested in 1978 and convicted of forming a political organization. During 1986 no reply was received from the Libyan authorities to any of Amnesty

International's communications about these 75 prisoners of conscience, some of whom were under sentence of death or serving life sentences.

Amnesty International received reports that political prisoners in Libya were often held without trial or after having been acquitted or having served their sentences. Among those reportedly held without trial were eight people arrested following an attack by members of the National Front for the Salvation of Libya on Colonel Gaddafi's headquarters in Bab al-'Aziziyah in May 1984. The organization also learned of dozens of political prisoners arrested since 1983 whose legal status and whereabouts had not been disclosed and was seeking further information on them.

In October Libya paid US$500,000 compensation to the Norwegian Government for the torture and ill-treatment of Norwegian sailors and the death under torture of one of them in May 1984 (see *Amnesty International Report 1985* and *1986*). However, the investigation into the death of the sailor, Bjorn Pedersen, promised by Libya in July 1985 was reported not to have taken place. During 1986, as in previous years, Amnesty International received little information on the treatment of prisoners. However, reports did confirm that torture methods such as *falaqa* (beating on the soles of the feet) and *farruj* (the prisoner is hung upside down from a perch inserted between the knees with wrists and ankles bound and is beaten intermittently) have been used in recent years.

Amnesty International received reports that Isma'il Hasan al-Sanussi Isma'il was executed on 1 August in the town of Waddan. He was believed to have been sentenced to seven years' imprisonment after his arrest in 1984. The organization did not know the charges on which he had been convicted and sentenced to imprisonment, nor was it aware of any further judicial proceedings before his execution. Amnesty International reiterated its unconditional opposition to the death penalty and recalled UN Resolution 35/172 of 15 December 1980 which set minimum standards for safeguarding defendants in capital cases, including guaranteeing the most careful legal procedures and the right of appeal.

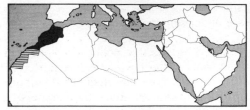

Morocco and Western Sahara

During 1986 Amnesty International was concerned about the continued imprisonment of 228 prisoners of conscience and possible prisoners of conscience; the detention of political prisoners; pre-trial and trial proceedings which did not appear to conform to internationally recognized standards; allegations of torture and ill-treatment of prisoners; and secret detention and continued detention after expiry of sentence.

Amnesty International continued to appeal for the immediate and unconditional release of 63 prisoners of conscience, and investigated the cases of 165 possible prisoners of conscience. Groups of these prisoners went on hunger-strike for limited periods on several occasions during the year to draw attention to their situation. Most of the prisoners of conscience had been sentenced to long prison terms in 1977 on charges including membership of various Marxist-Leninist groups. Among them was Hassan El Bou, whose mental health was believed to be deteriorating. Amnesty International was concerned about reports that he was not receiving adequate medical treatment.

During 1986 Amnesty International learned of the release of 23 adopted prisoners of conscience. Fifteen were released at the end of their sentences, and eight as a result of a royal pardon. Among those who benefited from the royal pardon were Azzouz Laarich and Abdelaziz Tribak, both sentenced to 30 years' imprisonment; and Mohamed Mechbal and Mohamed Loubnani, sentenced to 20 years' imprisonment. Four members of the *Union socialiste des forces populaires* (USFP), Socialist Union of Popular Forces, whose cases the organization was investigating (see *Amnesty International Report 1986*) were released upon completion of their prison sentences.

Amnesty International continued to investigate the cases of 31 individuals, mainly students, who were accused of being members of *Qa'idiyin*, a continuation of the underground movements *Ila-al Amam*, Forward, and *23 Mars*, 23 March. They were tried in 1984 and sentenced to prison terms of up to 15 years on charges including conspiracy to overthrow the government (see *Amnesty International Report 1986*). Amnesty International was concerned that many, if not all, might have been imprisoned for their conscientiously held beliefs, and sought information on the nature of the *Qa'idiyin* ideology and its position on violence. Amnesty International was also concerned about several aspects of their pre-trial and trial proceedings which appeared to fall short of internationally recognized standards for a fair trial: they were held in *garde à vue* (incommunicado) detention in police custody for several months; they alleged that their confessions were extracted under duress and later invoked as evidence in court proceedings; the pre-trial investigation in most of their cases was carried out without the presence of their defence lawyers; and defence lawyers did not have enough time to prepare the defence, and had difficulties in gaining access to the case dossiers. During the trial the court reportedly refused to investigate procedural irregularities and complaints by the defendants that their confessions were extracted under torture.

Amnesty International continued to investigate the cases of over 80 Saharans allegedly taken into custody by Moroccan security forces as long ago as 1976. In response to Amnesty International's appeals, the Moroccan authorities replied on a number of these cases, denying that they were in detention.

Amnesty International also investigated the cases of 41 individuals accused of belonging to the underground movement *Ila-al Amam*. Most were engineers, doctors, students or teachers belonging either to the *Union nationale des étudiants marocains* (UNEM), Moroccan National Students Union, or the *Syndicat national des enseignants* (SNE), National Union of Teachers. Forty-two were arrested in October and November 1985 (see *Amnesty International Report 1986*). Fifteen of them were tried and sentenced by the court of first instance in Casablanca on 31 January to prison terms of between three and four years, on charges reportedly related to public order offences during the riots of January 1984, membership of an illegal organization, and distribution of leaflets hostile to the government. Twenty-seven were tried by the Criminal Chamber of the Court of Appeal in Casablanca on 12 February on charges of conspiracy against the government. One was acquitted and 26 were sentenced to between three and 20 years' imprisonment. Amnesty International feared that some if not all of these prisoners may have been sentenced for their non-violent political beliefs. Amnesty International was also concerned about reports of irregularities in their pre-trial and trial proceedings. These included prolonged incommunicado detention in police custody; alleged torture during *garde à vue* detention; and convictions allegedly obtained on the basis of confessions extracted under torture or the threat of torture. Amnesty International expressed its concern to the authorities about these aspects of the case, asked whether the court had taken steps to investigate the torture allegations, and requested details of the charges and evidence produced against them. In reply, the authorities gave details of the charges against and date and place of trial of one of the group, Dr Mohamed Jaidi. However, the government did not answer in full Amnesty International's concerns on his case, nor did it give any information about the rest of the group.

On 31 October Amnesty International wrote to the authorities about the trial and imprisonment of five students sentenced to between two and six months' imprisonment by the court of first instance in Fez on 16 October for public order offences. They had reportedly been arrested on 6 and 8 October. Amnesty International expressed its concern at allegations of torture and ill-treatment during pre-trial detention, as well as about allegations that confessions extracted under torture had been used as evidence in court. Amnesty International requested details of the charges and evidence against them and urged an impartial and public inquiry into these allegations.

Amnesty International received reports of the arrest and prolonged incommunicado detention of a number of individuals, including students, trade unionists, and members of various political groups. On 7 February Amnesty International appealed on behalf of 10 phosphate miners, among them El Haj Mastour, Secretary General of the *Union générale des travailleurs du phosphate*, General Union of Phosphate Workers, who were arrested between 25 and 31 January in connection with a strike against dismissals and for better working conditions and wages. Amnesty International was concerned that they might have been detained to prevent them from exercising their rights of association and expression, and requested information about their legal position. Nine of the miners were released shortly afterwards and El Haj Mastour was released in May after more than three months in detention without trial. Amnesty International wrote again to the authorities on 31 October, asking for information about the arrest of Youssef Al Idrissi, a member of the *Organisation pour l'action démocratique et populaire* (OADP), Organization for Popular and Democratic Action, and Hassan Al Dradbi, a member of UNEM. Amnesty International was concerned that the two individuals had reportedly been kept in prolonged *garde à vue* detention since their arrest at the beginning of the month and urged them to be allowed access to lawyers and relatives. Amnesty International later learned that Youssef Al Idrissi had been released and that Hassan Al Dradbi had been presented before the court of first instance in Casablanca, reportedly accused of public order offences.

Amnesty International continued to receive reports of ill-treatment of political prisoners in various prisons. They were reportedly beaten and kept in isolation in dark, windowless, cold cells, and denied, or made to endure delays before receiving, medical treatment, in most cases needed for injuries resulting from torture during pre-trial detention. Amnesty International also received reports that their families were subjected to repeated interrogation and harassment. A number of prisoners in different prisons staged hunger-strikes in protest at their prison conditions. Amnesty International appealed on behalf of the group of 41 prisoners accused of belonging to *Ila-al Amam* whose cases the organization was investigating, following reports that they had staged a series of short hunger-strikes in protest at, among other things, their dispersal to a number of prisons. During these hunger-strikes they were reportedly subjected to various forms of ill-treatment, including beatings, and denied medical treatment. Amnesty International also continued to appeal on behalf of six prisoners who had gone on hunger-strike in April 1985, listing a number of demands including medical care (see *Amnesty International Report 1986*). Their families were reportedly not able to visit them or to obtain information about their health or where they were held, once they started their hunger-strike. No reply was received from the authorities.

Amnesty International continued to be concerned about the fate of approximately 100 military prisoners arrested following attempts on the life of King Hassan II in 1971 and 1972. According to Amnesty International's information, these individuals had been held in secret detention, incommunicado, since 1973. Reports indicated that they were kept in isolation in windowless, filthy and unventilated cells in extreme temperatures, with inadequate food, and given arbitrary punishment, and no medical care. Amnesty International feared that a number of these prisoners might already have died as a result of these conditions. Several had already completed their prison sentences, but were not released.

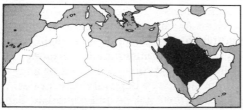

Saudi Arabia

Amnesty International was concerned about the long-term detention without trial, often incommunicado, of political prisoners, some of whom might have been prisoners of conscience; allegations of torture and ill-treatment, including the amputation of limbs as a judicial punishment; and the death penalty.

In 1986 Amnesty International documented the names of over 140 alleged political opponents or critics of the government reportedly detained in the eastern provinces of Saudi Arabia (see *Amnesty International Report 1986*). Those arrested were said to be Shi'a Muslims and included students, teachers, religious scholars and employees at oil installations. Among them was Makkiya 'Abdallah Hamdan who was reportedly arrested after midnight at her home on 24 July after trying to discover the whereabouts of her husband who had been arrested in May. Amnesty International was seeking further information on the arrests and the detainees' whereabouts.

At the end of 1986 Amnesty International was also seeking further information on the continued detention of 11 Egyptian nationals reportedly held without trial since 1979. Among them were Usama Awadh Sa'd, a medical student at Cairo University, and Abdul Moneim Abdul Hamid Bayoumi Sultan, a student at the Institute of Health in Cairo, Egypt. According to reports received from the detainees' families, the 11 were among a large group of pilgrims arrested following the seizure of the Grand Mosque in Mecca in November 1979 by an armed group. Following the arrests, 63 were tried and executed and 107 received prison sentences of varying lengths. Many were released after investigation but the 11, the majority of whom were students, remained in detention without trial.

In September Amnesty International appealed to the authorities to investigate the reported death in custody of Ahmad Mahdi Khamis, a Saudi national working at the British Bank of al-Dammam. Ahmad Mahdi Khamis was reportedly arrested on 11 August with several others from his village, Hillah Mahish, in the Eastern Province. The reasons for his arrest were not known but appeared to be connected with the appearance of opposition slogans on walls and the distribution of opposition leaflets in the village. The detainees were held incommunicado in al-Dammam Central Prison. On the night of 23 August his body was returned to his family with instructions that it should be buried without the customary funeral. Reports received by Amnesty International stated that his body bore the marks of torture.

In 1986 Amnesty International received several reports of torture and ill-treatment of detainees. As in previous years, torture or ill-treatment apparently occurred during the period immediately after arrest when detainees were held incommunicado. Among the practices described were beatings on the soles of the feet or all over the body; submersion in water; and sleep deprivation. Prisoners in cells were sometimes shackled by their ankles and some had been held in solitary confinement for over two years. Amnesty International was unable to investigate these reports fully but was concerned by their consistency, from a variety of sources, which appeared to indicate a pattern of torture and ill-treatment.

Amnesty International also expressed its concern about cruel, inhuman and degrading punishment being judicially imposed in the form of amputation of limbs. On 24 October four men had their right hands and left feet amputated ("cross-limb" amputation) in the town of Abha, 'Asir province. The four amputations, following convictions for burglary and armed robbery, brought to 11 the number of amputations documented by Amnesty International in 1986. These were also the first instances of "cross-limb" amputation to be brought to the organization's attention for several years.

In September 1986 Amnesty International informed the Minister of the Interior of its concern about reports that Mohamed Lazrak, a Tunisian national sentenced to death *in absentia* on 10 July by the Military Court of Tunis, had been returned against his will from Saudi Arabia to Tunisia. According to reports, Mohamed Lazrak was arrested by the Saudi authorities and handed over to the Tunisian authorities on 20 August. He appeared before the Military Court in Tunis on 23 August when the death sentence was upheld, and was executed on 2 September. Amnesty International reiterated its opposition to the involuntary return of individuals to any country where there are reasonable grounds to fear that they may be imprisoned for their non-violent conscientiously held beliefs or be subjected to torture or execution. Amnesty International sought clarification of the circumstances surrounding the return of Mohamed Lazrak to Tunisia and sought assurances that the necessary measures would be taken to ensure that such incidents did not recur. In response the Minister of the Interior stated that, contrary to Amnesty International's information, Mohamed Lazrak had not been forcibly returned but had returned to Tunisia of his own accord.

In 1986 Amnesty International learned of 24 executions. In all but one case they followed convictions for murder and were carried out after the relatives of the murder victims had demanded *Qisas* (retribution). Under the law relatives may demand *Qisas* in the form of the death of the murderer or by financial settlement, or they may waive such a claim. As well as Saudi citizens those executed included six Pakistanis, one Yemeni and one Egyptian. In August Ahmet Güneş, a Turkish worker in Jeddah, who had been convicted of the murder of his wife Eşe Güneş, was reported in the Turkish *Daily News* to have been reprieved after a Turkish Deputy intervened on his behalf with the victim's parents and obtained from them a document saying that Ahmet Güneş should not be executed. In several communications during the year to the Saudi authorities Amnesty International repeated its unconditional opposition to the death penalty and urged commutation of such sentences.

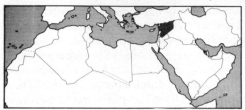

Syria

The main concerns of Amnesty International continued to be the detention without charge or trial of thousands of political prisoners under Syria's state of emergency legislation; the imprisonment of 275 prisoners of conscience; the long-term detention without trial of most political detainees and the detention of political prisoners after the expiry of their sentences; the routine use of torture by the security forces; "disappearances"; extrajudicial executions; and the death penalty. The authorities did not respond to any of Amnesty International's appeals in 1986.

During 1986 Amnesty International worked for the release of 275 adopted prisoners of conscience and was investigating the cases of 181 possible prisoners of conscience. The majority continued to be held without trial, some for over 16 years. It learned of the release of 67 prisoners on whose behalf it was working, of whom 66 were adopted prisoners of conscience.

Amnesty International learned of the release in May of Haitham Kamel Mustafa, a 20-year-old student detained without trial for six years. He was arrested for his involvement in establishing a prohibited organization, *Ittihad al-Nidal al-Shuyu'i*, Union for Communist Struggle (see *Amnesty International Report 1986*). He was reported to be in poor health upon release. In November 10 adopted prisoners of conscience were released. They were among a number of lawyers arrested in April and May 1980 after a one-day strike by the Syrian Bar Association on 31 March 1980 (see *Amnesty International Report 1984*). However, Amnesty International remained concerned about three lawyers from this group, 'Abd al-Majid Manjouneh, Salim 'Aqil and Thuraya 'Abd al-Karim, who continued to be held without trial. Amnesty International also continued to investigate the cases of over 150 doctors and engineers detained since 1980 because of their support for the strike.

Amnesty International learned that 56 members of the banned Communist Party Political Bureau (CPPB), had been released, three of them during 1986. Among them was the novelist Wadi' Ismandar who was freed in October. The organization continued to call for the release of 88 other party members held without trial since their arrest, some for over seven years.

Amnesty International continued to seek the release of 100 members of the banned Party for Communist Action (PCA), arrested at various times since 1980, none of whom had been charged or tried.

In 1986 several people suspected of involvement with the PCA were arrested, some of whom were arrested as hostages. Shafiqa al-'Ali was arrested on 28 April instead of her husband Faraj Birqadar, who had been wanted since 1984 because of his PCA membership.

Between February and June, over 180 Palestinians and Syrians were arrested by the security forces in Damascus and other cities, of whom 82 remained in detention without trial at the end of 1986. Among them were members of the PCA and several Palestinian groups, including *Fatah al-Intifadah* (Abu Musa's group) and the Palestine Liberation Front — Provisional Command. Several of the detainees were said to have been tortured, and one reportedly died in custody as a result. Among the detainees were whole families arrested as hostages: for example, the mother, three sisters, wife and sister-in-law of Samir al-Hassan, a Palestinian journalist, were arrested on 30 March. His mother was released when he was arrested on 1 April, and his other relatives were released in June.

In August Amnesty International appealed to the authorities on behalf of three members of a Jewish family held incommunicado without trial for over eight months. Shehade Besso and his sons Salim and Jacques were arrested in December 1985, reportedly because one of their relatives failed to return to Syria in accordance with guarantees given to the authorities. According to reports the three men were ill-treated during detention and the health of 70-year-old Shehade Besso had deteriorated seriously as a result. In October Amnesty International learned that they had been released.

Amnesty International sought further details about over 150 people detained without trial in the custody of *al-Amn al Siyassi*, the political security force. Most were arrested in September on suspicion of involvement with the prohibited *al-Tanzim al-Sha'bi al-Nasiri*, Popular Nasserist Organization. Among them were doctors, engineers and lawyers, several of whom were reportedly tortured.

In August Amnesty International appealed on behalf of 33 Lebanese nationals arrested by Syrian forces in Tripoli, Lebanon, between February and June. They were among a group of 38 people, five of whom were released in mid-1986, said to have been arrested in their homes at night and transferred to Damascus for interrogation. Some were reportedly tortured during detention, among them Tareq Marhaba, a teacher who reportedly had a heart attack as a result. He was released in December. At the end of 1986 Amnesty International learned that 12 detainees from this group had been released, but that 14 other Lebanese nationals had been arrested in Tripoli and Beirut and taken to Damascus.

Amnesty International continued to receive allegations of torture and ill-treatment of detainees in the custody of the security forces, among them adopted prisoners of conscience. In April the organization appealed on behalf of two adopted prisoners of conscience — Faisal Tahhan and Mufid Mi'mari — who were reportedly tortured to force them to sign declarations renouncing their political affiliations.

In August Amnesty International called on the government to investigate reports of the death under torture of Sulaiman Mustafa Ghaibur, a Syrian soldier from Hama, while in the custody of *al-Mukhabarat al-'Askariyya*, Military Intelligence. He died on 1 May and a coffin bearing his body was returned on the same day to his family, who were told that he had committed suicide and were instructed to bury the coffin immediately without opening it. According to Amnesty International's information, the coffin was opened and his body had bruises on the wrists and bullet wounds in the neck. It was alleged that he had been shot after his death under torture in order to simulate suicide.

In August and December Amnesty International also called for investigations into reports of the torture of four other detainees in the custody of *al-Mukhabarat al-'Askariyya*: Amina 'Omar, Mazin Rabi' and 'Ali al-Rifa'i, all Palestinians, and Karim 'Akkari, a Syrian. Two of them allegedly attempted to commit suicide after being tortured.

A number of appeals were issued during 1986 on behalf of detainees who were reportedly seriously ill and being denied adequate medical care. Among them was Mahmud Jalbut, a Palestinian clerk who was said to be in a critical condition as a result of a stomach haemorrhage. Appeals were also sent on behalf of four prisoners reported to be suffering from various ailments, including diabetes, inflammation of the oesophagus and kidney stones. The four — Husain Zaidan, Mustafa Fallah, Mahmud al-Fayyad and Jalal al-Din Mirhij — had been detained without trial since May 1985 when their 15-year sentences expired (see *Amnesty International Report 1986*). Amnesty International sought official clarification of the legal basis of their continued detention and urged their immediate release unless they were charged with a criminal offence.

In November Amnesty International learned that Tawfiq Draq al-Siba'i, a neurologist who "disappeared" following his arrest in May 1980, was alive and was being held in al-Mezze Military Prison, reportedly for involvement in matters affecting state security. In 1984 Amnesty International had received unconfirmed reports that he had been killed in a massacre at Tadmur Prison on 27 June 1980 (see *Amnesty International Report 1985*). Another prisoner, Khalil Brayez, "disappeared" two months after the expiry of his 15-year sentence in October 1985. He had not been released from prison. A former captain and intelligence officer in the Syrian army whose case the organization has been investigating since 1978, Khalil Brayez was last known to have been detained in al-Hassakeh Prison.

At the end of 1986 Amnesty International was seeking further information about reports of the killing of over 200 people by Syrian troops and Syrian-backed militia in Tripoli, Lebanon, in the third week of December. Some of those who died were said to have been killed during armed clashes between Syrian troops and militiamen of *Harakat al-Tawhid al-Islami*, Islamic Unification Movement. However, Amnesty International's information indicated that many of the victims were unarmed civilians summarily executed shortly after arrest. Hundreds of other people were reported to have been arrested in the Tripoli area by Syrian troops or to have "disappeared".

Amnesty International learned of eight officially confirmed executions in 1986. The victims had been convicted of crimes such as espionage and premeditated murder. During 1986 Amnesty International sent numerous appeals reiterating its unconditional opposition to the death penalty.

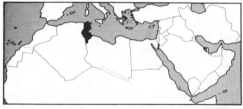

Tunisia

During 1986 Amnesty International was concerned about the imprisonment or restriction of prisoners of conscience and possible prisoners of conscience; prolonged incommunicado detention; and the death penalty.

Amnesty International adopted as a prisoner of conscience Moncef Ben Slimane, assistant university lecturer in sociology and Secretary General of the *Syndicat de l'enseignement supérieur et de la recherche scientifique* (SESRS), Union of Higher Education and Scientific Research. He was tried on 4 June by the court of first instance in Tunis and sentenced to one year's imprisonment for "defamation of the public order and public institutions". Amnesty International delegates observed his trial. The charge related to a letter sent by the SESRS to the Minister of Education criticizing government policies, and in particular its handling of disturbances at Tunis University. In October the Court of Appeal in Tunis reduced his sentence to six months, and he was released from prison on 14 November.

Amnesty International also adopted as prisoners of conscience Ahmed Mestiri, Secretary General of the *Mouvement des démocrates socialistes* (MDS), Movement of Socialist Democrats; Hassan Ben

Rabiha, an MDS member; and Omar Mestiri and Abdellatif Hermassi, both members of the political bureau of the *Rassemblement socialiste progressiste* (RSP), Progressive Socialist Assembly. They had all been arrested at the start of a non-violent demonstration in Tunis on 16 April in protest against the US raid on Libya. They were convicted by a cantonal court on 22 April of "assembling on a public highway" and each sentenced to four months' imprisonment, upheld on appeal on 14 June. The appeal hearing was attended by Amnesty International delegates. Three of the defendants were imprisoned and Ahmed Mestiri was placed under house arrest.

Amnesty International learned of the release upon expiry of his sentence on 14 June of adopted prisoner of conscience Beshir Essid, lawyer and Secretary General of the *Rassemblement nationaliste arabe* (RNA), Arab Nationalist Assembly Movement.

During 1986 Amnesty International continued to investigate the cases of 18 members of the Tunisian armed forces sentenced in 1983 to between five and eight years' imprisonment on charges including membership of the Islamic Liberation Party, a banned political group. These prisoners were among 29 individuals tried in August 1983 (see *Amnesty International Report 1986*).

Amnesty International appealed on behalf of a number of trade unionists arrested in various towns in November 1985, during a series of country-wide strikes and demonstrations which followed the breakdown of annual wage negotiations between the government and the *Union générale des travailleurs tunisiens* (UGTT), Tunisian General Workers' Union. They were tried in November and December 1985 and received sentences of between six and eight months' imprisonment on charges including the dissemination of information designed to disturb public order, and incitement to and participation in illegal strikes. Amnesty International was concerned that these prisoners may have been imprisoned solely for their non-violent trade union activities.

Amnesty International also continued to investigate the case of Habib Achour, Secretary General of the UGTT. He was sentenced to one year's imprisonment in December 1985 on charges of breaking into and taking control of a fishing cooperative in Sfax in 1982 (see *Amnesty International Report 1986*), the sentence being reduced to eight months on appeal. He was brought to trial for a second time in 1986 on charges of mismanagement of union funds, and sentenced in April to two years' imprisonment by the court of first instance in Tunis. The sentence was upheld on appeal. Amnesty International was concerned that Habib Achour may have been imprisoned to prevent him carrying out his trade union activities. It was also concerned because his first trial was held *in camera*, and may in other respects have fallen short of internationally recognized standards for a fair trial. Amnesty International repeatedly expressed concern about reports of a deterioration in his health as a result of inadequate medical attention in prison. He was reported to be suffering from diabetes, a heart condition and arthritis. He was reported to be in the military hospital in Tunis at the end of 1986. Amnesty International learned that Habib Achour was tried again in December and sentenced to a further four years' imprisonment by the Criminal Chamber of the Court of Appeal in Tunis on charges of complicity in the mismanagement of funds. At the end of 1986 Amnesty International was seeking more information about his latest trial.

In October Amnesty International raised with the authorities the cases of a number of individuals reportedly arrested between July and September and held in prolonged *garde à vue* (incommunicado) detention since their arrest. They included members of the *Mouvement d'unité populaire* (MUP), The Movement for Popular Unity, an unauthorized political organization, and members of the unauthorized *Mouvement de la tendance islamique* (MTI), Islamic Tendency Movement. Amnesty International requested details of their arrest and detention and of any charges against them, and urged that they be allowed immediate access to lawyers and relatives.

Amnesty International learned of 18 executions during 1986 and of two death sentences, all for the crimes of rape, murder, theft, assault and attempted murder, and appealed to the authorities in every case. Among those executed was Mohamed Lazrak, a Tunisian national sentenced to death *in absentia* on 10 July by the Military Court in Tunis for assault, theft and attempted murder. He was executed on 2 September following his return from Saudi Arabia. Amnesty International was concerned about reports that he had been forcibly returned from Saudi Arabia to Tunisia, and wrote to the Saudi Arabian Minister of the Interior (see *Saudi Arabia* entry). Amnesty International reiterated its opposition to the involuntary return of individuals to any country where they may face persecution for their conscientiously held beliefs, torture or the death penalty, and sought clarification of the circumstances surrounding the return of Mohamed Lazrak to Tunisia. The Saudi Arabian Minister of the Interior replied that, contrary to Amnesty International's information, Mohamed Lazrak had returned to Tunisia of his own accord.

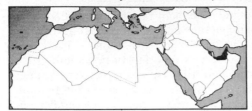

United Arab Emirates

Amnesty International's concerns during 1986 were the imposition by courts of floggings and death sentences and the introduction of new capital offences. The organization was also concerned about the possible deportation of Iranians who might become prisoners of conscience or face torture or execution if returned to their own country.

On 8 July Amnesty International appealed to Shaikh Zayed Ibn Sultan al-Nahayyan, President of the United Arab Emirates, following reports that four people had been flogged in Abu Dhabi on 20 June for intoxication and breaking the fast during Ramadan. Hussain 'Ali Ahmad, a Somali, 'Abd al-Karim Muhammad Jasim, an Indian, and Gharib Muhammad, a Qatari, were each sentenced to 80 lashes, and Mahmud Muhammad Da'ala, a Somali, was sentenced to 40 lashes. The organization reiterated its opposition to the judicial penalty of flogging as a punishment which constitutes cruel, inhuman and degrading treatment. No response was received.

Amnesty International received reports of two death sentences. On 28 November it learned that Khalid Maho 'Ali, an Indian, had been sentenced to death by a criminal court in Dubai for murder. Amnesty International appealed to Shaikh Rashid Ibn Sa'id al-Maktoum, Ruler of Dubai, to commute the death sentence, stating its unconditional opposition to the death penalty. On 15 December it appealed for the commutation of the death sentence passed on Paul George Nadar, an Indian national convicted of the premeditated murder of nine members of two Pakistani families. No responses were received to any of Amnesty International's appeals, and the organization did not know whether either sentence was carried out.

Amnesty International was concerned about the introduction of new capital offences. On 17 March Federal Law No. 6 of 1986 was passed, providing the death penalty for five drug-related offences. However, Amnesty International did not learn of any death sentences passed under this law in 1986.

During 1986 Amnesty International appealed on behalf of 14 Iranian nationals at risk of being forcibly returned to Iran, where they could have become prisoners of conscience, or been tortured or executed. On 20 January Amnesty International sought official confirmation of reports of the arrest and detention in Sadri Prison of 10 Iranians in the previous week. Amnesty International believed that they would be at risk of torture or execution because of their political activities if returned to Iran and sought assurances that they would not be returned. No response was received. On 31 January Amnesty International appealed on behalf of two other Iranians — 'Ali Akbar Khalvati and Abdul Reza Salimi — who risked being forcibly returned to Iran. They were reportedly arrested on 24 January and held in Abu Dhabi Prison. On 5 March and 17 April Amnesty International renewed its appeals on their behalf after receiving reports that the Iranian authorities had requested their return. No response was received. On 26 February Amnesty International appealed on behalf of Hamid Hosham, who had reportedly fled to Dubai from Iran, where he had been tortured. He was said to have been detained at Dubai airport and to be in danger of forcible return to Iran. The authorities responded to Amnesty International's appeals on 15 April, stating that no such person was detained in the United Arab Emirates. The organization subsequently learned that Hamid Hosham had been released and that his claim for political asylum was being examined by the United Nations High Commissioner for Refugees. On 21 October Amnesty International sent appeals on behalf of Gholamabbas Riathi, an Iranian refugee who was reportedly detained on or around 13 October and was being held near Abu Dhabi. The organization sought assurances that he would not be forcibly returned to Iran. No response was received.

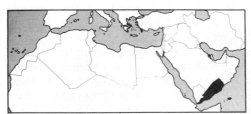

Yemen (People's Democratic Republic of)

Amnesty International was concerned about the fate of eight prisoners of conscience and 20 possible prisoners of conscience it knew of before fighting broke out in January, and about the reported detention of possible prisoners of conscience following the fighting. Some were held without charge, others were brought to trial and faced the death penalty. The organization was also concerned, following the changes in government, about the systematic use of torture and about reports of extrajudicial executions and of possible "disappearances".

On 13 January heavy fighting broke out in Aden between rival factions of the ruling Yemeni Socialist Party. Street clashes erupted following the assassination that day of a number of leading party and government officials, reportedly on the orders of the Head of State, 'Ali Nasir Muhammad. The civil strife lasted until the end of January and resulted in casualties officially estimated at over 4,000 dead. 'Ali Nasir Muhammad was ousted from power and Prime Minister Haydar Abu Bakr al-'Attas was elected Chairman of the Presidium of the Supreme People's Council on 8 February.

During 1986 Amnesty International remained concerned about the fate of eight prisoners of conscience and eight possible prisoners of conscience arrested between 1967 and 1975, and received confirmation of the release of one of them. Assafa Ainalen, an Eritrean civilian pilot arrested in 1975 and held in al-Mansura Prison in Aden, was released in July 1980. Amnesty International had been investigating his case since 1977 but had never received a response to its inquiries from the authorities, and only in 1986 was it able to confirm his release. Amnesty International also continued to seek information on 12 possible prisoners of conscience, members of the pro-Iraqi Ba'th Party, three of whom were sentenced to death in November 1985 (see *Amnesty International Report 1986*). The organization learned in November from the exiled former authorities that the death sentences had been commuted in December 1985, but the subsequent fate and whereabouts of the 12 prisoners remained unknown. Despite repeated appeals by Amnesty International, no information was made available by the new authorities on any of these cases, and the organization feared that several of the prisoners may have died in previous years or during the fighting in January.

Following the fighting in January, thousands of people were arrested by the new authorities and detained in prisons, military camps, schools and other public buildings. Many detainees appear to have been arrested solely because of their place of origin, particularly those from the provinces of Aden, Abyan and Shabwa, whose inhabitants were assumed to be sympathetic to 'Ali Nasir Muhammad. Detainees were released during the year, most of them under a general amnesty declared on 29 March. In September the authorities announced that 3,700 people had been released since the fighting. According to official figures, 700 people were in detention at the end of 1986, although opposition sources maintained that the number was still in the thousands. Amnesty International was concerned about several individuals arrested in January or February who were reported to be still held without charge or trial at the end of 1986. They included journalists, trade unionists, former government officials and military personnel. The organization believed that some of them may have been prisoners of conscience, detained because of their political beliefs or their personal relationships with former prominent government personalities. Appeals sent by Amnesty

International in April and July remained unanswered.

Ninety-four detainees arrested following the fighting in January were brought to trial on 2 December before the Supreme Court of the Republic in Aden, together with the former head of state and 47 others tried *in absentia* as they were abroad. All 142 defendants were charged with treason and faced the death penalty. Amnesty International was concerned that the defendants, some of whom might be prisoners of conscience, were reportedly held incommunicado for prolonged periods and might be sentenced to death with no right of appeal. On 28 December an Amnesty International delegate arrived in Aden to observe part of the trial.

Testimonies gathered by Amnesty International from victims and eye-witnesses revealed that, at least during the first months of the year, torture was used systematically in numerous detention centres. Reported methods included beating with rifle butts and wooden sticks; flogging with plastic-coated electric wires or cables; burning with cigarettes or with hot iron rods; and electric shocks. A few detainees were reportedly blinded by having their eyes gouged out. A method of torture reported to have been widely used — particularly in the Yemeni-Soviet Projects' compound and in the military camps of al-Fath and al-Sawlaban — involved placing parts of the victim's body in hot tar. Eye-witnesses reported that 12 men died in the Yemeni-Soviet Projects' compound in Aden between February and August after being forced into barrels containing hot tar. Former detainees also reported threats of execution and mock executions.

Five journalists were reported to have been tortured to death between February and August. Among them were Zaki Barakat, President of the Democratic Yemeni Journalists' Organization and Editor-in-Chief of the weekly *al-Thawri*, who was believed to have died in March after being tortured in al-Sawlaban Military Camp.

Eight extrajudicial executions, including three in which the victims were said to have been killed with electrical surgical saws, were reported to Amnesty International. The victims included journalists, judges, and a member of the Supreme People's Council. According to eye-witness accounts, mass executions took place during the first weeks after the fighting in January.

In April and July Amnesty International urged the authorities to investigate cases of torture, death under torture and extrajudicial execution in order to bring to justice those found responsible. No reply was received and further appeals were sent in December.

Amnesty International was informed of several people arrested following the fighting in January whose fate and whereabouts were still not known at the end of the year. The organization feared that some may have died in custody and was seeking further information.

MISSIONS: JANUARY–DECEMBER 1986

Date	Country	Delegate(s)	Purpose
January/February	Paraguay	Julio Raffo (Argentina)	Trial observation/Research
February/March	Turkey	Nicolas Ulmer (United States/ Switzerland)	Trial observation
February/March	Liberia	Ralston Deffenbaugh (United States) Staff member of International Secretariat	Research/Trial observation
February/March	Papua New Guinea	Dick Oosting (The Netherlands) Staff member of International Secretariat	Introduce Amnesty International to government
March	Malaysia	Desmond Fernando (Sri Lanka) Staff member of International Secretariat	Research
March	Uruguay	José Zalaquett (Chile) Staff member of International Secretariat	Discuss Amnesty International's concerns with government authorities
March	Yugoslavia	Alex Milne (United Kingdom) Staff member of International Secretariat	Trial observation
April	Uganda	Antonio Marchesi (Italy) Staff member of International Secretariat	Discuss Amnesty International's concerns with government authorities
April	Mexico	Staff member of International Secretariat	Research
April	United Kingdom (N. Ireland)	Staff member of International Secretariat	Observe appeal hearing
April/May	Haiti	Staff member of International Secretariat	Research
April/May	Dominican Republic	Staff member of International Secretariat	Research
May	Rwanda	Alpha Abdoulaye Diallo (Guinea) Staff member of International Secretariat	Discuss Amnesty International's concerns with government authorities

Date	Country	Delegate(s)	Purpose
May	United States	Staff member of International Secretariat	Research
May	India	Secretary General, Amnesty International Staff member of International Secretariat	Discuss Amnesty International's concerns with government authorities
May	Philippines	Secretary General, Amnesty International Two staff members of International Secretariat	Discuss Amnesty International's concerns with government authorities
May	Grenada	Alex Milne (United Kingdom)	Trial observation
May	Yugoslavia	Michael Freeman (United Kingdom) Staff member of International Secretariat	Trial observation
May	Liberia	Ralston Deffenbaugh (United States)	Trial observation
May	Chile	Jaime Miralles (Spain)	Research
May/June	Yugoslavia	Staff member of International Secretariat	Trial observation
June	Turkey	Johan van Lamoen (The Netherlands)	Research
June	Guinea Bissau	Amand d'Hondt (Belgium) Staff member of International Secretariat	Discuss Amnesty International's concerns with government authorities
June	Nigeria	Staff member of International Secretariat	Research
June	Finland	Two staff members of International Secretariat	Discuss Amnesty International's concerns with government authorities
June	Tunisia	Daniel Dumartheray (Switzerland) Staff member of International Secretariat	Research/Trial observation
June	German Democratic Republic	Douwe Korff (The Netherlands)	Trial observation
June	United Kingdom (N. Ireland)	Two staff members of International Secretariat	Research

Date	Country	Delegate(s)	Purpose
June	Thailand	Jorgen Worm (Denmark) Hans Draminsky Petersen (Denmark) Staff member of International Secretariat	Research
June	Yugoslavia	John Vervaele (Belgium)	Trial observation
June/July	Peru	Staff member of International Secretariat	Research
July	Haiti	David Weissbrodt (United States)	Trial observation
July/August	Brazil	Julio Raffo (Argentina) Staff member of International Secretariat	Research
July/October	Fiji French Polynesia New Caledonia Solomon Islands Tonga Vanuatu Western Samoa	Staff member of International Secretariat	Introduce Amnesty International to governments
August	Congo	David Weissbrodt (United States)	Trial observation
August	Comoros	Member of International Executive Committee Staff member of International Secretariat	Discuss Amnesty International's concerns with government authorities
August	United States	Stephen Owen (Canada)	Research
August	Peru	Yvon Le Bot (France) Secretary General of Amnesty International Staff member of International Secretariat	Discuss Amnesty International's concerns with government authorities
August/September	Sudan	Andrew Mawson (United Kingdom) Staff member of International Secretariat	Research

Date	Country	Delegate(s)	Purpose
August/September	Haiti	Staff member of International Secretariat	Participate in meeting on human rights protection
October 1986/ January 1987	Brazil	Staff member of International Secretariat	Research
October	Turkey	Johan van Lamoen (The Netherlands)	Research
October/November	Sierra Leone	Staff member of International Secretariat	Research
October/November	Egypt	Two staff members of International Secretariat	Research
October/November	Pakistan	Staff member of International Secretariat	Research
November/ December	United Kingdom (N. Ireland)	Wesley Gryk (United States) Staff member of International Secretariat	Observe appeal hearing
November/ December	Central African Republic	Biram Sy (Senegal)	Trial observation
December	Philippines	Member of International Executive Committee Staff member of International Secretariat	Discuss Amnesty International's concerns with government authorities/ Research
December	Kenya	David Weissbrodt (United States)	Discuss Amnesty International's concerns with government authorities
December	Argentina	Staff member of International Secretariat	Research
December	People's Democratic Republic of Yemen	Adel Amin (Egypt)	Trial observation
December	Colombia	Staff member of International Secretariat	Research
December	Peru	Staff member of International Secretariat	Research
December	Czechoslovakia	Riikka Pyykko (Finland)	Trial observation

APPENDIX I

Statute of Amnesty International
Articles 1 and 2

As amended by the 17th International Council, meeting in Espoo — Helsinki, Finland, 27 August — 1 September 1985.

OBJECT

1.　CONSIDERING that every person has the right freely to hold and to .express his or her convictions and the obligation to extend a like freedom to others, the object of AMNESTY INTERNATIONAL shall be to secure throughout the world the observance of the provisions of the Universal Declaration of Human Rights, by:

a) irrespective of political considerations working towards the release of and providing assistance to persons who in violation of the aforesaid provisions are imprisoned, detained or otherwise physically restricted by reason of their political, religious or other conscientiously held beliefs or by reason of their ethnic origin, sex, colour or language, provided that they have not used or advocated violence (hereinafter referred to as "prisoners of conscience");

b) opposing by all appropriate means the detention of any prisoners of conscience or any political prisoners without trial within a reasonable time or any trial procedures relating to such prisoners that do not conform to internationally recognized norms;

c) opposing by all appropriate means the imposition and infliction of death penalties and torture or other cruel, inhuman or degrading treatment or punishment of prisoners or other detained or restricted persons whether or not they have used or advocated violence.

METHODS

2.　In order to achieve the aforesaid object, AMNESTY INTERNATIONAL shall:

a) at all times maintain an overall balance between its activities in relation to countries adhering to the different world political ideologies and groupings;

b) promote as appears appropriate the adoption of constitutions, conventions, treaties and other measures which guarantee the rights contained in the provisions referred to in Article 1 hereof;

c) support and publicize the activities of and cooperate with international organizations and agencies which work for the implementation of the aforesaid provisions;

d) take all necessary steps to establish an effective organization of sections, affiliated groups and individual members;

e) secure the adoption by groups of members or supporters of individual prisoners of conscience or entrust to such groups other tasks in support of the object set out in Article 1;

f) provide financial and other relief to prisoners of conscience and their dependants and to persons who have lately been prisoners of conscience or who might reasonably be expected to be prisoners of conscience or to become prisoners of conscience if convicted or if they were to return to their own countries, to the dependants of such persons and to victims of torture in need of medical care as a direct result thereof;

g) work for the improvement of conditions for prisoners of conscience and political prisoners;

h) provide legal aid, where necessary and possible, to prisoners of conscience and to persons who might reasonably be expected to be prisoners of conscience or to become prisoners of conscience if convicted or if they were to return to their own countries, and, where desirable, send observers to attend the trials of such persons;

i) publicize the cases of prisoners of conscience or persons who have otherwise been subjected to disabilities in violation of the aforesaid provisions;

j) oppose the sending of persons from one country to another where they can reasonably be expected to become prisoners of conscience or to face torture or the death penalty;

k) send investigators, where appropriate, to investigate allegations that the rights of individuals under the aforesaid provisions have been violated or threatened;

l) make representations to international organizations and to governments whenever it appears that an individual is a prisoner of conscience or has otherwise been subjected to disabilities in violation of the aforesaid provisions;

m) promote and support the granting of general amnesties of which the beneficiaries will include prisoners of conscience;

n) adopt any other appropriate methods for the securing of its object.

The full text of the Statute of Amnesty International is available free upon request, from: Amnesty International, International Secretariat, 1 Easton Street, London WC1X 8DJ, United Kingdom.

APPENDIX II

Amnesty International News Releases 1986

28 January	Hundreds of thousands imprisoned on basis of race in *South Africa*, says AI report
4 February	AI urges new *Guatemalan* Government to end torture and killing
12 February	AI reports on human rights abuses in *Nicaragua*
5 March	AI launches campaign against human rights violations in *South Africa*
19 March	AI reports torture, killing and mass arrests in *Zaire*
2 April	Ethnic Turks imprisoned during *Bulgarian* assimilation campaign, AI reports
16 April	AI issues known figures for *death penalty* in 1985, says true total much higher
14 May	AI urges *Mexican* Government to act against torture and killings in rural areas
28 May	AI, 25 years old, cites human rights progress and calls for further action against abuses
11 June	Government critics face imprisonment and torture in *South Korea*, says AI
25 June	AI seeks fair trial for Muslim prisoners in *Indonesia*
14 July	AI announces appointment of next Secretary General
18 July	AI reports killings, torture in *Colombia*
3 September	*Chilean* security forces use clandestine groups, says AI
10 September	AI says *Sri Lankan* Government must explain "disappearances"
16 September	AI urges investigation of reports of torture in *Israeli*-occupied territory
30 September	*UK* procedures fail to answer key question on killings by security forces, AI says
8 October	AI cites killing and torture of tribal villagers in *Bangladesh*
15 October	AI's *annual report* says pressure grows for human rights
19 November	AI reports torture in *Afghanistan*

Regional News Releases 1986

28 February   Execution of 17-year-old in *Bangladesh* violates human rights
standards, says AI

8 July   AI mission confirms Kampuchean refugees were tortured
after arrest in *Thailand*

APPENDIX III

Amnesty International around the world

There are now over 3,740 local Amnesty International groups in over 60
countries around the world. In 44 countries these groups are coordinated by
sections, whose addresses are given below. In addition, there are individual
members, supporters and recipients of Amnesty International information
(such as the monthly *Amnesty International Newsletter*) in more than 150
countries and territories.

Section addresses

Australia: Amnesty International, Australian Section, PO Box A159, Sydney
South, New South Wales 2000

Austria: Amnesty International, Austrian Section, Esslinggasse 15/4, A-1010
Wien

Bangladesh: c/o Amnesty International, CMD, International Secretariat, 1
Easton Street, London WC1X 8DJ

Barbados: Amnesty International, Barbados Section, Breezy Hollow, Crane,
St Philip, Barbados, West Indies

Belgium: Amnesty International, Belgian Section (*Flemish branch*), Kerk-
straat 156, 2008 Antwerpen
Amnesty International, Belgian Section (*francophone branch*), 9 rue
Berckmans, 1060 Bruxelles

Brazil: Amnistia Internacional, Rua Harmonia 899, 05435 – São Paulo – SP

Canada: Amnesty International, Canadian Section (*English-speaking
branch*), 130 Slater Street, Suite 800, Ottowa, Ontario, K1P 6E2
Amnistie Internationale, Section canadienne (*francophone*), 3516 ave
du Parc, Montreal, Quebec, H2X 2H7

Chile: Señores, Casilla 4062, Santiago

Denmark: Amnesty International, Danish Section, Frederiksborggade 1,
1360 Copenhagen K

Ecuador: Señores, Casilla 240, Sucursal 15, Quito

Faroe Islands: Amnesty International, Faroe Islands, PO Box 1075, 3800
Torshavn

Finland: Amnesty International, Finnish Section, Munkkisaarenkatu 12 A 51, 00150 Helsinki 15

France: Amnesty International, French Section, 4 rue de la Pierre Levée, 75553 Paris Cedex II

Federal Republic of Germany: Amnesty International, Section of the FRG, Heerstrasse 178, 5300 Bonn 1

Ghana: Amnesty International, Ghanaian Section, PO Box 9852, Kotoka Airport, Accra

Greece: Amnesty International, Greek Section, 20 Mavromihali Street, Athens 106-80

Hong Kong: Amnesty International, Hong Kong Section, 216 Beverley Commercial Centre, 87-105 Chatham Road, Kowloon

Iceland: Amnesty International, Icelandic Section, PO Box 618, 121 Reykjavík

India: Amnesty International, Indian Section, c/o Dateline Delhi, 21 North End Complex, Panchkuin Road, New Delhi 10001

Ireland: Amnesty International, Irish Section, 8 Shaw Street, Dublin 2

Israel: Amnesty International, Israel Section, PO Box 23003, Tel Aviv, 61230 Israel

Italy: Amnesty International, Italian Section, viale Mazzini 146, 00195 Rome

Ivory Coast: Amnesty International, Section Ivoirienne, 1 rue de Commerce, Immeuble Nassar et Gaddar, 04 BP 895, Abidjan 04

Japan: Amnesty International, Japanese Section, Daisan-Sanbu Building 3F, 2-3-22 Nishi-Waseda, Shinjuku-ku, Tokyo 160

Luxembourg: Amnesty International, Luxembourg, Boîte Postale 1914, 1019 Luxembourg

Mexico: Sección Mexicana de Amnistía Internacional, Ap. Postal No. 20-217, San Angel, CP 01000 Mexico DF

Nepal: c/o Amnesty International, CMD, International Secretariat, 1 Easton Street, London WC1X 8DJ

Netherlands: Amnesty International, Dutch Section, Keizersgracht 620, 1017 ER Amsterdam

New Zealand: Amnesty International, New Zealand Section, PO Box 6647, Te Aro, Wellington 1

Nigeria: Amnesty International, Nigerian Section, 15 Onayade Street, Fadeyi-Yaba, Lagos

Norway: Amnesty International, Norwegian Section, Niels Juelsgt. 39, Oslo 2

Peru: Señores, Casilla 581, Lima 18

Portugal: Seccão Portuguesa AI, Apartado 1642, 1016 Lisboa Codex

Puerto Rico: Calle Cabo Alverio 562, Ext. Roosevelt Hato Rey, Puerto Rico 00918

Senegal: Amnesty International, Section Senegalaise, 126 rue Joseph Gomis (ex rue de Bayeux), B.P. 3813, Dakar

Spain: Amnesty International, Paseo de Recoletos 18, Piso 6, 28001 Madrid

Sri Lanka: Amnesty International, Sri Lanka Section, 79/15 Dr C.W.W. Kannangara Mawatha, Colombo 7

Sweden: Amnesty International, Swedish Section, Gyllenstiernsgatan 18, S-115 26 Stockholm

Switzerland: Amnesty International, Swiss Section, PO Box 1051, CH-3001 Bern

Trinidad and Tobago: Amnesty International, Trinidad and Tobago Section, PO Bag 231, Woodbrook PO, Port of Spain, Trinidad, West Indies

Turkey: c/o Amnesty International, CMD, International Secretariat, 1 Easton Street, London WC1X 8DJ

United Kingdom: Amnesty International, 5 Roberts Place, off Bowling Green Lane, London EC1 0EJ

United States of America: Amnesty International of the USA (AIUSA), 322 8th Ave, New York, NY 10001

Venezuela: Señores, Apartado 5110, Caracas 1010

Countries with local Amnesty International groups, but no section:

Aruba	Guyana	Sierra Leone
Argentina	Republic of Korea	Tanzania
Bangladesh	Mauritius	Thailand
Bermuda	Nepal	Tunisia
Colombia	Netherlands Antilles	Uruguay
Costa Rica	Papua New Guinea	USSR
Egypt	Philippines	Zambia

APPENDIX IV
International Executive Committee

Stephen R. Abrams	United States of America
Peter Duffy	United Kingdom
Whitney Ellsworth	United States of America
Wolfgang Heinz	Colombia
Peter Klein	Federal Republic of Germany
Santiago Larrain	Chile
Lesley Merryfinch	International Secretariat
Bacre Waly Ndiaye	Senegal
Franca Sciuto	Italy

APPENDIX V

The African Charter on Human and Peoples' Rights

The African Charter came into force on 21 October 1986. The text of the Charter was adopted unanimously by the Organization of African Unity (OAU) in 1981. It provides for the protection of basic human rights, including those which form the basis of Amnesty International's work — the right to life, the right to be free from arbitrary arrest or detention, the right to a fair trial and the right to freedom of conscience.

The African Charter provides for an African Commission on Human and Peoples' Rights, consisting of 11 members nominated by states which are parties to the African Charter and elected by the entire OAU Assembly of Heads of State and Government. The commission's responsibilities include promotion of human rights in the region and examination of allegations that a State Party has violated the Charter.

Amnesty International considers the Charter to be a major regional initiative in the protection of human rights. It is encouraging all OAU member states to become parties to the Charter as well as to the International Covenant on Civil and Political Rights and its Optional Protocol.

The complete text of the African Charter is available from the OAU.

Ratifications and signatures as of 31 December 1986

States which have ratified a convention are party to the treaty and are bound to observe its provisions. States which have signed but not yet ratified have expressed their intention to become a party at some future date; meanwhile they are obliged to refrain from acts which would defeat the object and purpose of the treaty.

OAU Member State	Signature/ Ratification	OAU Member State	Signature/ Ratification
Algeria	S	Central African Rep.	R
Angola	–	Chad	R
Benin	R	Comoros	R
Botswana	R	Congo	R
Burkina Faso	R	Djibouti	–
Burundi	–	Egypt	R
Cameroon	–	Equatorial Guinea	R
Cape Verde	S	Ethiopia	–

OAU Member State	*Signature/ Ratification*	*OAU Member State*	*Signature/ Ratification*
Gabon	R	Saharawi Arab	
Gambia	R	Democratic Rep.	
Ghana	–	(Western Sahara)	R
Guinea	R	Sao Tome and	
Guinea-Bissau	R	Principe	R
Ivory Coast	–	Senegal	R
Kenya	–	Seychelles	–
Lesotho	S	Sierra Leone	R
Liberia	R	Somalia	R
Libya	S	Sudan	R
Madagascar	–	Swaziland	–
Malawi	–	Tanzania	R
Mali	R	Togo	R
Mauritania	R	Tunisia	R
Mauritius	–	Uganda	R
Mozambique	–	Zaire	–
Niger	R	Zambia	R
Nigeria	R	Zimbabwe	R
Rwanda	R		

APPENDIX VI

Selected Statistics

By the start of 1987 there were Amnesty International sections in 44 countries and 3,744 groups worldwide. There were more than 500,000 members and subscribers in over 150 countries.

In 1986 a total of 4,247 prisoners were adopted as prisoners of conscience or being investigated as possible prisoners of conscience. During 1986, 1,792 new prisoner cases were taken up and 1,952 prisoners were released.

During 1986 Amnesty International initiated 391 Urgent Action appeals on behalf of almost 2,000 people in 73 countries. Of these, 142 were prompted by reports of torture, and eight were made on behalf of prisoners in a critical state of health and in need of medical treatment. Eighty were issued in cases of arbitrary arrest, prolonged incommunicado detention, detention without charge or trial, or unfair trial. Sixty-two related to extrajudicial killings or "disappearances" and 75 were on behalf of prisoners sentenced to death. Others were issued in cases where prisoners had died in detention, or were on hunger-strike in support of demands falling within Amnesty International's mandate.